KEYBOARD SHORTCUTS

Item ➤ Lock	⌘-L
Justified alignment	⌘-Shift-J
Leading dialog box	⌘-Shift-E
Left alignment	⌘-Shift-L
Ligature *AE* (Æ)	Option-Shift-'
Ligature *ae* (æ)	Option-'
Ligature *fi* (fi)	Option-Shift-5
Ligature *fl* (fl) *	Option-Shift-6
Maintain picture box aspect ratio	Shift-Option-drag
Maintain aspect ratio of box and picture	⌘-Shift-Option-click
Registered symbol	Option-R
Right alignment	⌘-Shift-R
Select line	triple-click
Select paragraph	quadruple-click
Select word	double-click
Select all	⌘-A (or quintuple-click)
Small caps format	⌘-Shift-H
Start of document	Control-A (or Home)
Tab dialog box	⌘-Shift-T
Trademark symbol (™)	Option-2
Underline format	⌘-Shift-U
View ➤ Actual Size	⌘-1
View ➤ Fit in Window	⌘-O
View ➤ Show/Hide Invisibles	⌘-I
View ➤ Show/Hide Rulers	⌘-R

Books that Work Just Like Your Mac

As a Macintosh user, you enjoy unique advantages. You enjoy a dynamic user environment. You enjoy the successful integration of graphics, sound, and text. Above all, you enjoy a computer that's fun and easy to use.

When your computer gives you all this, why accept less in your computer books?

At SYBEX, we don't believe you should. That's why we've committed ourselves to publishing the highest quality computer books for Macintosh users. Externally, our books emulate the Mac "look and feel," with powerful, appealing illustrations and easy-to-read pages. Internally, our books stress "why" over "how," so you'll learn concepts, not sequences of steps. Philosophically, our books are designed to help you get work done, not to teach you about computers.

In short, our books are fun and easy to use—just like the Mac. We hope you find them just as enjoyable.

For a complete catalog of our publications:

SYBEX Inc.
2021 Challenger Drive, Alameda, CA 94501
Tel: (510) 523-8233/(800) 227-2346 Telex: 336311
Fax: (510) 523-2373

Page Design with QuarkXPress 3.2

for the MAC

PAGE DESIGN WITH
QUARKXPRESS® 3.2
FOR THE MAC®

Patrick W. Fellers

SYBEX®

San Francisco • Paris • Düsseldorf • Soest

Acquisitions Editor: Dianne King
Developmental Editor: Kenyon Brown
Editor: David Krassner
Technical Editor: Celia Stevenson
Book Designer: Helen Bruno
Production Artist: Lisa Jaffe
Screen Graphics: John Corrigan
Typesetter: Deborah Maizels
Proofreader/Production Assistant: Janet K. MacEachern
Indexer: Anne Leach
Cover Designer: Ingalls + Associates
Cover Artist: Lynn Brofsky

Library of Congress Card Number: 93-62083
ISBN: 0-7821-1043-6

Manufactured in the United States of America
10 9 8 7 6 5 4 3 2 1

This book is dedicated to the relentless support of my wife, Mary Jane, and my children, Nicholas, Megan, and Cathleen. Mary Jane is the first person to recognize a glimmer of talent and style in my writings and "forced" me to stay at the keyboard until the task was complete. My kids were the recipients of many a "No-Dad" day and tolerated my absence well.

ACKNOWLEDGMENTS

My sincere thanks go out to the people who made this production a team effort. In particular, I wish to thank the people at SYBEX whom I have had direct contact with in the project, including Dianne King and Ken Brown for giving me the chance to produce for SYBEX; David Krassner, Celia Stevenson, and John Corrigan for making my text and graphics the highest possible quality, and the other team members who made this book a product they can all claim with pride. In teaching, we instruct students on the print production process, as it goes from the client to the designer, through each production stage until it hits printed paper. As each prepress step becomes one that can be performed on the computer, job specifications become blurred. Some may even say that from one computer desktop, an entire production can be assembled from start to finish. I would like everyone to know that publishing is still a "team sport" and efforts such as this book could not be accomplished without talents from many individuals. I thank you all!

I also would like to pay special note to the help given by William Buckingham at XChange. He gave me direct support in the area of XTensions, quickly and accurately. I hope we can work together on the next effort.

CONTENTS
AT A GLANCE

Contents

DOCUMENT CONSTRUCTION 65

PAGE LAYOUT 81

PART

MULTIPAGE DOCUMENTS

CREATING A
MASTER PAGE

APPLYING A MASTER
PAGE TO A DOCUMENT

PART

IIII

WORD PROCESSING

7 IMPORTING AND EXPORTING TEXT **157**

8 TEXT FORMATTING **173**

PART

VI

OUTPUTTING DOCUMENTS

APPENDICES

INTRODUCTION

Many business leaders and educators proclaim that we are now in the midst of a second Renaissance. This second Renaissance embraces computer technology as a vehicle to distribute information and communications. Technological advances in this area over just the past few years have been astounding, and so has the pressure for people to keep pace!

As a practicing graphic designer and educator, I have had the pleasure of seeing the metamorphosis of preprint production activities as they have evolved from dedicated typesetting machines to the fantastic hardware and software of today. My first job as a typesetter was on one of the first CompuGraphic typesetting machines in the early 1970's. Then, to change type size on a line, you had to stop the machine, physically remove a lens and replace it with another, to photograph a new size of the typeface. Twelve lenses were necessary to obtain the twelve basic type sizes. The font was in the form of a film strip. Employees were extremely careful when handling the $700.00 fonts.

Working on that equipment, one had to have knowledge of photography, typography, graphic design and a bit of computer savvy. My studies in Industrial Design at The Ohio State University gave me just what was needed for the job. It was difficult to find someone with the skills to operate and maintain this type of equipment in a small shop environment. Early phototypesetting equipment was prone to breakdowns and the operator had to know what to fix and when to call for repairs.

Today, the technology seems light years ahead of that CompuGraphic typesetter I worked on nearly two decades ago. Now you can not only set variable sizes on one line but do so in 0.001-point intervals. You can even augment the typeface in several electronic variations simultaneously. Today, the price of a high-level desktop publishing software, such as QuarkXPress, is lower than that of early film fonts.

File compression and telecommunications make it easy to download a needed font over the telephone line from an on-line service. Electronic fonts of today cost pennies compared to the cost of their old filmstrip counterparts. Frequently, software applications bundle "free" fonts with their product to encourage sales.

Today, we use the desktop computer for a variety of tasks, including text input. Special desktop publishing software allows the user to see the text and graphics on the page as the layout would suggest. They call it *WYSIWYG*—which stands for What You See Is What You Get. I tell my students it should be called WYSIWYHF—What You See Is What You Hope For! Nothing's perfect yet!

The closest thing to *perfect* we have today is a state-of-the-art desktop computer, decked out in proper RAM, CD-ROM, DAT, HD, 10-BASE-T and QuarkXPress software. To keep up with all the new acronyms is beyond hope.

Now, you can write copy, design the page, key the text, change type attributes, scan photos, position the print, proof and color separate the job all through QuarkXPress. Is this Heaven...or Hell?

We've come far in the past twenty years, since my work with the CompuGraphic machine, but one constant still remains. Exotic technology demands skilled people for proper operation.

As Associate Professor at Columbus State Community College in Columbus, Ohio, I field many calls from printing firms and in-plant businesses. Many companies are taking the plunge toward QuarkXPress as their prepress software. These shop owners and department managers face the same problem; that is, they need skilled people to conduct and oversee their QuarkXPress activities.

Today's problem with QuarkXPress is similar to those of twenty years ago. A company could afford typesetting equipment, but lacked skilled employees to operate and maintain their investment.

An obvious solution to the QuarkXPress training problem is to have people read the manuals! Unfortunately, this usually meets with little success. Manuals are traditionally written as references, using a somewhat random access approach to information. Students of all ages learn best by having a mentor, presenting one technique after another, methodically building upon each skill level.

I am on a constant lookout for QuarkXPress material presenting information properly matched with learning styles. Finally, I jumped into the market myself. This book is the culmination of my efforts. It is my attempt to help the sequential learner conquer a complex task. I feel confident that if you follow this book through from front to back, in sequence, you will gain a very good functional knowledge of QuarkXPress. Sure, you can also use the book as reference, but the ideal situation is to follow the chapters sequentially and build on your knowledge.

HOW THE BOOK IS ORGANIZED

Part I: Getting Started with QuarkXPress includes four chapters to get you started creating your first QuarkXPress document, to show you the anatomy of the program, and to explain the principles of document construction and page layout.

Part II: Multipage Documents contains two chapters to introduce you to the creation and use of master pages.

Part III: Word Processing consists of four chapters on the QuarkXPress word processor and other methods of putting text into your documents. Topics include importing and exporting text, formatting text, using spelling and dictionaries, and creating and using style sheets.

Part IV: Typography comprises four chapters that deal with the size, font, and leading of type. Also, this part covers kerning and leading, TrueType and PostScript fonts, and some advanced typographic maneuvers.

The three chapters of *Part V: Graphics and Pictures* introduce the world of graphic images. Included are discussions of manipulating pictures and graphics, combining text with graphics, and color concepts.

The final section of the book, *Part VI: Outputting Documents*, advises on the sometimes tricky task of printing out your work. There are chapters dealing with PostScript printing and printing in color. Because many XTensions are often concerned with printing or prepress operations, there is a chapter listing over a hundred XTensions.

Finally, two appendices round out your QuarkXPress Odyssey, the first being a list of resources for the program, and the second a library of palettes and menus, just in case you forget what's where!

FEATURES AND CONVENTIONS OF THIS BOOK

At the beginning of each chapter, you'll find two features that will help you navigate the chapter quickly and easily. First, a *Featuring* list tells you what topics the chapter covers. Then, a *Mac Track* lists the most basic and useful commands covered in the chapter, explaining briefly how to use them and directing you to the pages they can be found on.

The symbol ➤ has been used to indicate a menu command. The context you will usually see it in is *menu* ➤ *command*, as in File ➤ Save.

A FINAL WORD

If you have any suggestions or comments, I invite you to E-mail my CompuServe address. I also would like to hear from all freeware and shareware XTension developers (Mac and Windows). Contact me through CompuServe at 71202,3471.

—Patrick Fellers

GETTING STARTED WITH QUARKXPRESS

....

I

CREATING YOUR FIRST QUARKXPRESS DOCUMENT

- Options for launching QuarkXPress

- Creating your first QuarkXPress document

- Modifying the new document

- Formatting text by changing attributes

- Saving the document on the hard disk drive

- Printing the document

To place text in the automatic text box 17

select the Content Tool from the Tool Palette. Then click on the automatic text box created when you originated the document. You should have a cursor flashing in the top left corner of the text box. This indicates you are ready to type in your text.

To alter text attributes such as font, size, etc. 21

highlight the text, using the Content Tool. (Click and drag the mouse cursor over the text to highlight). Select the commands appropriate for change under the Style menu.

To adjust line spacing for text in your document 23

highlight all the text (click and drag). Adjust leading from the options in Style ➤ Leading.

To save the document to your hard drive 26

choose File ➤ Save. Find a location to save the document, give it a name, click on Save.

To print your document 28

make sure you are properly connected to a printer. Select File ➤ Page Setup and make adjustments where necessary in this dialog box. Exit the setup dialog box, go to File ➤ Print. Make adjustments and click on OK.

To give you a quick start in creating QuarkXPress documents, you will make a simple, one-page flyer. As you go through the tutorial you may have questions on QuarkXPress features, tools, and capabilities. Be patient; only basic information is given in Chapter 1. You will find more detail in later chapters. In this way, we will carefully guide you through QuarkXPress, building your knowledge and confidence.

CREATING YOUR FIRST QUARKXPRESS DOCUMENT

Begin QuarkXPress by launching the application from your hard disk (or network). There are several ways to launch the program.

If you have not done any customization to the program since loading it, the application icon should be in its original folder. Find and open the QuarkXPress Folder on your drive. Inside you will find the original QuarkXPress application. Double-click the icon to launch the program (see Figure 1.1).

It is awkward and time-consuming to launch programs from their folders, though, so frequent QuarkXPress users often move the application icon (or alias in System 7) to one of three locations for easier launching.

NOTE

The technique of storing applications in the Apple Menu was not available before System 7.

▸ First, the icon might be on the Desktop. Here, the program is in plain view and can again be quickly launched by double-clicking.

FIGURE 1.1

FIGURE 1.1

The QuarkXPress application icon is in the original QuarkXPress folder on your hard-disk after installation.

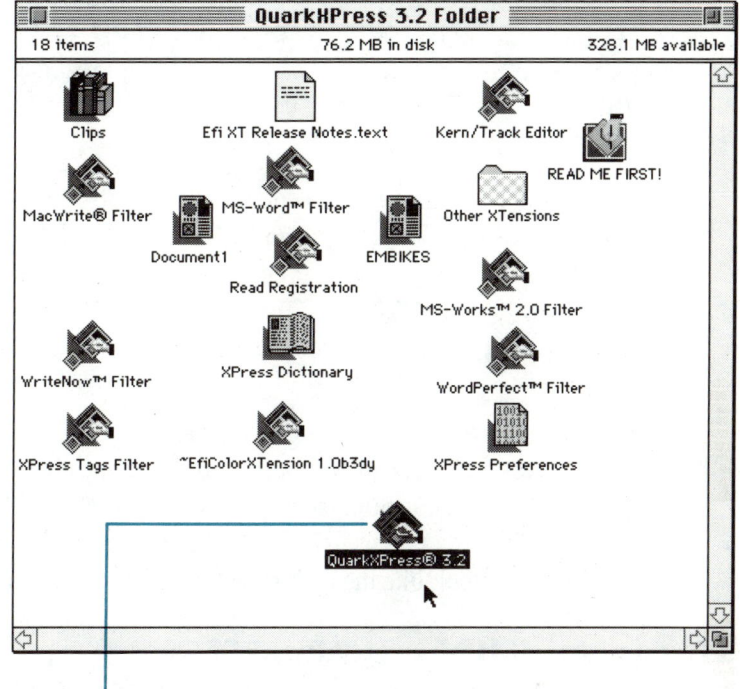

The QuarkXPress application icon

- A second location for the icon is the Startup Items Folder in the System Folder. This launches QuarkXPress upon startup, and is the quickest way to launch applications (see Figure 1.2).

- Finally, in System 7, the Apple Menu Items folder in the System Folder can house the application icon. This provides easy access of the icon from the Apple Menu (see Figure 1.3).

If you have any questions about positioning application icons or system approaches, reach for your set of Macintosh manuals. They are a great source of information.

FIGURE 1.2

The fastest way to launch QuarkXPress is by placing the application icon or its alias in the Startup Items folder.

The flyer you are about to create will demonstrate a few basic strategies for the QuarkXPress environment. You will: start the application; create a new document; key in text material; manipulate text; save your work; and finally, print the document. The flyer is a one page promo for a bicycle retailer. Your first QuarkXPress document will look like the flyer shown here (see Figure 1.4).

STEP 1: LAUNCHING QUARKXPRESS

Launch the software using one of the procedures described above. The program takes several seconds to load all pertinent files, filters, and extensions, in addition to checking your system configuration and network status. If a copy of QuarkXPress with the same serial number is open on the network, you will get an error message. You can't open two copies of QuarkXPress with the same serial number at the same time. Similarly, when upgrading, you cannot simultaneously open two versions of QuarkXPress with the same serial number.

FIGURE 1.3

Place an alias of the application icon in the Apple Menu Items folder, and you can easily launch QuarkXPress from the Apple Menu.

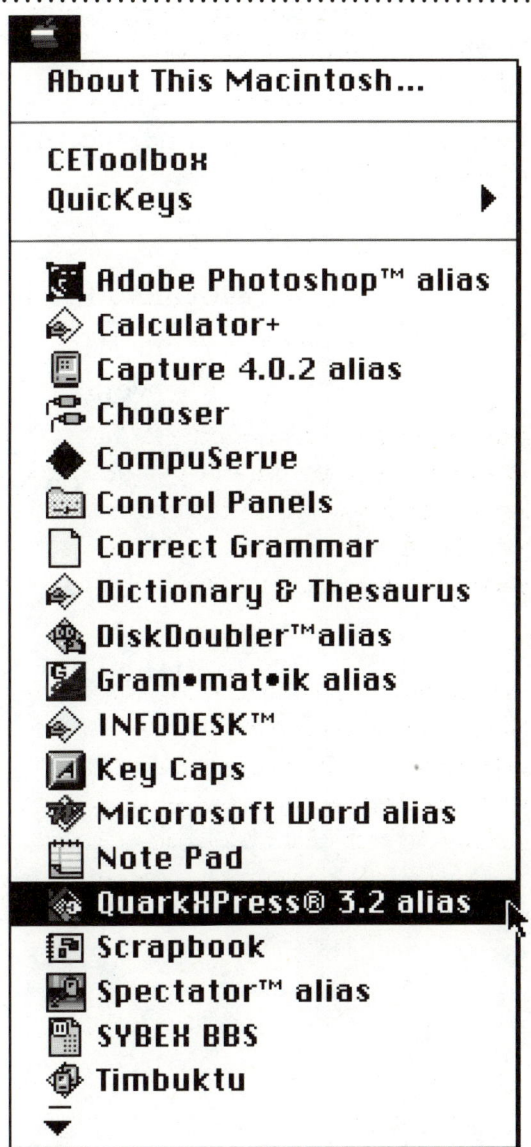

About This Macintosh...

CEToolbox
QuicKeys ▶

- Adobe Photoshop™ alias
- Calculator+
- Capture 4.0.2 alias
- Chooser
- CompuServe
- Control Panels
- Correct Grammar
- Dictionary & Thesaurus
- DiskDoubler™alias
- Gram•mat•ik alias
- INFODESK™
- Key Caps
- Micorosoft Word alias
- Note Pad
- QuarkXPress® 3.2 alias
- Scrapbook
- Spectator™ alias
- SYBEX BBS
- Timbuktu

FIGURE 1.4
Your first QuarkXPress document will be a one page flyer for Eddie Merrik Bicycles.

Eddie Merrik Spring Specials

NovaPed PR-12 Clipless Pedals
$149.95

Velloce Gel Saddles
$29.95

Scede MB3 Rims
$28.95

Sunlite Gamma Headsets
$39.95

Fujitaho Dura SK Brake Levers
$59.95

TIP

Mac users who are new to System 7 may have difficulty telling whether they are in an application or in the Finder. Beginners often launch QuarkXPress and then click on the Desktop, which takes them out of QuarkXPress and into the Finder. Then they can't understand why they the File ➤ New command keeps making new file folders all over the Desktop! Make sure the QuarkXPress application is active by examining the Application Menu, located at the far right side of the menu bar. The QuarkXPress icon will show if you are in QuarkXPress; if you are in the Finder, a little Mac will show there; other applications have their own icons.

The first indication that the program has launched is the QuarkXPress logo (see Figure 1.5). This will disappear after a few seconds, but to hurry the process, just click the mouse once. The logo screen has information concerning the version number and the registered user name. The same screen also appears if you select the About QuarkXPress option under the Apple Menu. For more information, see Chapter 2: Anatomy of QuarkXPress.

FIGURE 1.5

The QuarkXPress logo screen appears when you launch the application.

When the logo screen leaves, the work area appears to be transparent (see Figure 1.6). Before you open a document, there is no "work" area. This look may confuse the beginner; however, there are three clues that will tell you that you're in the properly opened QuarkXPress application.

First, look for QuarkXPress' floating palettes. You display these palettes using the Show/Hide options in the View menu. Shown options remain shown the next time QuarkXPress is open. For example, the Tools palette (see Figure 1.6) often remains shown. It is positioned on the left side of the screen's work area by default. The next time QuarkXPress is launched, the Tools palette will still show at the same location. The floating palettes consist of Tools, Measurements, Document Layout, Style Sheets, Colors, and Trap Information. The Library palette may be included, but it is located under the Utilities menu.

A second indicator of QuarkXPress activity is in the menu bar (also shown in Figure 1.6). The menu names differ from those of the normal Finder menu bar.

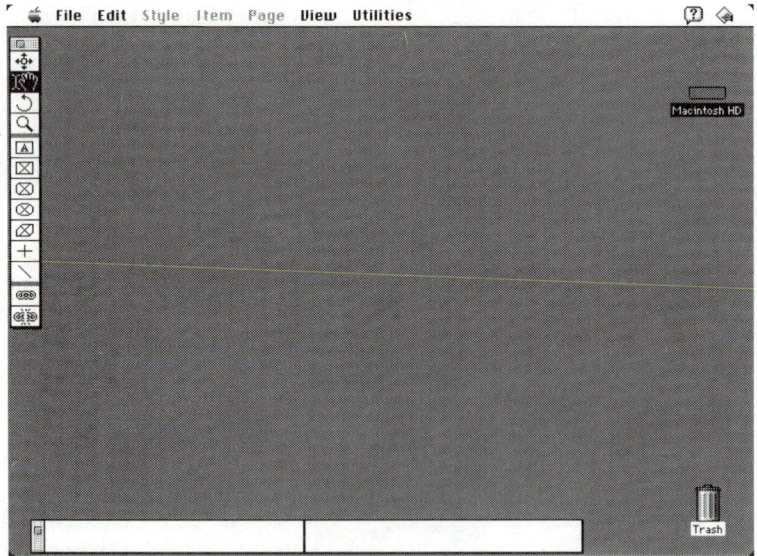

FIGURE 1.6

In System 7 or MultiFinder, it may be difficult to tell if QuarkXPress is properly launched. Without a document open, the application resembles the standard Mac Desktop.

NOTE

Clicking the application icon to find out which applications are running was not available before to System 7 (except with MultiFinder).

Finally, you can determine which application is active by looking at the icon at the top-right corner of the screen. Click and hold on this icon to see what programs are open. The active program will be checked (see Figure 1.7).

FIGURE 1.7
Click on the icon in the top-right corner of the screen (the Application Menu) to determine which application is active.

WARNING

There is a limited amount of memory in your Mac, and each open application consumes precious memory. Only keep necessary programs open.

STEP 2: CREATING A NEW DOCUMENT

As with most Macintosh applications, you start a new document by selecting the New option from the File menu (noted hereafter as File ➤ New). You should learn to use the keyboard equivalents whenever available to speed operations. The keyboard equivalent for New is ⌘-N. Once you've selected New, the New dialog box appears (see Figure 1.8). It includes options for Page Size, Margin Guides, Column

FIGURE 1.8

*The New dialog box in
QuarkXPress*

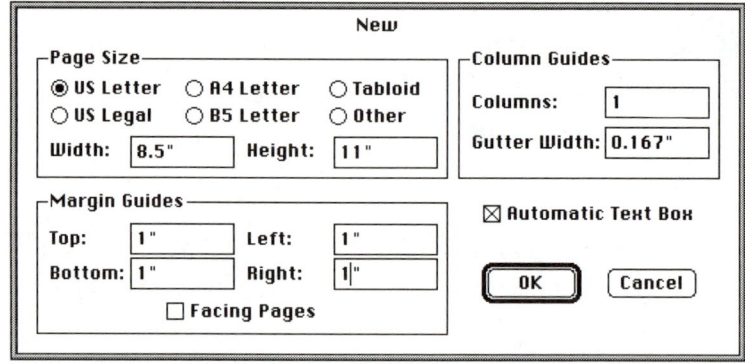

Guides, as well as the Automatic text box. Also, like most Macintosh dialog boxes, the New dialog box provides you the option of accepting your new settings (OK) or canceling them.

NOTE

Notice that some menu commands, such as New and Open, are followed by three periods (called ellipses). These indicate that the command leads to a dialog box.

We will look at each section of this dialog box later, but for now, key in the following configuration:

Page Size: Letter (Click on the radio button for US Letter if it is not already chosen)

Top: 1"

Bottom: 1"

Left: 1"

Right: 1"

Columns: 1 (gutter width doesn't matter)

Automatic text box: checked

When you're finished, click on the OK button. If you make a mistake and click on OK too soon, don't panic. Simply choose File ➤ New again and create another new document. Disregard any mistakes for now. You can close an erroneous document at any time.

Once you have clicked the OK button on the New dialog box, you're on your way! A new document work area appears on the screen (see Figure 1.9). This new document work area should be a full-size (100%) document page layout. Naturally, if you have a standard monitor, you won't be able to see the entire letter-size document on your screen. You can move around the page with the scroll bars.

NOTE

Not all users will have their QuarkXPress software configured exactly alike. Certain parts of the work area may show on some people's applications and hide in others. Why? Because QuarkXPress gives you a lot of flexibility about showing certain elements like the rulers, guide lines, tools, etc.

FIGURE 1.9

The screen as it may appear when opening a new document under QuarkXPress.

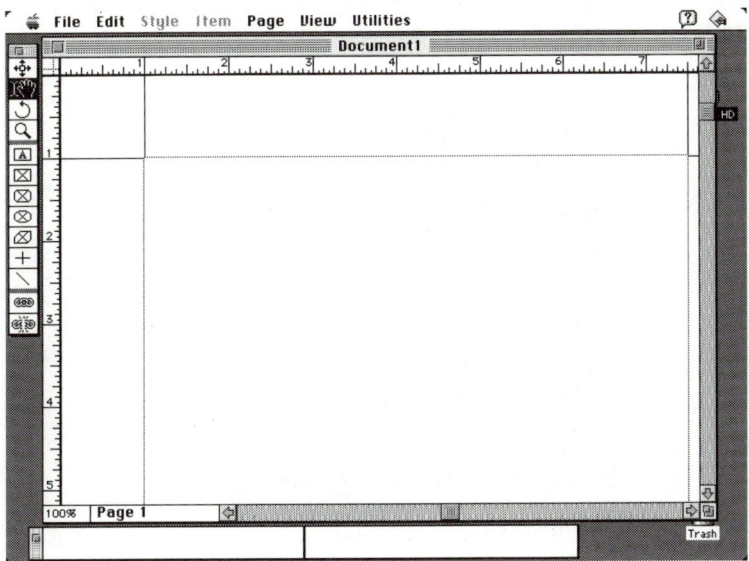

Depending on your configuration, certain parts of the work area may or may not be visible. The following list tells which items must be showing on your first QuarkXPress document, along with the settings you should use.

▸ The document work area is distinguished by the scroll bars on the right and bottom (see Figure 1.10). If you don't see this, go back and open a new document again (File ➤ New). If you still don't see the document work area, check to be sure you are still in QuarkXPress. Then select View ➤ Actual Size. The document may have been opened in a smaller size if your defaults have been reconfigured to a reduced size.

▸ You should be at Page 1, not Master or any other page (see Figure 1.10). Jump from Master page to Document page by using Page ➤ Display. Set it to Document. Use the vertical scroll bar to position yourself on the top left corner of Page 1, as shown in the graphic.

FIGURE 1.10

The document work area often shows scroll bars if the page is larger than the screen window can show.

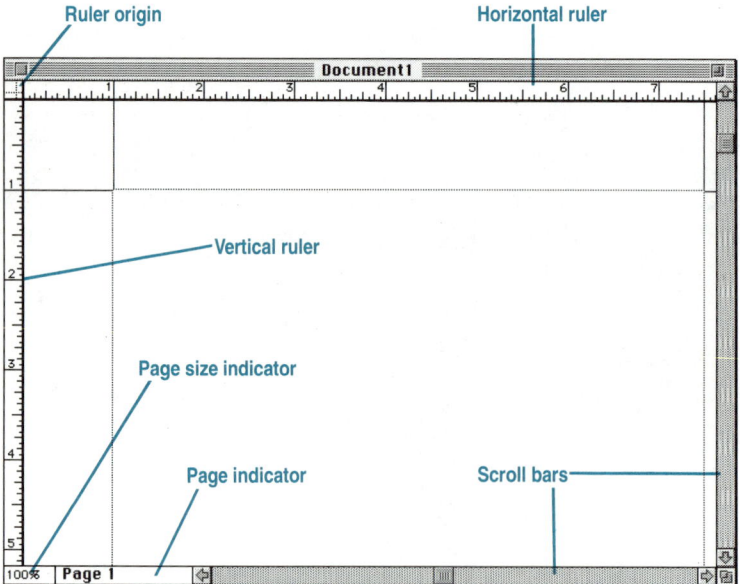

- You should be viewing the document at 100%. This represents the page size; double-click on this number and key in 100 if it does not already read 100%.

- You should show the horizontal and vertical rulers. You can do so by choosing View ➤ Show Rulers. In most cases the default will show rulers (see Figure 1.10).

- The Tools palette should be showing (you encountered this palette back in Figure 1.6). To show this floating palette, choose View ➤ Show Tools. You can move floating palettes anywhere using the usual Mac click and drag technique in the area at the top of the palette next to its close box.

- A text box was automatically created if you checked the Automatic Text Box option in the New dialog box (see Figure 1.11). If you do not have an automatic text box, it probably easiest to abandon your document and repeat the

FIGURE 1.11
The text box (created automatically) sits inside the original margins of the page.

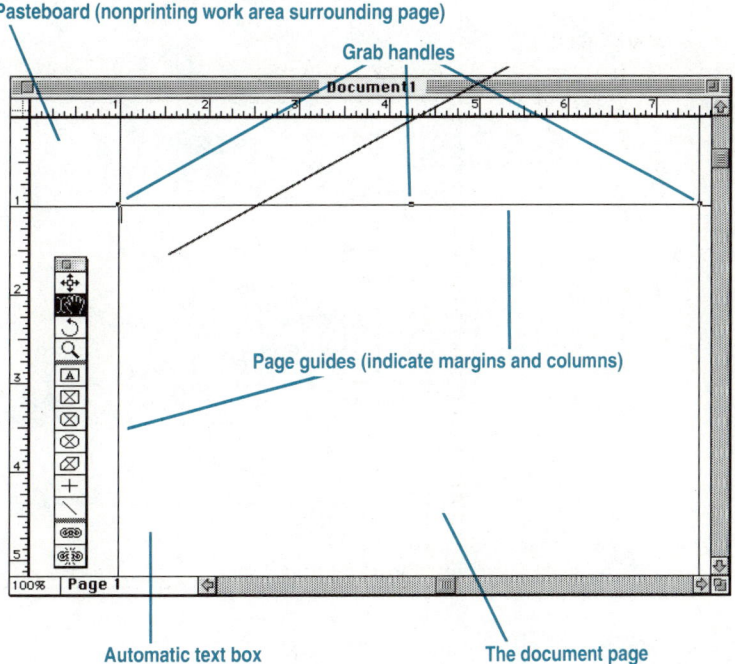

Pasteboard (nonprinting work area surrounding page)

Grab handles

Document1

Page guides (indicate margins and columns)

Automatic text box

The document page

first step of this section. Create another new document, this time making sure to check the Automatic Text Box. To view the entire text box, select View ➤ Fit in Window (see Figure 1.12). Then change it back to 100% for your work!

NOTE

If you are fortunate enough to have a large monitor to work on, your document may look slightly different than depicted in this chapter's graphic representations.

STEP 3: CLICKING IN THE TEXT BOX AREA

Now that everything is set on the work area you can key in the text. QuarkXPress works on the idea of text in text boxes. Graphic elements such as pictures and drawings go in graphic boxes (or picture boxes). This technique will quickly become second nature, even if you're more comfortable with other layout program styles. You can draw lines anywhere.

QuarkXPress is not a drawing program, but you can simulate basic geometric shapes through proper use of the tools. To create an outline geometric, you must create a text or picture box. For more complex graphic drawings, use the appropriate software application and import your picture into QuarkXPress.

NOTE

Remember, you cannot place text in a text box unless it is active.

To key in text, you must make the text box active. Place your cursor in the middle of the work area and click the mouse button. This activates the text box. When you click on the text box area, there should be a change in the box's outline. It will change to a solid line with the familiar grab handles (the little black squares—see Figure 1.13). This means that you have correctly highlighted (or made active) the text box. You can now place characters in the text box area.

At this point, your Tools palette should have either the Item tool (the top tool in the collection) or the Content tool (the second tool down) highlighted. You want the Content tool highlighted. Click it if necessary.

When used in a text box, the Content tool appears as a flashing cursor, similar to those in other word processors. The flashing cursor indicates that you can begin typing in the text box. QuarkXPress resembles a true typesetting program more so than other desktop-publishing programs. For this reason, when you click on the text area, the cursor will always go to the last keystroke position in the box. If it is a new box with no text, your cursor will take the first position in the box. You can edit and format type in the box using leading, alignment, and other kinds of typographic commands.

In the text box you have just clicked on, key in the following text, placing a return at the end of each line:

Eddie Merrik Spring Specials
NovaPed PR-12 Clipless Pedals
$149.95
Velloce Gel Saddles
$29.95

FIGURE 1.13
Click on the text box and the mouse cursor changes to the text editing tool. Note the word processing style cursor at the first keystroke position within the text box. Also, an active item has the traditional Mac grab bars at the corners.

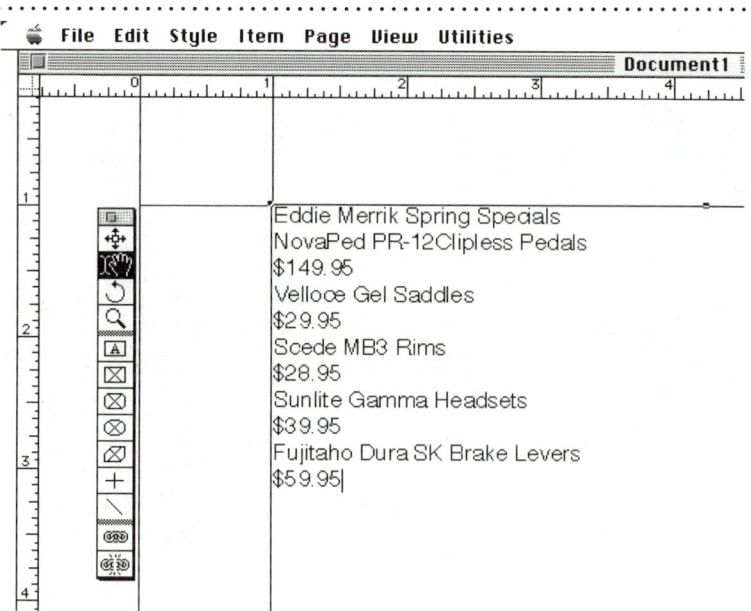

Scede MB3 Rims
$28.95
Sunlite Gamma Headsets
$39.95
Fujataho Dura SK Brake Levers
$59.95

Your screen should resemble the example (see Figure 1.14). This information will work together with other documents you construct throughout the book, building on the corporate communications needs of EM Bicycles, Inc.

STEP 4: CHANGING THE FONT

QuarkXPress allows you to change font information at any time. You are going to take advantage of this ability now. Change the text just keyed in to the font Times (chosen only because every Mac has this typeface) by highlighting all the text you have just keyed in. Click and drag over the text or just press ⌘-A, for Edit ➤ Select All. Your highlighted text should look like the example (see Figure 1.14).

FIGURE 1.14
Key into the text box the text for your first QuarkXPress document.

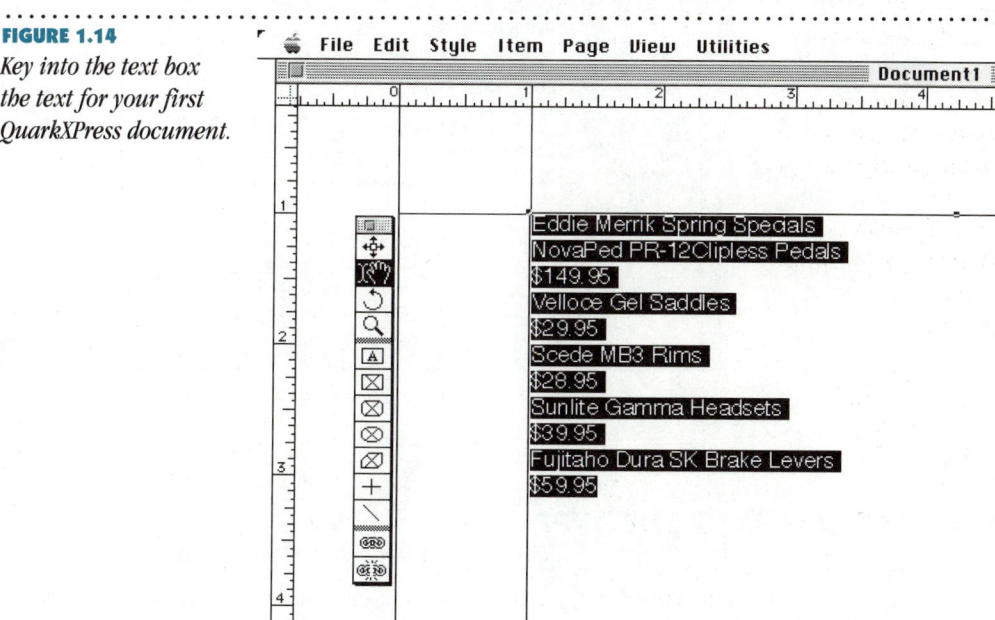

21

NOTE

Menu commands with right-pointing arrows, such as the Font, Size, Type Style, and Color options on the Style menu, indicate that the command leads to another menu (a submenu).

Next, select Style ➤ Font and choose Times (see Figure 1.15). Your highlighted text should change to Times. Look familiar? Every Macintosh owner is familiar with Times (and Helvetica, Courier, Geneva, and Chicago).

FIGURE 1.15

Choose Style ➤ Font, after highlighting the text, to change its type font.

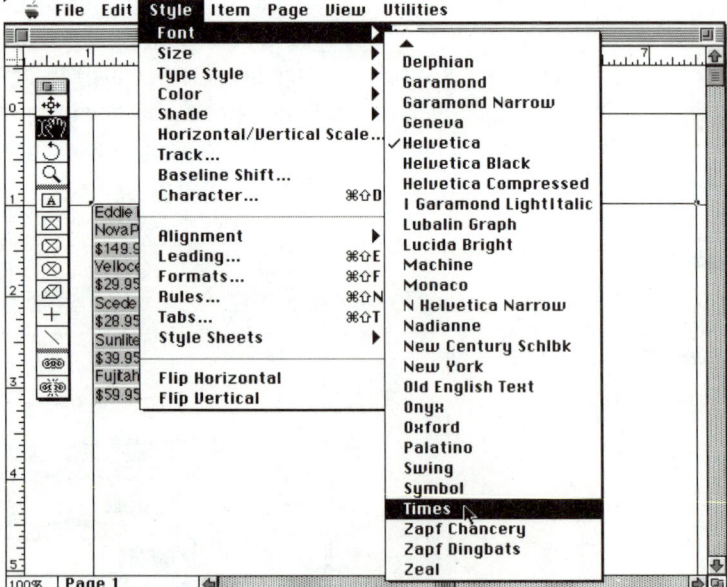

STEP 5: CHANGING THE TYPE SIZE

Highlight the text again if it's not still selected. Then, choose Style ➤ Size and select 36 point. Your highlighted text should change to 36 point size (see Figure 1.16).

FIGURE 1.16

*Your document will
look something like this
after you have changed
the size of the type.*

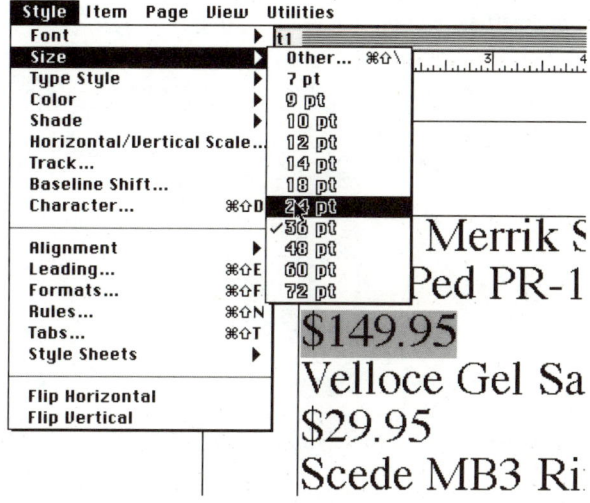

STEP 6: CHANGING THE LEADING FOR THE COPY

Highlight all the text again if it isn't already and choose Style ➤ Leading. The
setting is probably Auto; this is the default. Change leading to 30, representing
30 points of leading. Then click on OK (see Figure 1.17).

STEP 7: CHANGING THE SIZE OF THE PRICE TYPE

This time you will have to highlight each price individually, since there is no way to
highlight every other line. First, click and drag over the $149.95. Then, choose
Style ➤ Size and select 24 point as the type size. Repeat this for each of the other
prices until they are all each 24 point in size. Your document should look like the
example shown in Figure 1.18.

STEP 8: ADJUSTING THE LINE SPACING

Now you are going to work on placing additional leading or line space in the document. This will help shape the look of the page. Line space is an integral part of
good design. To begin, you will place an additional 30 points in key locations of
the text to space lines for the layout. Since the leading is set at 30 points, you can
use the Return key to give additional lines, i.e., 30 points line space, in specific
locations.

FIGURE 1.17

In the Leading dialog box, key in the leading you want in points.

Position the cursor before the *E* in *Eddie*, then click the mouse button. Press the Return key twice. This gives 60 points of additional line space in that location. Next, place the cursor before the *N* in *NovaPed*; then click the mouse button. Press the Return key three times (90 points leading). Then put the cursor after each price. Click the mouse button again to position the cursor; press Return once after each price (30 points line space in each location). Caution: Don't add any additional lines or line space after the last price because it may spill over and cause a second page to form. Your page layout is shaping up; it should now look like Figure 1.19).

FIGURE 1.18
Once you change the size of the type for the prices, your document will have two different type sizes.

Eddie Merrik Spring Specials
NovaPed PR-120 Pedals
$149.95
Velloce Gel Saddles
$29.95
Scede MB3 Rims
$28.95
Sunlite Gamma Headsets
$39.95
Fujataho Dura SK Brake Levers
$59.95

STEP 9: CENTERING THE TEXT IN THE TEXT BOX

To improve the look of this page, let's center the text. Highlight all text elements in the box. Use Edit ➤ Select All (⌘- A) or simply click and drag. Then choose Style ➤ Alignment ➤ Centered.

FIGURE 1.19
Proper use of the Return key gives you an additional 30 points of leading per line.

Eddie Merrik Spring Specials
NovaPed PR-120 Pedals
$149.95
Velloce Gel Saddles
$29.95
Scede MB3 Rims
$28.95
Sunlite Gamma Headsets
$39.95
Fujataho Dura SK Brake Levers
$59.95

STEP 10: SAVING THE DOCUMENT TO YOUR HARD DISK DRIVE

Choose File ➤ Save. Since you haven't saved this document yet, the Save As dialog box appears (see Figure 1.20). This dialog box gives you the option of where to save the document and what name to give it. Once the document is saved, this dialog box will not show unless you explicitly choose the Save As option.

Choose File ➤ Save to save your document to the hard disk. The Save As dialog box will appear, since you've not yet saved this file to disk.

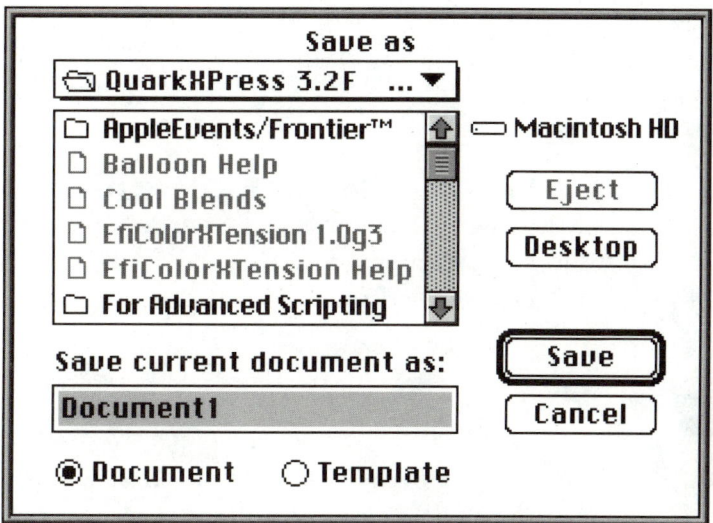

TIP

The rule of thumb about saving is…Save Early, Save Often. That means that practically before the first line of text, save the document. Then about every 15 to 30 minutes, press ⌘-S to save document changes.

TIP

Since it is an excellent idea to save frequently, you might consider purchasing an automatic save utility program. This kind of program will automatically save your work every few minutes, without your having to remember. A utility like this could be a good investment in a production environment. Nothing is quite as frustrating as working on a new document for four hours and have a system glitch take it all away!

Save this document in the existing folder (which should be the QuarkXPress folder) under the name EM Specials, as shown in Figure 1.20. Click on the OK button to accept. Your document is now saved under the name EM Specials, in the QuarkXPress Folder, on the hard-disk. Your document's new name will now appear in its title bar.

STEP 11: PRINTING THE FLYER ON YOUR LASER PRINTER

This step assumes that your Mac is connected to an output device of fairly high quality, such as a laser printer. If not, just follow along. You really do need such a printer to proof QuarkXPress documents.

TIP

To really take advantage of all of the remarkable power and versatility of QuarkXPress, you will need a high-quality printer, such as a laser printer, or at least access to one.

Select the laser printer through the Chooser option the menu Apple. Next choose File ➤ Page Setup and the Page Setup dialog box will appear. This dialog box has many important options, which we will explore in more detail later in the book. For now, just click on Printer Type and change the printer type to match your connected printer. If your machine is not listed here try another printer name. Often unlisted printers work well with LaserWriter (see Figure 1.21). Click OK to close the Page Setup dialog box.

You are now ready to print a copy of your first QuarkXPress document EM Specials. Select File ➤ Print. Again, a dialog box pops up with options. Ignore them for now; just click on OK to print.

Congratulations! You've printed your first QuarkXPress document. Welcome to the club! To quit QuarkXPress, like most other Macintosh programs, you choose File ➤ Quit (⌘-Q).

FIGURE 1.21

In the Page Setup dialog box, set the Printer Type to match your equipment.

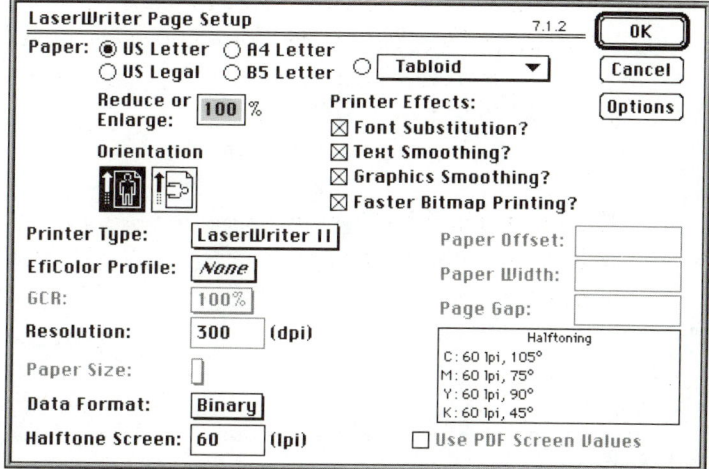

SUMMARY

To create your first QuarkXPress document (The EM Special flyer) you followed these steps:

1. Launch QuarkXPress

2. Create a new document

3. Click in the text box

4. Change the font

5. Change the size

6. Change the leading

7. Adjust the line spacing

8. Center the text

9. Save the document

10. Print the document

In general, to create, store, and print any new QuarkXPress document, you follow these procedures:

1. Launch QuarkXPress
2. Select File ➤ New, adjusting the settings as needed
3. Save under a new document name
4. Input text (and graphics)
5. Save
6. Edit text and graphics
7. Save
8. Print
9. Quit

Anatomy of QuarkXPress

FEATURING

▸ The menu bar and its submenu commands in QuarkXPress

▸ QuarkXPress floating palettes

▸ The menu items of Window and Help as applied to QuarkXPress

▸ The QuarkXPress Environment

properties and capabilities. This is where your document activities occur. It includes the document window with scroll bars, rulers, grid lines, page number indicator, page size indicator, pasteboard and any text, line or graphic elements you may create.

you simply open or create as many as you need. Resize and relocate the documents as necessary on your screen using the new Tile or Cascade options.

on the screen, use either of two techniques. You can select the View menu and an appropriate resize option, or simply highlight the size percentage number at the bottom left corner of the window, then overstrike with your new view (from 25% to 400% in 1% increments).

TRACKS

QuarkXPress, as it appears on the screen, consists of three main components the work area, the floating palettes, and the menu bar. This chapter dissects the three main areas of QuarkXPress.

THE WORK AREA

The work area includes the document window with its scroll bars, rulers, grid lines, page number indicator, page size indicator, pasteboard, and any text or graphic elements of the document page, as you saw in Chapter 1.

The work area only shows if a document is open, so when you launch QuarkXPress, no work area will show. If you launch QuarkXPress by opening a QuarkXPress document, though, you will immediately start with the document's work area.

BASIC COMPONENTS OF THE DOCUMENT WINDOW

Once you open a document, a sizable document window shows. It has scroll bars, scroll arrows, a zoom box, a size box, a close box, and a title bar (see Figure 2.1). You can manipulate the size and location of this window like any other Macintosh window.

WARNING

A document created in earlier versions of QuarkXPress may not be able to open simply by double-clicking the document icon. You may have to launch QuarkXPress and open the document through the File ➤ Open option in the application. The File ➤ Open option is really the best way to open a document anyway!

FIGURE 2.1

The QuarkXPress document window

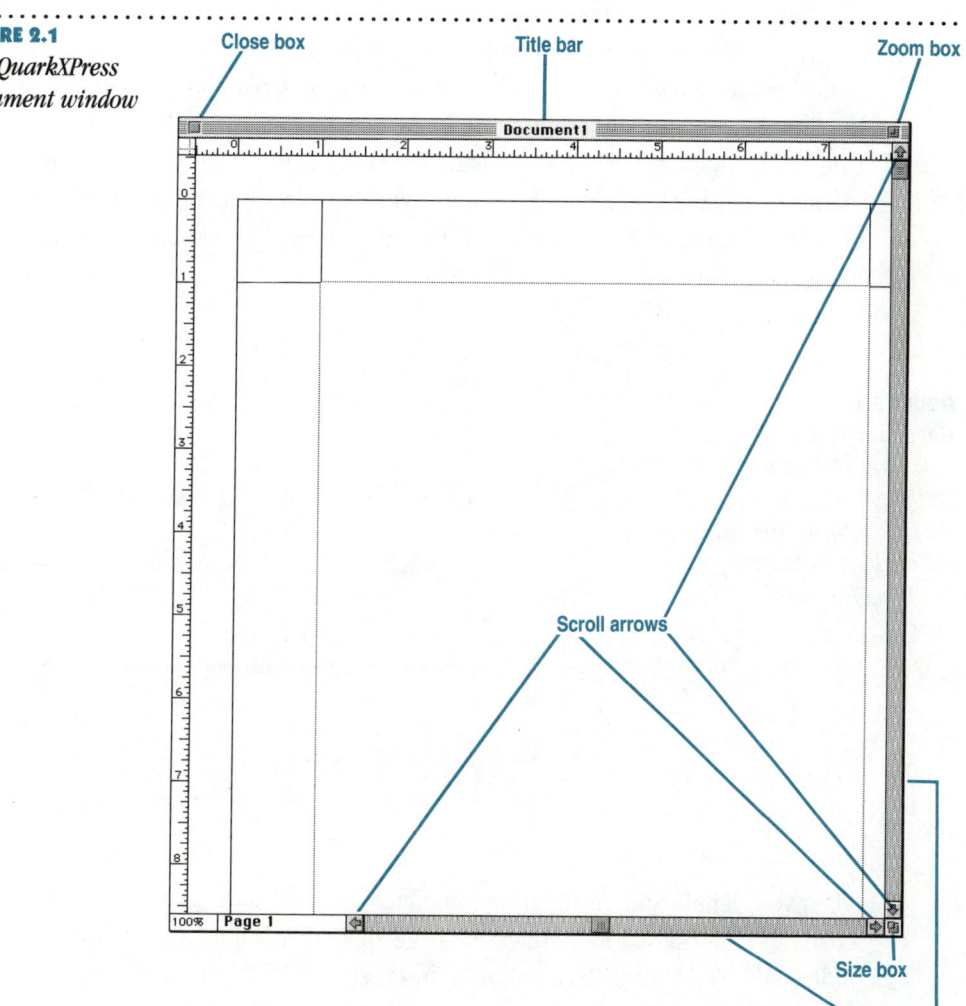

Close box Title bar Zoom box

Document1

Scroll arrows

Size box

Scroll bars

You can open up to seven document windows at a time. The active window will have horizontal parallel lines in the title bar. This is the way the Mac works with most other multiple window situations to indicate which is the active window. You can make changes only in the active window.

The QuarkXPress document window has two additional items that enhance its functionality. They are the page size indicator (the percentage of full size) and the page indicator (see Figure 2.2). You can change the page size on the screen by changing this percentage number. Just type in the new size and press Return or Enter. Later in the book, we will discuss using the Zoom (magnifying) tool and the View menu options to change the size of the page. Page sizes may range from 10 percent to 400 percent. A size called "Thumbnail" is also available through the View menu. Thumbnails do not show a percentage.

FIGURE 2.2

You can change the page size, as it appears on the screen, and see the page number you are working on in this location of the work area.

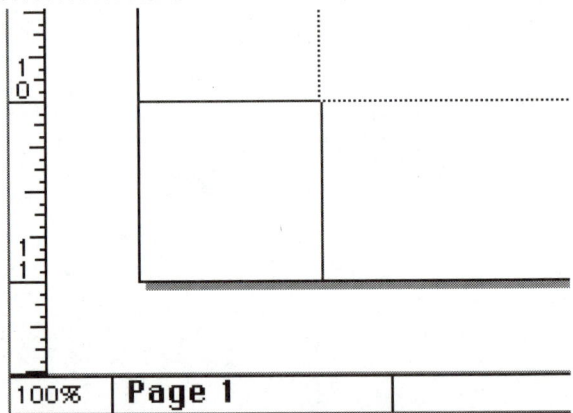

The page identification is the page number, telling which page of the document is currently showing. (If more than one page appears at a time, the top-most page is indicated). The Master Page option is an exception. When chosen, the page identifier reads Master. If parts of two or more pages show, the page number identifies the first page in that sequence. If pages are facing (side-by-side), the page number lists the left or first in the sequence.

You can move the page within the window by a variety of methods. The scroll bars enable you to scroll through the document from page to page. The Apple Extended Keyboard has Page Up, Page Down, Home, and End keys that are very helpful for moving around the document. The Page ➤ Go To option allows you to jump directly to the page of your choice.

A great method of jumping from page to page is through the Document Layout palette. Show this palette by selecting it from the View menu. To change from page to page, double-click on the page icon of your choice (see Figure 2.3).

The Document Layout palette allows you to move from page to page by double-clicking on the page you want.

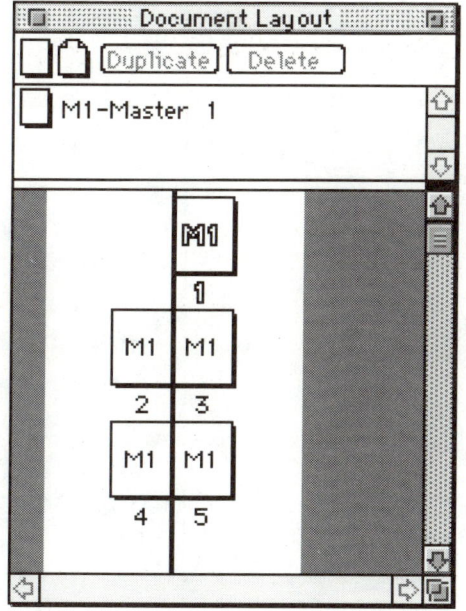

There are other parts of the QuarkXPress document window that may not appear immediately because they are options you can choose to display or hide by choosing Show or Hide from the View menu (see Figure 2.4). They are guides, the baseline grid, the rulers and invisibles. Also included under the View menu are the floating palettes, except for the Library palette, which you must open by using the File ➤ Open command.

RULERS AND GUIDES

Most QuarkXPress users leave the rulers showing. It's convenient, first, because it tells where you are in the page layout, and second, because you can use the rulers to create additional guides. Guides may also be called page guides. They are the

FIGURE 2.4

*The View menu with its
numerous Show and
Hide options*

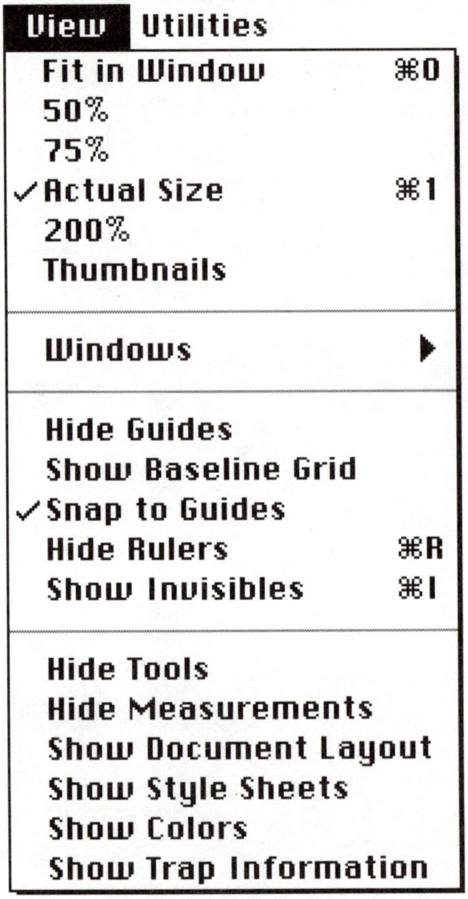

View Utilities	
Fit in Window	⌘0
50%	
75%	
✓**Actual Size**	⌘1
200%	
Thumbnails	
Windows	▶
Hide Guides	
Show Baseline Grid	
✓**Snap to Guides**	
Hide Rulers	⌘R
Show Invisibles	⌘I
Hide Tools	
Hide Measurements	
Show Document Layout	
Show Style Sheets	
Show Colors	
Show Trap Information	

nonprinting lines added to help position items on the page. Guides function as an artist's non-photo blue guide lines on a mechanical layout. In QuarkXPress, guides appear colored (dotted on monochrome monitors). Margin guides and ruler guides are examples of page guides. To make a vertical guide, click in the vertical ruler and drag to the right. Once the guide is in place, release the mouse button. You bring horizontal guides down analogously from the horizontal ruler.

TIP

To create and see the guides properly, first make sure the Edit ➤ Preferences ➤ General setting is set to Guides: In Front; also, choose View ➤ Show Guides if the guides are not showing.

To relocate a guide, click and drag it (outside a text or picture box area) to a new location (see Figure 2.5). To remove a single guideline, simply drag it back to the ruler. To eliminate all vertical or all horizontal guides, move the cursor to the appropriate ruler, hold down the Option key, and click the mouse button. Horizontal

FIGURE 2.5

To relocate a guide (horizontal or vertical), just click and drag. (Be careful to click on the guide outside of a box area, otherwise you may inadvertently move the box rather than the guide.) To eliminate a single guide, drag it back to the ruler. To eliminate all guides, hold down the Option key while clicking on the ruler (you must remove horizontal and vertical guides independently).

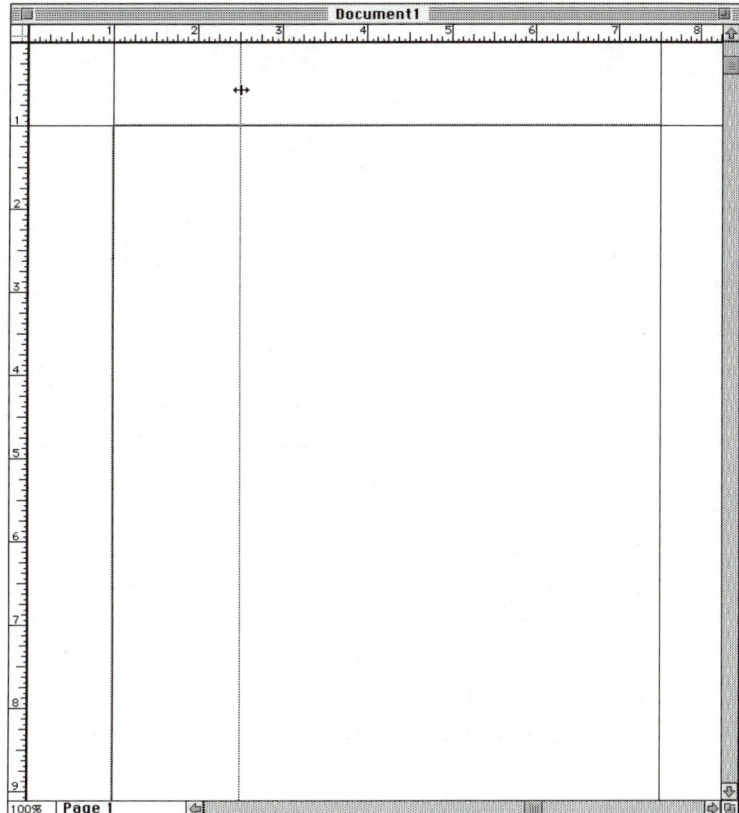

and vertical guides cannot be removed at the same time by this method. To hide all guides, choose View ➤ Hide Guides. This does not actually delete the guides, it just hides them from view.

TIP

To eliminate all vertical guides in the document, press the Option key then click on the vertical ruler. To eliminate all horizontal guides, press Option and click on the horizontal ruler. You cannot eliminate both the horizontal and vertical guides at the same time in this version of QuarkXPress. Be aware that this operation cannot be undone.

The Show/Hide Guides menu option also affects the original guides of your document page, the margin guides (see Figure 2.6).

THE BASELINE GRID

Another group of lines that may show on the work area is the baseline grid. Select View ➤ Show Baseline Grid to see it (see Figure 2.7). It consists of a gridwork of horizontal lines, their positions based on the settings in the Typographic Preferences area—choose Edit ➤ Preferences. This is helpful in graphic design for aligning text or graphic elements. The problem with the baseline grid option is that you might expect the linework to follow the text baselines, as the name implies, but it doesn't. Instead, it is a predetermined numerical value. If the text changes in size or leading, it may not conform to the baseline grid any longer. The baseline grid value is changed only when you change the Typographic Preferences Baseline Grid option yourself.

You can have the rulers show a variety of measurement systems. Choose Edit ➤ Preferences ➤ General . The horizontal and vertical rulers can even act independently. The available units of measure are inches, inches decimal, picas, points, millimeters, centimeters, and ciceros (see Figure 2.8).

FIGURE 2.6

This is a reduced page layout, showing the margin guides. These can be shown or hidden from the View menu along with all the other guides.

Regardless of the measurement system chosen, the top left corner of the document page always defaults to the 0,0 position on the ruler. This 0,0 position can be repositioned by clicking and dragging the ruler corner box (see Figure 2.9).

FIGURE 2.7

The baseline grid lines as they appear when you choose Show Baseline Grid. These are only guides; they will not print.

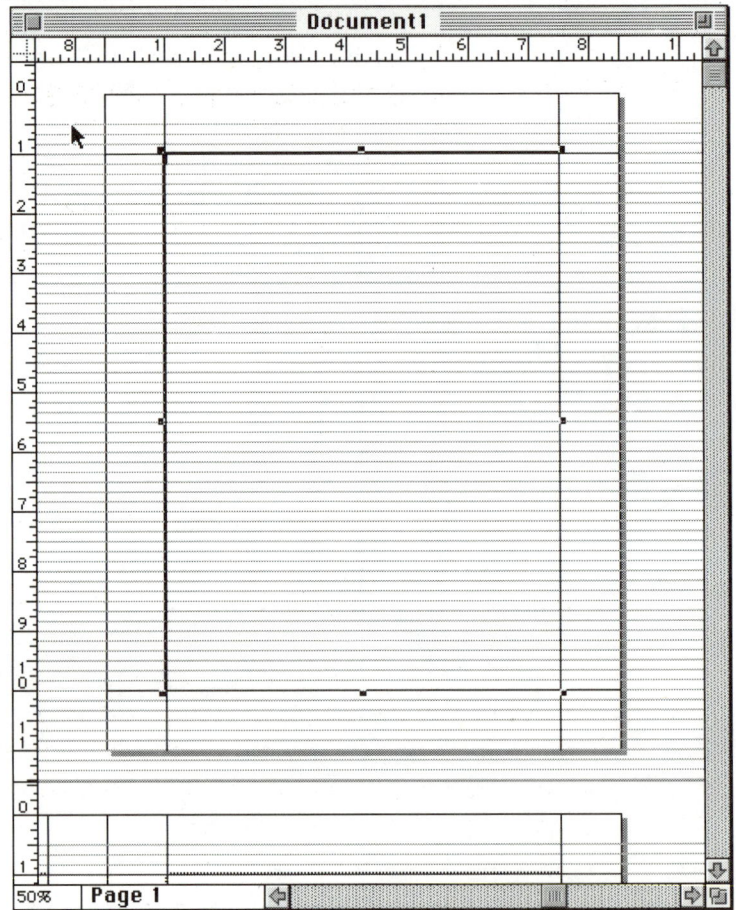

Another useful option under the View menu is Show Invisibles. Invisibles are those characters or keystrokes that are not normally seen, such as spaces, returns, and tabs. Showing invisibles can be handy for complex projects to keep track of your progress within the document. It doesn't take a very complex layout before you wonder where these keystrokes are (see Figure 2.10).

FIGURE 2.8

Select the unit of measurement to use from a variety of options. You may choose horizontal measurement independent of the vertical measurement system.

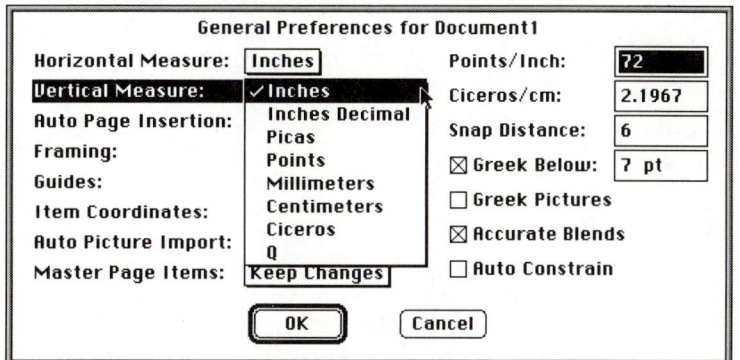

General Preferences for Document1

Horizontal Measure: | Inches

Vertical Measure: | ✓Inches
Inches Decimal
Picas
Points
Millimeters
Centimeters
Ciceros
Q

Auto Page Insertion:
Framing:
Guides:
Item Coordinates:
Auto Picture Import:
Master Page Items: | Keep Changes

Points/Inch: | 72
Ciceros/cm: | 2.1967
Snap Distance: | 6
☒ Greek Below: | 7 pt
☐ Greek Pictures
☒ Accurate Blends
☐ Auto Constrain

[OK]   [Cancel]

THE FLOATING PALETTES

There are separate windows of information within QuarkXPress called floating palettes (see Figure 2.11). You can show, move, and often resize these to fit your needs. Rarely would you want to have all palettes showing at once; but if you had multiple monitors, you could use one just for floating palettes and the other for documents. With just one standard monitor, though, they would needlessly waste screen space. For instance, you don't need Trap Information when working on a document that you intend to print in black-and-white. Trap Information is useful when you are working on a full-color job you intend to separate on the imagesetter. You will soon learn to be selective of the vast array of options within QuarkXPress!

NOTE

At a recent QUI (Quark User International conference), the attendees were informally polled as to their use of large monitors when working on QuarkXPress. Nearly 90 percent of the attendees indicated that they use large monitors. This is ideal for placing floating palettes on the screen while working on the document. Naturally, the larger the monitor the better, but cost is a major factor here.

FIGURE 2.9

Click and drag the corner from its original 0,0 position to relocate the 0,0 indicator. To revert to the default, double-click on the original 0,0 box.

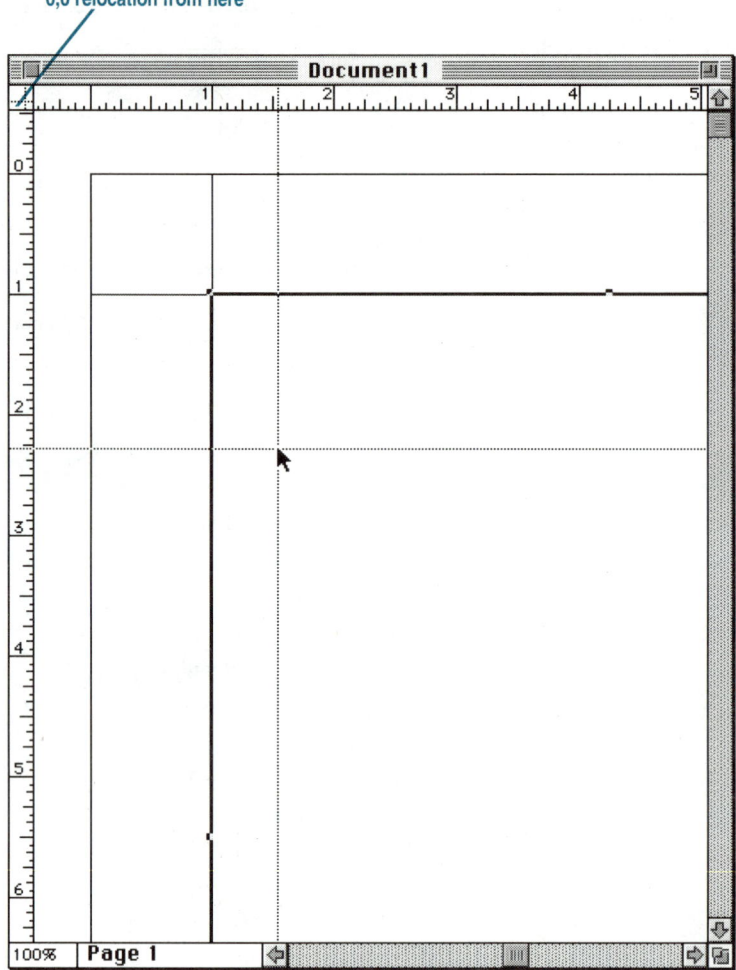

0,0 relocation from here

We will discuss the floating palettes, which are called Tools, Measurements, Document Layout, Style Sheets, Colors, and Trap Information, later in the book as applicable.

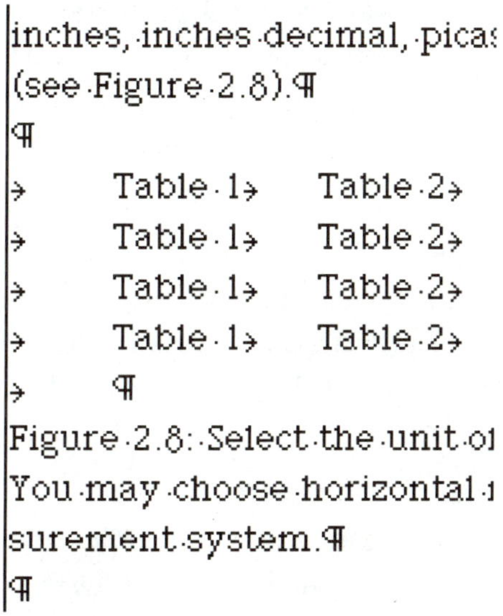

FIGURE 2.10

You can Show or Hide Invisibles from the View menu. Invisibles show keystrokes such as spaces, tabs, and returns.

inches,·inches·decimal,·picas

(see·Figure·2.8).¶

¶

→   Table·1→   Table·2→

→   Table·1→   Table·2→

→   Table·1→   Table·2→

→   Table·1→   Table·2→

→   ¶

Figure·2.8:·Select·the·unit·of

You·may·choose·horizontal·i

surement·system.¶

¶

FIGURE 2.11

You can show as many of the floating palettes as you like, but it is best to use them judiciously to save screen space.

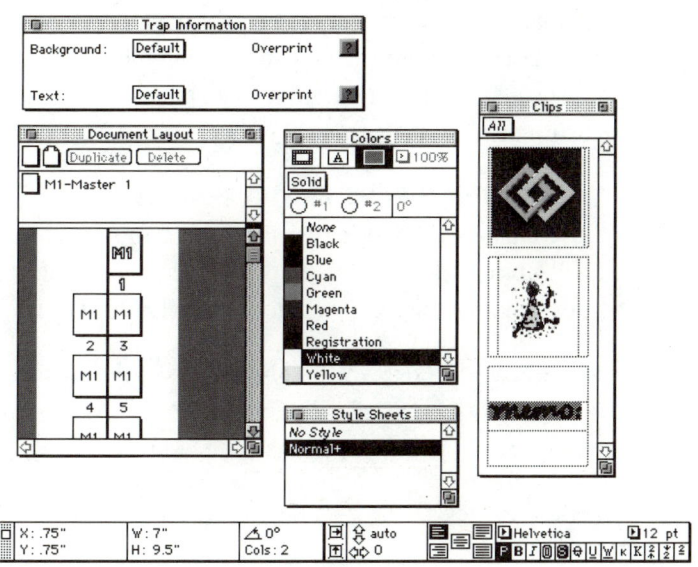

THE MENUS

A third major area in the anatomy of QuarkXPress is the menu bar. It consists of the Apple, File, Edit, Style, Item, Page, View, and Utilities menus. In System 7, there are also the Help and Application Menus.

THE APPLE MENU

The options on your Apple menu will depend on the particular desk accessories and other items you have in your Apple Menu Items folder. At any rate, its contents are independent of QuarkXPress with the exception of the About QuarkXPress option (see Figure 2.12).

WARNING

Every program has its "quirks" and QuarkXPress is no exception. You may have certain applications, inits, or desk accessories that are not compatible with QuarkXPress.

The About QuarkXPress option shows the QuarkXPress logo screen, complete with registration information and version number. If you hold down the Option key while choosing About QuarkXPress, an information box appears, called QuarkXPress Environment (see Figure 2.13).

THE QUARKXPRESS ENVIRONMENT BOX

Since this box is important, a short run through of its contents is in order. The following briefly details each bit of information. (When you are finished perusing the information in this box, you close it by clicking OK.)

XPRESS VERSION: 3.2   This pertains to the version of the QuarkXPress application loaded. You may also have other versions on the hard drive at the same time, but this refers to the one that is open at present.

FIGURE 2.12
The Apple menu options available while in QuarkXPress. Yours may look different.

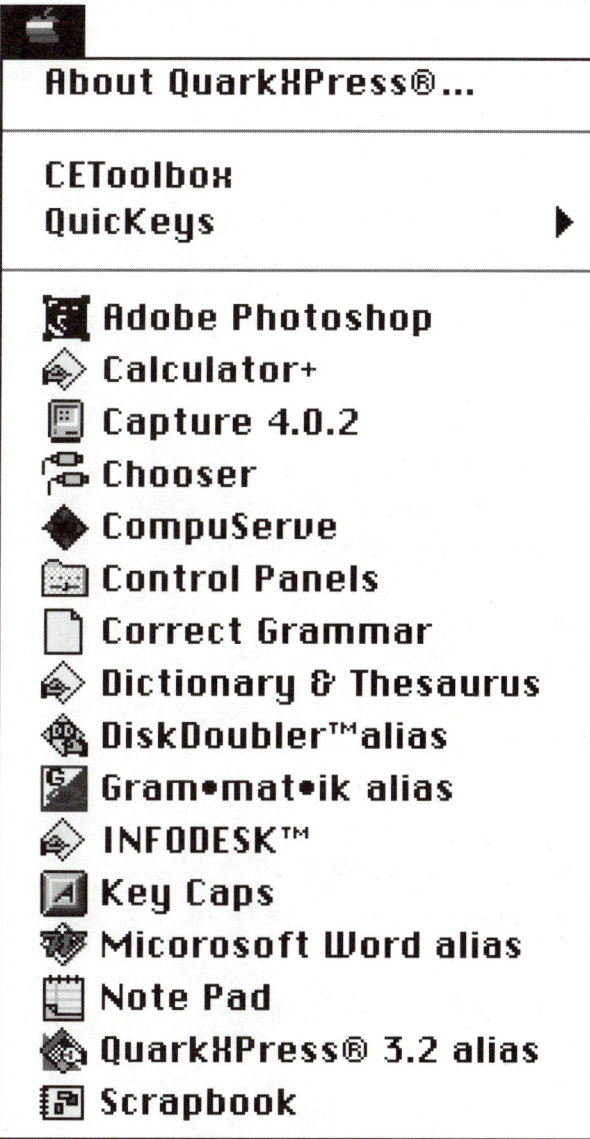

FIGURE 2.13
About QuarkXPress brings up the standard logo box unless you press the Option key while selecting About QuarkXPress. This brings the QuarkXPress Environment information box.

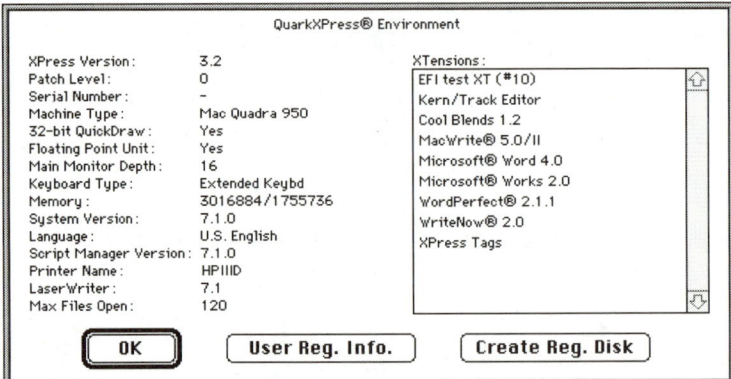

PATCH LEVEL: 0   This tells the patch version number. A patch is a program fix shipped to you after the main program is released. If someone determines that a glitch occurs under certain situations (e.g., the letter z is dropped when output on Saturdays) and that it is a significant problem, programmers will release a few lines of code which enables the program to work around this problem. These lines of code are called a patch or zap. This example shows no patches loaded at this time. Hopefully, there is no need to have a patch loaded!

SERIAL NUMBER: -   The serial number shows the registration of this specific copy of QuarkXPress; each registered user copy has a specific serial number. In a network, the same serial numbered copy can be open on only one machine, regardless of its physical location. QuarkXPress checks the network to make sure no identical serial numbered copies are already open. No serial number is shown in the example, as this is a beta copy supplied for writing purposes.

MACHINE TYPE: QUADRA 950   This identifies the type of Macintosh computer the software is loaded and running on. In this example, the machine running QuarkXPress is Macintosh Quadra 950. It is not important that the exact model be identified here. For example, if you have a Mac LCII, the machine type may be listed as simply LC. Frequent changes in Mac models often outpace the software revisions for this, so if your machine is not properly identified, don't worry!

32-BIT QUICKDRAW: YES   This refers to an option you may select (if your Mac allows) to create images on the screen in QuickDraw 32-bit quality. QuickDraw is Apple's name for the proprietary technology that draws images on the computer's monitor. The highest resolution available at this time is 32-bit quality. See your Mac owner's guide for further information in this area.

FLOATING POINT UNIT: YES   This option indicates the installation of a floating point unit (FPU) microchip that allows for faster math computation when required. Some Macintosh units come with this as a standard while others have it available as an option. The cost for a typical FPU chip for the Mac is around $150. It is a recommended option.

MAIN MONITOR DEPTH: 16   This represents the number of bit combinations available to create colors on your computer's monitor. This example of 16 represents 16 bit-per-pixel color graphics, giving tens of thousands of colors. Higher quality may use 24 bit-per-pixel images, which may require the installation of an optional graphics board, or video RAM, in your machine.

KEYBOARD TYPE: EXTENDED KEYBD   Apple has two keyboards available: the standard keyboard (without a function key array) and the larger extended keyboard (with fifteen function keys). The extended keyboard is superior for extra functionality and its "touch" or feel of the keys.

TIP

Buy the extended keyboard! It is invaluable when working on extensive publication data, especially when you team up the program with a utility such as QuicKeys.

MEMORY: 3016884/1755736   The memory category has two factor numbers: the first represents the approximate amount of memory recommended for QuarkX-Press to load and function; the second represents the amount of memory left after loading and document opening. As you open more documents, the memory remaining will decrease.

TIP

Buy more memory! Today memory is relatively inexpensive. You can buy a megabyte of memory for under $50 through most mail-order outlets and install it yourself. Although QuarkXPress can run on almost any Mac with a minimum of 2 Mb, it really runs best with more memory on a faster machine. If you are going to use the new EFIColorXTension, QuarkXPress requests a minimum partition of 3 Mb in RAM. Try to get 4 Mb of memory as a minimum, 8 Mb as a comfortable medium, and 2 gigabytes as optimum. Just kidding! But if you can afford to get 2 gigs of memory in your Mac, why not spend the money on a new Quadra instead, then buy 16 Mb simms?

SYSTEM VERSION: 7.1.0   This number tells you the version of the Macintosh operating system.

LANGUAGE: U.S. ENGLISH   The current language you have loaded the system to work under. QuarkXPress is available in over a dozen languages for use around the world.

TIP

If you are in the business of producing foreign language documents, you may be interested in a new product from Quark called Passport. This is a new version of QuarkXPress that comes with fifteen different foreign languages within the same package.

SCRIPT MANAGER VERSION: 7.1.0   This is a reference to the programming within System 7.

PRINTER NAME: HPIIID   This is the name of the printer last selected under the Chooser. Printers can be renamed, e.g., Ralph's Printer, Graphics Department Printer, etc., by many programs, so you have to be careful what printer to select on your network.

LASERWRITER: 7.1   This is the version of LaserWriter software that outputs to the printer.

MAX FILES OPEN: 120   The maximum calculated number of files that can remain open based on this Macintosh's hardware and software capabilities.

XTENSIONS: XTensions are programs added to QuarkXPress that give it more capabilities for certain situations. Several of those shown in the example are filters that allow the importing of word processed documents, retaining their original indents, tabs, etc. For more details on XTensions, see Part VII: QuarkXTensions.

THE FILE MENU

The File pull-down menu has five separate areas of operation (see Figure 2.14). The first section deals with opening or creating a new document, which you used in Chapter 1.

Next, there are commands for saving and closing documents. Also, if there is a mistake, the Revert to Saved option retrieves the last saved copy of the document. The Revert to Saved option is your friend! Anytime you make a mistake, consider using this option.

NOTE

EPS stands for Encapsulated PostScript. This is one of the highest quality images you can work with on the Macintosh because a PostScript file can be resized without loss of quality when imported or exported to other PostScript-compatible programs. In addition, EPS files will print equally well at almost any size.

The Get Text (or Picture), Save Text, and Save Page as EPS options allow you to import or save document elements. Get Text (in a text box) allows you to import text

FIGURE 2.14
*The File menu in
QuarkXPress*

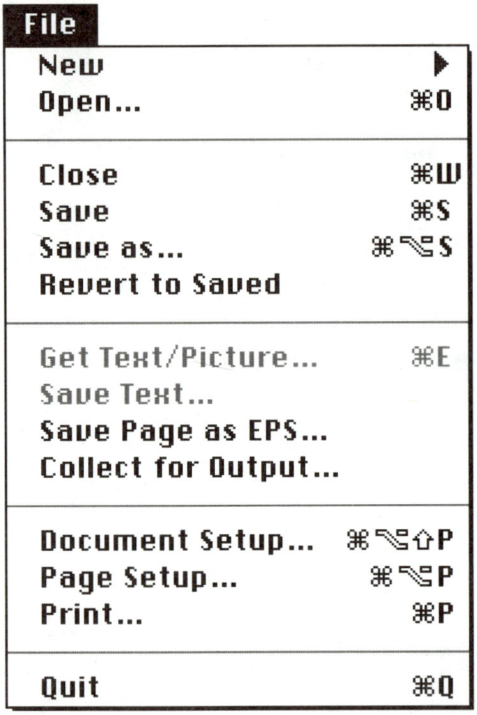

File	
New	▶
Open...	⌘O
Close	⌘W
Save	⌘S
Save as...	⌘⌥S
Revert to Saved	
Get Text/Picture...	⌘E
Save Text...	
Save Page as EPS...	
Collect for Output...	
Document Setup...	⌘⌥⇧P
Page Setup...	⌘⌥P
Print...	⌘P
Quit	⌘Q

from a word processed file directly into a text box. In a graphic box, the option reads Get Picture, allowing you to import a photograph or graphic element into a picture box. The Save Text option exports text to a separate ASCII file format. The Save Page as EPS option takes a "snapshot" of the page and saves it as a separate Encapsulated PostScript (EPS) file for future use in QuarkXPress or other applications.

The next section under the File menu consists of Document Setup, Page Setup, and Print. Each option brings up its own dialog box, allowing you to fine-tune certain options. Document Setup lets you change the page size or specify facing pages (see Figure 2.15). The Page Setup option determines various configurations for the output printer (see Figure 2.16). The Print option brings a dialog box that determines number of copies, specific pages, and other printing variables (see Figure 2.17).

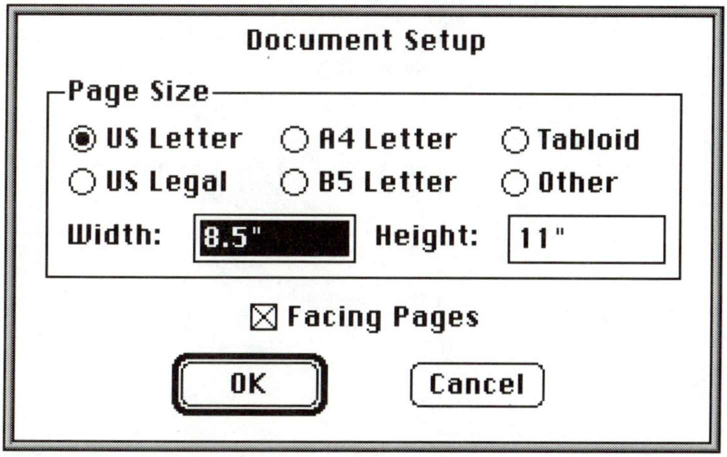

FIGURE 2.15
The Document Setup dialog box allows modification after the document has been created.

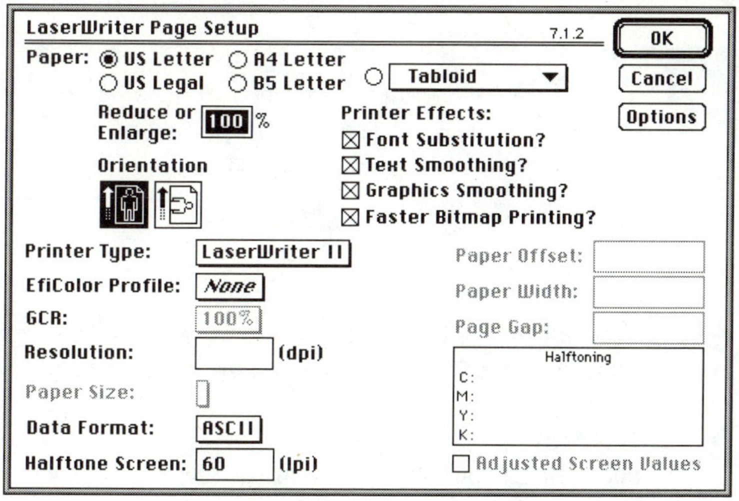

Document Setup

┌─**Page Size**─────────────────────────────┐

⦿ **US Letter**   ○ **A4 Letter**   ○ **Tabloid**

○ **US Legal**   ○ **B5 Letter**   ○ **Other**

Width: `8.5"`   **Height:** `11"`

⊠ **Facing Pages**

[**OK**]   [**Cancel**]

FIGURE 2.16
The Page Setup dialog box allows you to preset output specifications for your printer.

LaserWriter Page Setup   7.1.2   [**OK**]

Paper: ⦿ **US Letter**   ○ **A4 Letter**   [**Cancel**]
           ○ **US Legal**   ○ **B5 Letter**   ○ [**Tabloid** ▾]

Reduce or Enlarge: `100`%   **Printer Effects:**   [**Options**]
                                 ⊠ **Font Substitution?**

Orientation   ⊠ **Text Smoothing?**
                                 ⊠ **Graphics Smoothing?**
                                 ⊠ **Faster Bitmap Printing?**

Printer Type: `LaserWriter II`   **Paper Offset:** [   ]

EfiColor Profile: `None`   **Paper Width:** [   ]

GCR: `100%`   **Page Gap:** [   ]

Resolution: [   ] **(dpi)**   **Halftoning**
                                        C:
Paper Size: [ ]   M:
                                        Y:
Data Format: `ASCII`   K:

Halftone Screen: `60` **(lpi)**   ☐ **Adjusted Screen Values**

FIGURE 2.17
The Print dialog box contains options for QuarkXPress specific to imagesetter and color output.

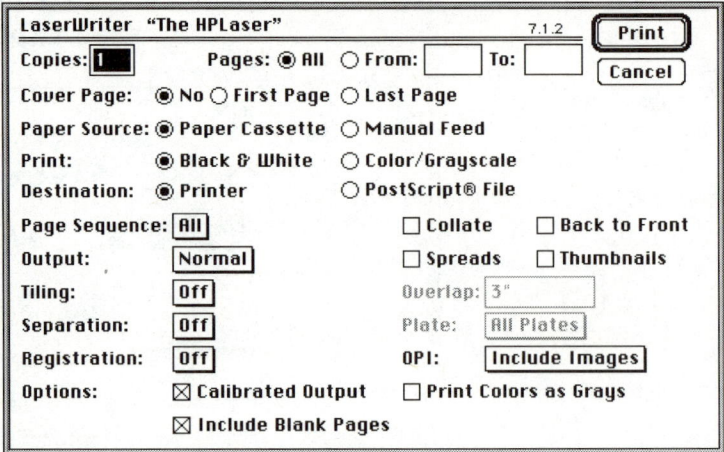

TIP

The Quit command is available only in applications, not in the Finder. If you are working with QuarkXPress and accidentally get into Finder (in MultiFinder or System 7), one way to check is to look for the Quit command on the File menu.

As customary in most Mac programs, the File menu command also contains the Quit command. This and other commands can be selected by keyboard equivalents, in this case, ⌘-Q. These shortcuts are listed on the menu.

THE EDIT MENU

Under the Edit pull-down menu are five separate categories for changing the document. The first area is your "safety net." It is the Undo command. Every QuarkXPress user relies heavily on the undo command! It will undo the last edit or command; this can be a change of type style, deletion of text, or any other single action. As long as the error is noticed before another action, it can be reversed with the Undo command. Be aware, though, that not everything can be undone.

Next are the infamous Cut, Copy, Paste, Clear, and Select All commands. These work the same in QuarkXPress as they do in any other application. However, use caution when cutting and pasting across software applications. Sometimes, QuarkXPress items like text and graphic boxes don't cross over to other applications. For example, you may not be able to copy a picture box in QuarkXPress and paste it in a Microsoft Works document. You can, of course, cut, copy, paste, and drag various elements from one QuarkXPress document to another (see Figure 2.18).

FIGURE 2.18
The Edit menu in
QuarkXPress

Edit	
Can't Undo	⌘Z
Cut	⌘X
Copy	⌘C
Paste	⌘U
Clear	
Select All	⌘A
Subscribe To...	
Subscriber Options...	
Show Clipboard	
Find/Change	⌘F
Preferences	▶
Style Sheets...	
Colors...	
H&Js...	⌘⌥H

NOTE

At a recent QUI, discussion was given to the topic of the Subscribe To command within QuarkXPress. Basically, it was an option that nobody used. Many said they avoided Subscribe To by importing through the network or exchanging disks. Others just did not have a need for this function. They also complained about the limitation of Subscribe To; namely, that it can only import PICT format pictures, rather than the higher quality EPS and TIFF images.

The Edit Menu in QuarkXPress 3.2 has Subscribe To and Subscriber Options, useful only if you are linked to another Mac and both are running System 7. In the proper environment, this Publish and Subscribe team allow each Mac in a networked environment to act as a file server. You can establish authorization for certain people to access your files. In turn, other Mac users have established rights to file access on their machines. QuarkXPress includes a built-in authorization option.

You might wonder why would anyone use this option if you can already import text and picture material. There are probably several reasons, but unless you are in a business that really needs this function it seems like a wasted feature. Consider the situation where a TIFF (tagged image file format) picture is on file somewhere down the network. If you are working on a document and someone else is retouching the photo on a different Mac, you can subscribe to that file. Simultaneous production can take place and when the photo is ready, it is already updated through the Publish/Subscribe capability. Just a thought! Maybe you have a better idea? Review your Publish and Subscribe material in the Macintosh user manuals. Maybe you will think of something for the publishing environment.

The Show/Hide Clipboard command gives a window that has the last item saved there with the Cut or Copy commands. It can hold only one "item" at a time. To store several images, use a Library file.

The last area under Edit combines several seemingly unrelated features. First, the Find/Change command allows the user to search and replace a particular word or phrase. One beautiful feature of Find/Change is the ability to Find/Change type attributes. You can use the Find/Change for type attributes if a specific range of text is noted to find and replace. In this event, the Find/Change dialog box resembles much of the Font Usage dialog box (Utilities ➤ Font Usage). The two options differ in that Find/Change must find a character or range of characters to alter type attributes. The Font Usage dialog box does not require searching for any text; you can search for attributes only and change according to your needs.

An extremely important command on the Edit menu that may alter all your documents created in QuarkXPress is Preferences. It has four subcategories: Application, General, Typographic, and Tools. The Preferences dialog boxes enable the user to establish certain criteria for the application or document, such as the color of guides, automatic leading, etc. In most of the preferences areas, changes to a dialog box affect the entire application, not just the document open at the time.

Style Sheets is a command that allows a predetermined type, look, and arrangement for a text area. For example, create one style sheet for the paragraph text of a document. It contains information in the type font, style, size, indentation, and any other pertinent material for that text block. Use that stored information in the style sheet again for other blocks of type that require those specifications. You can also assign a "hot key" to the style sheet. This means you can just highlight paragraph text and press one predefined style sheet key, like F5, perhaps F6 is the style sheet key for subheads and F7 is the key for headings. This feature is a real time-saver in document processing!

The Colors command allows you to determine which colors will be available from the color palette at any one time. QuarkXPress has a wide range of color options, including six color models: Pantone, Focoltone, Trumatch, HSB (Hue, Saturation, Brightness), RGB (Red, Green, Blue), and CMYK (Cyan, Magenta, Yellow, Black). It would be impossible to position all colors on one color palette, so QuarkXPress shows a limited number of colors at one time. A major thrust of version 3.2 is that of color separation potential, through the use of the EFIColorXTension. This will be detailed later in the book, but keep the thought of higher level color potential as you go through the chapters.

H&Js is the last command on the Edit menu. It enables you to determine the scope of hyphenation and justification use in the document. Selection of this option brings up a new dialog box for the H&J area.

THE STYLE MENU

The Style Menu has two areas that control the typographical look of the document (see Figure 2.19). First, commands are available for selecting the proper type font, size, style, etc., plus color and kerning. These change the individual type character's looks. Then the bottom section of this pull-down menu contains selections for how the entire line or group of lines will look. It includes selections for leading, alignment, tabulations, etc.

FIGURE 2.19

The Style menu in QuarkXPress changes depending on the item involved. Shown are the Style menus for Text, Picture, and Line items, respectively.

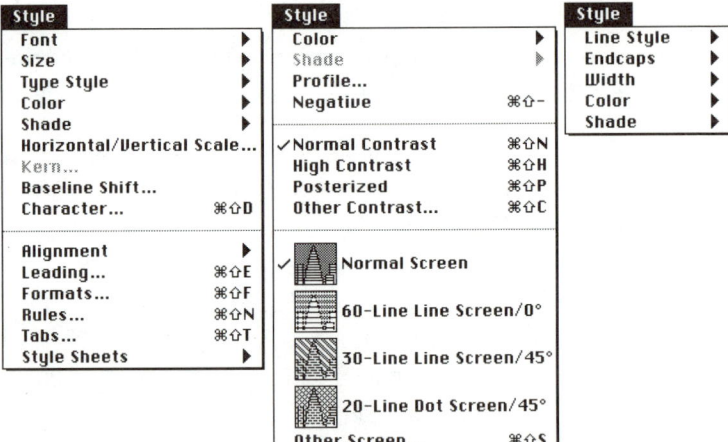

THE ITEM MENU

This menu controls "items" defined as text boxes or picture boxes (and their enclosed elements) or lines. There are five areas of interest on the Item menu (see Figure 2.20). The first area includes Modify, Frame, and Runaround. These commands bring up dialog boxes that control certain capabilities of the text and graphic boxes. They control such capabilities as placement, size, layers, and frames of the box areas. Once an item is selected as a text box, picture box, or line element, you can manipulate it using one or more of these dialog boxes.

FIGURE 2.20

The Item menu in
QuarkXPress

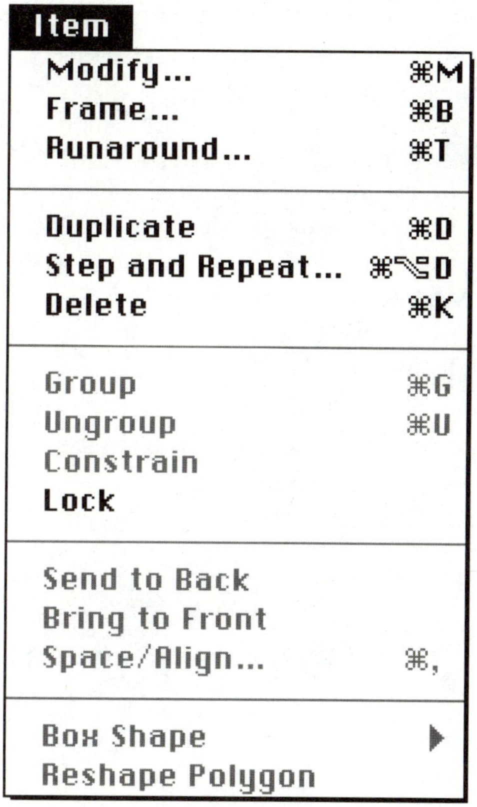

Item	
Modify...	⌘M
Frame...	⌘B
Runaround...	⌘T
Duplicate	⌘D
Step and Repeat...	⌘⌥D
Delete	⌘K
Group	⌘G
Ungroup	⌘U
Constrain	
Lock	
Send to Back	
Bring to Front	
Space/Align...	⌘,
Box Shape	▶
Reshape Polygon	

The second group of commands also works with selected items. The Duplicate, Step and Repeat, and Delete options reproduce or delete items.

The commands of Group, Ungroup, Constrain, and Lock control several groups of elements for movement control. Group combines several elements into one for movement or duplication; Ungroup reverses the Group command; Constrain combines one or more elements to be constrained in the box; and Lock makes sure that you can pin down an item so it will not be repositioned (moved) on the page accidentally. You can Unlock locked items for future repositioning.

The Send to Back and Bring to Front commands give control to layering of elements. Each item sits on a separate layer controlled by these options. The Space/Align option aligns objects on the same plane (vertical and horizontal positioning, as opposed to layering).

Picture or graphic boxes can take on shapes other than simple rectangular dimensions. The last group of commands—Picture Box Shape and Reshape Polygon—on the Item menu allow the user to control the graphic box shape.

THE PAGE MENU

The Page menu encompasses all commands for page manipulation (see Figure 2.21). It includes functions to add, delete, and move pages, as well as to group and display pages. It also has commands for maneuvering through the document from page to page. This menu group gives the user the ability to jump from document pages to master pages.

FIGURE 2.21

Page menu options in
QuarkXPress

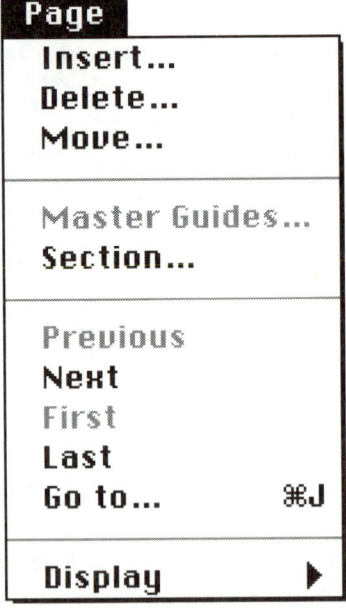

THE VIEW MENU

This menu has multiple components, starting with a resize option for the display of the page (see Figure 2.22). Specifically, the options for resizing include Fit in Window, 50%, 75%, Actual Size, 200%, and Thumbnails size layouts. Fit in Window and Actual Size have the keyboard shortcuts ⌘-O and ⌘-I.

As described earlier, this is one method of resizing the page as it appears on the monitor. Other methods include editing the Size Percentage box in the document window and using the Zoom tool from the Tools palette.

The remaining two sections under the View menu include the Show/Hide commands. The first area includes functions to hide or display various document parts, including guides, invisible keystrokes, grid lines, and rulers. These are all available to help you in the layout of the page elements. They are not mandatory for function of QuarkXPress and certain options are often hidden.

The floating palette Show/Hide options are in the next group. They allow you to display any of the floating palettes, including Tools, Measurements, Document Layout, Style Sheets, Colors, and Trap Information.

THE UTILITIES MENU

The last QuarkXPress menu is Utilities (see Figure 2.23). As the name suggests, this menu contains additional tools intended to make your job a little easier and to give you a great deal of quality control. There are several areas under the Utilities menu.

FIGURE 2.22

The View menu with its many Show/Hide commands

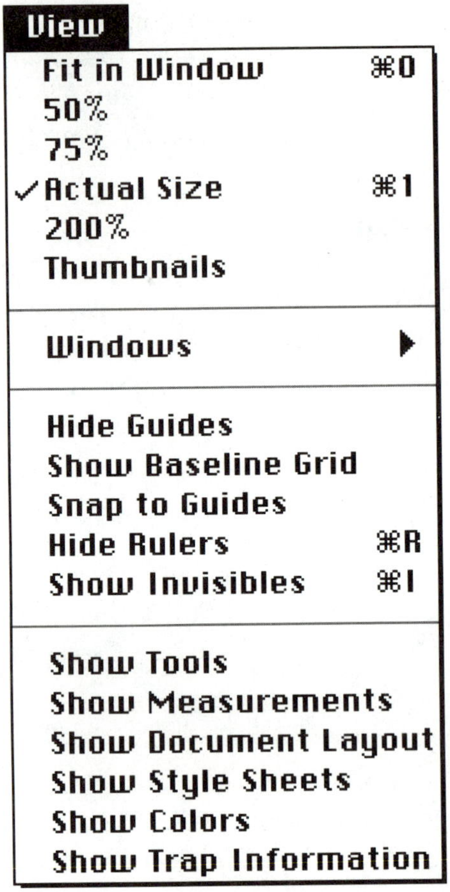

View

Fit in Window	⌘0
50%	
75%	
✓**Actual Size**	⌘1
200%	
Thumbnails	
Windows	▶
Hide Guides	
Show Baseline Grid	
Snap to Guides	
Hide Rulers	⌘R
Show Invisibles	⌘I
Show Tools	
Show Measurements	
Show Document Layout	
Show Style Sheets	
Show Colors	
Show Trap Information	

The first section comprises the dictionary and spell-checker. It allows spell checking from a listed dictionary or from supplemental dictionaries you create.

Next, a dialog box involving hyphenation control is available through Suggested Hyphenation and Hyphenation Exceptions options. The Library command follows, giving you control over archive folders of graphic materials.

FIGURE 2.23

The Utilities menu has, among other things, the Library floating palette.

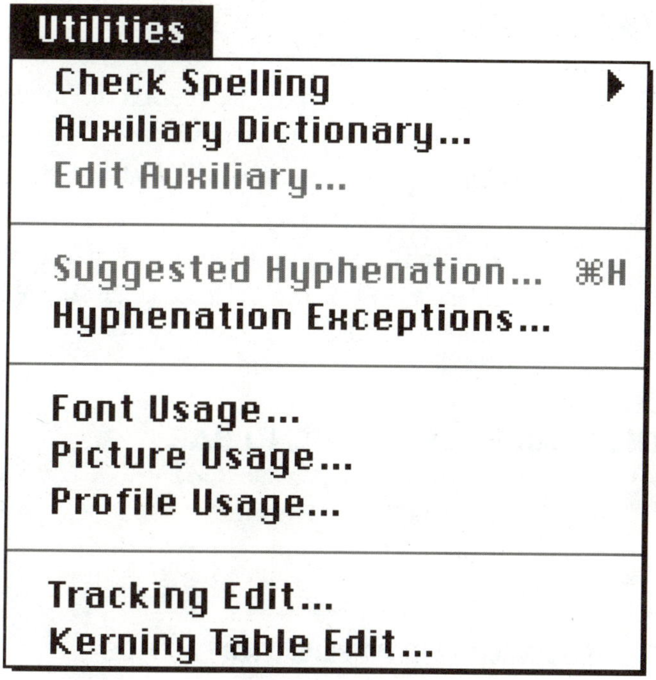

Utilities

Check Spelling ▶

Auxiliary Dictionary...

Edit Auxiliary...

Suggested Hyphenation... ⌘H

Hyphenation Exceptions...

Font Usage...

Picture Usage...

Profile Usage...

Tracking Edit...

Kerning Table Edit...

The Font Usage and Picture Usage commands are in the next group. Font Usage is similar to the earlier Find/Change command under the Edit menu. It does everything the Find/Change command does, but in font information only; this option does not search for character or word information. It is invaluable for changing font options throughout a document. For example, you can key in copy using a font that is easy to read on the screen, then change it later for high print quality. The Picture Usage command allows you to scroll through a visual representation of all pictures within the document.

WARNING

If you get involved with QuarkXPress XTensions, they may alter the appearance or contents of the menu bar. Be aware that the menu items may vary from one machine to another depending on the XTensions loaded in that version of QuarkXPress.

The last commands under the Utilities menu include controls for editing tracking and kerning tables by typeface. Selective editing of the kerning and tracking tables for a font will allow those changes to take place for that font in each combination of letters changed.

OTHER PARTS OF THE MENU BAR

The last two items on the Menu bar are generic to the Macintosh operating System 7 and are not QuarkXPress features specifically. They include the Help and Application menus. Check your System 7 manual for more information on these options.

THE HELP AND APPLICATION MENUS

Although the QuarkXPress Help area is available in non-System 7 applications, it resides under the Help pull-down menu here (see Figure 2.24). Look for it under the Apple menu in System 6.X installations.

The Application Menu tells you what application you are currently working in. You can use it to switch between applications or to return to the Finder. Simply click and hold on the icon and a menu will drop. Then choose the application you wish.

FIGURE 2.24

If the help files were loaded during installation, both the QuarkXPress Help and the EFIColorXTension Help will be accessible from the Balloon help area of System 7.

Document
Construction

TRACKS

To drag or copy items from one document to another 76

open both documents, the one containing the element to copy, and the one to target. Resize and relocate so they are both seen on the screen (you can use View ➤ Windows ➤ Tile Document). Maneuver the windows so that both the item and its recipient area is shown. Click on the item and drag it from its present location, across the border to the recipient document, then drop (release the mouse button).

To insert page(s) at specific locations in the document 77

use Page ➤ Insert. This gives a dialog box enabling you to select the number of pages and their insert locations. Location choices include before current page, after current page, or at the end of the document.

To save a document page as an EPS (Encapsulated PostScript) file 79

you can select the option Edit ➤ Save Page as EPS. This saves the entire document page and its contents as an EPS file which can be later imported into an appropriate application or output directly to a PostScript printer.

QuarkXPress has several fantastic features that make it the leader in its software category, desktop publishing. In fact, desktop publishing, as the phrase was originally coined, is perhaps an inaccurate description of the function of QuarkXPress today. A better moniker today is electronic publishing.

Electronic publishing may be a more appropriate description for QuarkXPress as it is used in the printing industry. Software in this area is designed to be an appendage of the printing process. Unlike desktop publishing software, which was originally designed to print on the desktop laser printer, electronic publishing software is best utilized on a professional laser imagesetter. This product is then converted to film and used for the printing plate image.

To differentiate a desktop document maker from a true professional publishing package we must examine certain aspects of the software. Let's first consider document construction.

QUARKXPRESS PAGE SIZE CAPABILITIES

QuarkXPress has five predetermined page sizes available when you create a new document. This is a quick way to input data to page size rather than inputting each width and height dimension (see Figure 3.1). You can also specify special dimensions for a page that may not be listed in the five standard page sizes.

FIGURE 3.1

Choosing File ➤ New brings up the New dialog box, where you can select from five predetermined page sizes or create your own special size, ranging anywhere from as small as 1" square to as large as 48" square.

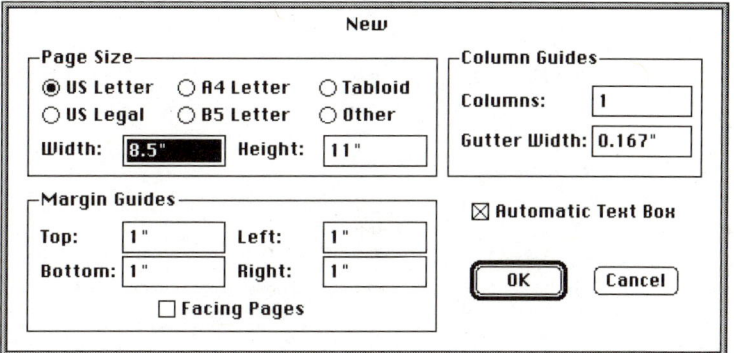

TIP

QuarkXPress has the capability of changing the measurement system and adapting to your needs. For example, if the measurement system were placed in inches in Edit ➤ Preferences ➤ General, but you needed to make a new document in pica measurements, just place the pica measurement in the page size fields. Be sure to include the units (such as pt for points), though! QuarkXPress will convert it to inch measurements for you. This applies to all measurement systems in QuarkXPress.

The letter ($8\frac{1}{2} \times 11''$), legal ($8\frac{1}{2} \times 14''$), and tabloid ($11 \times 17''$) sizes are most commonly used in the United States, while the A4 and B5 letter sizes are predominant in European paper sizes. The A4 dimension works out to 8.268" wide by 11.693" high, which is equivalent to 210 mm × 297 mm (see Figure 3.2). The B5 size is 176 mm × 250 mm (6.929"×9.843").

If you want to change the page size after the document is already created, choose File ➤ Document Setup. Adjustments in this dialog box change the document size

FIGURE 3.2

The page size fields reflect the measurement system you have set in preferences. In this example, Millimeters are set. A4 and B5 options are more prevalent in European layout.

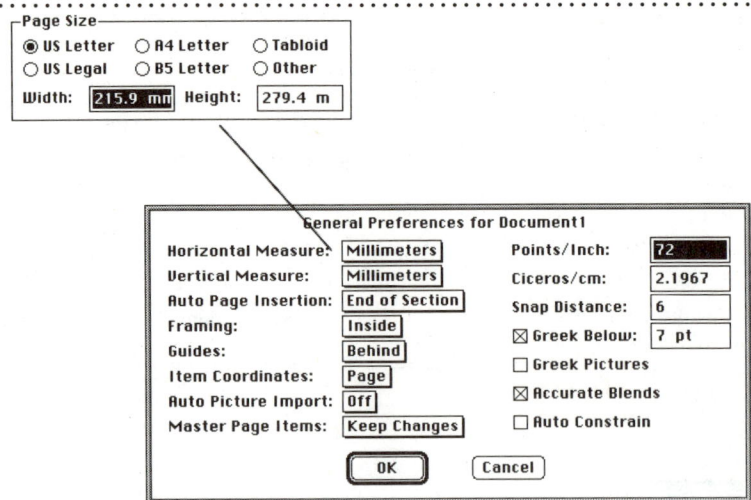

even in the middle of document construction (see Figure 3.3). As before, the option to create a custom page size in QuarkXPress allows document sizes from 1″×1″ to as large as 48″×48″. If you change the page size after starting the document, you may affect items on that page. Usually, a warning will appear in QuarkXPress indicating that you may have problems if you change the page size.

FIGURE 3.3

You can change the document size after the document is in progress by choosing File ➤ Document Setup and making changes in the Document Setup dialog box.

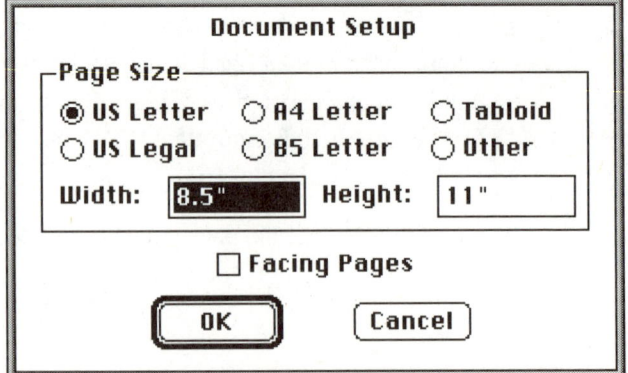

 **TIP**

To tile a large document means to print it in pieces, which you must then assemble. You will probably have to do this any time your document is larger than tabloid size.

Larger documents often must be printed by tiling them, at least until a 48" image-setter is developed. Tiling is an operation where a document larger than the size of the printer paper is broken up into smaller pieces and printed. The smaller pages resemble a puzzle of sorts, which you must piece together to form one large mural. To enable tiling, use the Tiling option in the Print dialog box (see Figure 3.4).

MAXIMUM DOCUMENT LENGTH

A feature which must be annoying to the "page-making" desktop publishing software companies is that QuarkXPress can create documents up to 2,000 pages long or 2 gigabytes in file size (whichever comes first). Document length was one of the first areas to differentiate page-making software from software that could be used in a publishing environment. Publishing implies the process of creating a document of some length, such as a newspaper, magazine, or book. Software that purports to be designed for publishing must therefore be able to create hundreds, if

FIGURE 3.4

The Tiling option in the Print dialog box enables you to print larger documents than the printer can make. This is done by breaking them down into pieces in a puzzle-like manner.

LaserWriter "The HPLaser"		7.1.2	Print
Copies: 1	Pages: ● All ○ From: □ To: □		Cancel
Cover Page:	● No ○ First Page ○ Last Page		
Paper Source:	● Paper Cassette ○ Manual Feed		
Print:	○ Black & White ● Color/Grayscale		
Destination:	● Printer ○ PostScript® File		
Page Sequence: All		☐ Collate ☐ Back to Front	
Output: Normal		☐ Spreads ☐ Thumbnails	
Tiling: ✓ Off / Manual / Automatic		Overlap: 3"	
Separation:		Plate: All Plates	
Registration: Off		OPI: Include Images	
Options: ☒ Calibrated Output	☐ Print Colors as Grays		
☒ Include Blank Pages			

not thousands, of pages to compete in the publishing market today (see Figure 3.5). It seems that most traditional publishing houses of fine magazines and books are moving toward or have already converted to the desktop publishing environment. Many well-known publishing houses were represented at the 1992 Quark User International conference in New York City, including Gannett, Inc., Readers Digest, Time, Hearst, Prentice Hall, Standard Publishing, Life Magazine, and Simon & Schuster. These companies are all incorporating QuarkXPress in their publishing plans.

FIGURE 3.5

QuarkXPress documents can range up to 2000 pages in length. You may insert from 1 to 100 pages at one time, before or after a specific page number. The program also allows you to have as many as 254 Master Pages to select from.

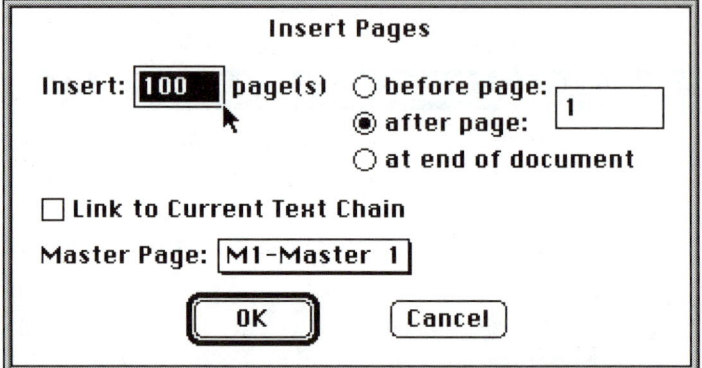

MULTIPLE PAGE SPREADS

QuarkXPress allows the creation of multiple page spreads so the user can see from page to page how the document will appear in print (see Figure 3.6). By use of the Document Layout palette, you can arrange up to five standard size pages side by side. A large monitor is best when working on a double page layout because it allows you to work on both pages simultaneously. Remember, QuarkXPress is a production tool; if production can be created faster with higher quality, it is a more profitable environment. A large, high-resolution monitor is almost a must for a high-volume, quality-conscious QuarkXPress environment. The Document Layout palette lets the QuarkXPress user arrange document pages regardless of the predetermined single or facing page document (see Figure 3.7).

FIGURE 3.6

QuarkXPress allows you to work on multiple page spreads.

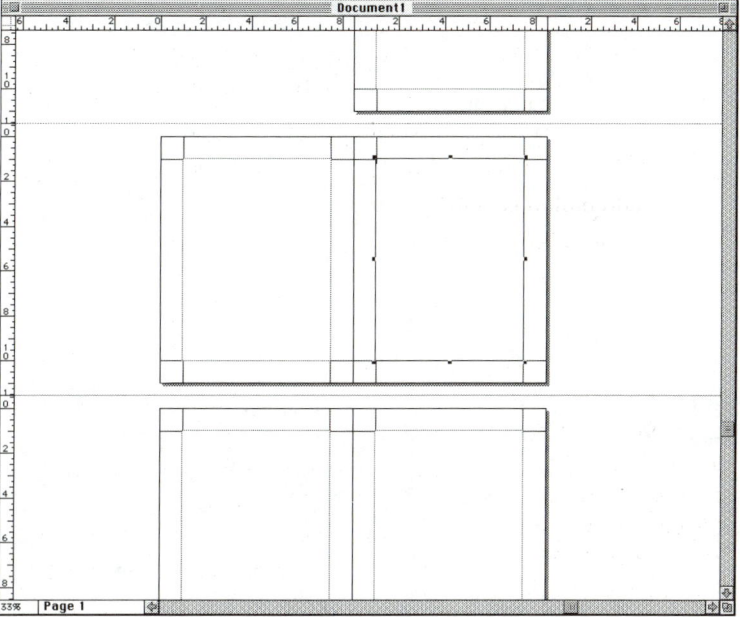

FIGURE 3.7

The Document Layout palette lets you arrange multiple page spreads for your convenience while working. Here, three different arrangements of the same project are shown.

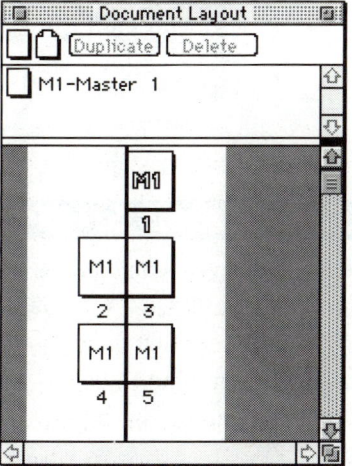

USING TEMPLATES

Templates are available in QuarkXPress so you can create and reuse a base form or layout. That base layout can be used to create other documents without altering the original template layout. When you first save a new document, you have the opportunity to choose whether the layout will be saved as a template or document. Documents can be called up and altered. Templates cannot be altered after they are saved. You can alter a template by saving it under any file name. This takes more time, but does the function of preventing accidental changes to the file (see Figure 3.8).

FIGURE 3.8

*You have the option of
saving a new document
as a document or a
template.*

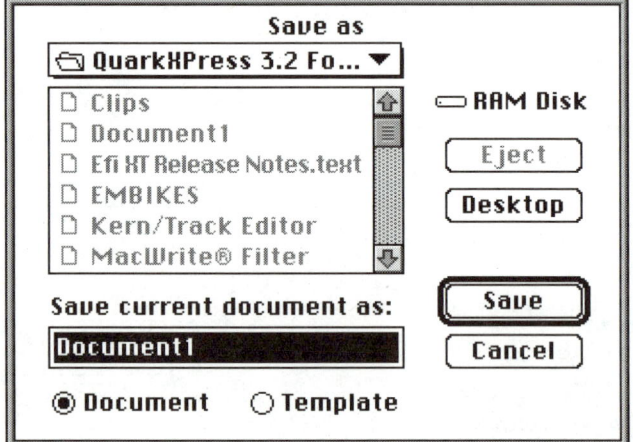

GRIDS, GUIDES, AND SNAPPING DISTANCES

When you create a new document, a default grid system will be in place. This can be shown or hidden with View ➤ Show/Hide Baseline Grid. It displays horizontal lines (baselines) as specified in the Typographic Preferences dialog box (Edit ➤ Preferences ➤ Typographic). The Baseline Grid system can be changed; the increments for baseline grid can be anywhere from 1 to 144 points. The baseline grid is hidden by default.

If the Snap to Guides option in the View menu is checked, the edges of items you move or resize will snap to the grid, similar to the way they snap to other page guides. To specify the distance at which objects snap, enter a value in the Snap Distance field, located in the General Preferences dialog box. You may specify a Snap Distance value from 0 to 216 pixels. The default value is 6 pixels. Keep in mind that a pixel on one machine may be closer or farther apart than pixels on other machines. This depends on the resolution quality of the monitor and graphic card of your Macintosh.

WARNING

Use the Item tool to select and move a guide line; using the Content tool will select the text box, picture box, or line beneath the guide.

Guides can be generated by clicking and dragging in the ruler. As we mentioned back in Chapter 2, you can move them by selecting them with the Item tool (the topmost tool in the Tool palette, it resembles a compass). New for version 3.2 is the ability to drag a ruler guide even when the pointer is over an item. In previous versions of QuarkXPress, you had to click on the guide somewhere other than over the item.

MASTER PAGES

QuarkXPress allows the creation of Master pages (maximum of 254) for a document. The master page contains items which are to be shown on all subsequent document pages. For example, a line running across the head of each document page should be created once on the master page. This displays the line on each page, even though it was drawn only once. Page numbers are also frequently placed on the master page.

NOTE

Only pages originating from a master will take on the changes of that master. Pages originated from some other master will take on changes only from the "parent" master page.

Even after the master page and subsequent document pages are created, you can still go back to the master and make changes as needed. Your changes will be reflected in all document pages that originated from that master. Individual items from the master page can be edited on the document page as well. Those changes will be reflected on the master page, as well as all subsequent document pages. For example, if you place a heading on the master page, it will appear on all subsequent document pages. If you then noticed the line needed a greater thickness, this could be edited on the existing document page. The changes would appear on the master and thus on all document pages. There is more information and examples on master pages in Part II.

DRAGGING PAGES BETWEEN QUARKXPRESS DOCUMENTS

A really unique feature in QuarkXPress is its facility for dragging a page layout and its contents from one document to another, providing multiple documents are open. To do this, follow these steps:

1. Change the view to Thumbnails.

2. Open a second document and change the view to Thumbnails here, too.

3. Click to highlight a page of the first document and drag it across the monitor to the second document (see Figure 3.9).

This might take a bit of practice to get the page where you want it. There are several advantages to this feature, such as the ability to drag and create multiple master pages. If you drag a page from one document to another and they have different master page specifications, the new document will have both styles, a M1-Master 1 and M2-Master 2. The feature is also good for quickly duplicating a page layout or multiple elements of a page, such as the text and graphic boxes. In a

FIGURE 3.9

You can work on multiple documents simultaneously and drag page layouts or independent elements from one document to another.

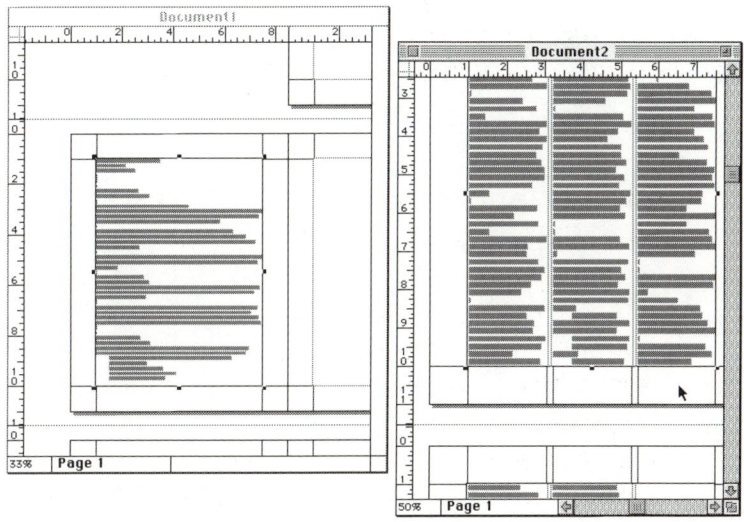

work-group publishing environment you can combine several documents into one using this QuarkXPress feature.

MULTIPLE PAGE MANIPULATION

QuarkXPress has the ability to insert, delete, and move multiple pages (see Figure 3.10). You can choose from three automatic page insertion options or insert pages manually. These are time-saving options. Trying to do these operations with other desktop publishing packages can get frustrating, because you must constantly be aware of adding more pages as the document length increases. QuarkXPress gives the option of adding pages automatically as needed, linking sequential text, or placing pages in as needed quantities in a manual fashion anywhere in the document. These page manipulations are part of the Page menu options, or you can use the Document Layout palette.

Frequently, you will have no idea how many pages a document will have prior to inputting its contents. The options in QuarkXPress that allow you complete control over the addition or subtraction of pages at anytime are extremely helpful.

FIGURE 3.10

You can manipulate pages using the options on the Page menu or by using the Document Layout palette.

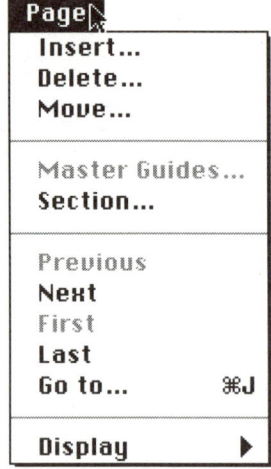

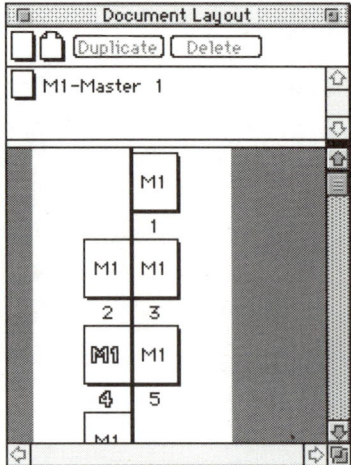

SECTIONS

Each document can be subdivided into sections. Sections can have their own page numbering sequence, even though they are still a part of the original, larger document. For example, in this book, the pages near the front are numbered in the i, ii, iii sequence (Roman numerals), while the text is numbered in a 1, 2, 3 fashion (Arabic). Thus, this book as a document would contain two sections. These settings are controlled by using the Page ➤ Section command (see Figure 3.11).

Page numbers in any section or in the entire document can be placed in automatic sequence, or you can specify an automatic Continued on and Continued from page number. You can insert the character for Previous Box Page Number (⌘-2) or the character for Next Box Page Number (⌘-4). These refer to the page numbers of the previous or next linked boxes. They can be used after phrases such as *continued from page* and *continued on page*. The correct page number will appear automatically.

FIGURE 3.11
*You have several
choices for numbering
style in the Section dia-
log box.*

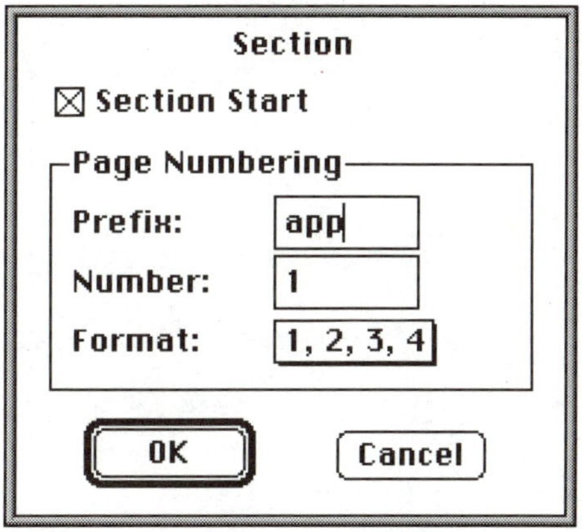

Section

☒ **Section Start**

┌─ **Page Numbering** ─────────┐

Prefix: `app`

Number: `1`

Format: `1, 2, 3, 4`

[OK]   [Cancel]

ENCAPSULATED POSTSCRIPT PAGES

Each page can be saved as an Encapsulated PostScript (EPS) file. This allows you
to import it into other software applications, such as illustration programs, for
further enhancement (the command is File ➤ Save Page as EPS). It can also be
imported back into a QuarkXPress document picture box. Saving anything as a Post-
Script file allows you to manipulate and resize it in other documents that take
PostScript format. For example, you may want to save a page as the EPS format to
later be retouched by a photo retouching program. This would allow you to import
the EPS file directly into the retouching program and edit as needed.

Page Layout

To create a picture box   85

you must create it using one of the picture box tools from the Tools Palette.
There are four choices to pick from, depending on the shape you want the
picture box to take. Select from the Rectangle, Rounded Corner, Oval, or
Polygon Picture Box Tool. To form the picture box, click and drag as you did
to form a new text box.

To form a new line item   85

select from one of the line drawing tools in the Tools palette. Choose from
the Orthogonal line or Line drawing tools. To use these, click and drag
where you want the line to be on the document page.

To form a grouped item   86

click on or encircle (lasso) a group of two or more items. After you see the
grab bars for all items chosen you can select Item ➤ Group. The individual grab bars will disappear, indicating that all items are grouped as one.

QuarkXPress has a great many options for manipulating items in your document. You may find many of these invaluable if you are doing a lot of prepress work. In this chapter, we'll explore those features, options, and tools that allow you to manipulate or edit items on the document layout page.

ITEMS IN QUARKXPRESS

QuarkXPress works through the manipulation of what it calls items. An item can be any of four different elements: the text box, the picture box, a line, or a grouped element. Throughout the book, emphasis is placed on the text box, picture box, and line as items. The grouped item is manipulated in much the same manner as the three other kinds.

THE TEXT BOX AS AN ITEM

The text box is considered an item on the page and may be created either automatically or manually. To create a text box automatically, you must check the Automatic Text Box option in the New dialog box (File ➤ New). This places a text box on your first page and sets up automatic linking of similarly placed text boxes on subsequent pages. For example, with Automatic Text Box checked, you can import a five-hundred page document into a text box on page 1. Once the box fills with text, other pages with text boxes will be added to accommodate all imported text.

NOTE

Both the Item and Content tools can be used to resize box items. To relocate an item, use the Item tool or the Modify dialog box (Item ➤ Modify). The Item tool is typically used to relocate an item.

The other way to create a text box item is to generate it manually using the Text Box tool. You select the tool, then click and drag to form a new rectangle on the page. This rectangle will be your text box. You can place text in it using the Content tool. Once drawn, the text box can be resized by manipulating the grab boxes of the item. Click and drag them as you would resize other items in Macintosh style. When resized, the text flows throughout the box according to its new size.

THE PICTURE BOX AS AN ITEM

The Picture Box has many of the same attributes as the Text Box. That is, you can create it manually with a selected tool from the tool palette. Once created, you can manipulate the image in the picture box by importing files (File ➤ Get Picture) and through the Content tool. A picture box can be resized and relocated using the Item tool. You can also frame it and apply specific runaround features.

You can use any of the following tools to create a picture box:

- The Rectangular Picture Box tool

- The Rounded-corner Rectangle Picture Box tool

- The Oval Picture Box tool

- The Polygon Picture Box tool

NOTE

Any item style, text box, picture box, line or grouped item can be rotated using the rotation tool. Text and Picture boxes can also be rotated with the rotation option in the Measurements palette.

The characteristics of each are the same, only the shape differs. You can resize or reshape a picture box with the Item tool or Content tool and the grab boxes (once the item is selected). The Item tool can also be used to reposition the picture box item.

THE LINE AS AN ITEM

The line element is an item in a QuarkXPress document because it has several of the same manipulation characteristics as the picture or text box items just described. That is, you can manipulate it (style, color, endcaps, width, and shade). The line item can have runaround features, like the box items. It can also be manipulated through the Item and Content tools.

GROUPED ITEMS

Any combination of items can be grouped together as a single item. Grouping allows you to move entire element clusters together as one. Once moved they can be ungrouped.

NOTE

You can also rotate grouped items. Use either the Rotation tool or the rotation field in the Measurement palette to manipulate the grouped item. After rotation, you still can ungroup as necessary.

You can manipulate grouped items the same way that you would to any single item. They may be cut and pasted, moved, rotated, and so on.

ROTATING LINES, TEXT BOXES, AND PICTURE BOXES

QuarkXPress is the leading desktop publishing program in the area of item rotation. As explained above, the three main elements of any QuarkXPress page are the text box, picture box, and line. Any item can be rotated in increments of as little as 0.001°. Rotation is accomplished by one of two techniques.

The first technique is to do the rotation manually. Follow these steps:

1. Highlight the item by clicking on it. (The grab boxes indicate that an item has been properly highlighted.)

2. Click on the rotation tool (see Figure 4.1). The cursor changes to a register mark icon.

3. Use this new cursor to click and drag on a grab bar of the item to rotate. The movement of your drag will dictate the angle of rotation.

FIGURE 4.1

The Rotation tool on the
QuarkXPress Tool palette

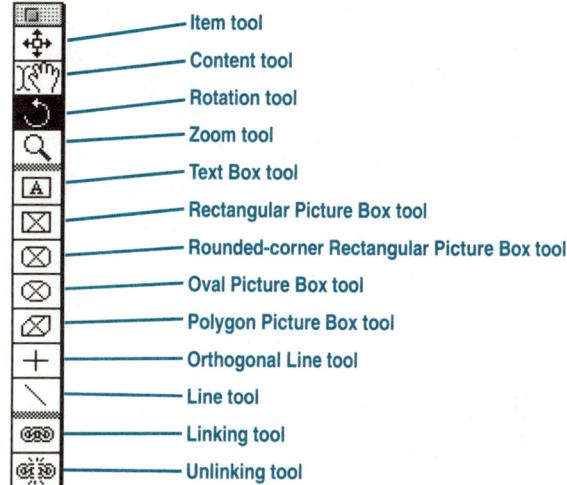

- Item tool
- Content tool
- Rotation tool
- Zoom tool
- Text Box tool
- Rectangular Picture Box tool
- Rounded-corner Rectangular Picture Box tool
- Oval Picture Box tool
- Polygon Picture Box tool
- Orthogonal Line tool
- Line tool
- Linking tool
- Unlinking tool

The finished product may not appear as crisp on your screen as it did before rotation, but it will print fine using the PostScript language. Text, especially when in a small type size, is next to impossible to read after rotation on a standard Macintosh screen, so it is a good idea to do any editing before you rotate it (see Figure 4.2). However, QuarkXPress does allow complete text editing after rotation.

The disadvantage of rotating by eyesight is that you may want to be more accurate, which is difficult to do in a manual rotation. A better method for accuracy rotations is to use the Measurement palette, which is perhaps more simple. Follow these steps:

1. First, make sure the Measurement palette is shown (see Figure 4.3).

2. Then, as before, click on the item to see the grab handles.

3. Next, highlight the number next to the rotation icon in the Measurement palette.

4. Edit the number to suit your rotation angle. When you're done, press Return. The item is rotated precisely as specified!

FIGURE 4.2

Text blocks can also be rotated even if they are more difficult to read (on the screen) after rotation.

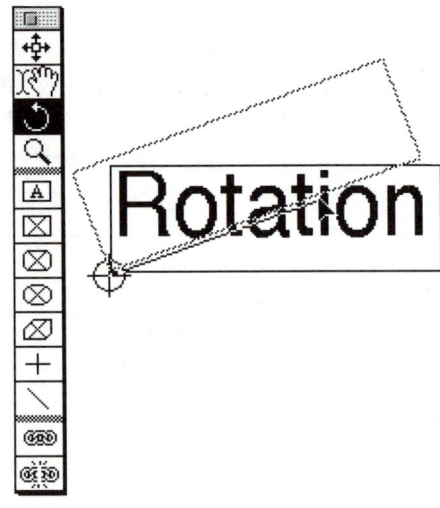

NOTE

Text box items can be edited while in their rotated form. You do not necessarily have to unrotate a text item to edit it as long as you can read the copy.

FIGURE 4.3

Use the Measurement palette for accuracy to 0.001° in rotation.

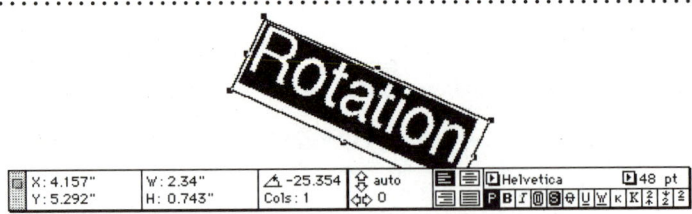

EXTENDING AND BLEEDING ITEMS

Page layouts have been a problem in the electronic environment in that items could be placed on the page only and could not extend beyond the boundaries of that page. The technique of extending items to bleed off the page or to spread across multiple pages is taken care of handily in QuarkXPress 3.2. It is so simple it hardly warrants discussion.

To make an item bleed off the page, simply enlarge the item box and, if necessary, the item itself. Move the item beyond the boundary of the page (see Figure 4.4). When you print, include trim marks and your bleed should also print. Some software programs assume that these overextended items are to be carried to the next page of the document. QuarkXPress simply understands a bleed as a bleed.

FIGURE 4.4

The screened area is to bleed off the page in this example. It extends beyond the page boundaries.

WARNING

Use caution in selecting spreads, though, because, in a signature, the design spread pages may not be exactly across from each other. The printers "spread" or method to lay out pages for production will differ from the way it is naturally done in QuarkXPress. XTensions are available to help work with the conversion.

To move items across multiple pages of a spread, just design them to occur on your document layout. In Figure 4.5, the picture item is intended to range across the spread. Select the Spreads option of in the Print dialog box (File ➤ Print). QuarkXPress will break the item where necessary.

WORKING WITH MULTIPLE ITEMS

Multiple items on a page or spread can be selected simultaneously by one of two methods. One method is the tried and true Macintosh-lasso approach, in which the Item tool encircles a selection of items until their grab bars all show at the same time. The second method is to select one item at a time while holding down the Shift key. The Shift key enables you to keep accumulating items that have grab

FIGURE 4.5
The picture item is stretched across a two page spread.

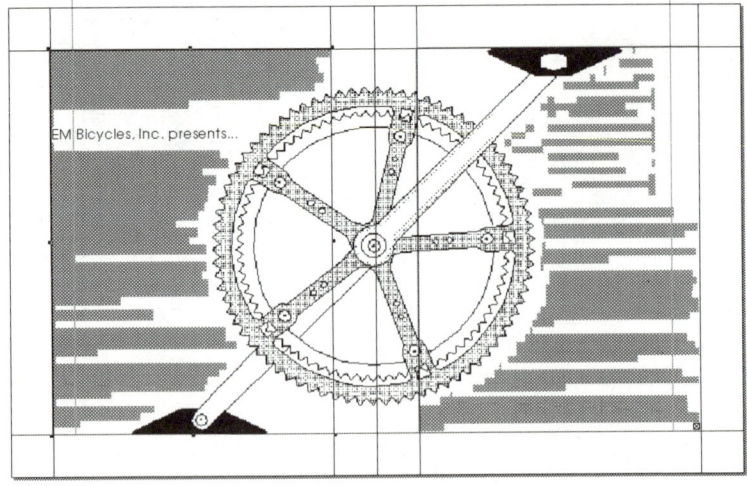

bars. Once multiple items are selected they can be grouped together as one item by selecting the Item ➤ Group option. The advantage in grouping items comes in moving or duplicating the new grouped item (see Figure 4.6). If desired, the items can later be ungrouped. Once the Item ➤ Ungrouped option is used, each element in the larger grouped item becomes independent once again.

TIP

You can save a great deal of time if you group certain items and "store" them on your pasteboard area. For example, in working on a form, you may want to draw a ruled line, repeat it as many times as possible, then group them all as one item. This item can then be placed off to the side (on the pasteboard) for future use. When needed just click and drag it into position.

FIGURE 4.6

You can group multiple items of different types together. In this example, a text box and a picture box are lassoed with the item tool and grouped together (Item ➤ Group). They can now be manipulated as if they were one item.

You can cut, copy, paste, duplicate, drag, or rotate single or grouped items (see Figure 4.7). Single or grouped items can also be dragged between documents.

Multiple duplicates can be created automatically and positioned through using the Item ➤ Step and Repeat command. This command saves a tremendous amount of time in production of the layout. It allows automatic control of alignment and space when items are duplicated multiple times. The Step and Repeat dialog box allows you to duplicate single or multiple items in the horizontal or vertical dimension of your choice.

LOCKING AND UNLOCKING ITEMS ON THE PAGE

When working on a page layout creating elements and positioning them on the page, accuracy becomes very important. Occasionally, situations arise when a simple click of the mouse button causes an item to highlight and somehow move. To avoid any accidental movement of elements on the page QuarkXPress allows you to

FIGURE 4.7

Grouped items can be manipulated for rotation as well as step and repeat. This example shows the grouped elements of a text and picture box grouped, then rotated. Finally, the group was duplicated with the step and repeat option (Item ➤ Step and Repeat).

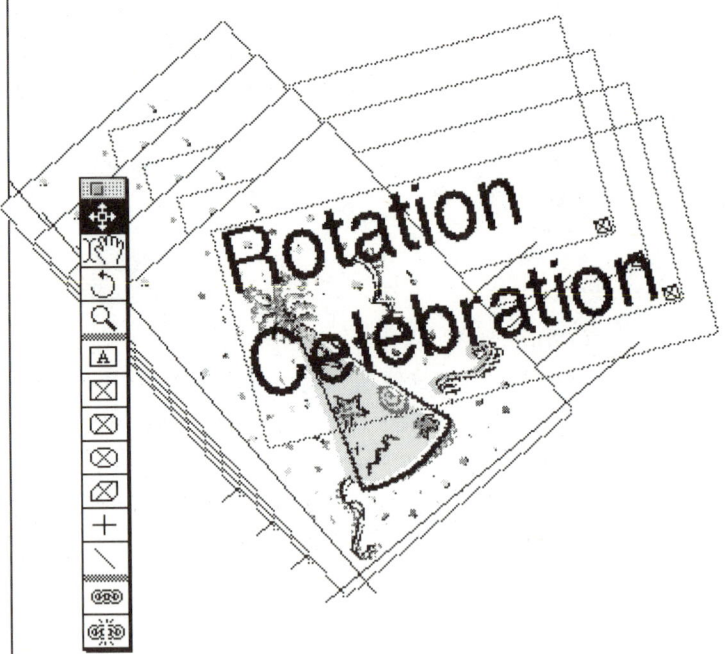

lock items in position on the page. Once locked, the item cannot be repositioned until unlocked. This helps avoid the time-wasting mistakes that may occur in electronic layout. The Lock and Unlock options are under the Item menu.

TIP

Locking and unlocking items becomes extremely helpful as you prepare more sophisticated layouts with QuarkXPress. With dozens of elements in close proximity, invariably you will accidentally select the wrong element and move it. Even slight movement may be enough to damage your layout. Avoid accidental selection and movement by locking the item once in place. You can unlock it later if it needs manipulation. Text can be edited within a locked text box.

NUDGING

A problem working with the mouse or roller ball is they sometimes are not very accurate. There seems to be that last moment slip as the button is lifted. To help solve this dilemma, the good people at QuarkXPress have included an option that allows the nudging of items. You simply click on the desired item with the Item tool to highlight it, then use the arrow keys (up, down, left, right) to reposition the item as desired.

NOTE

CompuServe is a great source for locating those hard-to-find, or nearly trivial programs for your production. In the Desktop Publishing Forum you will find a program or programs to tweak QuarkXPress capabilities just a bit beyond normal. This note was given here because a program is available for adjusting the Nudging capability of QuarkXPress.

The increment of nudge is one full point for each arrow press. If the Option key is held down and then the arrow is pressed, the nudge is in $\frac{1}{10}$-point increments. This can be a very useful feature.

VIEWING ITEM CONTENTS WHILE DRAGGING OR ROTATING

Again, this capability, like so many others in the software, saves a great deal of "designer agony." With some programs, moving an item by dragging removes it from view on the screen while the move takes place. After the move is complete, the item reappears. This makes for too much trial-and-error layout. QuarkXPress allows the item and its contents to be viewed during the move, at your option. The same feature is available for rotations.

RUNNING TEXT AROUND OR BEHIND ITEMS

Any desktop-publishing program worth its salt should allow you to integrate text and graphic items in any way you desire. You should be able to place text on top of the graphic, and vice versa. You should also be able to place text so it runs around graphics, and be able to control runaround specifics.

QuarkXPress gives you several options in runarounds. It allows you to form a runaround where the text goes around the contour of the graphic item (see Figure 4.8). Item ➤ Runaround allows you to control the distance separating the graphic from text. You decide how close the text gets on each side of the graphic.

FIGURE 4.8

The Runaround Specifi-cations dialog box (Item ➤ Runarounds) allows you to determine the distance to text around your item. This prevents text from touching the item.

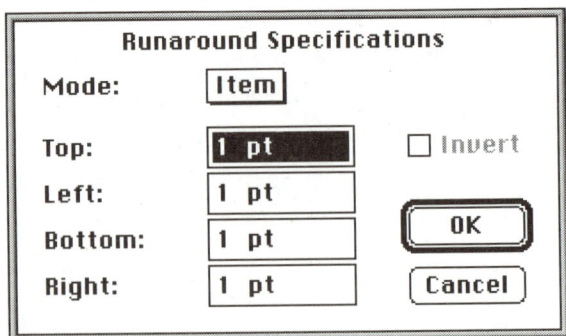

By selecting Item from the Runaround Specifications dialog box you can specifically choose the runaround distances. Other options include None, Auto Image, and Manual Image modes (see Figure 4.9).

FIGURE 4.9

Select the mode of choice to runaround the targeted item.

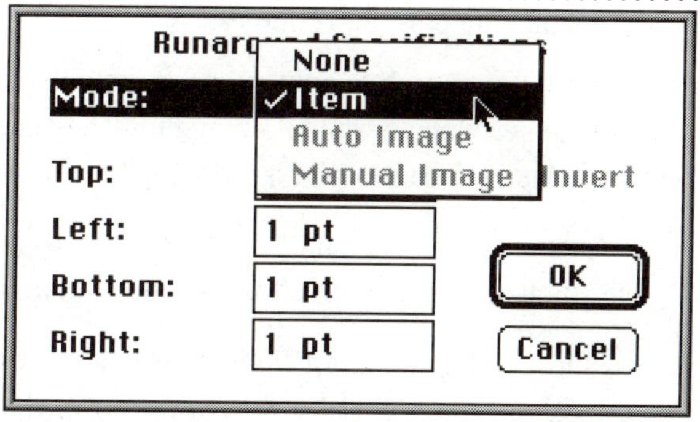

If the item is an irregularly shaped picture, you may wish to conform the runaround more to the shape of the item than the picture box containing it. The Runaround dialog box enables you to choose a Manual Image runaround or an Auto Image runaround (see Figure 4.10). In the manual option, QuarkXPress creates a polygon around the item and you control the distance and flow by moving

FIGURE 4.10

The Manual Mode of runaround allows you to change the shape of the polygon surrounding the item.

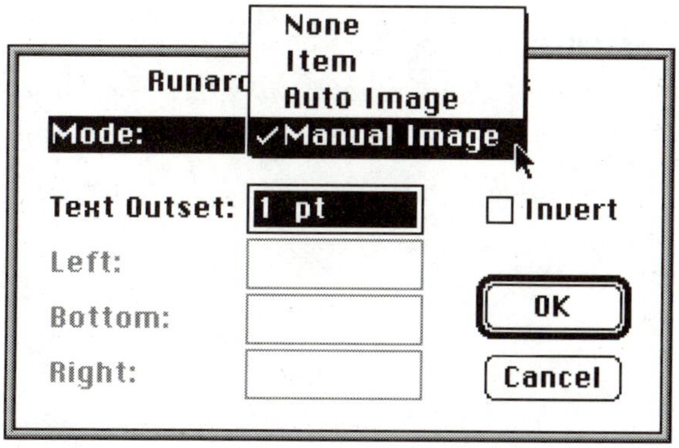

the polygon's handles. If you move the box containing the picture, the runaround polygon moves as well.

To change the shape manually, follow these steps:

1. Click on one of the grab handles of the odd shaped polygon.

2. Drag it and the polygon reshapes.

3. To create a new grab handle, click on the polygon outline where you want the new handle while holding the ⌘ key down. This forms a new grab handle in that location which can be used to reshape.

The results of the manual and automatic methods are essentially the same, although you have more control with the manual option.

Finally, there is the option for None. This enables you to remove the runaround and give the text the right-of-way to flow over or through the graphic item. This may be used in situations where you would want to have an overprint effect.

FLOWING TEXT INSIDE A PICTURE SHAPE

A QuarkXPress capability similar to a runaround is that of flowing text inside a picture shape. This can be used in certain design situations when you want that extra bit of something in the layout (see Figure 4.11). This feature is a bit goofy in that you really have to play around with it to master its full potential. At first it appears to be rather cute, then as you work with it, it is one of those features you hope you never need!

WARNING

Although placing text inside an irregularly shaped area is unique, it is a trick that can easily be misused. Remember, bad design is still bad design, regardless of the tool.

FIGURE 4.11

Often inverted text doesn't exactly fill the area as you had planned..

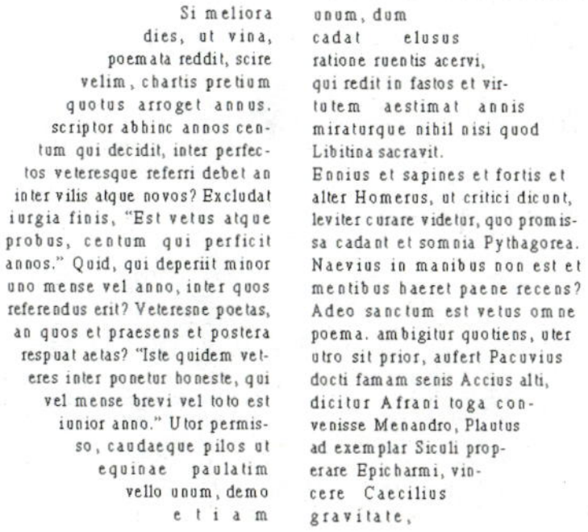

Si meliora dies, ut vina, poemata reddit, scire velim, chartis pretium quotos arroget annus. scriptor abhinc annos centum qui decidit, inter perfectos veteresque referri debet an inter vilis atque novos? Excludat iurgia finis, "Est vetus atque probus, centum qui perficit annos." Quid, qui deperiit minor uno mense vel anno, inter quos referendus erit? Veteresne poetas, an quos et praesens et postera respuat aetas? "Iste quidem veteres inter ponetur honeste, qui vel mense brevi vel toto est iunior anno." Utor permisso, caudaeque pilos ut equinae paulatim vello unum, demo etiam unum, dum cadat elusus ratione ruentis acervi, qui redit in fastos et virtutem aestimat annis miraturque nihil nisi quod Libitina sacravit. Ennius et sapiens et fortis et alter Homerus, ut critici dicunt, leviter curare videtur, quo promissa cadant et somnia Pythagorea. Naevius in manibus non est et mentibus haeret paene recens? Adeo sanctum est vetus omne poema. ambigitur quotiens, uter utro sit prior, aufert Pacuvius docti famam senis Accius alti, dicitur Afrani toga convenisse Menandro, Plautus ad exemplar Siculi properare Epicharmi, vincere Caecilius gravitate,

Here is a basic example of how to create text inside an irregularly shaped object. You should play around with it to get the full benefit. To flow text inside an irregular shape, you need to perform the following steps:

1. For this example, create a new document with two columns. Select two columns from the option in the New dialog box. Size and margin information is not too important in this example.

2. Click on OK to accept information in the box.

3. A new document page appears with the text box divided into two columns. Key in text, any text, to fill the two columns. Remember, this is to show that text will flow in an area, so you don't have to read the text to demonstrate that! You might want to type a paragraph, then copy and paste it until the page is filled.

4. Using the Select All command (⌘-A), highlight all the text and justify it (Style ➤ Alignment ➤ Justified). This makes the text in your example fill the shape better.

5. Create a circular picture box anywhere on the document page. Create this with the appropriate picture box tool (the Oval Picture Box tool). Hold down Shift while drawing the picture box to create a circle. To draw the box, click in the work area and drag diagonally. The same technique is used to create all other picture or text boxes. For the sake of this example, make a

circle that is approximately 3–4″ in diameter. You may want to change the View to Fit in Window so you can see the whole document page.

6. Using the Item tool, click on the circular picture box to select it.

7. Move it to the approximate center of your two column text area if it isn't already there.

8. Select Manual Image mode from in the Runaround Specifications dialog box (Item ➤ Runaround). Then select Invert. Click on OK to accept the settings.

9. Presto! Your text follows the circular shape. You might have straggler lines that have to be attended to; some fine-tuning is usually necessary.

As stated earlier, using the inverting technique take a bit of practice. You can invert and fill text to a picture box shape, or if you're feeling brave, fill text in a picture shape within the picture box. Remember, practice makes perfect. Good luck!

When Invert is used to place text inside the polygon, text beyond the limits of the polygon is unaffected. Only text that will fit inside the polygon will move. Click on the original item with the edit tool and press the Delete key. The shape remains with text flowing inside it, while the original item disappears.

FRAMING TEXT AND PICTURE BOXES

In QuarkXPress, you can frame both text or picture boxes by using Item ➤ Frame. You must first have a text or picture box selected. You may use either the Item or Content tool to select the item. When you select Item ➤ Frame, a dialog box appears giving you options for the frame's style, width, color, and shade (see Figure 4.12). You may select from a variety of frame styles in the library.

NOTE

Not all frame styles are available for all picture or text box shapes. Certain rectangular frame shapes are not appropriate on oval boxes and are therefore not shown as an option in the frame selections.

FIGURE 4.12
After a box is selected, go to the Frame Specifications dialog box (Item ➤ Frame).

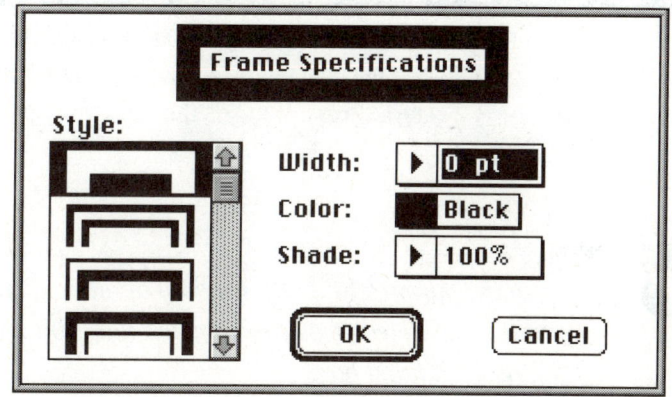

Custom frames can be generated by another program, Frame Editor. It is probably located within the QuarkXPress folder. It enables you to customize the look of any given frame, new or existing, on a pixel-by-pixel basis (see Figure 4.13). Any box can have a frame, including Text Boxes.

FIGURE 4.13
Frame Editor, a stand-alone program that comes with QuarkX-Press, allows you to customize your own frame library. It should be in the QuarkXPress folder.

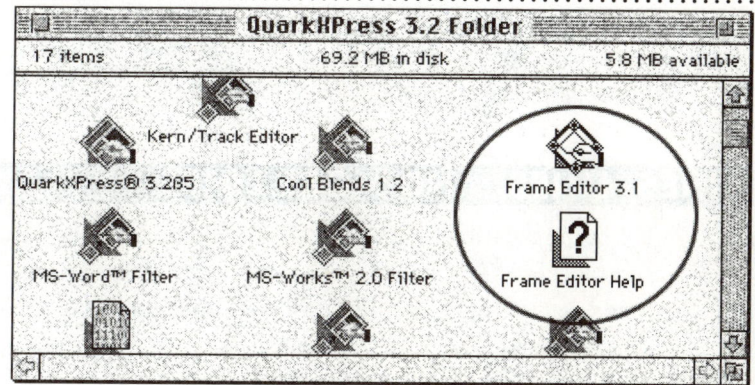

ANCHORING ITEMS TO TEXT

Although the concept of nesting in QuarkXPress is probably long gone by the everyday user, there may be a few who have to draw up documents created on pre-version 3.2 QuarkXPress. If this is the case, you may have to contend with nested items.

NOTE

To use the parent/child relationship of older versions of QuarkXPress, select the Auto Constrain option in the General Preferences dialog box.

Earlier versions of QuarkXPress had a system of "nesting" items on the page. It would enable any item created within a larger item to become the "child" item of its parent. If the parent were moved, the child was moved along with it. Apparently, this was a radical departure from other competitors and many users were uncomfortable with the operation. Since version 3.0, QuarkXPress has enabled people to use the conventional "non-nested" style of page layout. But for the old timers who have become accustomed to this and use nesting as a manipulation tool, QuarkXPress has it as a selectable option. Choose Auto Constrain option under the General Preferences dialog box (Edit ➤ Preferences ➤ General). This is an all-encompassing function; you cannot nest certain items and not others.

LINES, LINES, AND MORE LINES

The last in the trio of items in QuarkXPress is lines. The simple line has many options in QuarkXPress; it takes on a character of its own. You can draw lines in perpendicular fashion using the Orthogonal Line tool from the Tool palette. Or, if you would rather, the regular Line tool allows you to draw lines at any angle on the page. Both tools use the click-and-drag technique.

Lines can be manipulated in a variety of ways. First, you may want to draw a line and highlight it. Then go to the Style menu. The Style menu options change specifically for lines. You may also wish to manipulate line information directly from the Modify dialog box (Item ➤ Modify). In this dialog box, you can change several specification options at once.

Finally, you can use the Measurement palette. When a line is highlighted, the information on that line appears in the Measurement palette. You can change any of this information directly in the Measurement palette. Once you've made your changes, press Return, and the changes are reflected in your line.

ROTATING LINES

Line rotation in QuarkXPress is differs slightly from that of other items through use of the Measurement palette. Yes, you can still use the Rotation tool, just as you do with other items. Select the item; select the tool; move a grab bar. It is relatively straightforward.

For finer control, use the Measurement palette. First select the line. Then in the Measurement palette, click the option showing Endpoints, Midpoint, Left Point, Right Point (see Figure 4.14). Select an option other than Endpoints, and the Rotation field will appear, as shown. To replace the rotation angle, highlight the angle degree value and replace it with your own value. Activate by pressing Return (or Enter).

FIGURE 4.14

Rotate lines by first selecting Midpoint, Left Point, or Right Point from the Measurement palette. Then change the rotation angle and press Return or Enter.

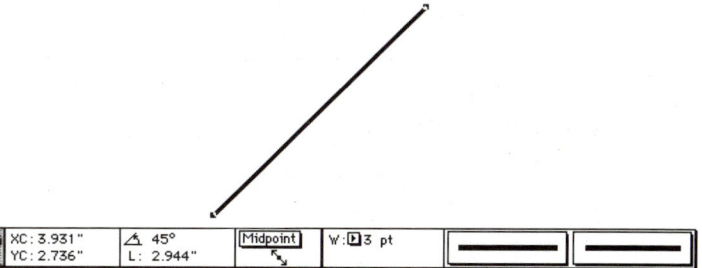

MANIPULATING MARGIN GUIDES

You have already seen how QuarkXPress gives a complete set of margin guides to help locate the main text area of the page. This is established as you create a new document, in the Margin Guides area of the New dialog box. This information sets the text box size and the Margin Guides.

WARNING

Changing the Document Setup option after a document has already been created may have an affect on elements you have placed on the page. Be careful if you choose to make document size changes on existing documents.

To change the Margin Guides after a document has been started you must use the Document Setup dialog box (File ➤ Document Setup).

OTHER GUIDES

Just like the layout artist who needs the help of a non-repro blue line for placement of items on the page, QuarkXPress helps by allowing you to place guides as needed on the layout. These guides are obtained by dragging them from the rulers. Just click and drag from the ruler, horizontal or vertical. You can place as many guides on the page as you want. You can manipulate or move these guides by clicking and dragging them (outside a box area).

To change the colors of any guides, choose Edit ➤ Preferences ➤ Application. Click on the guide you wish to change and a color wheel appears. It gives you options for selecting the color of that guide. Regardless of the colors selected, the guides will not print out when you send your product to the laser printer or imagesetter.

SNAP TO GUIDES

Another of the many options available to you is the ability to dictate the Snap to Guides distance. This is the distance at which an item—text, line, or picture—will jump to the next guide when repositioned. Choose Edit ➤ Preferences ➤ General and adjust the Snap Distance option (in pixels). A setting of 6 indicates that anywhere within six pixels of the guide, an item will jump to that guide. This capability helps alleviate problems of inaccuracy that layout artists had for years in the manual format.

MULTIPAGE
DOCUMENTS

II

CREATING A MASTER PAGE

To define the original master page when creating a new document   110

create a new document. The New dialog box (File ➤ New) information is used not only for your document page but also as a basis for the first Master Page of your document. Guides and other information can change later at your discretion, but initially, information in the New dialog box constructs the Master Page.

To specify the master to be a two page spread   111

check the option for Facing Pages in the New dialog box (File ➤ New). This will give you, initially, a two-page traditional layout. You may later alter this to be as many as five pages abreast in the layout.

To make alterations in the page size and facing pages   112

select the Document Setup dialog box (File ➤ Document Setup). This allows you to change the size of the document page and/or facing pages option after the document has been originated.

first, change to the Master Page of the document. Make your changes on that master and all subsequent document pages based on that master will have these changes also.

you can simply use Document ➤ Insert. The submenu option will allow you to select the type of master the new page should be formed after or simply a blank page from no master.

A master page is a non-printing page used as a template or format for other pages in your document. As you add new pages to the document, they automatically follow the format of a master page. Master pages can contain elements that print on the document pages (such as page numbers or headers) even though the master page itself does not print.

DEFINING MASTER PAGES WHEN YOU CREATE A NEW DOCUMENT

After you launch QuarkXPress, you often want to create a new document (File ➤ New). This brings a New dialog box. Changes in the New dialog box affect the document pages and master pages. It includes an option of page size, guides, facing or non-facing page options, an automatic text box option and column information.

NOTE

Page size ranges in QuarkXPress from 1" by 1" to 48" by 48" for non-facing pages, with a maximum of 24" wide by 48" tall for facing pages. Column gutter width, as set up in the New dialog box, can range from 3 to 288 points (4"). You may set the number of columns anywhere from 1 to 30.

Not only are you establishing the look of your document page in this New dialog box, but you are also establishing the look of the first master page. Your master pages will follow the format in page size, guides, columns and automatic text box in the default master page, M1-Master 1.

MASTER PAGES OF FACING AND NON-FACING PAGES

As you create a document (File ➤ New), QuarkXPress immediately gives two or three master pages, depending on the type of document. If the option for facing pages is unchecked on the New dialog box, you will have non-facing pages. Facing pages and non-facing pages help in your layout for imposition and bindery planning. Facing pages spread open to each other, while non-facing pages are independent single pages. Your Document Layout palette (View ➤ Document Layout) will represent these facing or non-facing pages for the length of your document (see Figure 5.1).

FIGURE 5.1

Specifications given in the New dialog box will reflect on the Master Pages of the document.

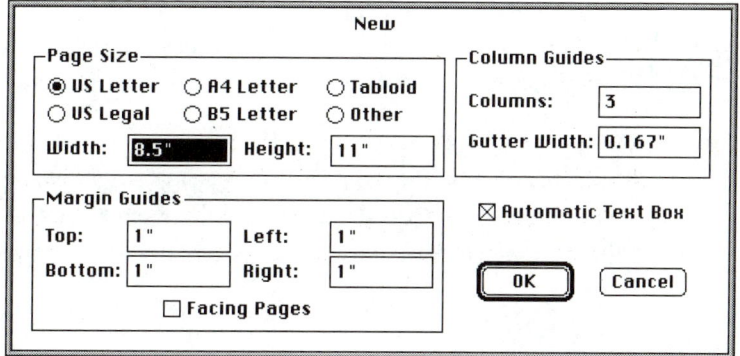

NOTE

After a new document is created, show the Document Layout palette (View ➤ Show Document Layout) to see icon representations of document and master pages.

TIP

Blank master pages have multiple uses. One such purpose involves creating a new document page based on the blank for a place-holder in your document. This can hold position for a photograph or advertisement. All editorial material will link or run around this blank page. Page numbers will also continue to work in sequence, taking into account the placeholder page.

Non-facing pages have two initial master pages (plus an original document page). The two master pages consist of one blank master page, and one M1-Master 1 page designed with the guides and text box information from the New dialog box. The blank master page can create other master pages or blank document pages. Blank pages have no items or guides such as on a M1-Master 1 page.

Check the Facing Pages option in the New document dialog box and you get page layouts in spreads. That is, page one is a single right hand page, two is a left hand page of a two-page spread, facing page three, and so on. See the Document Layout palette for an icon inventory of master and document pages.

Facing pages have three master pages at the start. One master page is the blank page, just like that given to the non-facing document. Another master page is M1-Master 1. Again, the M1-Master 1 page follows guides and text box information outlined in the New dialog box, as you created the document. The third master page, unique to the facing pages layout, contains another type of blank master page. It is a blank facing-page master page. Use this to create other facing page document pages or other facing page master pages. The facing-page master page also includes information detailed in the New dialog box.

THE DOCUMENT SETUP DIALOG BOX

You have created a document in the New dialog box, giving size, guides, etc. As you work on the document, however, there may be changes necessary. You can make some changes in document layout through the Document Setup dialog box (File ➤ Document Setup) shown in Figure 5.2.

FIGURE 5.2

*The Document Setup dia-
log box allows you to
change dimensions after
the document is set up.*

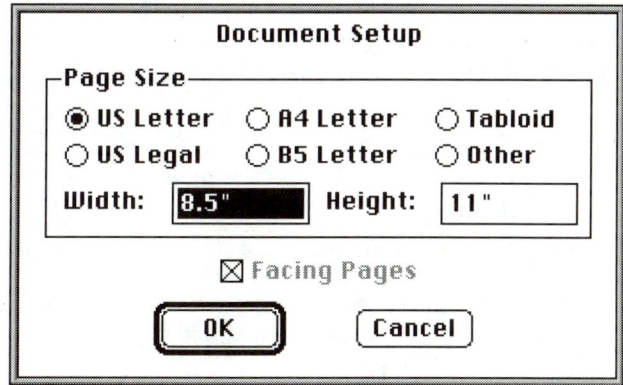

The Document Setup dialog box allows document changes to page size for the current document. You must be careful here, as changes may affect existing document
items. Figure 5.3 shows a message box warning for existing page items.

FIGURE 5.3

*Improper field input will
result in a message box
informing you of your
limits.*

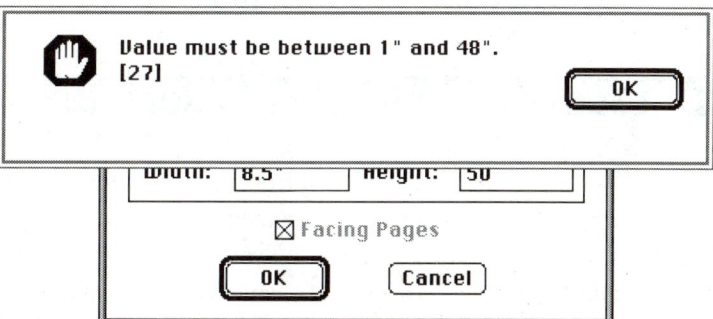

REPEATING ELEMENTS

Master pages can contain all elements you wish to repeat on each page of your
document. This may include page numbers, any header and footer information, or
graphic elements. Certain items, such as page numbers will reflect numerical
changes in their accompanying document pages, as you will see in Chapter 6. You
may also place boxes, lines, or grouped items on a master page.

You can modify any of the elements contained within the master page at any time. You can make changes right on the master itself or on the document page related to it. The changes will be reflected in all document pages related to that master page.

When you apply a new master page to an existing document page (from another master page) you can specify to Keep Changes or Delete Changes. Access these choices in the General Preferences dialog box (⌘-Y). In this dialog box, the Master Page Items option gives these choices through a pop-up menu.

Typically, when you apply the new master page to a document page, any unmodified master items are deleted on the document page. The default setting is Keep Changes. This enables old modified master page items on the document page to remain as you apply a new master page design to that document page. If you choose Delete Changes, both modified and unmodified master page items on document pages will be deleted.

Use this feature when modifying master pages of a document, such as updating a newsletter or magazine. If you want the changes for the document pages, apply Keep Changes. If you want changes to only apply to existing document pages, select Delete Changes in the General Preferences dialog box.

MASTER PAGES IN THE DOCUMENT LAYOUT PALETTE

You can manipulate master pages with the Document Layout palette (View ➤ Show Document Layout). You can resize and move this palette around like other QuarkXPress palettes. The Document Layout palette is probably one of the floating palettes you will want to have on your screen always. Unfortunately, it takes up so much space, that leaving it showing is impractical on a 13″ monitor.

TIP

To help your performance in QuarkXPress, get a large monitor or a second monitor (and graphics card). The second monitor can even be monochrome, because all you really need to use it for is to house your floating palettes.

Master pages are also helpful in the creation of new document pages. Again, use the Document Layout palette. Drag the icon of a particular master page down to the document area (see Figure 5.4). Drop the icon where the new document page should be. Once you release the mouse button (on the drag sequence), the new document page icon appears in that location. To see all pages of the Document Layout palette you can scroll horizontally or vertically with the scroll bars. This palette can also be resized. You can enlarge the palette to see several master and document page icons at the same time.

FIGURE 5.4

One way to create a new document page is to click and drag the master icon down to the page document area in the Document Layout palette.

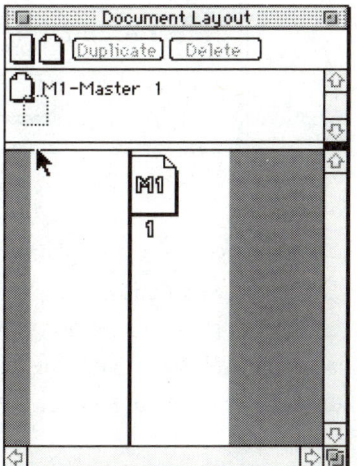

NOTE

All Master Pages and Document pages appear as icons within the Document Layout palette. Use this palette to create new pages based on the master pages.

You can also add pages by using Page ➤ Insert. This allows you to add a single page or multiple pages anywhere in the document. It also gives you the option of choosing the master from which to form the new document page (see Figure 5.5).

FIGURE 5.5

Use Page Insert to create new pages.

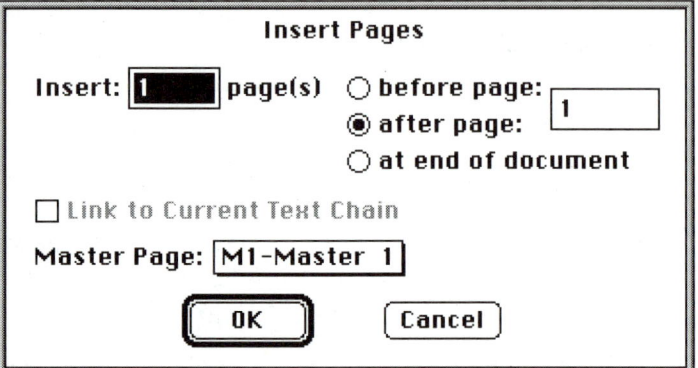

The blank master page will have no guides, but M1-Master 1 conforms to the guidelines set in the New dialog box (see Figure 5.6). You can create other masters by dragging a copy of the plain master over the M1-Master 1 area, renaming the new masters M2-Master 2, M3-Master 3, etc., as necessary. These then show as icons in the Document Layout palette.

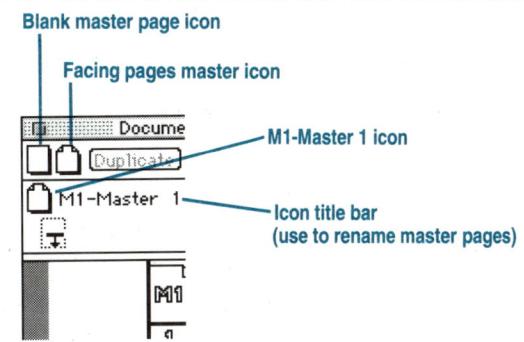

FIGURE 5.6
Create a new master page by dragging a copy of the plain master over to the M1-Master 1 area. This gives you a M2-Master 2.

Blank master page icon

Facing pages master icon

M1-Master 1 icon

Icon title bar
(use to rename master pages)

CREATING MASTER PAGES

If you need more master pages in the document, create more. One way to create a new master page is to use the Document Layout palette.

WARNING

When dragging a blank master page, do not try to place it on the M1-Master 1 page icon, otherwise it will replace M1-Master 1, which could be disastrous. If this happens, immediately choose Edit ➤ Undo (⌘-Z).

Across the top are the standard master page icons, including one blank, a facing-page master page, and a M1-Master 1 page. The M1-Master 1 page sits between two arrows. To create a new master, e.g., M2-Master 2, click and drag on the blank master page at the left. Drag it between the two arrows near the M1-Master 1 page (do not try to place it on the M1-Master 1 page or it will replace M1-Master 1). Release the mouse button when you have the page positioned, and a M2-Master 2 page icon will appear. You may rename any master in the space immediately below the master page icons. If you have more masters than will show on the Document Layout palette, the arrows act as scrolling arrows to allow you to see each master page created.

WARNING

If you insert new pages into your document using the click-and-drag technique on the Document Layout palette, be careful about where you drop new pages. When you drop new pages, all succeeding pages will renumber, which can be very confusing if you've dropped in a new page in the wrong place.

When using the Document Layout palette to form new pages, if a page is dropped anywhere in the document icon layout it is inserted within the document group. Pages will renumber accordingly. For example, if you click and drag a copy of M1-Master 1 into the document layout icons between pages 1 and 2, the new page becomes page 2. The old page 2 changes to page 3, etc. This insertion technique can be useful, but be careful. Page sequence can easily get confusing (see Figure 5.7)

FIGURE 5.7

Be careful to remember page sequence when adding pages within the document. It can be confusing on the Document Layout Palette.

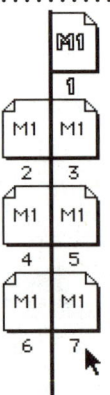

EDITING MASTER PAGES

You have two options to view and modify a master page. One option is to choose the master page you want to view from the Display submenu (Page ➤ Display). Select the page you want and it will display in your work area (see Figure 5.8). You can edit the master page as you would any document page. If you select Document from the submenu options, QuarkXPress displays a full view of the last document page viewed.

FIGURE 5.8

Page ➤ Display shows you the inventory of document and master pages.

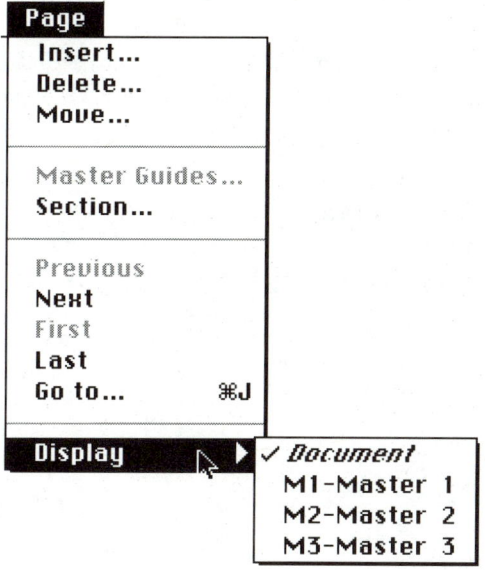

NOTE

To modify only the master page guides, choose Page ➤ Master Guides. Select this when you are viewing a specific master page, as not all master pages will have the same guides. Reposition the margin guides by changing the appropriate values in the dialog box. The master page you are viewing will change according to the new values entered.

The second method to view and modify a master page is through the Document Layout palette. This useful window enables you to select a particular page icon, master or document. Just scroll to find the icon of choice and double-click on that page. Your selection opens in full view for you to modify as necessary.

DELETING MASTER PAGES

To delete a master page from the Document Layout palette, simply click to select and click the Delete button. The page will disappear, and all pages within the document will renumber as necessary, automatically. You will get a warning to confirm the deletion.

RENAMING A MASTER PAGE

Use the Document Layout palette to rename the Master Pages for more informative layout work. For example, on the Document Layout palette, click once on a master page and its name appears right beside it. You may wish to rename this particular master page according to its function in the publication (see Figure 5.9). Highlight the original name and type in the new name or description of your choice.

FIGURE 5.9

Rename the master pages by highlighting the name on the Document Layout palette. Replace the name with your own name or description.

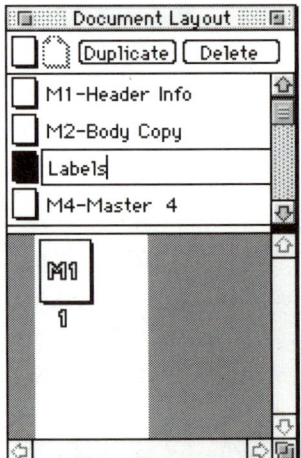

As you know, publications will often have several layouts within a single document. The frontmatter of a book may take on one layout, the bulk of the text another, and the glossary or index, still another. QuarkXPress allows you to have multiple masters within the same document. You should rename the pages to give more appropriate descriptions, rather then leaving them as M1-Master 1 or M2-Master 2.

COPYING MASTER PAGES

Another method for incorporating multiple master pages within a document is by copying a master from another document. When you copy a page from one document to another, its master layout follows, becoming an additional master page. To see how this works, follow these steps:

1. Open two different documents (preferably with two different page layouts).

2. Resize the work area so that the two documents can rest side-by-side on the screen.

3. Change both documents to Thumbnails view by choosing View ➤ Thumbnails (see Figure 5.10).

4. Now you can copy a selected page. Click and drag a page of one document to the other document. Position it where desired and release the mouse button. Since QuarkXPress allows you to open as many as seven documents simultaneously, you can use this technique of copying page layouts (and master pages) for up to seven documents at a time. After duplication, the Document Layout palette will indicate an additional master page as well (see Figure 5.11).

Multiple master pages will not automatically follow page number sequence from one page to another. That is, if the first few pages of the document were formed after M1-Master 1 and the next few pages were in M2-Master 2, page numbering from M1-Master 1 will not automatically follow to the B pages. You must start page numbering sequences anew on each master. See *Page Numbering* and *Sections* in Chapter 6.

FIGURE 5.10

Copying pages from one document to another also copies their master pages. Document 1 on the left will inherit the master page of the document page copied from Document 2.

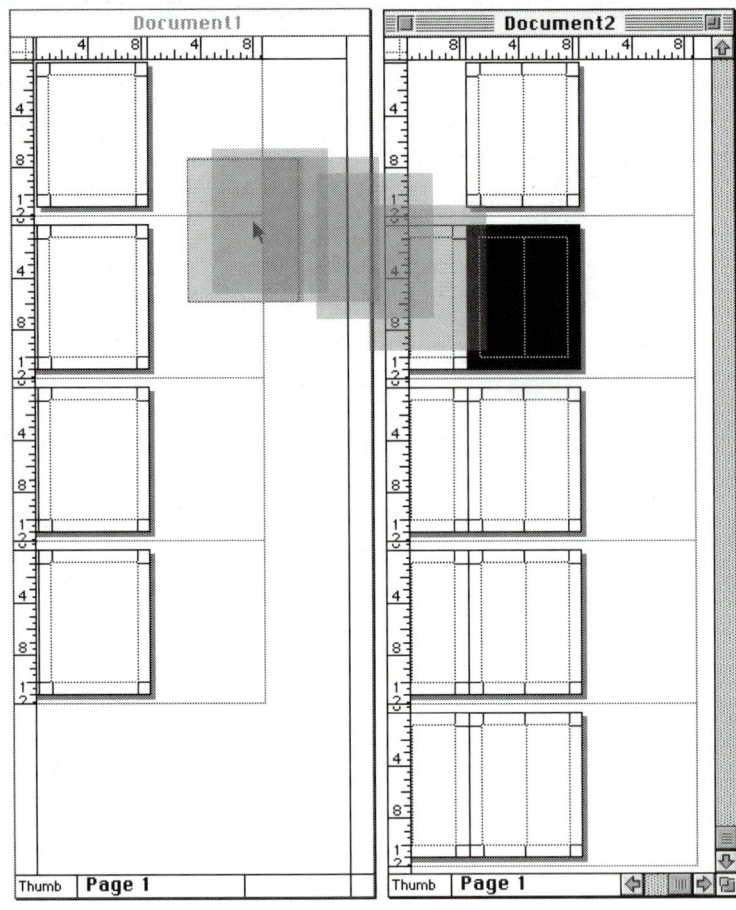

FIGURE 5.11

This illustration shows the Page ➤ Display submenu, indicating the document has two master pages. Each master page can be displayed and edited as necessary.

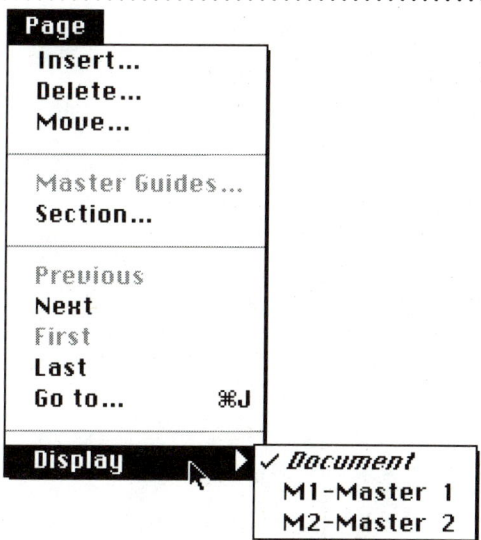

Applying a Master Page to a Document

When you have a job that requires only a few pages, the master page capability of QuarkXPress seems less important. If, however, you are like so many QuarkXPress users who routinely produce documents dozens of pages in length, master page is a boon! This chapter shows you how to apply master pages to your documents and to get the most of them.

You spent some time in the last chapter learning how to get a master page for your document and how to duplicate them as necessary. But what is the functional side of a master page? What can you do with them to increase productivity? What are some tricks that help you create master pages quicker? What kind of hints will enable you to be more efficient in the master page applications? We will explore the answers to all these questions in this chapter.

DELETING PAGES AND MASTERS

To delete a document or master page using the Document Layout palette, select the page or master and click the Delete button. Page deletions cannot be undone unless you choose to revert to the last saved version of the file (File ➤ Revert to Saved). Another way to delete a page is through the Page ➤ Delete option, which brings up a dialog box. Key in the page number(s) to delete then press OK. Pages cannot be undeleted, but again, you may choose File ➤ Revert to Saved.

TIP

When you see a button with the thick, dark frame around it (for example the OK button), you can select it from the keyboard by pressing Return. This works only when the button has the thick frame around it.

VIEWING PAGES

There are three ways for you to view the pages in your document. First, you can use the Document Layout palette to view document and master pages. To do this, open the Document Layout palette, then double-click on the page (document or master) you wish to view. This page shows in full size in the work area. Use this technique to close the page and view another if you wish. In each case where you view a page in the work area, the appropriate icon will highlight in the Document Layout palette. Also, the document window indicates the page number identification near the bottom left corner of the work area. Using the Document Layout palette allows you to select any particular page to view.

NOTE

The Document Layout palette is a versatile feature that enables you to see or scroll through all page icons of the document. It can be resized and relocated like any standard Macintosh window. You can also use the scroll bars to scroll horizontally or vertically. Arrows are also provided next to the master page icon list to scroll through these if you have more than are visible.

Another method of viewing the document or master page is using the Page ➤ Display submenu. You can choose between the document view and a master page view in the work area. This is not quite as selective as using the Document Layout palette, because it does not let you go to a specific document page on the work area. Finally, the third method is to use Page ➤ Go to.

MODIFYING THE MASTER PAGES

You can modify master page items on the master itself or on one of the pages related to it. Relating to a master page means the document page originated from a particular master page. When you create the document page, it includes master items. The document page becomes a clone of the original master page. You can create a document page based on a particular master in one of two ways. First, you can drag the master page icon down into the document icon area in the Document Layout palette. The second method would involve the use of the Page ➤ Insert option. Remember these, because the example later in this chapter shows you how to set up master pages for a newsletter, but the example does not cover making document pages from those masters! If you do find you need to refresh your memory, take a look at Chapter 5.

TIP

To create a new master page based upon items within an existing master page, first go to the Document Layout palette. Click on the master page icon that you are using as a model. After it highlights, choose the Duplicate button. The new master page icon appears below the master icon selected as the model. It is automatically given a name given in the M1-Master 1 sequence style. You can alter the new master page icon immediately after its creation. This saves a lot of time in creating a design that is only slightly different from others, because you have only to make a few changes rather than working from scratch.

Your document may have several master pages within the construction of the product. Each document page is molded from one of the master pages. The problem of having multiple masters for the new user is that certain key items do not carry over from one master (and document page) to another. Sequential page numbering, for example, does not follow from one master to another.

PAGE NUMBERING AND SECTIONING TECHNIQUES

The Previous Box Page Number (⌘-2) and the Next Box Page Number (⌘-4) are handy for creating automatic page number lines such as "Continued from page…" and "Continued on page…". Page numbers are displayed and updated automatically if you insert the proper Page Box Number code. Even as pages get repositioned in the document, the previous/next page codes reflect the new changes.

TIP

To use the Page Box Number codes, often it is best to use them on the Master Pages of the document. This will prevent the redundancy of placing them on each document page. Also, if you use the Previous Box Page Number and Next Box Page Number codes, place them in their own text box, but position the box on the Master Page inside the master text box (automatic text box). They will not work if placed outside the automatic text box area.

Use these page box number codes in the Format option of the Section dialog box (see Figure 6.1). The Section dialog box enables you to specify starting page number of the section and number type, as well as to preface the page number with a

FIGURE 6.1
The Section dialog box

```
┌──────────────────────────────────┐
│            Section               │
│ ⊠ Section Start                  │
│  ┌─Page Numbering────────────┐   │
│  │ Prefix:    [          ]   │   │
│  │ Number:    [ 15      ]    │   │
│  │ Format:    [ 1, 2, 3, 4 ] │   │
│  └───────────────────────────┘   │
│    ( OK )      ( Cancel )         │
└──────────────────────────────────┘
```

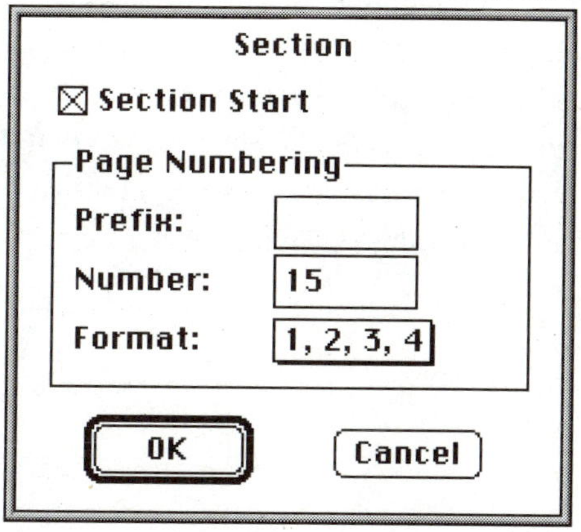

four character information piece. This could be useful for example, in prefacing the appendix pages with *App-*, to indicate the appendix in your document.

TIP

Get the Section dialog box from Page ➤ Section or from the Document Layout palette. In the Document Layout palette first click on the document page you want to begin the section, then click on the page name area of the Document Layout palette. TheSection dialog box will appear.

COMMAND	SHORTCUT COMBINATION
Previous Box Page Number Character	⌘-2
Current Box Page Number Character	⌘-3
Next Box Page Number Character	⌘-4

USING AUTOMATIC PAGE NUMBERING IN SECTIONS

Another use for multiple master pages is creating sections within your larger document. Sections are small, isolated groups of pages, typically with special activity or emphasis in your publication (e.g., index, appendix. or glossary). You should treat these with automatic page numbers highlighting their uniqueness. For these areas, use the Section option. To specify a document page or group of pages as a section, go to the first page in that sequence. Look at the page number in your document to confirm the page you are on. Then select Page ➤ Section. The Section dialog box appears. Check on the Start Section option. Controls in the page numbering area become active (black not gray). At that point the current page becomes the first page of the new section.

NOTE

Page numbering and sections are detailed in this chapter of this book because you will often number pages from the master pages. Working from page to page is all right for smaller documents, but remember… larger documents yield tighter deadlines. For some reason, it seems that the larger the project, the less time you have for it. Automatic page numbering and sectioning on the master pages saves a lot of agony if done right!

To specify a sequential page number for the current document page, place the starting page number in the page number field (see Figure 6.2). To specify the format of page numbering, click and select from the page number section (see Figure 6.3). When you are finished, click OK.

FIGURE 6.2

You may use up to four characters in the prefix area of the Section dialog box. This prefix will go before page numbers in the Section.

```
┌─────────────────────────────────────┐
│              Section                 │
│  ☒ Section Start                     │
│  ┌─Page Numbering──────────────────┐ │
│  │                                  │ │
│  │  Prefix:      ┌──────────┐       │ │
│  │               │ app      │       │ │
│  │               └──────────┘       │ │
│  │  Number:      ┌──────────┐       │ │
│  │               │ 1        │       │ │
│  │               └──────────┘       │ │
│  │  Format:      ┌──────────┐       │ │
│  │               │ 1, 2, 3, 4│      │ │
│  │               └──────────┘       │ │
│  └──────────────────────────────────┘ │
│     ┌────────┐      ┌──────────┐      │
│     │   OK   │      │  Cancel  │      │
│     └────────┘      └──────────┘      │
└─────────────────────────────────────┘
```

FIGURE 6.3
You can choose from a variety of page number formats within the Section dialog box.

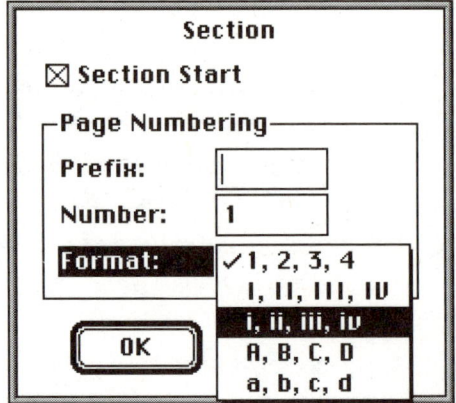

CUSTOMIZING PAGE NUMBERS

To make the page numbers look the way you want, including the font, style, size, etc., work from the master document. Make the automatic box page number a part of the master page. Start by creating a text box, in approximately the position you want to have the page number. Then key in the automatic box page number (⌘-3). This will ensure that all future document pages from that master will have proper page numbers. Then customize the page number by highlighting the <#> characters of the automatic box page number. While highlighted, change the type characteristics as you would any normal type. Those type characteristics will reflect in the document page numbers.

ABSOLUTE PAGE NUMBERS

Combining a series of automatic page numbers and section numbers can get quite confusing. To print out certain groups of pages, the print dialog box lists only From and To. This doesn't help much if you have three page 1s in the document. To get around this, QuarkXPress has Absolute Page Numbers. This means that if you want to print "physical" page 6 through "physical" (or absolute) page 21, you input the From and To fields as +6 and +21 respectively (see Figure 6.4). Regardless of the page sequence and section names, QuarkXPress calls the first absolute page +1, the second +2, and so on, throughout the document.

FIGURE 6.4

Use Absolute Page Numbers when printing a document with various sections. Section page numbers are not accurate for printing specific pages.

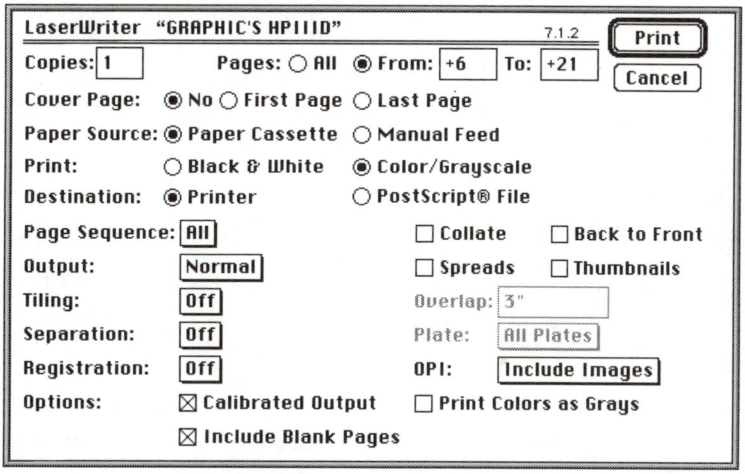

LaserWriter "GRAPHIC'S HPIIID"		7.1.2	Print
Copies: 1	Pages: ○ All ● From: +6 To: +21		Cancel
Cover Page:	● No ○ First Page ○ Last Page		
Paper Source:	● Paper Cassette ○ Manual Feed		
Print:	○ Black & White ● Color/Grayscale		
Destination:	● Printer ○ PostScript® File		
Page Sequence: All	☐ Collate	☐ Back to Front	
Output: Normal	☐ Spreads	☐ Thumbnails	
Tiling: Off	Overlap: 3"		
Separation: Off	Plate: All Plates		
Registration: Off	OPI: Include Images		
Options: ☒ Calibrated Output	☐ Print Colors as Grays		
☒ Include Blank Pages			

LINKED TEXT BOXES ON THE MASTER PAGE

You establish information for new documents in the New dialog box (File ➤ New). One of the options here is Automatic Text Box (see Figure 6.5). Checking this option creates an automatic text box in the M1-Master master page (following established margin guides). It also automates the creation of similar new text boxes on all future pages related to this master page. These text boxes will link

FIGURE 6.5

If you check Automatic Text Box in the New dialog box, a text box is created with linking capabilities.

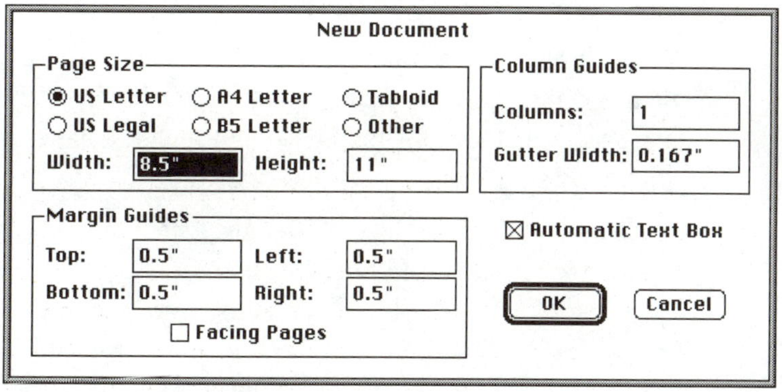

New Document

Page Size
● US Letter ○ A4 Letter ○ Tabloid
○ US Legal ○ B5 Letter ○ Other
Width: 8.5" Height: 11"

Column Guides
Columns: 1
Gutter Width: 0.167"

Margin Guides
Top: 0.5" Left: 0.5"
Bottom: 0.5" Right: 0.5"
☐ Facing Pages

☒ Automatic Text Box

OK   Cancel

automatically. Linked text boxes allow type to flow from one text box to another. If you bring the master page up to the document area, you will notice a link icon at the top-left corner of the page (if you have checked the Automatic Text Box option).

TIP

It is often easiest to link and unlink graphically by reducing the view to a small percentage (Thumbnails won't work, though), selecting the Linking or Unlinking tool from the Tools palette, andclicking on a text box.

As detailed earlier, edited items on the master page reflect on all related document pages. The exception is that of the linked text box. QuarkXPress will not allow you to place text inside an automatic text box on the master page. You must place any text on the master page in its own unlinked box. Select linking and unlinking through the appropriate tool in the Tool palette.

The automatic text link icon on the master page indicates that, as text flows into the text box, if the text is a greater quantity than will fit, it may need to go beyond that box. If so, QuarkXPress adds a new page to the end of your document with an automatic text box the same size, shape, and position as that of the preceding page. The remaining text flows on to the new page, and so on, until all text is taken care of and positioned.

If you chose multiple columns on the New dialog box, then text flows first in column one, then two, etc., for the entire page. More text will cause the addition of other pages and text will continue to flow in like manner on the new pages.

WARNING

Mixing manual linking with automatically linked text boxes can get confusing. Try to keep track of where your type is by keeping a saved copy in reserve.

You can also have manual control of text flow through use of the Linking and Un-linking tools on the Tools palette (see Figure 6.6). To link two text boxes so that the text will flow from one chosen text box to another, select the Linking tool. Click on the first text box. Then click immediately on the linked text box. An arrow will show indicating the direction of text flow from the original text box to the linked text box. To break a link (Unlink) select the Unlinking tool. Then click on a text box until the arrow appears, then click with the Unlink on the end or "feather" part of the arrow. The link is now broken.

Linking frequently, but not exclusively, occurs through master pages. In small documents, as noted to earlier, you may not have the same need for master pages as perhaps in a larger document.

FIGURE 6.6

The Tool palette with tools identified that you will use throughout this chapter.

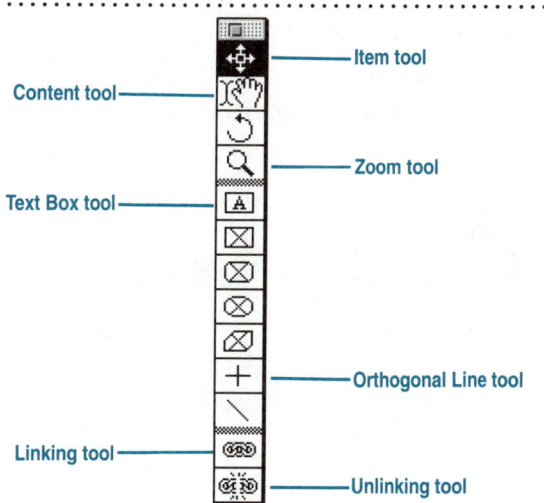

ANCHORING ITEMS ON MASTER PAGES

Sometimes the feature that allows you to change Master Page items on related document pages is unwanted. This may be true primarily if you are working with a complex document page and accidentally click on a master page element. You may move it slightly or accidentally delete it. To avoid these problems, it is wise to "lock" certain items on the master pages. The procedure is simple. Click on the item and select Item ➤ Lock (⌘-L). This anchors the item, preventing it from accidental movement or deletion. You can still edit text and graphics on the master page or the related document page. Remember, QuarkXPress works through item boxes: text goes in text item boxes and graphics are placed in picture boxes. While anchored in position, the text or picture box cannot be moved, but its contents can be edited. Locking only anchors the box!

YOUR SECOND QUARKXPRESS DOCUMENT

Now you get an opportunity to place this newfound knowledge of master pages to work in your second QuarkXPress document. You will be creating a master page document layout for a future EM Bicycles newsletter…QuickRelease. It's rather simple, and you are only working on the master pages in this example. You can add more to it later if you wish to see how it prints. For now, the master pages are of primary focus.

Begin by creating a new document with the specifications shown in Figure 6.7. This will be a two column layout. Guides will be $\frac{3}{4}''$ on all sides. Check the Automatic Text Box option, but DO NOT check the Facing Pages option. This newsletter will have equal margins and you don't need to worry about bindery options yet. Once all fields are setup accordingly, click on OK to accept.

 **NOTE**

Remember, you can accept any dialog box options by pressing the keyboard Return or Enter keys, when the OK is surrounded by a double outline.

FIGURE 6.7

Use the specifications shown in this illustration for your new document.

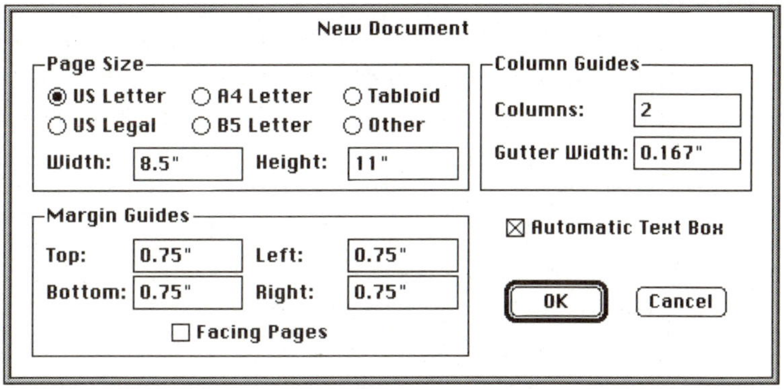

New Document

Page Size
- ◉ US Letter   ○ A4 Letter   ○ Tabloid
- ○ US Legal   ○ B5 Letter   ○ Other

Width: 8.5"   Height: 11"

Column Guides
Columns: 2
Gutter Width: 0.167"

Margin Guides
Top: 0.75"   Left: 0.75"
Bottom: 0.75" Right: 0.75"
☐ Facing Pages

☒ Automatic Text Box

[OK]   [Cancel]

Your screen should show part of page 1 (100% size). If the size is not 100%, select View ➤ Actual Size. Another way to select 100% is to use the keyboard equivalent (⌘-1).

Now, make sure your Tools and Document Layout palettes are showing (see Figure 6.8). The Document Layout palette shows icons representing one document page, one blank master page and one M1-Master 1.

 **NOTE**

In this example, the left/right master icon is gray, or unavailable, because the Facing Pages option was not checked when creating the new document.

You are going to set up a format for the newsletter to make it easier to produce month after month. Repeatable information will be on master pages. A total of three applied master pages are needed for this newsletter.

▸ The first master will be for the cover page of QuickRelease.

▸ The next master will be for all inside material.

▸ The third master page will be set up for the back cover of the newsletter, with material such as mailing information.

FIGURE 6.8
*Make sure the Tools and
Document Layout pal-
ettes are showing.*

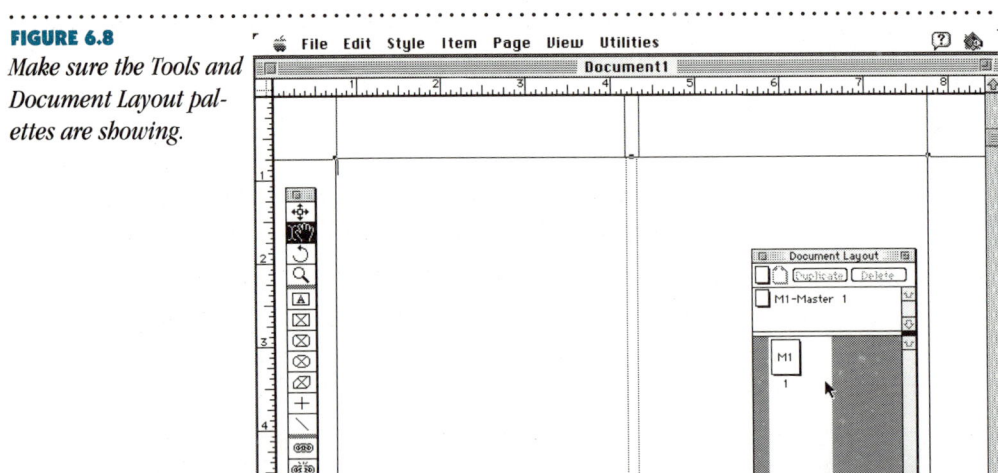

CREATING TWO NEW MASTER PAGES

First you should create two new master pages. Until you rename them, they will be
M2-Master 2 and M3-Master 3 respectively. There are two techniques you can use
to create new master pages at this time in your document construction. The first
technique involves cloning the M1-Master 1 page. Since there is no information on
it yet, this technique is fine for your example here. To clone a page you will use the
Duplicate button located on the Document Layout palette. Create the M2-Master 2
page by clicking on the M1-Master 1 icon to identify it as the master to clone.
Next, click on the Duplicate button in this palette. Immediately, a new icon appears under the M1-Master 1 page icon, named M2-Master 2. To create another,
repeat the procedure, that is, click on the M1-Master 1 icon, then the Duplicate
button. As you clone a master page, its duplicate appears right under the original,
perhaps disturbing your sequence, M1, M3, M2, etc. This can be easily remedied
as you can click and drag the master page icons to the sequence of your
preference.

The sequence of Master page icons in this area really have no bearing on the
document at this time other than for your organization. However, it may be less

confusing if master pages were properly numbered in succession, so change them as needed.

NOTE

To create more master pages in a duplicate manner, clone the last master page icon in the sequence. This way the newest master will be numbered and placed in the last position in the palette window. Remember, though, the object of duplicating a master page is to copy its layout and contents, so be selective.

Another method to create more master pages involves a simple technique. All you have to do is click on a master icon from the inventory area of the palette. This is where the icons for the plain and left/right master pages reside. After you click on it, drag it down to the location, before or after, the M1-Master 1 page icon rests. You will then have two master page icons, M1-Master 1 and M2-Master 2. You can continue this to get the number of master pages you need. Both methods of creating new master pages are simple, but only you can select a technique that works best for your production situation.

To see all icons in the Document Layout palette, you may want to manipulate the palette by one of several methods. First, you can scroll to examine other areas of that window. You may want to enlarge this window of the palette by use of the "split-window" position on the scroll bar. This is the dark part of the scroll area that separates the main two windows in this palette. To use this, click and drag down on the "split window" icon. You may also want to enlarge the palette's total size on the screen. To resize the Document Layout palette, use either the Macintosh Zoom box or the Size box of the palette (see Figure 6.9). You can use these box icons in a standard Macintosh manner.

Next, you should rename the master pages. M1-Master 1, M2-Master 2 and M3-Master 3 are too impersonal for such an elegant document. To change the default name of master pages, click the default name and overstrike with your new name.

FIGURE 6.9

The Document Layout palette, when enlarged slightly, will show icons for all master pages in your project.

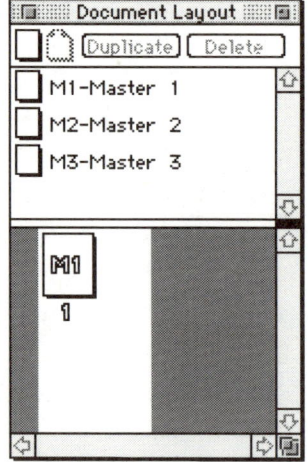

First, change the name of M1-Master 1. Call it QR Cover (see Figure 6.10). As you can see, the M1 designation remains and the new name of your master page is M1-QR Cover. Next, click the M2-Master 2 icon, select the name, and rename it QR Body. Finally, rename the M3-Master 3 to QR Mailer.

FIGURE 6.10

Highlight and replace the generic name of the master pages with more descriptive monikers.

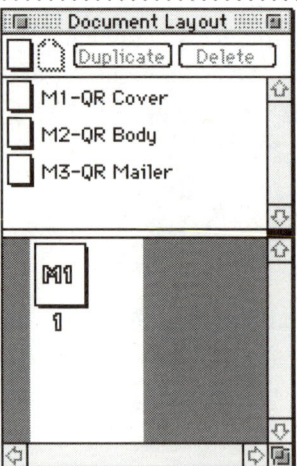

These new master pages and their given names reflect in the Page ➤ Display submenu. Remember, you can use this menu option to select a document or master page instead of using the Document Layout palette (see Figure 6.11).

FIGURE 6.11

The Page ➤ Display option will show document and master page names.

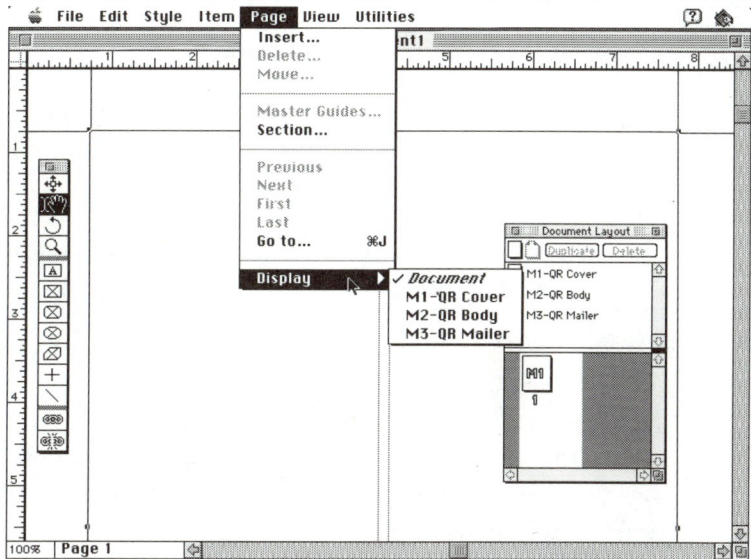

NOTE

You may want to save this document now that you have put some time into it. The earlier you start saving a document, the better off you will be in case of a disaster. Save this under the name of QR Newsletter.

EDITING THE MASTER PAGES

Next, you will edit each of the master pages. That is, you are going to include text or graphic elements which will repeat on each issue of the newsletter in their respective pages. In the Document Layout palette, double-click on the M1-QR Cover icon (formerly, M1-Master 1). This opens up the master page QR Cover to the full size in the document work area.

NOTE

Adjustments made on the M1-QR Cover master page will not affect the layout of other master pages cloned from the original M1-Master 1 page.

Start by preparing a banner for the newsletter. To do this, you must adjust the size of the automatic text box in this master page. You are going to lower the top of this text box so a new text box containing the banner will appear at the top of the page. You don't want the two text boxes to interfere with each other.

Create a new text box using the text box tool. Click on the new text box once with the Item or Content tool and you will see grab handles appear at the corners and mid-points of the text box outline. Next, key in ⌘-M (equivalent to Item ➤ Modify) to bring up the Text Box Specifications dialog box. Change the Origin Down field to 2.75 and the Height field to 7.5 (see Figure 6.12). Click OK. These changes will give an additional 2″ for the banner.

CREATING QUICKRELEASE BANNER

To create the banner, you are going to have to create a new text box at the top of this master page, M1-QR Cover. First select the Text Box tool from the Tool palette. Next, click and drag, forming a new text box in the work area. Specific size and placement of the new text box is unimportant when creating the box, because it will be adjusted in the Text Box Specifications dialog box. After the new text box is drawn, click on the new text box with the Content tool and the text editing cursor will be flashing. Key ⌘-M to get the Text Box Specifications dialog box for this item. Change the size fields as shown in Figure 6.13. Click OK. This will give you two text boxes in the master page QR Cover.

FIGURE 6.12

Match the specifications given here for your text box.

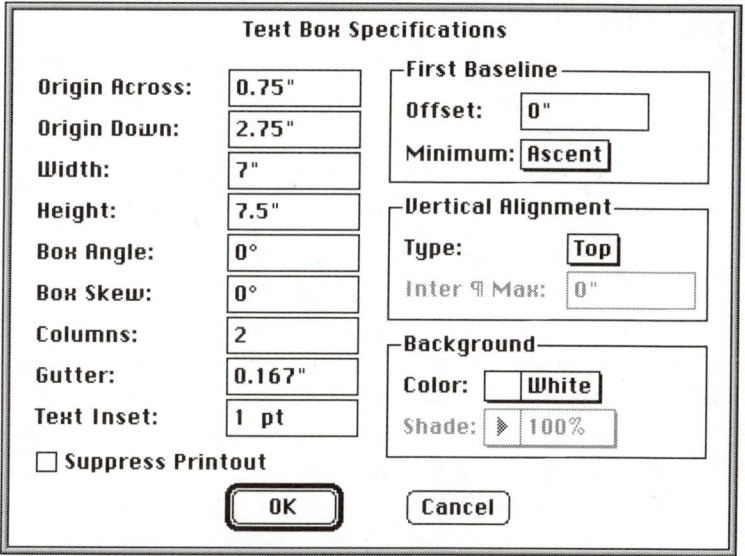

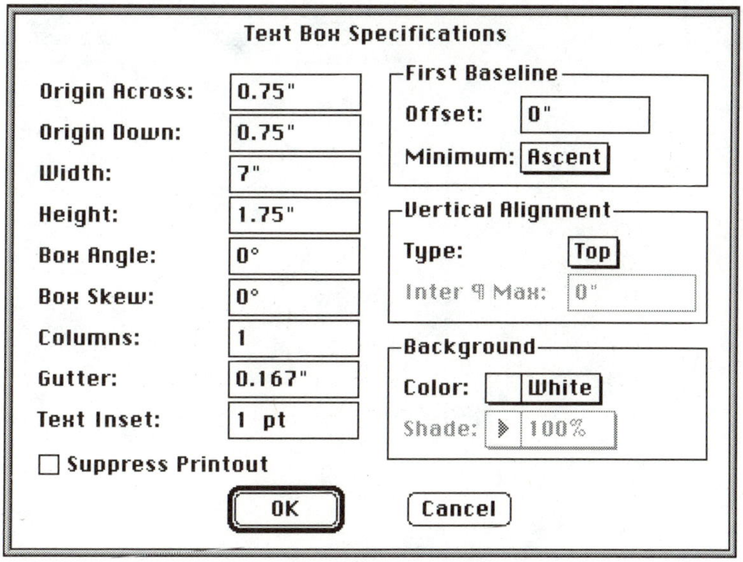

Text Box Specifications

Origin Across: `0.75"`

Origin Down: `2.75"`

Width: `7"`

Height: `7.5"`

Box Angle: `0°`

Box Skew: `0°`

Columns: `2`

Gutter: `0.167"`

Text Inset: `1 pt`

☐ Suppress Printout

First Baseline

Offset: `0"`

Minimum: `Ascent`

Vertical Alignment

Type: `Top`

Inter ¶ Max: `0"`

Background

Color: `White`

Shade: ▶ `100%`

[OK] [Cancel]

FIGURE 6.13

The text box item, housing the banner, is set up through the Text Box Specifications dialog box.

Text Box Specifications

Origin Across: `0.75"`

Origin Down: `0.75"`

Width: `7"`

Height: `1.75"`

Box Angle: `0°`

Box Skew: `0°`

Columns: `1`

Gutter: `0.167"`

Text Inset: `1 pt`

☐ Suppress Printout

First Baseline

Offset: `0"`

Minimum: `Ascent`

Vertical Alignment

Type: `Top`

Inter ¶ Max: `0"`

Background

Color: `White`

Shade: ▶ `100%`

[OK] [Cancel]

APPLYING A MASTER PAGE
TO A DOCUMENT
....

CH. 6

TIP

You can nimbly leap from field to field in a dialog box by using the Tab key.

Choose the Content tool and click on your new text box, if it isn't already selected. Key in the following text: QuickRelease. Then press Return. On the next line, key in Volume X, Number X (see Figure 6.14). Naturally, you will replace the X on each issue with the appropriate number.

NOTE

Have you thought of saving the document yet? You probably should save any new document as soon as you can to avoid any possible frustration! Don't wait to complete the document; save it as soon as a good foundation is established, such as you have here. Save this project under the name QR Newsletter.

FIGURE 6.14

Key in the text for your banner as shown here.

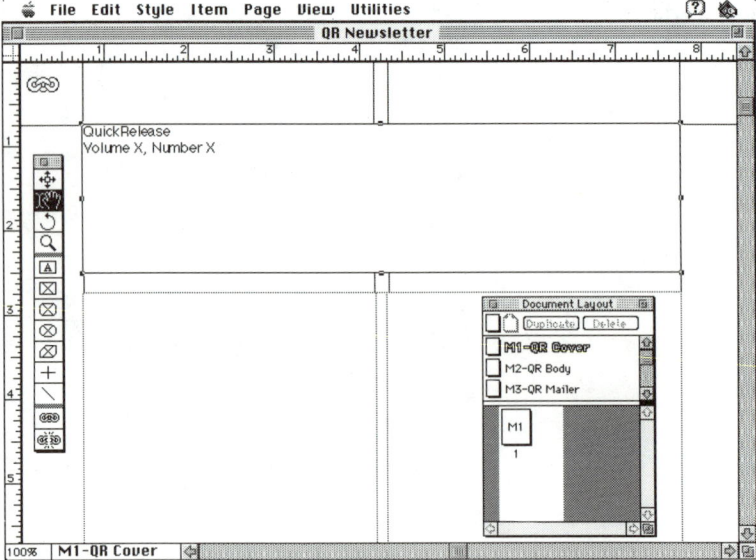

Now change the type characteristics of the letters by highlighting the first line only (highlight QuickRelease). Select Style ➤ Character (or the keyboard equivalent, ⌘-Shift-D). In the Character Attributes dialog box, make changes to reflect those in Figure 6.15. Include not only the type font, style, and size, but also the horizontal scale and tracking information. Click OK when the information is correct. Next highlight the second line of text, Volume X, Number X. Choose Style ➤ Character again, and change the settings to Font: Times-Plain; Size: 12 pt; Horizontal Scale: 150%; and Track Amount: 0. When you are finished, click OK.

FIGURE 6.15
Key in specifications to match this dialog box for the title.

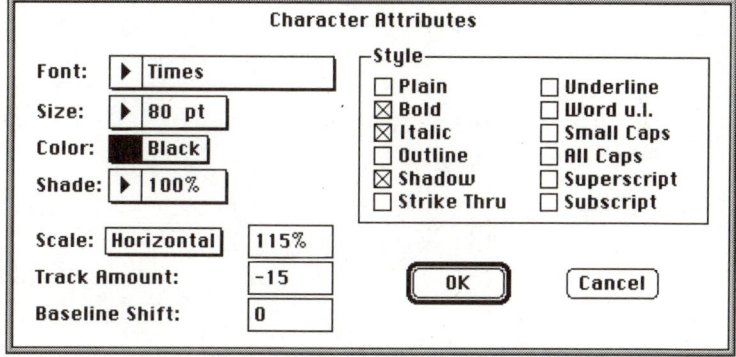

NOTE

Your text may not look good on the screen. The Times font was chosen for this example because all Macs have this font. System 7 furnishes a TrueType Times font as well. If you don't have the TrueType or ATM (Adobe Type Manager) installed to help your type look better on the screen, you may have poor type quality (on the screen) in this project. Please remember, though, that screen quality is not what counts, printed output does! Your document should print fine to a PostScript printer or imagesetter.

Now you should center both lines of banner text. To select both lines, place your cursor in the text box and use the shortcut ⌘-A (Select All), then ⌘-Shift-C (Style ➤ Alignment ➤ Centered). . The text should resemble that in Figure 6.16.

FIGURE 6.16

Once you've changed the typeface and size and centered the text, your document should look something like this.

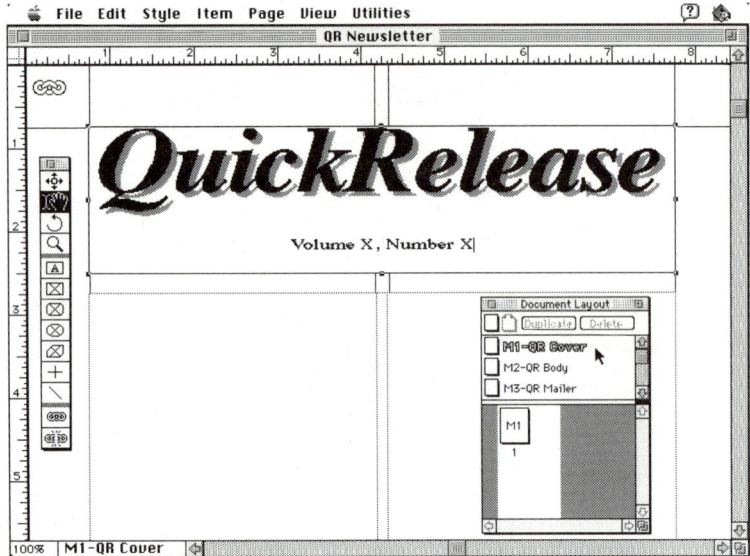

Finally, you will add a line to this master page that separates the banner from body copy. Use the Orthogonal Line tool. Click and drag to form a line.

NOTE

In this example you cover many new techniques in QuarkXPress. To try to limit the "confusion factor", you are asked to reposition items using Item ➤ Modify according to numerical specifications. Later in the book, you will have an opportunity to explore manual methods of item manipulation. For now, this is the quickest technique.

Use the Item tool and click on the new line to select it. If properly selected, you should see the typical Mac "grab bars" for the item. Then choose Item ➤ Modify (⌘-M) and change the specifications as shown in Figure 6.17. Then click on OK to accept changes.

Ta da! You have created and edited your first master page.

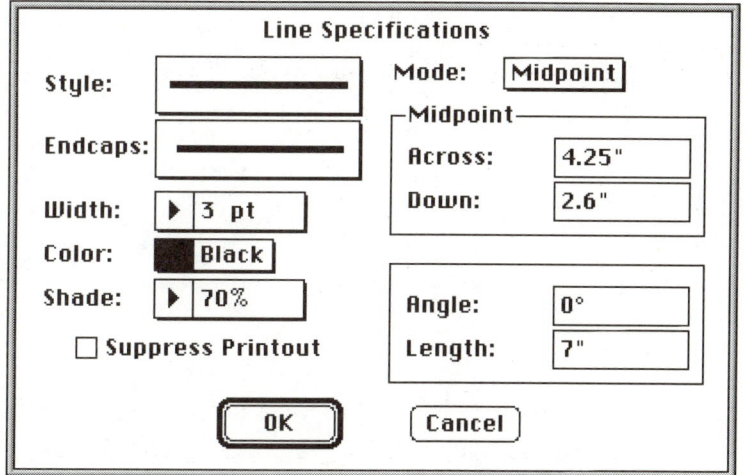

EDITING THE QR BODY MASTER PAGE

Editing the QR Body master page will be much simpler. You only have to place a page number at the top center of the page. To begin, open the appropriate master page through one of two techniques. You can choose Page ➤ Display ➤ M2-QR Body option or double-click in the Document Layout palette on the M2-QR Body (previously, M2-Master 2) page icon.

With the M2-QR Body master page showing at Actual Size in the work area, click on the Text Box tool, from the Tools palette. Click and drag in the document work area to create a new text box. Then, while the new text box is still active, go to the Text Box Specifications dialog box, Item ➤ Modify (⌘-M). Change it according to the settings in Figure 6.18. Press the Return key or click on OK.

FIGURE 6.18

*Modify the page number
text box to match these
Text Box Specifications.*

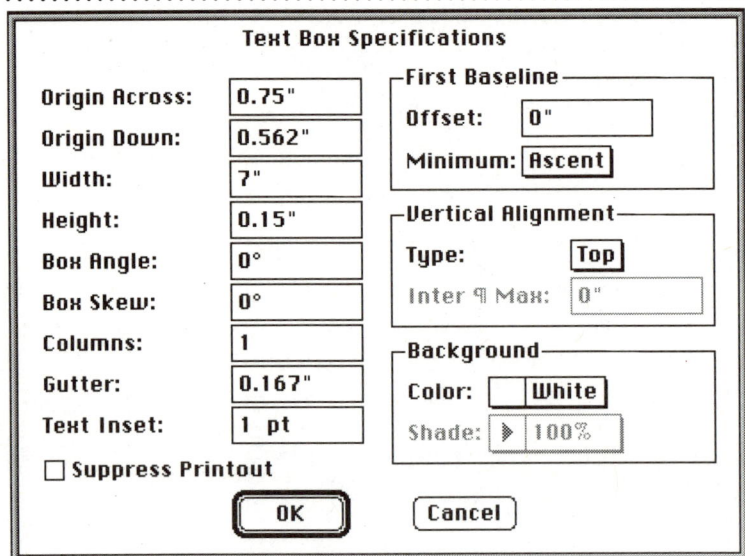

Now, to work on this text box, you should temporarily enlarge it. Click on the text box with the Item or Content tool. This shows the grab handles of the text box item. Click and drag on a corner grab handle to enlarge the box. Next, using the Content tool, click on the text box; the cursor should change to the text cursor. Key in the Automatic Box Page number (⌘-3). Highlight and change the text to Times, 9 point. This will later be centered on the page. For now, after altering the type, change the text box back to fit the specifications shown in Figure 6.18.

To center your copy on the page, simply highlight (click and drag) over the copy with the Content tool. It will allow you to make changes. Center the copy high-lighted by pressing the ⌘-Shift-C (Style ➤ Alignment ➤ Centered). Your text should resemble Figure 6.19.

FIGURE 6.19

The page number box should resemble this illustration on the master page.

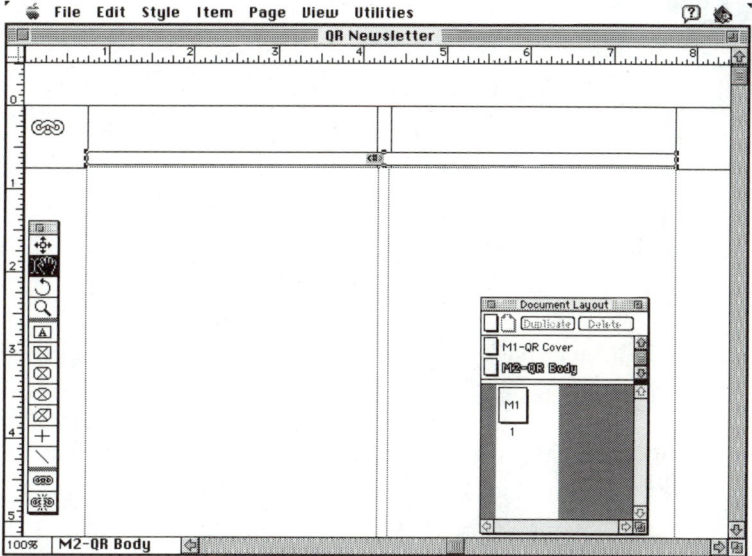

THE BACK PAGE OF YOUR NEWSLETTER

The back page of your newsletter (M3-QR Mailer), will also have a page number, identically placed and styled as in the body pages. There are a few ways to get this page number on the M3-QR Mailer. You could:

▸ Duplicate the master page you have just modified. This makes an exact copy with all your changes. The problem here is that you already have established a third master page. What would become of the existing M3-QR Mailer master page?

▸ You could copy just the text box, with its contents for the page number. Then leave the M3-QR Body master page, open the M2-QR Mailer, and paste the copied text box into proper position.

▸ You could just go to the existing M2-QR Mailer master page and edit the page, as you did in the M3-QR Body. In essence, you could repeat the steps just completed, but apply these on the M3-QR Mailer page.

NOTE

The philosophy throughout this book has been one of productivity. You will no doubt face production problems frequently in the document creation process. Your success depends greatly on what decision(s) you make.

The quickest way to produce the page number text box on this master page is to duplicate the M2-QR Body master page, then modify as necessary to make it the M3-QR Mailer. Start by activating the Document Layout palette. This means to show the palette, if its not shown. Use the View ➤ Show Document Layout menu option if it is not showing.

Steps to take include deleting the existing M3-QR Mailer master page, duplicating the M2-QR Body master and renaming it to be the new M3-QR Mailer. Sequentially, perform the following steps:

▸ Scroll if necessary to see the icon and name of the M3-QR Mailer in the Document Layout palette.

▸ Click once on the M3-QR Mailer icon to identify it. It will darken when highlighted.

▸ Click on the Delete button in the Document Layout palette, while the M3-QR Mailer is highlighted. The master page is deleted.

▸ Click on the M2-QR Body master page icon to identify it.

▸ Click on the Duplicate button of the Document Layout palette, while the M2-QR Body master page is highlighted. It duplicates to form a new M3-Master 3 master page.

▸ Highlight the name of the new page, M1-Master 3, overstrike with the new name, M3-QR Mailer.

That's it. Sometimes the quickest way to duplicate specific information on one master page is to duplicate the entire page.

Next, you have to modify the page to accept the mailer information. To do this you will modify the large text box on the page and add a second at the bottom for the company address.

Select Page ➤ Display ➤ M3-QR Mailer or double-click on its icon in the Document Layout palette. Click on the large text box with the Content or Item Tool. Then, go to the Text Box Specifications dialog box (⌘-M). Change the size and location of the box to Origin Across: 0.75; Origin Down: 0.75; Width: 7; and Height: 4. Click OK.

NOTE

You could also have made adjustments from the Measurements palette. To use this palette, select Show Measurements from the View menu. Any changes to the numerical values you see on the palette can be made by overstriking. Activate by pressing the Enter key.

Now you must make another text box on the bottom of this page. Select the Text Box tool from the Tool palette. Create a new text box and modify it according to Figure 6.20.

FIGURE 6.20
Text box specifications for the address box.

X: 0.75" Y: 6"	W: 7" H: 4"	⊿ 0° Cols: 1	

Now key in the return address. Change to the Content tool (from the Tools palette) and click on the new text box. The cursor will show that you are ready to type. Key in the following address:

```
EMBicycles, Inc.
1325 Pontiac Street
Detroit, MI 54236.
```

After each line, press Return to go to the next line. Highlight all the text and choose Style ➤ Character. Then use the Character Attributes dialog box(⌘-Shift-D) to change attributes to Times, 12 point. Click on OK to accept information in this dialog box and Voila, your newsletter is finished (at least as far as this chapter is concerned)! Save the document, if you haven't already, under the name *QRNewsletter*.

NOTE

When saving a document in QuarkXPress, you have two options at the bottom of a new save dialog box. These include the options to save your work as a Document or a Template. To save as a Document, your work is able to be opened, edited and saved as you are familiar with other Macintosh documents. Select Template to make the project a master that you can build from, without changing the original. For a real newsletter, you may want to save the work just performed as a Template. That way, you can open it each time a new newsletter is to be produced, edit and save under a new file name. The original Template is not altered, allowing it to be used as a master for the next newsletter. Version 3.2 also has a nifty new AutoSave feature; after you have saved a document once, AutoSave periodically records your changes to disk, thereby reducing the possibility of data loss.

PRINTING MASTER PAGES

Master Pages normally do not print when you output the document; however, you can print information contained on a document page. When the master page is displayed in the document window, all controls of the Page Setup dialog box are available. You also have access to controls in the Print dialog box (except All, From and To). When facing page master pages are displayed, both left and right pages print. So as a final exercise, choose File ➤ Print (⌘-P) to print out the master pages, and prepare to admire your work!

WORD
PROCESSING

III

Importing and Exporting Text

MAC TRACKS   MAC TRACKS   MAC TRACKS   MAC TRACKS   MAC

To import text and maintain style tags 166

click on the Include Style Sheets check box in the dialog box for Get Text (File ➤ Get Text).

To import certain word processing file formats 169

in QuarkXPress make sure you have the proper filter included in the QuarkXPress folder.

To export text and maintain style tags 169

use the XPress tags in QuarkXPress that enable you to associate traditional command code sequencing for specific attributes.

QuarkXPress has an abundance of word processing capabilities. It allows you to import text from a wide variety of word-processing software packages. If you choose, you can even use the built-in QuarkXPress word processor, without the need for an outside one. It has many of the functions you may be looking for in a dedicated word processor. Once you import or generate text, you can manipulate it with a wide array of features including kerning and tracking.

WORD PROCESSING IN QUARKXPRESS

Perhaps the easiest way to get text into QuarkXPress is to create it with a separate word processor and to import it. Importing and exporting word processed material is really almost transparent these days.

In a publishing environment, there is often a staff of quick-typing individuals who work at word-processing stations. They may be working on Microsoft Word or MacWrite on the Macintosh. They may even be working in DOS or the Windows environment with analogous programs. Today, it really doesn't matter. All you need to bring text in from a foreign application is a little cooperation and communication at the outset.

WHY OUTSIDE WORD PROCESSORS?

Why would anyone advocate using an outside word processor with that function built into QuarkXPress? The answer is simple: Word processing should be left to the word processor! Although QuarkXPress has word-processing features, it cannot compete in that arena with a full-fledged word processing program. Also, there are people highly skilled in those specialized programs. The philosophy to follow for highest productivity is leave specialty work to the specialists and let them use the tools they work with best.

NOTE

QuarkXPress has built-in filters for some word processors, while others can be purchased through outside vendors. All popular word-processing packages are supported in some fashion, so you need not worry about migrating files into QuarkXPress.

HOW TO GET TEXT FROM OUTSIDE WORD PROCESSORS

One method of bringing text from an outside word processor starts with communicating your needs. Often, word processing applications today are on a Macintosh, DOS or Windows platform. Most give you options on the formats you want to save in. For example, in MacWrite II, you can save a file as a MacWrite document or as Text—see Figure 7.1. Saving as text is equivalent to saving as ASCII.

NOTE

ASCII is an acronym for American Standard Code for Information Interchange. It is an industry standard, text-only format. QuarkXPress can import and save text in ASCII format.

CONNECTING TO PCS

Although DOS translation software is serviceable, sometimes information is lost when converting to QuarkXPress. For those individuals who work daily in a multi-platform environment, the new version of Apple File Exchange is a better solution (see Figure 7.2).

FIGURE 7.1

The Save dialog box in MacWrite II allows you to save your document as a generic text format.

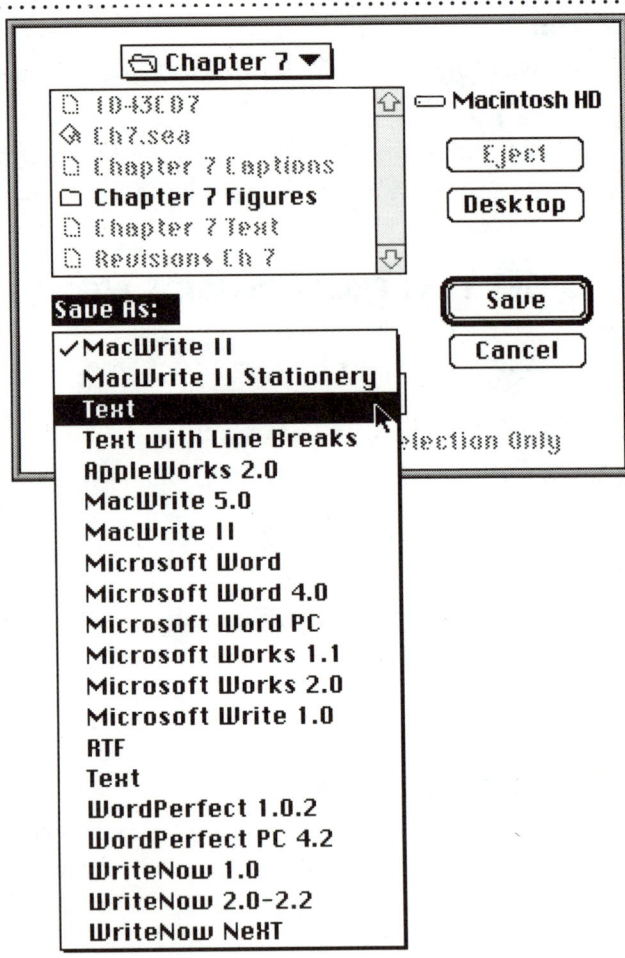

FIGURE 7.2

The Apple File Exchange folder

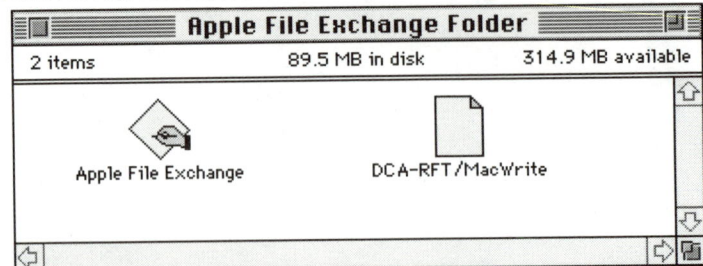

WARNING

One of the problems between moving information from one machine format to another is that of the physical connectivity. There are numerous solutions on the market for Mac/PC connectivity. The solution that may be easiest to work with is a combination of software application and "sneaker net" (also known as "shank's mare"—it means walking the file from one machine to another). Get a copy of DOS Mounter or equivalent that enables your Mac floppy drive to read and write in a DOS format. Once loaded, this software enables you to place a DOS disk in your Mac and exchange information with other Mac applications.

Apple File Exchange is a translation utility that will take PC files and turn them into Mac files (and vice versa). It is quite intuitive to use, and supports many common formats. For details on the Apple File Exchange, see your Macintosh documentation.

HOW TO IMPORT TEXT

If you can physically connect outside data to the Macintosh environment (through a Superdrive or through a network) QuarkXPress can usually import any ASCII (text) files you want to use. The procedure is simple. Create a text box in your QuarkXPress document if you did not check the Automatic Text Box option when you created the new document.

NOTE

If you have checked the Automatic Text Box option when creating a new QuarkXPress document, a text box will show on the master page (within the margins). A text box of like size will also be on the first document page. In a text import situation, Master A has a linked text box. This means that if the imported text takes up more room than there is in the text box, other pages will be added, and the text will automatically flow from one page to another. If the text box on the Master Page is not linked, you must do all this work manually. Thus, it may be best, until you gain more experience, to check the Automatic Text Box option when you create a new document for importing text.

Once the text box is in place, select the Content tool from the Tool palette. (Hint: it's the second tool down; it is the I-beam/Hand combination.) It is important to select this tool, because you can only import text with the Content tool.

TIP

Be sure to use the text box on the first page of the document, otherwise, you'll get a warning about not putting text in a master documents text box.

Make sure that you have clicked on the text box to select it. The Mac and QuarkXPress have no idea where to place the text if you don't first identify the text box!

Next choose File ➤ Get Text (see Figure 7.3) or press ⌘-E. The Get Text option is available only when the Content tool is in use and a text box is active. If you identify a picture box with this tool, the option says Get Picture instead of Get Text. We will discuss how to import picture material in Chapter 14.

FIGURE 7.3
*Use File ➤ Get Text to
import a text file.*

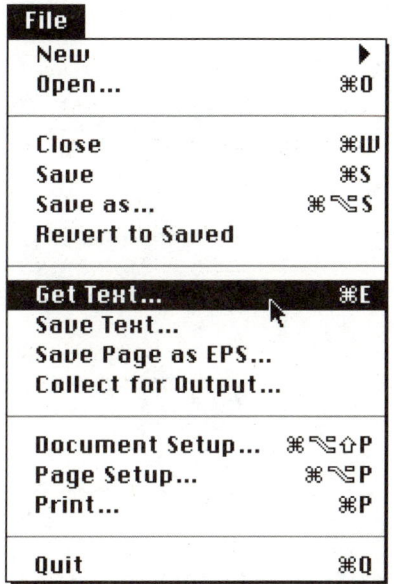

Once you select Get Text, a dialog box appears (see Figure 7.4). The Get Text dialog box should be familiar to experienced Mac users. It resembles the "open file" style of dialog box. You can look anywhere on any connected floppy disk, hard drive, or network drive that you have access to.

CONVERTING SYMBOLS AND QUOTES IN QUARKXPRESS

QuarkXPress gives you the option of using traditional word-processing quotes ("") or the more stylized typesetting quotes (""). Typesetting quotes are different (they look like a 66 and a 99), while word-processing quotes look the same on both ends (they look like hash marks). Conversion also works on double hyphens and single quotation symbols.

To import text and automatically convert double hyphens (--) to the typographer's equivalent, the em dash (—), as well as converting foot (') and inch (") marks to apostrophes (') and typesetter's quotes ("), check the Convert Quotes option. If you do not want to convert these symbols, leave the option box unchecked.

FIGURE 7.4
The Get Text dialog box enables you to search from among several drives or network connections to find the file you wish to import.

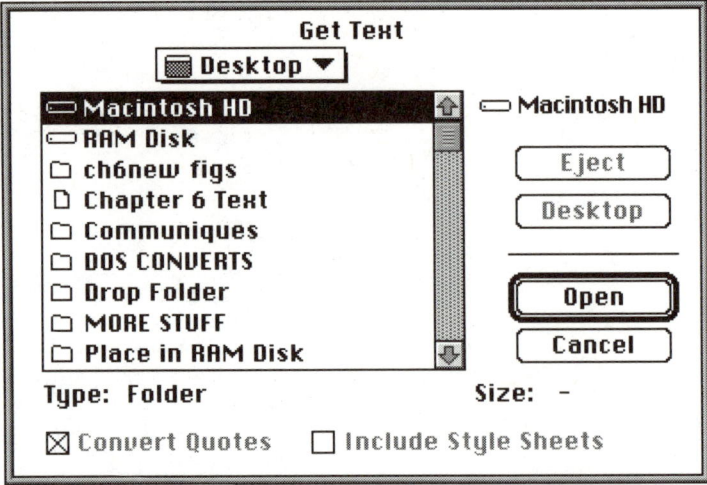

STYLE SHEETS OF IMPORTED TEXT

In the Get Text dialog box (File ➤ Get Text or ⌘-E), there is an option box called Include Style Sheets. This specifically works at this time on Microsoft Word style sheets. To append an MS Word style sheet to an active document's list of available style sheets, check the Include Style Sheets option.

OTHER INFORMATION IN THE GET TEXT DIALOG BOX

Other information in the Get Text dialog box are the Type and Size fields. Once you have identified a particular file to import, the Type field indicates the style (text, ASCII, WordPerfect, etc.) of the document (see Figure 7.5). Size represents how big the total file of text is in (disk storage) size.

FIGURE 7.5

*The dialog box will iden-
tify the type and size of
the file you have flagged
for import.*

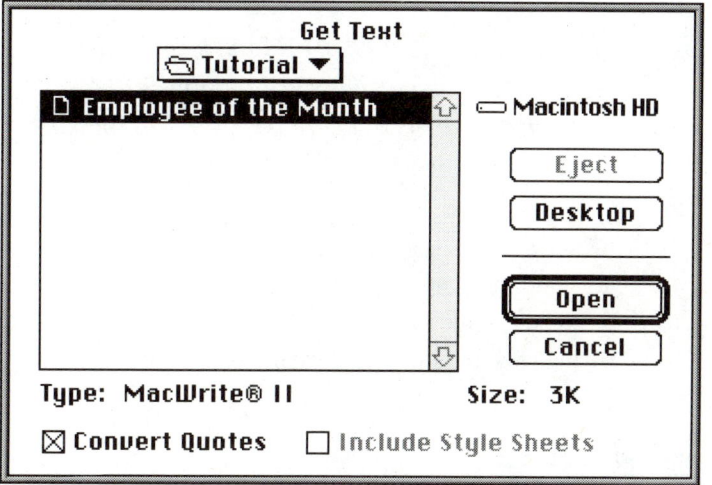

WARNING

*Be aware of the type file size when importing. Although you can
have up to 2000 document pages in QuarkXPress, it may be easier
to work with in smaller chunks. Consider breaking large word-
processing files down into manageable-sized chunks, and then
import them as necessary. That is, unless you have taken earlier
advice from Part I of this book, and purchased a gigabyte of
memory! As a Mac user, you know how frustrating it is to suddenly
run out of memory. Working with large documents is likely to
cause this problem and therefore is not advised.*

To format imported ASCII text, specify attributes and paragraph formats at the text-insertion point in QuarkXPress before you bring in the text. Otherwise, establish these in QuarkXPress style sheets to apply later.

When you import a file, the original file remains untouched. Only a copy of the text imports from the original file. Once the copy imports, there is no need for the original text file disk or network connection. This is not a tagged file, but rather it is an actual duplication of each character of the primary text file.

WARNING

If you use a data compression program, particularly one that renames the file, QuarkXPress may not recognize it as a text file, in which case it will not import it. You should first decompress the file and store it where accessible.

Once the Get Text dialog box is acceptable, click Open. After a pause, the text will stream from the host file into your QuarkXPress text box. More pages and text boxes will form as needed.

WARNING

Often in the process of creating a new document and importing text, it is common to omit a crucial step—you must save the document. This can be a life-saving step, particularly when you work with large text blocks.

After the text imports, you can make changes in the QuarkXPress document. Chapter 8 explores text formatting and other manipulation techniques.

WHAT IF YOUR WORD-PROCESSED TEXT IS NOT PLAIN TEXT?

If the word-processed document is not ASCII text, there are alternatives. QuarkXPress comes with filters for several popular word processors (see Figure 7.6.). Consider the use of an extra sub-folder that you can move filters in and out of as needed for the application of the day.

FIGURE 7.6
These icons represent various filters.

MS-Works™ 2.0 Filter

MacWrite® Filter

WriteNow™ Filter

WordPerfect™ Filter

These filters, when installed, allow QuarkXPress to import specific word-processing formats.

XPRESS TAGS

XPress Tags are keyboard command codes for certain operations that transfer through ASCII text. You can use XPress Tags in imported text as well as in text you intend to export from QuarkXPress. XPress Tags' codes may come from an outside word-processing system or text to import to QuarkXPress (see Figure 7.7).

FIGURE 7.7

*A sample listing of
XPress Tags*

Begin Kerning............	<Knnn>
Bold	<B>
Color Index	<Cnnn>
Font	<nnn>
Italics.......................	<I>
Line Break	<R>
Point Size	<Pnnn>
Resume Normal.........	<D>
Small.........................	<S>
Strike thru.................	<H>
Subscript	<v>
Superscript................	<^>
Underline...................	<U>

NOTE

*WYSIWYG is an acronym for "what you see is what you get." It
more appropriately should be WYSIWYHF—what you see is what
you hope for!*

CONVERTING XPRESS TAGS

To convert XPress Tag codes, check Include Style Sheets in the Get Text dialog box
(⌘-E). If unchecked, tags do not convert; they display in the imported text. This
can make a big difference in bringing in outside keystrokes. For example, if you
were to use style sheets in MS Word, they would include information such as font,
style, size, etc., all pertinent material for the publication. If you do not import this,
all these details will have to be restructured once the text is imported in QuarkX-
Press. Also, you may have additional coding structures to delete after import.

NOTE

The Get Text dialog box lists only ASCII files and files from word-processing programs for which an import/export filter is available. QuarkXPress filters must be stored in the QuarkXPress folder or the System Folder. If you need a particular text format filter, store it properly before you launch QuarkXPress.

XPRESS TAGS IN EXPORTING TEXT

If you wish to use the XPress Tags capability in exporting text from QuarkXPress, insert specific codes in your text structures (see Figure 7.7). These codes are similar to what some word processors call style sheets. Quark has taken a proprietary naming of them in the QuarkXPress program: XPress Tags.

TIP

To export all the text contained in a text box or a chain of linked text boxes, activate the text box by clicking on it. Then select File ➤ Save Text. To save and export a selected range of text, highlight that range of text only, then choose File ➤ Save Text. Although the export feature is available in QuarkXPress, it is not known to be applied widely throughout the QuarkXPress user community. This is due to the growing number of XTension programs available from third party developers. In most cases, you can perform every manipulative function to text either before it is imported to QuarkXPress or through XTensions. See Chapters 19 and 20 for more information on XTensions.

You can automatically insert specific style codes when you save text with QuarkXPress. Save the text as XPress Tags and the ASCII file you create will contain all embedded style tag codes. You can also exchange XPress-tagged text with any program that supports this format.

8

TEXT FORMATTING

click and drag to highlight the text you want to change (it can be a letter, word, phrase, or even the entire document), then select a new typeface from the Style ➤ Font menu.

click and drag to highlight the text you want to change (it can be a letter, word, phrase, or even the entire document), then select a new size from the Style ➤ Size menu.

(from 7 to 192 points), press ⌘-Shift->. To decrease the size through this same fixed range, press ⌘-Shift-<.

highlight it with the Content tool. Then use the keyboard equivalent. For example to change the highlighted text to italics, press ⌘-Shift-I. See keyboard equivalents listed beside the menu item name.

To change the space between two characters   183

anchor the cursor between those two. With the cursor flashing, select Style
➤ Kern. A numerical dialog box appears allowing you to input a numerical
value. You can specify a kerning value from -500 to 500 in increments as
fine as .000005 em. The default is zero. A negative value decreases the distance between two characters, while a positive number increases the
distance.

To adjust spacing with the measurement palette   184

press either of the kerning arrows in the palette. This will increase or decrease space between two characters in increments of 0.05-ems. A numerical dialog box appears allowing you to input a numerical value. You can
specify a kerning value from -500 to 500 in increments as fine as .000005
em. To adjust in increments of 0.005-ems, hold down the Option key while
clicking on the kerning arrows.

To use the keyboard shortcuts to adjust the
baseline   186

highlight the characters of choice again, then press ⌘-Option-Shift-+ to
move the text above the baseline in one-point increments. Press ⌘-Option-
Shift-hyphen to move the text below the baseline in one-point increments.

An essential part of word processing today is the ability to assign your keystrokes a proper font, size, style, etc. This chapter introduces you to the QuarkXPress feature directly dealing with these type attributes, the Style menu.

TEXT FORMATTING AND THE STYLE MENU

The Style Menu has three different appearances. It looks one way when using it for text boxes, another when adjusting style for the picture boxes, and yet another when editing style for a line item (see Figure 8.1). The focus in this chapter is to see how the Style menu works for text boxes.

TIP

As you read along, you will note a recurring theme. Whenever you want to change text, you must use the Content tool to highlight it. Only then can you alter it.

The Style menu is only accessible if you are using the Content or Item tool. Also, you can only use Style if you have highlighted an item. Remember, you can tell an item is highlighted by the familiar black grab boxes.

FIGURE 8.1

The Style menu changes for the type of item you have selected. Different style menus are available for the picture box item, the line item and the grouped item.

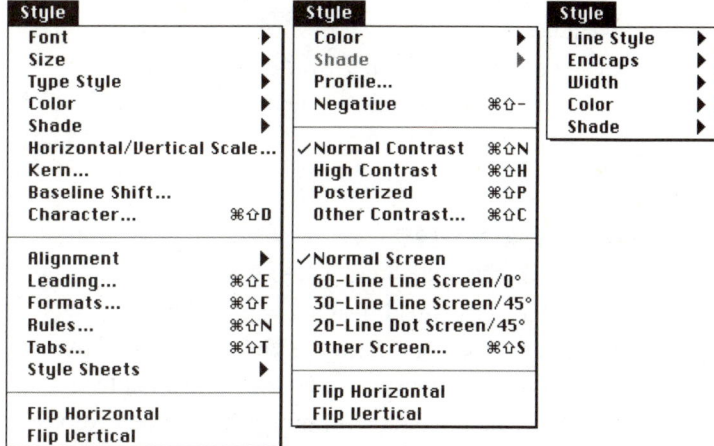

NOTE

Several of the options listed under the Style menu are also accessible through the Measurement palette and keyboard equivalents. If frequent changes are necessary, it may be a good idea to keep the Measurement palette in the document work area all the time. To change Measurement palette data, highlight and overstrike. Overstriking replaces the new measurement or name. When finished with your changes, press Return or Enter. Specific keyboard shortcuts are listed in this chapter as well as on the inside front cover of this book.

THE FONT COMMAND

The Font command allows you to select from a variety of typefaces. You must have each typeface resident in your system to select it. If you don't have a particular font in your machine's System Folder, you will not find it on the Font submenu.

177

To change the font of a section of text, click and drag to highlight the text you want to change (it can be a letter, word, phrase, or even the entire document), then select a new typeface from the Style ➤ Font menu. Once you have selected the typeface with the cursor, release the mouse button. The highlighted text changes to the new typeface.

THE SIZE COMMAND

The size command allows you to select from a list of type sizes. You must identify the text to be resized through highlighting. Then select Style ➤ Size. The size menu consists of several type sizes, measured numerically in points (a printer's measurement system based on the days of hot lead typesetting). The point size numbers that are outlined represent typeface sizes whose files are resident in the System. These sizes look good as screen fonts; non-outlined fonts may not look very good on the screen (see Figure 8.2). Use of Adobe Type Manager (a separate

FIGURE 8.2

The Style ➤ Size submenu shows what sizes are available to you. Sizes that appear in outline type will look better on your screen than solid ones. All sizes should print equally well.

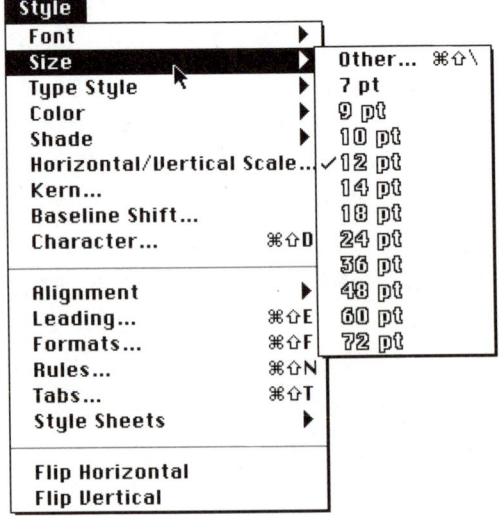

software application) will allow your fonts to look better on the screen even when you don't have the appropriate screen font size.

Regardless of how it looks on the screen, the printed version of the font probably looks better than that on the monitor. See Chapter 13 for more details.

USING OTHER SIZES

If you want a size not listed, select the command Other (⌘-Shift-\). Selecting Other allows you to key the size you need, exactly! QuarkXPress allows you to select sizes ranging from 2 to 720 points. Not only that, you can select type sizes in increments as small as 0.001 of any measurement unit. That is, you can use points, inches, metric, etc.; any measurement system you have chosen in QuarkXPress can also apply to type sizes. Remember, odd sizes may not look good on the screen, but they should look fine when printed.

CHANGING FONT SIZES WITH THE KEYBOARD

It was noted earlier that you can change type sizes with the Style menu as well as through the Measurement palette. One additional technique you should be aware of is keyboard shortcuts. To increase the type size through a range of preset sizes (from 7 to 192 points), press ⌘-Shift->. To decrease the size through this same fixed range, press ⌘-Shift-<.

To increase size in one point increments from 2 to 720 points (the total range), press ⌘-Shift-Option-<. To decrease in one point increments, press ⌘-Shift-Option->.

THE TYPE STYLE COMMAND

Again, if you are somewhat familiar with other Macintosh programs, you will understand the notion of changing the style or "look" of type. The Type Style command (Style ➤ Type Style) determines if the type will look outlined or plain, underlined or strike-through, etc.

NOTE

You can combine several options from the Type Style menu (e.g., Bold Outline type).

To adjust the type style of a section of text, highlight it with the Content tool. Then select Style ➤ Type Style. There are several ways you can change the highlighted text. Slide the mouse cursor down to highlight a choice or use the keyboard short-cut (the shortcuts are listed on the menu to the right of each format). If you choose to use the keyboard equivalent, simply highlight the text and key in the appropriate key combinations for the change you want to make. For example to change the highlighted text to italics, press ⌘-Shift-I. Figure 8.3 shows the Type Style submenu with all the keyboard shortcuts.

THE COLOR COMMAND

To color the text of your choice, again select the Content tool. Highlight the text to apply color to. Then select the Style ➤ Color submenu. This allows you to choose from a color palette. To add or augment colors, see Chapter 17.

FIGURE 8.3

All styles on the Type Style submenu have handy keyboard equivalents.

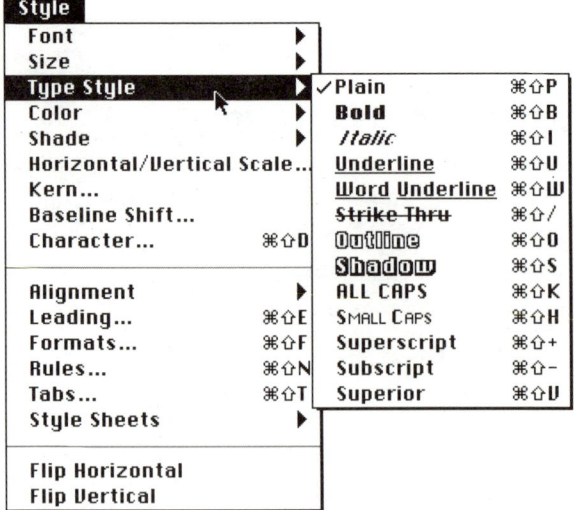

THE SHADE COMMAND

In addition to the other stylistic options, you can shade type. This means you are adding some kind of shading to the text. To shade text, select the Content tool, highlight the text to change, and select Style ➤ Shade. This command gives you percentages of color or shade. If your text is black, it gives you percentages of black in grayscale. The scale is 0–100 percent in ten percent increments (see Figure 8.4). Like the Size submenu, there is an Other command. Selecting this allows you to key in the exact percentage of shade desired. You can select from 0 to 100 percent in 0.1 percent increments. Once you have keyed in the size you want, click on the OK button.

THE HORIZONTAL SCALE COMMAND

This command allows you to expand or condense the width of type. The original width of the type is a default of 100 percent. To use the Horizontal Scale command you first use the Content tool to select the text. Then select Style ➤ Horizontal/Vertical Scale and a dialog box appears. (Horizontal shows in the dialog box, if you want to change the Vertical value, click on the popup menu). The number is already in percentage, so there is no need to key in the percent sign.

FIGURE 8.4

The Shade submenu

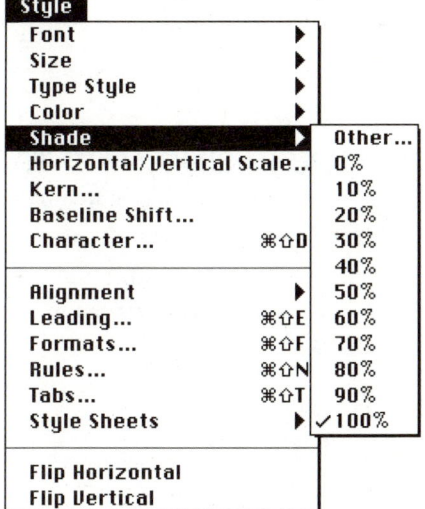

FIGURE 8.5

A line of type whose set width has been changed.

Lines of type altered with horizontal scale.

Lines of type altered with horizontal scale.

A number less than 100 compresses the width of the type. Some typographers call this normal width the *set width*. A number greater than 100 expands the width of the type design. This does not alter type height and size. The increment may range from 25 to 400 percent, in increments as small as 0.1 percent (see Figure 8.5).

THE VERTICAL SCALE COMMAND

This command allows you to expand or condense the height of the type characters. The original height of the type is a default of 100 percent. To use the Vertical Scale command, you first use the Content tool to select the text. Then select Style ➤ Horizontal/Vertical Scale and a dialog box appears. Click and hold on the Scale popup menu to change it from Horizontal to Vertical. Then change the value, just as if it were a Horizontal Scale command. The number is already in percentage, so there is no need to key in the percent sign.

A number less than 100 compresses the type. A number greater than 100 enlarges the height of the type characters without altering the basic design characteristics. The increment may range from 25 to 400 percent, in increments as small as 0.1 percent.

KERNING, LETTERSPACING, AND TRACKING

One of the capabilities that electronic publishing programs have, that few word processors provide, is the ability to kern. Kerning means adding or taking space from between two characters. This improves the appearance of type character combinations. When multiple characters or words are spaced, the proper name for it is tracking. This material is covered in greater detail in Chapter 12.

KERNING COMMANDS

To change the space between two characters, anchor the cursor between those two. With the cursor flashing, select Style ➤ Kern. A numerical dialog box appears allowing you to input a number from −500 to 500. The measurement unit for this manual kerning is 0.000005 em-space. The default is zero. A negative value decreases the distance between two characters, while a positive number increases the distance.

NOTE

Normally, an emspace is a square the size of the point size. This is a relative term, meaning that if the point size is 10 points, its EM em-space would be a non-printing space 10 points wide by 10 points tall. If the point size were 12, the em-space would be 12 by 12, and so on. (The em-space comes from hot lead type, where it was used as a nonprinting, spacing unit. Typesetters used it in combination with other nonprinting spacing units for alignment and indentation purposes.) QuarkXPress adds a new dimension to the em-space. It defines the em-space as the width of two zeros in the current font. This sounds rather computer programmer-like, doesn't it?

KERNING WITH THE KEYBOARD

To use the keyboard for kerning purposes, anchor the cursor between the two characters of choice. To increase space in increments of 0.05-ems, press ⌘-Shift-}. To increase letterspacing in increments of 0.005-ems, press ⌘-Option-Shift- }. To reduce space between characters, key ⌘-Shift-{ for increments of 0.05-ems or ⌘-Option-Shift-} for increments of 0.005-ems.

MAKING SPACE ADJUSTMENTS IN THE MEASUREMENT PALETTE

To adjust spacing with the T palette, press either of the kerning arrows in the palette (see Figure 8.6). This will increase or decrease space between two characters in increments of 0.05-ems. To adjust in increments of 0.005-ems, hold down the Option key while clicking on the kerning arrows.

FIGURE 8.6
You can kern directly from the Measurement palette.

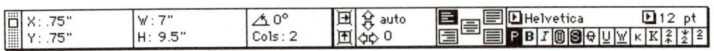

The Measurement palette method of kerning is wonderful because you can see the text as changes occur. Also, it is quicker to make repetitive changes than bringing down a dialog box from the menu.

TRACKING

Tracking takes advantage of all the techniques outlined for kerning. The primary difference between kerning and tracking is that in tracking you must highlight the group of characters to change. In kerning, simply positioning the cursor between two characters is sufficient to identify the location.

NOTE
Kerning and tracking occupy the same slot in the Style menu, but when you highlight a group of characters or lines (as opposed to simply placing the cursor), the command changes from Kern to Track.

Highlight a group of characters using the Content tool and then select Style ➤ Track. If no groups of characters are highlighted, the Kern command shows (see Figure 8.7).

FIGURE 8.7

*The Style menu com-
mand changes from
Kern to Track depend-
ing on your needs.*

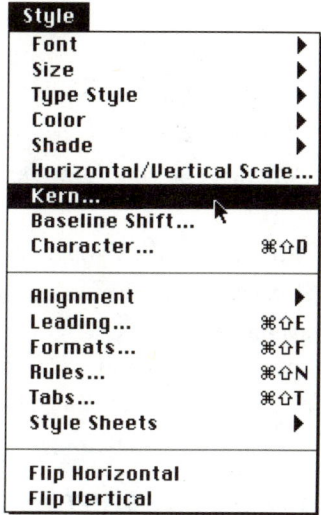

OTHER COMMANDS

Kerning and Tracking commands go far beyond manual adjustments mentioned
here. You have automatic adjustments, kerned pairs, etc. See Chapter 12 for more
details on customizing the kerning capability in QuarkXPress.

THE BASELINE SHIFT COMMAND

The bottoms of most type characters rest upon an imaginary line known as the
baseline. QuarkXPress has a feature that allows you to raise or lower the type characters from its original baseline (see Figure 8.8).

FIGURE 8.8

*An example of a base-
line shift*

The great Mountain Bikathon!

WARNING

Even when you use baseline shift on a line, the line still "remembers" its original baseline. This may cause confusion on your part if you must highlight the text again for another action. The text's new and old locations highlight together.

To implement a baseline shift, highlight the character or group of characters you want to move from the baseline. Then select Style ➤ Baseline Shift. This will bring up the Baseline Shift dialog box. Enter a number in the Baseline Shift field. A positive number represents the number of points you want the highlighted character(s) to rise above the baseline. A negative number moves the characters below the baseline. The range is −42 to 42 points.

EFFECTING A BASELINE SHIFT WITH THE KEYBOARD

TIP

Use the Baseline Shift command in combination with different point sizes and other character attribute commands.

From a production point of view, anything you can do from the keyboard without having to go to the menu is often faster. In the case of the Baseline Shift command, you can use a keyboard shortcut without using the menu commands. To use the keyboard shortcuts, highlight the characters of choice again, then press ⌘-Option-Shift-+ to move the text above the baseline in one-point increments. Press ⌘-Option-Shift-hyphen to move the text below the baseline in one-point increments.

THE CHARACTER COMMAND

NOTE

You will probably find yourself using the Character Attribute command more than any other style command simply because it is like one-stop shopping. You can change everything in that one box and change multiple attributes simultaneously.

The Style ➤ Character selection opens a dialog box that contains a combination of most of the previously listed options (see Figure 8.9). You can directly access all the preceding list of Style options from this one dialog box (keyboard shortcut: ⌘-Shift-D).

FIGURE 8.9

You can access most style commands from the Character Attributes dialog box.

Character Attributes

Font: ▶ Helvetica

Size: ▶ 12 pt

Color: Black

Shade: ▶ 100%

Scale: Horizontal 100%

Kern Amount: 0

Baseline Shift: 0

Style
- ☒ Plain
- ☐ Bold
- ☐ Italic
- ☐ Outline
- ☐ Shadow
- ☐ Strike Thru
- ☐ Underline
- ☐ Word u.l.
- ☐ Small Caps
- ☐ All Caps
- ☐ Superscript
- ☐ Subscript

OK   Cancel

MANIPULATING TYPE LINES THROUGH THE STYLE MENU

Often, in processing words with a desktop publishing application, you have to decide how to align paragraph lines. This alignment takes the form of horizontal, left to right, and, today, you can even align vertically throughout the column. QuarkXPress has the ability to align in both horizontal and vertical directions.

ALIGNING TEXT WITHIN A TEXT BOX

Alignment refers to how the text sits within the text box. There are four options in alignment: Left (ragged right), Right (ragged left), Centered, and Justified (see Figure 8.10).

The default for alignment is flush left, at least in the United States version of QuarkXPress. To enforce a different alignment, activate the text box and select an appropriate alignment. Without further identification, the alignment change will affect all paragraphs in this indicated text box. If you want only an isolated paragraph to change, position the cursor within that paragraph. With the paragraph selected, choose Style ➤ Alignment and your selection, or use the keyboard equivalent. You can also make the change from the Measurement palette by selecting the appropriate icon.

Again, from a production standpoint, you will find yourself using the keyboard equivalent or Measurement palette methods more often than the menu command. The keyboard shortcuts are listed next to the Alignment commands on the menu.

FIGURE 8.10

You have four horizontal alignment options for text.

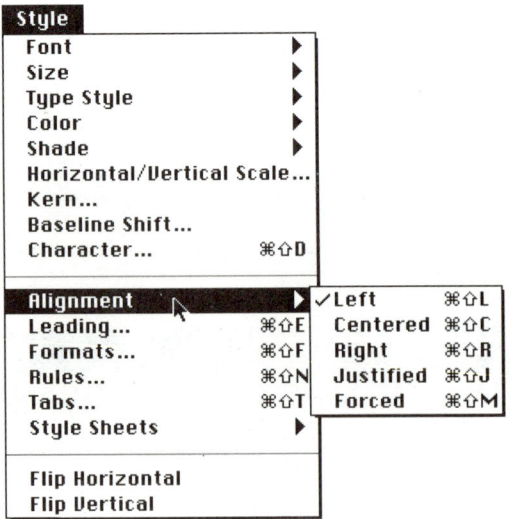

188

WHAT EXACTLY IS JUSTIFICATION?

Justification is a complex process whereby the computer decides how many characters will fit on a line. Of these words, perhaps the last word can hyphenate. Anyhow, a certain amount of extra (non-character space) remains. With justification, the extra space is distributed throughout the line, first between words, then between characters. If evenly distributed, the text appears flush left and flush right (justified). If you choose Left (ragged right), all extra space is added at the end of the line, moving type left. In Flush Right, all extra space is added at the beginning of the line, moving the type to the right. With centered text, the space is evenly distributed on both sides of the line. Often the Left, Right, and Centered commands have no hyphenated words. The Justified command, though, usually requires hyphenation to work best. That is why hyphenation and justification together are known as H & J. Chapter 14 discusses hyphenation and justification in more detail.

VERTICAL ALIGNMENT

QuarkXPress has an option that allows vertical alignment or justification of paragraphs. To use this, you select the text box to align (click on the box with the Content tool). Next choose Item ➤ Modify (⌘-M). The Text Box Specifications dialog box appears (see Figure 8.11).

FIGURE 8.11
You can specify the vertical alignment of paragraphs in the Text Box Specifications dialog box.

Text Box Specifications

Origin Across:	0.75"
Origin Down:	0.75"
Width:	7"
Height:	9.5"
Box Angle:	0°
Box Skew:	0°.
Columns:	2
Gutter:	0.167"
Text Inset:	1 pt

☐ Suppress Printout

First Baseline
Offset: 0"
Minimum: Ascent

Vertical Alignment
Type: Justified
Inter ¶ Max: 0"

Background
Color: White
Shade: ▶ 100%

OK   Cancel

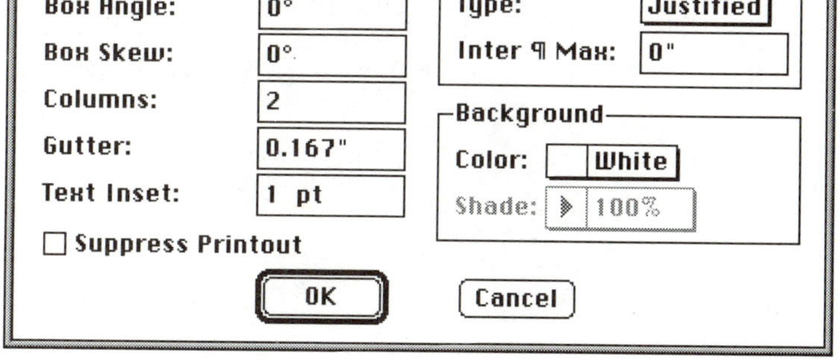

From the Vertical Alignment Type menu, select Top, Centered, Bottom, or Justified. If you select Justified, enter the maximum amount of space between paragraphs that you wish to allow in the Inter ¶ Max field. A Inter ¶ Max of zero distributes the space between lines and paragraphs evenly. The process is somewhat similar to that just described in Justification above. Only this time, a finite number of lines will fit within a specific text box height. The last fraction of a line distributes according to the setup.

SPELLING AND DICTIONARIES

MAC TRACKS· MAC TRACKS MAC TRACKS MAC TRACKS MAC

Any desktop publishing program worth purchasing today has a spell-checking dictionary of some type built in. What differs in QuarkXPress is the depth of its spell-check capabilities and capacity of dictionaries. Even though it was suggested to use an outside word processor, QuarkXPress does a handy job internally, especially when it comes to making sure you spell right!

SPELLING AND DICTIONARIES

QuarkXPress allows you to check the spelling of a single word, of an active story, of the entire document, or of the text on master pages. A copy of the file Xpress Dictionary must be located either in the QuarkXPress folder or the System Folder.

CHECKING THE SPELLING OF A SINGLE WORD

To check the spelling of a single word, highlight the word or place the text insertion bar (the Content tool's I-beam cursor) within or immediately to the right or left of that word. Select Utilities ➤ Check Spelling ➤ Word (see Figure 9.1). If the

FIGURE 9.1

The Check Spelling menu options

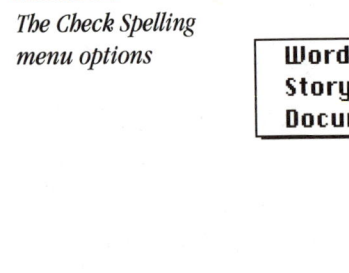
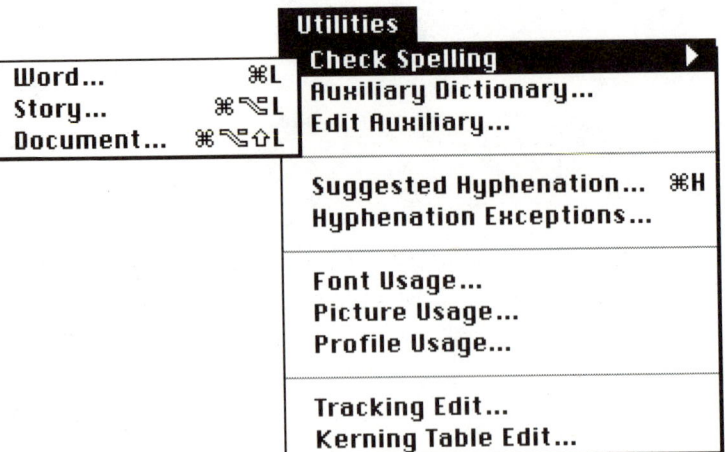

Word...	⌘L
Story...	⌘⌥L
Document...	⌘⌥⇧L

Utilities
Check Spelling ▶
Auxiliary Dictionary...
Edit Auxiliary...

Suggested Hyphenation... ⌘H
Hyphenation Exceptions...

Font Usage...
Picture Usage...
Profile Usage...

Tracking Edit...
Kerning Table Edit...

word is not in the Xpress Dictionary or other open auxiliary dictionaries, the Check Word dialog box appears (see Figure 9.2). Here, you have the option of selecting a replacement word or of canceling the operation and returning to the document. To replace a word, click on the desired replacement word and click on the Replace button. Another technique is to double-click on the replacement word. Once you select the replacement, it takes the place of the misspelled word in your document and the dialog box closes. The spell-checking sequence is complete.

FIGURE 9.2

*The Check Word
dialog box*

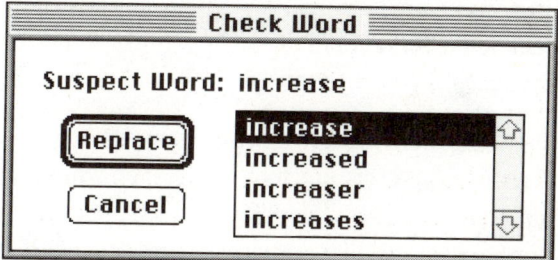

CHECKING A STORY

To check the spelling in a story, activate the text box (click on it with the Content tool). Then select Utilities ➤ Check Spelling ➤ Story. First a Word Count dialog appears (see Figure 9.3). The Word Count dialog box displays three fields of information, Total, Unique, and Suspect.

 **NOTE**

QuarkXPress understands a story to be all text within a single text box or in a chain of linked text boxes.

Total is the total number of words checked. Unique represents the number of unique words identified, as opposed to repetitions of words. Suspect represents the number of words not in the Xpress Dictionary or in any open auxiliary dictionary.

FIGURE 9.3
*The Word Count dia-
log box*

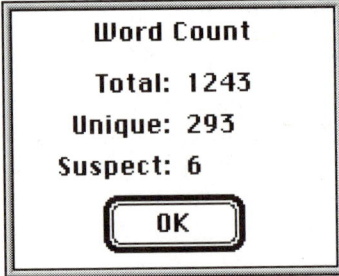

```
Word Count

Total: 1243

Unique: 293

Suspect: 6

   OK
```

If no words are identified as possibly misspelled, it displays 0 in the Suspect Word field of the Word Count dialog box. Press Return or click on OK to return to the document.

If anything other than 0 appears, when you click OK the Check Story dialog box displays. This acts very much like the Check Word dialog box in the way you select a replacement words. The difference is that in the story there may be more than one word to check. If that is the case, after each word, the checker goes to the next word in question. You then must decide its replacement, and so on. Eventually, after all suspect words of the story are replaced or skipped, the process ends and you are taken back to the text.

The Check Story dialog box also includes a Replace With field. This enables you to key in a new word for replacement. It also includes buttons of Lookup, Skip, and Keep.

NOTE

You can add to Auxiliary Dictionaries; you may not, however, alter the Xpress Dictionary. There are 120,000 words contained in the Xpress Dictionary.

Lookup displays similarly spelled dictionary words in the scroll lists. Skip allows you to overlook the word in question. After all, it may be correct even if it is not in the Xpress Dictionary. You can add the word to an auxiliary dictionary by clicking on the Keep button. Keep allows you to record a word identified as suspect into a currently opened auxiliary dictionary.

CHECKING A DOCUMENT

Another option for spelling is that of Utilities ➤ Check Spelling ➤ Document. Use this the same way you would use Check Spelling ➤ Story. The difference is that checking the spelling of the document covers all stories in the document.

WORKING WITH AUXILIARY DICTIONARIES IN QUARKXPRESS

You may be working in an environment with specialized words not contained within the 120,000 in the Xpress Dictionary. This may call for an auxiliary dictionary to be created. Auxiliary dictionaries augment the Xpress Dictionary and make checking your words faster, because the checker flags fewer suspect words.

Open an auxiliary dictionary by choosing Utilities ➤ Auxiliary Dictionary. Auxiliary dictionaries have their own names and you can open and close an auxiliary dictionary at any time. You can create as many dictionaries as you want, but only one can remain open at a time. Any number of documents can use the same auxiliary dictionary.

CREATING A NEW AUXILIARY DICTIONARY

To create a new auxiliary dictionary, select Utilities ➤ Auxiliary Dictionary. The Auxiliary Dictionary dialog box displays. Click the New button. Then enter a name for the new dictionary in the New Auxiliary Dictionary field. If you create the new dictionary without a document open, it becomes the New Default Auxiliary Dictionary. Use the dialog box controls to select the location where you wish to save the dictionary.

EDITING AN EXISTING AUXILIARY DICTIONARY

To make changes to an open existing auxiliary dictionaries, you should select Utilities ➤ Edit Auxiliary. The Edit Auxiliary Dictionary dialog box appears, giving you the opportunity to Add, Delete, Save, and Cancel.

 **WARNING**

The Auxiliary Dictionary augments the Xpress Dictionary. You cannot use an auxiliary dictionary if the Xpress Dictionary is not in the QuarkXPress folder or System Folder.

CREATING AND USING STYLE SHEETS

FEATURING

- Creating new style Sheets
- Defining styles in a style sheet
- Applying style sheets

 **TRACKS   MAC TRACKS   MAC TRACKS   MAC TRACKS   MAC**

To alter such attributes as indents, leading, spacing, alignment, and drop caps in a style sheet 206

click on the Formats button in the Edit Style Sheet dialog box. A Paragraph Formats dialog box appears. Edit according to your needs.

To manipulate text to match the QuarkXPress grid 208

click on Lock to Baseline Grid in the Paragraph Formats dialog box and the text "snaps to" the baseline grid. Leave it unchecked, and items will not snap to the baseline grid.

To place a tab stop in position in the style sheet tabs option 213

select one of the styles of alignment (i.e., Left, Center, Right, Decimal, Comma, or Align On) from the tab icons, then click on the tab ruler where you want the tab to position. For more accurate positioning you may key in the numerical ruler value in the field of the tab (style sheet) dialog box.

A very handy feature of the QuarkXPress word processor is the style sheet. Style sheets enable you to predetermine how a particular section of type will look. A style sheet is essentially a group of text formatting commands all stored together in one place for the sake of convenience. You can use style sheets to change unformatted text into heads, subheads, captions, body copy, or whatever. You can access style sheets through a menu selection or more conveniently, by using keyboard shortcuts.

There are two big advantages of style sheets:

▶ You will get a consistent look to your documents.

▶ It is easier to change attributes for a particular design element, because you can just change the style sheet applied to the element. This saves you from having to change each occurrence of the element individually.

ESTABLISHING STYLE SHEETS FOR YOUR DOCUMENT

New documents have one default style sheet (that applied to the general text). This may not suit your needs, however, so you should create your own. Using style sheets is essentially a two-part process:

1. You establish each style sheet's attributes.

2. You apply a style sheet while editing a document. Applying a style sheet means associating text with it.

NOTE

Style Sheets consist of up to four main settings groups: character, format, rules, and tabs. These four are identical to the Character, Formats, Rules, and Tabs control available in the Style menu. Therefore, description of these features will appear in detail only once here in this chapter.

NOTE

What may be considered a global style sheet is one not attached to a particular document. Instead, this style sheet may be made generally available in QuarkXPress, similar to the way you change preferences for the entire application. To create a global style sheet, use the same procedures as described for the document style sheet. However, create the style sheet and save it while there are no documents open. That is, either close all document windows and create a style sheet with no "working" area, or, immediately after launching QuarkXPress, before opening a document, create and save your style sheet.

CREATING A NEW STYLE SHEET

To create a new style sheet, select Edit ➤ Style Sheets (see Figure 10.1). A dialog box appears giving you the option of editing the default style sheet (called Normal), of creating a new style sheet, or of importing one from another document. The default style sheet is not for general use, but rather to guide you in creating your own as necessary.

NOTE

Remember, only style sheets created while a document is open will apply to that document. Style Sheets created without an open document will become Global Style Sheets. You can also append style sheets from other documents to one in which you want them to appear.

The dialog box enables you to edit any existing style sheet. A new document has only one style sheet (Normal) and applies those attributes to the text. The preset Normal style sheet values are Helvetica 12-point plain black text, auto leading with no tracking, no horizontal scaling, and 100% shading. When you modify this style sheet, all text that it applies to changes. If you modify the Normal style sheet with no documents open, the changes will apply to new documents only.

FIGURE 10.1
Select Edit ➤ Style Sheets to get the Style Sheets dialog box. It allows you to edit an existing style sheet or create a new one.

Edit	
Can't Undo	⌘Z
Cut	⌘H
Copy	⌘C
Paste	⌘V
Clear	
Select All	⌘A
Subscribe To...	
Subscriber Options...	
Show Clipboard	
Find/Change	⌘F
Preferences	▶
Style Sheets...	
Colors...	
H&Js...	⌘⌥H

You can edit existing style sheets to suit your needs or create new ones by clicking on the New button. The New option displays the Edit Style Sheet dialog box. This dialog box includes fields for you to input the name of the style sheet and its keyboard equivalent. You must give each style sheet a unique name; of course, it is preferable to use a name that reflects the function of the style sheet (e.g., Body Copy, Heads, Subheads, etc.). A keyboard equivalent is not necessary but will save you time in production. To add a keyboard equivalent, type in the key or key combination you want to use for this style sheet.

The Based on pop-up menu gives you the opportunity to base a new style sheet on an existing style sheet in the inventory. If you don't want to use another style sheet as a reference, choose No Style.

TIP

Due to the amount of detail in a style sheet, you may want to save blank documents with style sheets recorded. Then, if you need those style sheets, use the document as a template to develop your new material.

Information near the bottom of this box lists the default attributes of a style sheet. It includes Character Attributes, Paragraph Formats, Paragraph Rules, and Paragraph Tabs, if any. You may include any or all of this information in a style sheet. Select and modify this information through the four buttons on the dialog box, Character, Formats, Rules, and Tabs.

THE CHARACTER OPTION IN STYLE SHEETS

Click on the Character button in the Edit Style Sheet dialog box and a typical Character Attributes dialog box appears. This is the same type of Character Attributes dialog box you can get from selecting Style ➤ Character when editing text.

All the Style command options are available in the Character Attributes dialog box. The advantage is that, as a style sheet, the attributes can be applied as a group to a specific kind of text, along with the characteristics of format, rules and, tabs. See Chapter 8 for more details on type-style attributes and the Character Attributes dialog box.

THE PARAGRAPH FORMAT DIALOG BOX

The Formats option brings up the Paragraph Formats dialog box, which should also be familiar to you (see Figure 10.2). The Paragraph Formats dialog box is the same one that appears when you choose Style ➤ Formats.

TIP

When keying a value into a numerical (measurement) field, use nearly any form of measurement you are comfortable with, QuarkXPress will translate. Of course you must keep within the given measurement systems available in QuarkXPress. It is best to keep away from such measurements as "hands" or "stones" though!

The Paragraph Formats dialog box contains information for such attributes as indents, leading, spacing, alignment, and drop caps, among others.

THE LEFT AND RIGHT INDENT FIELDS

The Left and Right Indent fields give you the option of indenting paragraphs on the left or right side. Left Indent indicates how far the entire paragraph will indent from the left side (toward the right). The Right Indent indicates how far the entire paragraph will indent on the right (toward the left).

FIGURE 10.2

The Paragraph Formats dialog box enables you to specify how each paragraph will look, including all indentation and alignment options.

Paragraph Formats	
Left Indent: `0"`	Leading: `auto`
First Line: `0"`	Space Before: `0"`
Right Indent: `0"`	Space After: `0"`
☐ Lock to Baseline Grid	☐ Keep with Next ¶
☐ Drop Caps	☐ Keep Lines Together
Alignment: `Left`	
H&J: `Standard`	(OK) (Cancel)

TIP

You may want to include a tab key (for indentation) at the beginning of the paragraph, just out of habit. Be careful, as this may be indented in addition to the first line indent you set up in this Formats section. You don't want twice the amount of indent.

FIRST LINE INDENT

The First Line Indent field is to establish the traditional indentation that goes with indenting the first line of each paragraph. You may use this concurrent with the Drop Caps option, also in this dialog box. See more information on Drop Caps later in this chapter.

LEADING

The term leading stems from the use of hot lead typesetting, wherein typesetters would place a strip of lead between lines of type. This would space them out, providing non-printing white space between lines of type in the paragraph. The distance between each line was leading. The distance from the baseline of one line to the baseline of another was line space, but as computer programs got into the typesetting business, somehow the terms got confused. Thus, today, the distance from baseline to baseline is called leading.

The Leading field controls leading for that paragraph. It has the same leading capability as the Leading menu command (Style ➤ Leading). Leading is usually measured in points (see Figure 10.3).

The value placed in this field must be within the range of 0 to 1080 points. Auto leading is the default. Auto leading is usually default valued at 20 percent above the point size. This is changeable through the Typographic Preferences dialog box (Edit ➤ Preferences ➤ Typographic).

FIGURE 10.3

The distance, baseline to baseline, from one line of text to another is the leading.

Leading is known as the
distance from one baseline
to the next baseline.

Baseline
Baseline

SPACE BEFORE AND SPACE AFTER THE PARAGRAPH

There are times in which you want to have some white space before or after the paragraph for design reasons. This is especially true if you choose not to distinguish your paragraphs with a first line indentation. Remember, if you place space before and after, it will double between paragraphs, and you may have more space than desired.

TIP

QuarkXPress is savvy enough to know that if you specify Space Before and the paragraph you apply the style to is at the top of the page, it will not put the space before (which would be aesthetically displeasing). Very nice!

LOCK TO BASELINE GRID

As mentioned earlier in the book, QuarkXPress places an invisible gridwork under your text. You can display or hide the grid through the View ➤ Show/Hide Baseline Grid command. You can customize the grid by choosing Edit ➤ Preferences ➤ Typographic.

WARNING

If you check Lock to Baseline Grid, it will override leading for all the text. For example, if your leading is 14, but the baseline grid leading is 12, the Lock to Baseline Grid option will split the lines to rest on every other (12 point) baseline.

An underlying gridwork is helpful from a layout point of view in that you can manipulate text to match the grid across the design. Click on this option and the text "snaps to" the baseline grid. Leave it unchecked, and items will not snap to the baseline grid.

DROP CAPS

The Drop Caps option, once checked, presents two more input fields (see Figure 10.4). They are the Character Count and Line Count. The Character Count determines the number of characters at the beginning of the paragraph that you want to enlarge and drop. The Line Count determines the height of the dropped character(s); that is, you must specify how many lines the enlarged character will consume (see Figure 10.5).

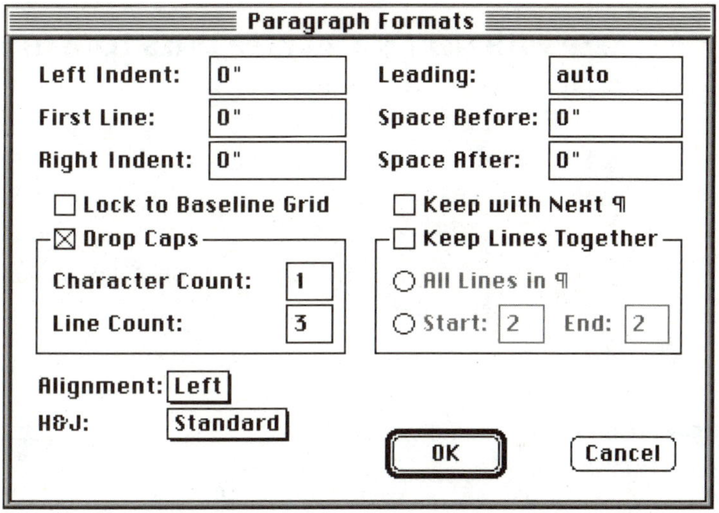

FIGURE 10.4

The Drop Cap option, if checked, provides two more fields of information for you to interact with: Character Count and Line Count.

Paragraph Formats

Left Indent:	0"	Leading:	auto
First Line:	0"	Space Before:	0"
Right Indent:	0"	Space After:	0"

☐ Lock to Baseline Grid ☐ Keep with Next ¶

☒ Drop Caps ☐ Keep Lines Together

Character Count: 1 ○ All Lines in ¶

Line Count: 3 ○ Start: 2 End: 2

Alignment: Left

H&J: Standard

[OK] [Cancel]

FIGURE 10.5

This example shows a Drop Cap of with a total drop of three lines.

If you have removed QuarkXPress version 3.0 from your computer, you cannot open documents that were created in version 3.0 by double-clicking on them in the Finder. If you try, you will receive the standard system alert stating that the application cannot be found. You must first launch version 3.2 and then open these documents with the Open command (File menu).

When you open and modify a version 3.0 document in version 3.2, the modification date and creator may not be updated properly when the folder or disk window displaying the document is open in the Finder.

*The Drop Caps option, if active, works on all paragraphs with that
style applied. You probably would not want this to occur, though.
It may be best to establish a separate style sheet with the drop cap
option for the initial paragraph. All other paragraphs can have a
similar style sheet but without the Dropped Cap. This is an
excellent application for the Based on option in the Edit Style
Sheet dialog box.*

KEEP WITH NEXT ¶ AND KEEP LINES TOGETHER

To prevent paragraphs from becoming separated at the bottom of a column or a
page, check the Keep with Next ¶ option. (A classic example is keeping a figure
and its caption together on the same page.) To keep all lines of a selected paragraph in the same column or on the same page, check the Keep Lines Together option. Once checked, another small dialog box appears. This gives the alternative of
having the option apply to All Lines in ¶ or of designating Start and End line numbers (see Figure 10.6).

FIGURE 10.6

*The Keep Lines Together
option, if checked, al-
low you to keep all lines
together in the para-
graph or only specific
lines.*

Paragraph Formats

Left Indent: `0"`   Leading: `auto`

First Line: `0"`   Space Before: `0"`

Right Indent: `0"`   Space After: `0"`

☐ Lock to Baseline Grid   ☒ Keep with Next ¶

☒ Drop Caps   ☒ Keep Lines Together

Character Count: `1`   ◉ All Lines in ¶

Line Count: `3`   ○ Start: `2`   End: `2`

Alignment: `Left`

H&J: `Standard`

[OK]   [Cancel]

ALIGNMENT

Alignment is similar to the alignment option you had in the Style menu (Style ➤ Alignment). Its purpose is to help you align the lines of the style sheet in one of four fashions: Left, Right, Centered, or Justified. Click on the drop-down menu and drag to select the alignment option of your choice. Once selected with your cursor, release the mouse button. Your choice will alter all lines with this style sheet applied.

Be sure to consider the settings in the H & J option when determining your alignment. Regardless of your choice, the H & J setting will influence your type.

H & J OPTIONS

Click and hold on the drop-down menu for H & J to choose from an assortment of H & J settings. These settings are established by choosing Edit ➤ H & Js. The default option is Standard, and no other options will be available if you do not create custom H & J settings.

NOTE

H & J is the heartbeat of good typograph; without it, all characters would take on a monospaced look, like typewriters give. This is also the most difficult part of the program to get high-quality results. QuarkXPress is among the best on the market for providing quality H & J for desktop computers. It has nearly caught up to high-level electronic publishing programs in use for minicomputers and dedicated systems.

THE PARAGRAPH RULES DIALOG BOX

Check the Rules button in the Edit Style Sheets dialog box to reach the Paragraph Rules dialog box. You can place rules above or below the text (of your style sheet). If you click on either option, other settings appear, allowing you to set the size, style, and location of the rule. In essence, this is the same dialog box you get when you choose Style ➤ Rules. This rule option applies only to the style sheet that you are editing. You may set either or both rules options (see Figure 10.7).

FIGURE 10.7

*If you check both Rule
Above and Rule Below,
you get specifications
for lines in both areas.*

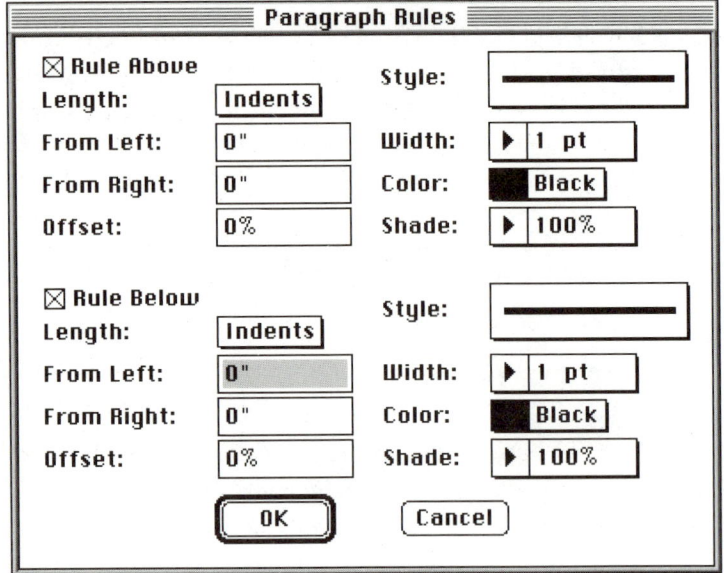

The Length drop-down menu gives you the option of making the rule as long as the
Indents or Text. To choose one of these two options, click and hold on the Length
drop-down menu, then select.

From Left, From Right, and Offset allow you establish line coordinates relative to
paragraph text. Select the Style, Width, and Shade options from an inventory or key
in your own. The Color option allows you to choose from a drop down menu of
the existing color palette for that document. Add other colors through the Edit ➤
Colors option.

NOTE

*At QUI 1992, several members expressed discontent with the fact
you could resize text as EPS, but the linework remained
unchanged. Apparently, the Rule Above and Rule Below options
edit differently than type.*

THE PARAGRAPH TABS DIALOG BOX

Tabs enable you to place text exactly within a line and keep the position constant from one line to the next. You would use tabs when you wanted to set up your text in a column format or when you wanted to isolate a word or phrase somewhere on the line. QuarkXPress has six options for tabs: Left, Center, Right, Decimal, Comma, and Align On.

NOTE

Remember, Tabulation can be used in style sheets as well as adjusted outside style sheets (Style ➤ Tabs). To differentiate between the two, the tab controls outside of style sheets are referred to as "standard" tabulation. Tabs set in style sheets will apply only to that text the style sheet is applied to. They are saved and may be reused as needed throughout your document. Standard tabs are available only for a range of highlighted text. Changes are isolated in standard tabulation. If similar changes are needed later in the document, the tab operation must be repeated for the new text.

The last button of the Edit Style Sheets dialog box is Tabs. Tabs in style sheets work the same as any tabs in QuarkXPress. Click the Tabs button to get the Paragraph Tabs dialog box (see Figure 10.8).

In this setup box there is a special ruler that corresponds to the text box you are setting tabs within. The ruler starts at the beginning of the text box with the 0 mark. This makes it slightly different from the primary ruler that appears over your document. The primary ruler has a 0 point at the top left edge of the document page. You must specify the type of tab stop before placing a new tab on the ruler.

There are two options available to set up each tab stop. You can visually set up each tab stop by clicking on the ruler or you can be more precise and use the numerical input for exact tab stop placement. Even when you have positioned a tab stop on the ruler, you can relocate it.

FIGURE 10.8

*The tab options include
aligning text Left, Center,
Right, on the Decimal, on
the Comma, or on a des-
ignated character
(Align On).*

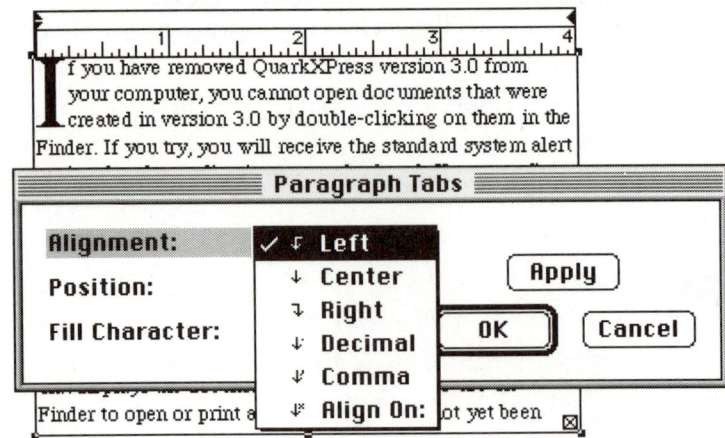

To place a tab stop in position, select one of the styles of alignment (i.e., Left, Center, Right, Decimal, Comma, or Align On). The Left alignment option means that
your text, when sent to this tab stop on the line, will reside in a flush left, ragged
right location at that point. Center will center the text around the tab mark. The
Right option means that your text will stop flush right at that location on the line.
Align on Decimal or Comma is a bit tricky until you experiment. With these options, your text will be centered around either decimals or commas; in other
words, some of the text will come before the decimal or comma, and some after it.
This is particularly good for column material such as in annual reports, where you
would probably want numbers to align on the decimal or comma. The final option
is Align On. Click on this option and a new field appears, allowing you to keystroke in one character. This enables you to use any single printing character as a
tab stop.

After you choose the alignment option, click on the tab ruler to place the tab. You
can achieve greater accuracy by keying a numerical coordinate into the Position
field. After all tab stops are identified, click on OK.

Any tab stop can have a Fill Character. The fill character will repeat as many times as necessary to fill up any white space on the line (these are often called leaders). The Fill Character field allows you to keystroke in the single character you want to use as the fill character.

TAB INDENTATION

The Tabulation setup dialog box for style sheets is very similar to the standard Tab dialog you reach from the Style menu (Style ➤ Tabs). The primary difference is in indentation controls. In style sheets, indentation is manipulated through the use of the (Paragraph) Formats option.

NOTE

Standard tab controls available through Style ➤ Tabs have a slightly different look than tabs in style sheets.

Another difference is that the Style Sheets Tabulation dialog box does not have an Apply button. This button, in standard tabulation, enables you to see tab variations prior to final application. You can see the text move to the tabulation you have established. Standard tabs apply to selected text (that you have on the screen). Highlight a range of text, then set your tabulations. You can use Apply and see changes in your text, make adjustments, then execute. Apply is available only on the Tab commands outside style sheets (Style ➤ Tabs). In style sheets tabs, you establish criteria before inputting text.

You can also set up the tab ruler to modify indents on the paragraph. On the left side of the ruler there are a pair of triangles. The top triangle represents first line indent; the bottom triangle controls left side indent. The right side of the tabulation ruler has another triangle. It moves right side indent for the text. Any modifications made with these indentation triangles in the tabulation ruler reflect numerically in the indentation fields for Paragraph Formats. See Figure 10.9 for an indication of the indentation triangles.

FIGURE 10.9
*Set the indentation tri-
angles in the tabulation
ruler (changes are re-
flected in the Paragraph
Formats indentation
fields).*

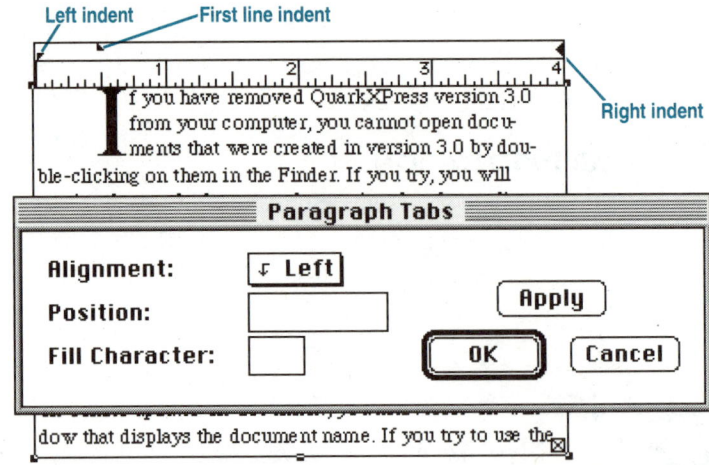

Another QuarkXPress 3.1 feature in standard tabulation is the Right Indent Tab.
Prior to version 3.1, it was difficult to establish a flush right tab equal to the right
hand margin of the paragraph. Now you can! To apply the Right Indent Tab, create
a right indent by pressing Option-Tab. This tab stop takes the characteristics of the
right-most tab on the line. If that tab is flush right, the Option-Tab will make text
appear flush right at the right margin. If you have a fill character on the far right,
tab Option-Tab will use that fill character.

APPLYING STYLE SHEETS

After you edit information for each style sheet, press Save to record your changes
and exit the Edit Style Sheet dialog box. Now, in working on a document, you may
at any time apply a style sheet. To do this, highlight a range of text to change, then
select the style sheet (or key in its keyboard equivalent). You may select the style
sheet first, and then key in or import the text. This new copy will reflect specifications of that style sheet. You may also show and select from options in the Style
Sheet palette—choose View ➤ Show Style Sheets—(see Figure 10.10).

FIGURE 10.10

*Use the Style Sheets pal-
ette to select a
particular style sheet
from the inventory.*

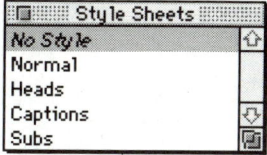

NOTE

*To select a recorded style sheet, you have three options. These
include selecting the appropriate style sheet from the submenu in
Style ➤ Style Sheets, using a keyboard equivalent that you
programmed when making the style sheet, or picking the
appropriate choice from the floating Style Sheets palette (View ➤
Show Style Sheets).*

TYPOGRAPHY

IV

SIZE, FONT, AND LEADING

11

To change global settings for any and all type attributes   224

you must do so when there are no documents open. Open documents make the changes apply to that document only.

To select from a wide variety of measurement systems   225

select the Horizontal and Vertical Measure options in the General Preferences dialog box (Edit ➤ Preferences ➤ General).

To work in the measurement system of your choice   226

ignore the selected system for your input values. Use the values in a measurement system you want; QuarkXPress will convert it.

To use either Typesetting or Word Processing modes of leading   227

select from the Typographic Preferences dialog box (Edit ➤ Preferences ➤ Typographic). The default option is Typesetting. It measures leading from the baseline.

To Set The Automatic Leading Value In A Percentage Value Relative To The Type Size   227

change the Auto Leading percentage. The default is at 20% and the total vertical line space will be 120% of the type size on that line.

The amount of space between lines of type, known as leading, is expressed in points or fractions of a point. There is no predefined rule about line space for good typography. Too much or too little leading in a paragraph is undesirable. Certain typefaces may need more or less leading due to their design. In fact, the only constant with leading is that it's measured in points, part of the printer's measurement system.

NOTE

Initial and global settings for text attributes such as size, font, etc., are established in the default style sheet called Normal. You can change this or add your own global style sheets. Global style sheets, those that apply to any document, must be created before you open a document.

THE PRINTER'S MEASUREMENT SYSTEM

In the United States, the standard for type measurement is the pica and the point. There are approximately 72 points in one inch. That would make each point approximately 0.0139 inches high. There are twelve points in a pica. Six picas equal one inch.

NOTE

The reason you find approximate numbers for the exact size of a point is that no one has ever standardized on the exact size of a point. Indeed, different typesetting equipment manufacturers use different standards as to point size. However, the measurement is small enough that the rule of thumb is that there are 72 points to the inch.

SELECTING MEASUREMENT SYSTEMS IN QUARKXPRESS

In the General Preferences dialog box (Edit ➤ Preferences ➤ General), you can choose from a variety of measurement systems, including points, picas, inches, metric, and ciceros. In this way, you can use a system required by a specific project or simply the one you feel most comfortable with. A beautiful feature of QuarkXPress is that you can enter a value in any measurement system you want by including the abbreviation for that system (e.g., " for inches, mm for millimeters, etc.). QuarkXPress will automatically convert your entered value to the measurement system of the document.

Another measurement system available is the cicero. The cicero is a unit of measurement more prevalent in the European Didot system. A cicero is slightly larger than a pica (1 cicero equals .178 inches). However, the world has not standardized the size of a cicero, either, and you can customize the cicero in the General Preferences dialog box (⌘-Y) along with the point.

LEADING IN A QUARKXPRESS DOCUMENT

Traditionally, leading is defined as the nonprinting white space between lines of text. This came from the hot lead typesetting era when a typesetter would place strips of lead or copper between lines of type to space them out. No extra strips of lead would make the paragraph set solid. The amount of space that each line took up, including the text and leading, was known as line space.

The computer generation in the cold type era redefined the term. Today, leading means the measurement from the baseline of one text line to the baseline of the next (see Figure 11.1).

FIGURE 11.1

Leading is the distance from the baseline of one text line to the baseline of the next.

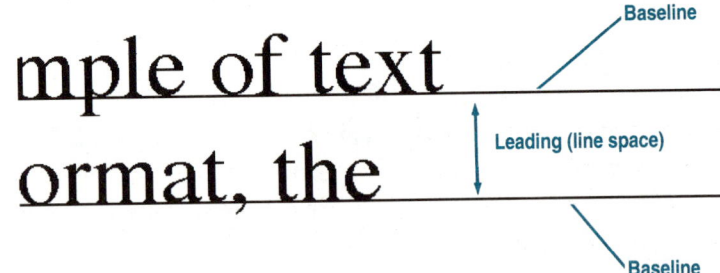

NOTE

You can choose to use either Typesetting or Word Processing modes of leading from the Typographic Preferences dialog box (Edit ➤ Preferences ➤ Typographic). The default mode is Typesetting. It measures leading from the baseline. The Word Processing option uses an older technique of measurement from the text ascent line, that is, measurement to the top cap or ascender of the next line. It is available only to keep QuarkXPress compatible with the few word processors that still use that system.

Although the standard is to use points for leading measurement, QuarkXPress will allow you to enter any value system. So if you need to specify leading in thousands of an inch, QuarkXPress is happy to oblige. Additionally, QuarkXPress will translate all sorts of measurements into points. This is true for all measurement systems available in QuarkXPress.

THE LEADING RANGE IN A QUARKXPRESS PARAGRAPH

It should come as no surprise that QuarkXPress has a superior leading capability. The program allows you to enter leading values in increments as small as one-thousandth of a point! (Can you even imagine a job that would require this leading accuracy?) You make these adjustments by choosing Style ➤ Leading (⌘-Shift-E).

NOTE

If you try to type in a number smaller than $\frac{1}{10000}$ of an inch, the leading will default to auto.

The minimum amount of leading allowed in the program is −1080 points in a minus leading situation; the maximum is 1080 in positive leading. Changing the value to 0 causes the leading to revert to its default (auto leading).

LEADING OPTIONS IN A QUARKXPRESS DOCUMENT

The QuarkXPress application gives the user three different styles of leading to choose. The choices are percentage, automatic incremental relative, and absolute.

NOTE

QuarkXPress uses the term "absolute" leading to refer to a number you place as the leading value that cannot automatically be changed. For example, if you place a numerical value of 12 in leading, that leading will be 12 regardless if the point size is 10 point size, 20 point size or 400 point size.

AUTOMATIC LEADING

The default leading is auto percentage leading. You can key in text without setting any specific leading and not worry about the spacing values. You enter automatic percentage leading in the Typographic Preferences dialog box (Edit ➤ Preferences ➤ Typographic). This percentage is tied to the type size. Set the automatic leading percentage at 20% and the total line space will be 120% of the type size on that line. Set the value at 30% and the total line space will be 130% of the type size on that line, and so on. In automatic percentage leading mode, as you change your text size the leading changes along with it.

NOTE

A popular value for paragraph leading is 20% beyond the type size. That is why the default value is 20%.

PROBLEMS WITH AUTOMATIC PERCENTAGE LEADING

Automatic percentage leading is generally a well-liked feature, but can also have a negative side. When there is more than one type size or adjustment on a line, the automatic percentage leading feature favors the largest size (see Figure 11.2).

WARNING

Leading in QuarkXPress is set on a paragraph to paragraph basis. You cannot lead only one line of a paragraph separately from other lines. The feature to use for this kind of manipulation is the Baseline Shift option (Style ➤ Baseline Shift). This allows you to move a highlighted range of text above or below the baseline.

FIGURE 11.2

When you have multiple sizes on a text line problems can arise with automatic leading, because the largest text size is favored.

This is an example of text in paragraph format. As you change the size of type within the paragraph, automatic leading compensates giving less than desired results.

In addition, manipulated text lines, through baseline shift, play havoc with automatic percentage leading (see Figure 11.3). Most typesetters who work with QuarkXPress will not use the automatic leading option because of possible problems later in the document.

AUTOMATIC INCREMENTAL RELATIVE LEADING

The automatic incremental relative leading capability allows you to add a prescribed amount of leading to the type size (e.g., +4 pt.). Just enter the number with a plus sign in the Auto Leading field (Edit ➤ Preferences ➤ Typographic). If, for example, the type size is 10 with an automatic incremental relative leading of +3, the line space would be 13 points. Change the text to 12 point and the new line space becomes 15 point (12 points plus 3 points).

NOTE

Text with applied style sheet values overrides the automatic values. In leading, placing auto or automatic incremental relative leading values for a paragraph can be overridden by applying a style sheet with different leading values in its format.

As you change a value in the auto leading field of the Typographic Preferences dialog box, it applies to all auto-leaded lines in the document. Text baselines in auto-leaded paragraphs are automatically replaced with their new value, that is, auto lead plus your value.

FIGURE 11.3

This illustration represents the baseline shift with manipulated text in an automatic leading mode.

This is an example of text in paragraph format. As you change the baseline shift within the paragraph, automatic leading compensates giving less than desired results.

ABSOLUTE VALUES FOR LEADING

The most common form of leading is absolute leading, which allows the user to specify the exact leading value. Then the leading value remains constant, regardless of text manipulation and size changes in the chosen area of the document. For example, if the leading were 12 points, it would remain 12 points if the text were 10 points in size or 72 points in size. The leading value for a chosen range of text remains constant, unless changed again.

TECHNIQUES FOR CHANGING THE LEADING

There are a variety of ways to establish and use leading values in this application. Depending upon what you want to do, one or another will be most expedient. You can view and manipulate leading by choosing Style ➤ Leading (⌘-Shift-E). Click on a text box with the Content tool to activate the text Style menu, then select Style ➤ Leading. Type a value for the leading and click OK.

The auto-leading value is established in the default style sheet, called Normal. One of the attributes set in the Normal style sheet is that of leading. The default leading option in this style sheet is "auto." Because this style sheet is the default for any new text created in a new QuarkXPress text box, the leading for new text is auto.

You can change Normal style sheet's leading option to a value more to your liking or create a new style sheet. Either way, the second method of controlling leading values is using style sheets (see Figure 11.4).

NOTE

Leading affects the entire paragraph unless indicated otherwise. Click in a text paragraph with the Content tool and the entire paragraph will change through the leading options. To change multiple paragraphs, highlight a range of text. That highlighted range will change as you modify leading values.

The third method for manipulating leading values is to use the Measurement palette's leading arrows or type in a value. To change leading with this palette, click on the text area with the Content tool. This ensures you are in text edit mode. Then

FIGURE 11.4
One of the ways to change leading is through style sheets.

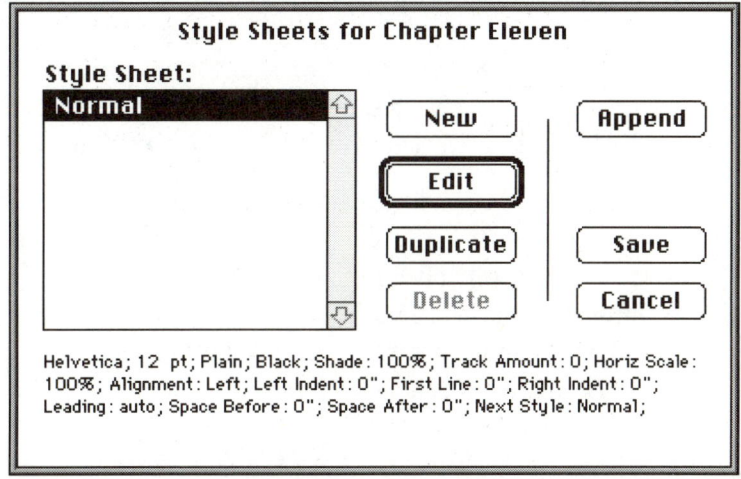

display the Measurement palette (View ➤ Show Measurements) if it's hidden. Change leading for a paragraph by clicking on that text to position the cursor, then click on the leading arrows to increase or decrease leading. You can also key in an absolute number, auto, or an automatic incremental value in the field next to the leading arrows (see Figure 11.5). Highlight a range of text to change if you want to change leading in several paragraphs.

FIGURE 11.5
You can use the leading arrows and field in the Measurement palette for manipulation.

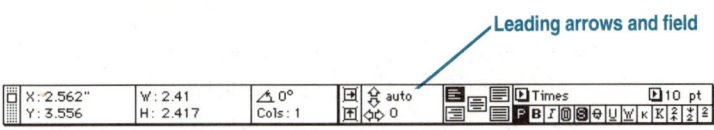

VERTICAL TEXT ALIGNMENT OPTIONS

QuarkXPress gives you four options for manipulating the vertical line spacing in the column of text material in your document. You can align text with the Top, Centered, Bottom, or Justified options. Vertical alignment can be adjusted from within the Text Box Specifications dialog box (Item ➤ Modify).

The rationale behind vertical text alignment is similar to that of justifying characters on a line. In justification, there is only so much space on a line and only so many words will fit of a selected style and size, remaining space is distributed throughout the line. Similarly, in vertical alignment, only so many lines and paragraphs will fit in the vertical space of the column or text box. Any additional space is distributed throughout the column vertically.

If you choose Top, the lines are placed with the top of the first line positioned as specified in the First Baseline field of the Text Box Specifications dialog box (see Figure 11.6).

FIGURE 11.6

The Text Box Specifications box allows you to specify Vertical Alignment options.

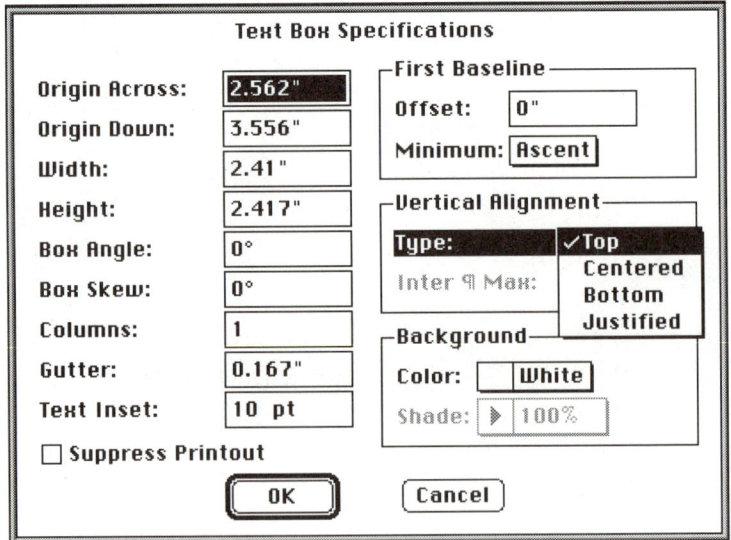

Center-aligned text will center between the top and bottom of the box. The text box fills from the center as you enter text. All remaining space fills in equally at the top and bottom of the text box or column.

NOTE

Vertical text alignment works within the boundaries of Text Inset established under Item ➤ Modify. The Text Inset value represents how much border or nonprinting space you want from the edge of the text box item to where your type will start. This represents a safety zone of sorts protecting your type from possibly being too close to the edge. This becomes apparent when you shade the text box or place a border frame around it. Values for the Text Inset are usually in points but may take formats from other measurement systems.

If you choose Bottom, the text starts at the bottom of the text box with remaining space located at the top. The last line in the text box will be the last line flush with the text inset position at the bottom of the text box.

NOTE

In center-alignment, when Lock to Baseline Grid applies, text lines position so they lock to the grid increments closest to where the baselines would be if the text were truly centered.

In text boxes specified as Justified, text lines start at the First Baseline position, the last line flush with the text inset position at the bottom of the box, and remaining lines justified in between. Justified vertical alignment allows you to specify a value of maximum distance between paragraphs in the Inter ¶ Max box (see Figure 11.7).

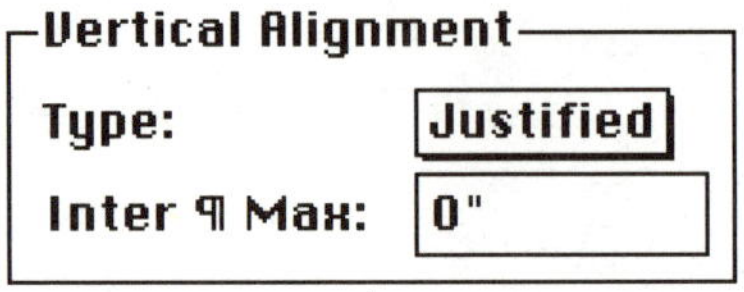

FIGURE 11.7

*QuarkXPress allows you
to enter a maximum
vertical distance.*

```
┌─Vertical Alignment──────────┐
│                             │
│  Type:      │Justified│     │
│                             │
│  Inter ¶ Max:  │0"      │   │
│                             │
└─────────────────────────────┘
```

Vertical alignment is a great timesaver for preparing your layout. Place the extra space between paragraphs as you want, electronically. Control paragraph spacing through justified vertical alignment by selecting the amount of space you allow between paragraphs. This feature works great! It takes the cut and paste out of column alignment.

KERNING AND TRACKING

12

To use keyboard equivalents for kerning and tracking   246

press ⌘-Option-Shift-} to add space in $\frac{1}{200}$ em space increments. Press ⌘-Option-Shift-{ to subtract space in the same increments. To track using keyboard equivalents, highlight the range of characters to alter the letterspacing.

To track negatively   246

press ⌘-Option-Shift-{; to track positively, press ⌘-Option-Shift-}. Both track in $\frac{1}{200}$ em space increments.

To adjust kerning or tracking in 0.005 ($\frac{1}{200}$) em space increments   247

use the keyboard commands ⌘-Shift-{ to decrease and ⌘-Shift-} to increase.

To enter a breaking flexible space   248

press Option-Shift-spacebar. Enter a nonbreaking flexible space by pressing ⌘-Option-Shift-spacebar.

You have the option in QuarkXPress of increasing and decreasing the amount of space between characters. In typesetting jargon, changing space between characters has been known as letterspacing. Negative spacing between two characters is kerning. Positive spacing between characters is letterspacing. Adjusting space between characters in a range, that is, several characters, lines or paragraphs, is tracking. The QuarkXPress application calls both positive and negative changes kerning, relative to the value you establish; it does not use the word letterspacing. This chapter explores the capability within QuarkXPress to use kerning and tracking capabilities.

. . . .

NOTE

The kerning and tracking values are based on the em space. The em space is a non-printing spacing unit, measured as a square whose sides are equal to one unit of the relative point size. For example, ten point type has an em space ten points tall and ten points wide; a twelve point type size has an em space of twelve by twelve, and so on.

KERNING AND TRACKING IN QUARKXPRESS

Every type character has a certain amount of non-printing space on either side of it. This is based on original designs in hot metal typesetting. In this way when two characters were next to each other, no other spacing units were necessary to prevent them from touching when printed.

Typography today is a carry-over from a trade that is centuries old. The tools have changed, but the need for good typography remains. Good typography in today's electronic publishing industry is not different from quality standards of fifty or one hundred years ago.

Electronic publishing tools today allow you to place type characters as close or as far apart as you want. Without any manipulation on your part, type characters still have a suitable letterspacing. This is because most type characters, as in hot type, have a preset amount of non-printing white space on either side. In hot type, that non-printing space is the shoulder (all parts of letters in hot-lead typesetting had descriptive names). Today, type emulates the look of lead type, but not all the names apply.

In some cases, though, the defined non-printing space of a type character is not aesthetically pleasing. Typically this is the situation when two specific type characters rest next to each other. Figure 12.1 shows twenty of the more common kerning problem pairs.

Kerning in QuarkXPress is similar to its traditional predecessor. You can adjust the space between a pair of kerned characters. Where QuarkXPress departs from tradition is that it calls both positively and negatively adjusted space kerning.

The space between the characters is called the kerning value. In QuarkXPress you can input this kerning value or take it from an information table. The kerning table is a file in QuarkXPress that has a combination of various character pairs with the kerning values installed for each one, specific to the style and size of the font.

Tracking in QuarkXPress is similar to kerning, but is applied to a range of characters. Kern or Track values can be adjusted through the Tracking Edit (Utilities ➤ Tracking Edit) and Kerning Table Edit (Utilities ➤ Kerning Table Edit) dialog boxes. Like kerning, tracking can be automatic or manual.

FIGURE 12.1
Twenty of the more popular kerning problem pairs.

Yo	We	To	Tr	Tr
Wo	Tu	Tw	Ya	Te
P.	Ty	Wa	yo	we
T.	Y.	TA	PA	WA

THE RANGE OF KERNING AND TRACKING VALUES IN QUARKXPRESS

In version 3.2 of QuarkXPress, you calculate the kerning value range in em spaces. An em space, to use the traditional phrase, is a unit of measurement relative to the point size. It is a square with sides equal to the point size; that is, in ten-point type, the em space is ten points wide by ten points tall.

The em space is another carry-over from hot lead type. Typically, to space type characters for indentation purposes, a specific non-printing "character" had to be available in the typesetter's job case. There were several sizes of these, to use depending on the need. These included the em, en, and thin space. The em is the square of the point size, approximately the same width as the capital M character (see Figure 12.2). The en space was half that wide; the thin space was about one-fifth as wide as an em. It took up about as much space as a period or comma.

As typesetting moved from metal to computer, manufacturers began to use fractions of an em as a measuring system. They broke the em down into further divisions called units. One manufacturer may claim to kern in 54 units to the em,

FIGURE 12.2

The em space is a non-printing spacing unit that is measured relative to the point size. The width and height are equal to the point size.

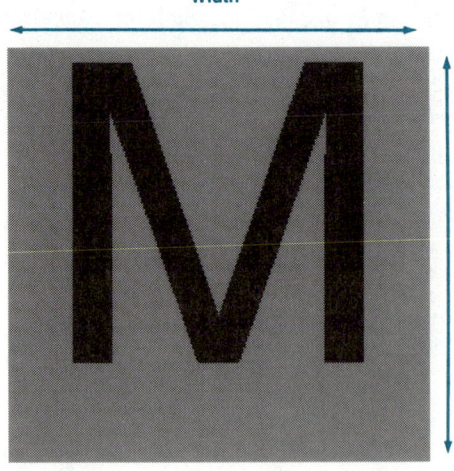

Width

Height

while another may claim 128 units to the em. The idea was that, the finer you could manipulate letterspacing, the better your typography would be. It was not uncommon to have people working full-time in typesetting shops to program their own specific kerning tables with this newfound capability. Kerning was a major factor in separating the craftsman from the guy down the block who could afford to buy a cheap typesetting machine.

The typesetting industry has come a long way in a short amount of time! Now the "guy" down the street may be a woman (the industry was dominated by males for centuries), and she may have a desktop computer running QuarkXPress, which allows her to control kerning in finer increments than imagined just a few years ago. QuarkXPress kerning (or tracking) is calculated in em units and can be specified in values from −500 to 500 as measured in units of em space (see Figure 12.3). Today, the typesetting house is now a service bureau. Quality is QuarkXPress and laser imagesetter output.

FIGURE 12.3

QuarkXPress breaks the em space into 200 equal units for kerning and tracking purposes.

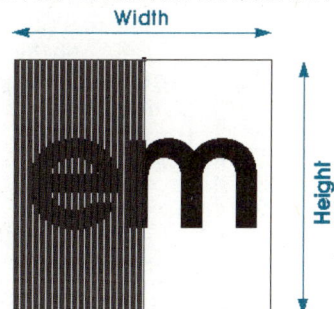

KERNING AND TRACKING TABLES IN QUARKXPRESS

Kerning and tracking are very similar in nature, but have slightly different control features in QuarkXPress. Kerning, as used in QuarkXPress, gives you the capability to select from a predetermined spacing between two type characters, or adjust that

spacing in a variety of ways. Tracking affects a wider range than just the space between two characters. It affects how much space is between character pairs for a
group of characters. This group or range to be affected by Tracking can be as
small as two characters or as large as the entire document. You can use Tracking
to adjust space between characters through a predetermined spacing value or adjustments you make manually for the range chosen.

THE KERNING TABLE EDIT COMMAND

You open the Kerning Table Edit dialog box by choosing Utilities ➤ Kerning Table
Edit (see Figure 12.4). The Tracking Edit dialog box is opened similarly: choose
Utilities ➤ Tracking Edit (this is also shown in Figure 12.4.). This dialog box

FIGURE 12.4

*Selecting the Tracking
Edit (top) and the Kern-
ing Table Edit (bottom)
options from the Utili-
ties menu brings up
these two dialog boxes.*

enables you to select the font and style to edit kerned values. Select the font/style combination and click on the Edit button for changes. Once the selection is made, the Kerning Values dialog box opens specific to the font and style of your choice (see Figure 12.5).

FIGURE 12.5

Once you decide what font and style to edit, the Kerning Values dialog box enables you to selectively edit the kerning for a particular pair of characters. Once edited you can export a copy of these specifications; you can also import kerning values.

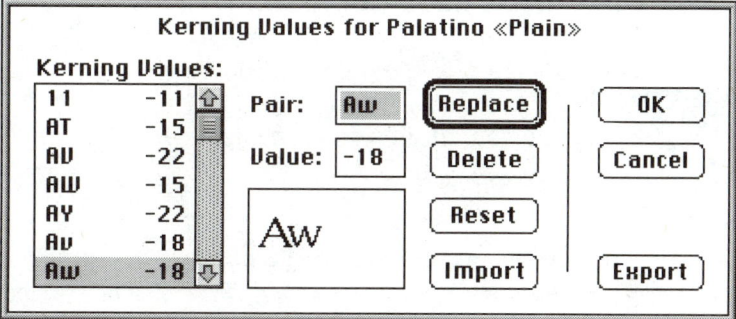

NOTE

If you type a new pair of characters in the Pair entry box, the Replace button changes to Add.

The Kerning Table Edit dialog box gives several options for making changes. You can choose to edit an existing character pair, create and modify a new pair, delete a kerned pair, import similar kerning values, or export these values to another file. The numerical kerning values run in em space increments. As you adjust a particular kerned pair, you can preview the change in the kerning window. Once the settings meet your satisfaction, click on Replace to change the pair or OK to exit the dialog box without changing. You can also click Cancel.

Information in the Kerning Values dialog box applies to the document in all situations with that pair in that font and style. So if you have edited the *Aw* combination in Palatino Plain type, they will always kern at the value specified (−18 in Figure 12.5). You need not revisit the Kerning Values dialog box while working unless a character combination needs revision.

THE TRACKING EDIT COMMAND

TIP

If you goof up in setting the tracking, you can click Reset to get the default setting back; then you can try again.

To edit the tracking settings, select Utilities ➤ Tracking Edit to bring the Tracking Edit dialog box (see Figure 12.4). This dialog box is similar to the one for kerning, but does not have style choices. Tracking values do not take type style into account. The Tracking Values dialog box applies to each major font size group (see Figure 12.6). Click on the value bar in the graph to move the tracking values per font size. The normal tracking value is 0. Values below 0 create tight tracking, while those greater than 0 extend tracking. Once you have modified the graph to reflect your tracking preferences, click on OK to save the changes.

NOTE

Some nefarious fonts, obtained through bulletin boards or on-line services, do not work accurately in the kerning and tracking tables as described here.

FIGURE 12.6

The Tracking Values dialog box (shown for Palatino) indicates the size and tracking value you desire. Click on the floating "cursor" in the graph and drag it to the appropriate tracking value for each size.

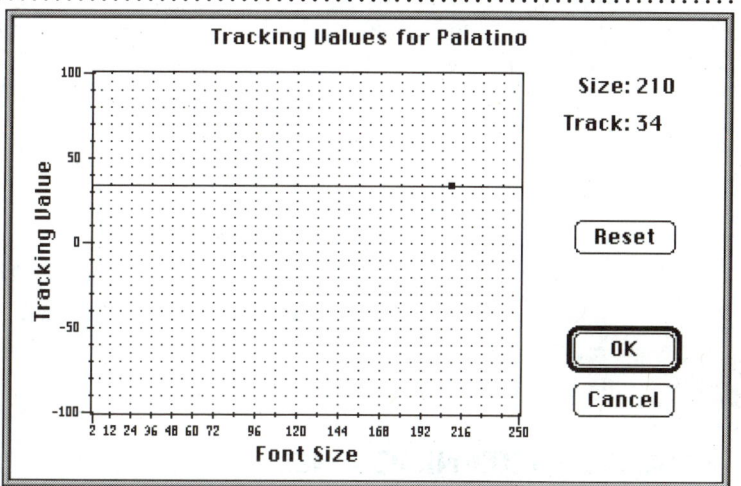

APPLICATION OF KERNING AND TRACKING CONCEPTS IN QUARKXPRESS

In QuarkXPress you can implement kerning and tracking either automatically or manually. To automatically change values, edit the appropriate dialog boxes as described above.

NOTE

Changing kerning or tracking to one font does not change all fonts, or (with kerning) even styles within that font. You must make several changes for kerning and tracking.

To manually apply the kerning and tracking values, select the character or characters you want to modify. To change a kerning value between two characters, anchor the cursor between the two characters and change the kerning value. You can change the kerning value in one of three ways: from the Measurements palette, by using the menu options (Style ➤ Kern or Style ➤ Character), or by keyboard shortcuts.

The menu options include both kerning and tracking under the Style menu. If you are seeking to change kerning at a location between two characters, the menu will show the *Kern* option under Style. If you have a range of characters highlighted, the program assumes you mean to change tracking. Therefore, the name under the Style menu is changed to *Track*. Regardless of Kern or Track, once you choose the option, a small dialog box enables you to insert a numerical value of your kern or track change. After the value is inserted, close the dialog box and your change is implemented.

CHANGING KERNING AND TRACKING FROM THE MEASUREMENTS PALETTE

Display the Measurements palette (View ➤ Show Measurements) and locate the kerned pair to edit. Click between the characters to anchor the cursor. While the cursor is flashing, adjust the kerning arrows or field of the Measurements palette (see Figure 12.7). Pressing on the kerning arrows changes kerning in a predefined 10 number range ($1/200$ em space increments). When finished press Return or Enter.

In similar manner, you can change the tracking of a range of characters. Start by highlighting the range of characters to track. Using the Measurements palette, change the tracking for the entire highlighted range. This range can be as small as a few characters or as large as your entire document text.

KEYBOARD SHORTCUTS FOR KERNING AND TRACKING

You can also kern and track using keyboard equivalents. Press ⌘-Option-Shift-} to add space in $1/200$ em space increments. Press ⌘-Option-Shift-{ to subtract space in the same increments. To track using keyboard equivalents, highlight the range of characters to alter the letterspacing. To track negatively, press ⌘-Option-Shift-{; to track positively, press ⌘-Option-Shift-}. Both track in $1/200$ em space increments.

FIGURE 12.7

Kern the A and W closer together using the Measurements palette.

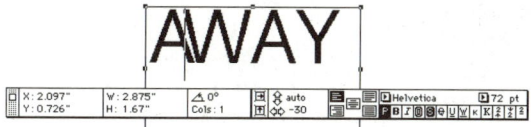

To adjust kerning or tracking in 0.005 ($\frac{1}{200}$) em space increments, use the keyboard commands ⌘-Shift-{ to decrease and ⌘-Shift-} to increase.

RELATED FEATURES IN QUARKXPRESS

A couple of features similar to the kerning and tracking in QuarkXPress are the Flex Space Width capability and use of Ligatures.

FLEX SPACE WIDTH

A new feature in version 3.2 is flex space width, located in the Typographic Preferences dialog box (Edit ➤ Preferences ➤ Typographic). Flexible space is a variation of the en space that you can modify. To specify the width of a flexible character or word space, enter the value in the Flex Space Width field.

NOTE

Remember, the en space is a portion of the em space. The en space is half as wide as the em space, but the same height (e.g., a 12 point em will have an en space 6 points wide, 12 points tall).

The flex space width is a percentage of the normal en space relative to the font and size (see Figure 12.8). You may use a percentage value ranging from 0% to 400% in 0.1% increments. The default value for Flex Space Width is 50% (relative to the en space).

FIGURE 12.8

*Change the Flexible
Space Width value in
the Typographic Prefer-
ences dialog box. Also
from this dialog box,
you have the option of
selecting Ligature use,
as available in the font.*

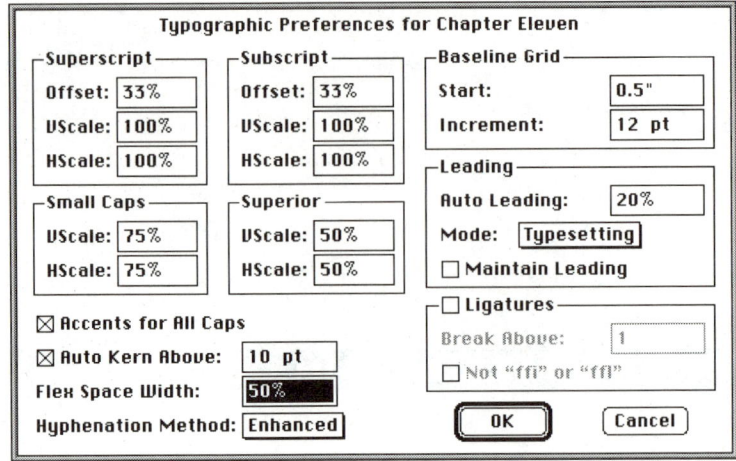

Typographic Preferences for Chapter Eleven

┌─Superscript─┐ ┌─Subscript─┐ ┌─Baseline Grid─┐
Offset: 33%   Offset: 33%   Start: 0.5"
VScale: 100%   VScale: 100%   Increment: 12 pt
HScale: 100%   HScale: 100%

┌─Small Caps─┐ ┌─Superior─┐ ┌─Leading─┐
VScale: 75%   VScale: 50%   Auto Leading: 20%
HScale: 75%   HScale: 50%   Mode: Typesetting
                                ☐ Maintain Leading

☒ Accents for All Caps   ┌─☐ Ligatures─┐
☒ Auto Kern Above: 10 pt   Break Above: 1
Flex Space Width: 50%   ☐ Not "ffi" or "ffl"
Hyphenation Method: Enhanced   [OK] [Cancel]

To enter a breaking flexible space, press Option-Shift-spacebar. Enter a nonbreaking flexible space by pressing ⌘-Option-Shift-spacebar.

A new feature for QuarkXPress 3.2 is flex space width. This is a resizable en space
(half the width of an em). It not only resizes relative to the type size used, but flex
space width gives you control over more width. You can control the space to be
within a percentage value, from 0% to 400%. This enables the en space (that is to
say, the flex space width) to be used for spacing where you previously had limited
or no space options available.

NOTE

*This option further demonstrates the lengths to which Quark has
gone to make this a professional electronic publishing product.
Prior to this, you only had options of this magnitude on highly
specialized and extremely costly typesetting programs. Although
this option may be used by only a few users demanding perfection
at every character, it is available to all users of QuarkXPress!*

Use the flex space width when you want to move a type character over slightly but don't want to bother setting up a tab for one occasion. It is a tool to help you manipulate type, this time through nonprinting spacing units.

The default value is 50%. You may obtain a breaking flexible space +/−50% through the keys Option-Shift-spacebar. A nonbreaking flex space width (50%) can be obtained through using the ⌘-Option-Shift-spacebar.

LIGATURES WITHIN THE FONT

Hot type has a finite amount of space between characters. You could place the characters only so close, as the lead bodies would touch. To remedy this it was sometimes necessary to saw off part of the shoulder to allow for a tighter kern. Popular type character combinations requiring tight kerning were molded together as one.

Two or more characters designed as if they were one distinct unit are called ligatures (see Figure 12.9). Typically, there are five f-ligatures, the fi, ff, fl, ffi and ffl, and the diphthongs of æ, and œ. Not all fonts have these available in ligatures for electronic publishing. They are more prevalent in book publishing than advertising typography.

FIGURE 12.9
Examples of ligatures available in the Times font

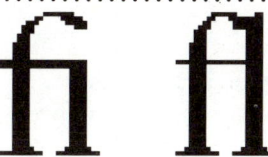

TIP

If you are a ligature fan, you can create your own when not otherwise available. Use the Kerning Table Edit dialog box to place a specific pair together as you desire. You can also use this technique for certain typographical logotypes.

Certain fonts may have ligatures available. To allow QuarkXPress to use available ligatures, select the option from the Typographic Preferences dialog box (see Figure 12.8).

AN EXERCISE IN KERNING

To practice kerning, you can revisit your restaurant newsletter, QuickRelease, introduced earlier. Any good newsletter will have a masthead relating the title of the publication. Any typographically correct masthead will be kerned to perfection.

NOTE

Kerning and tracking are visually aesthetic features. There is no specific rule regulating how much or how little space to use.

STEP 1: ADDING THE TEXT

Start by opening up your saved copy of the newsletter project and go to the cover master page. Highlight the name QuickRelease and key the word QuickRelease right over the original. This gives you a clean start without having to retrofit any previous kerning or tracking. Starting fresh, now you can key in the text for the masthead, that is QuickRelease. Then, highlight and change attributes through Style ➤ Character (⌘-Shift-D) as follows:

- Times font

- 72 point size

▶ Horizontal Scale: 95%

▶ Style both Bold and Shadow

When you are finished, click OK to exit the Character Attributes dialog box.

NOTE

In the original newsletter example, you altered tracking in the Character Attributes dialog box. In this example, you will include it manually, by highlighting the range of characters and changing the Measurements palette. As you initially key in and alter your text, the two words will take up two lines. Don't worry; as you change kerning and tracking, they will condense to fit on one line.

STEP 2: ADJUSTING THE KERNING AND TRACKING

Once the text is in and modified, it is time to start the kerning and tracking process. Begin by making sure you have the Measurements palette showing (View ➤ Show Measurements), as well as the Tools palette (View ➤ Show Tools).

Select the Content tool and highlight the word QuickRelease if not already highlighted. Then highlight the tracking field on the Measurements palette. Change this value to read −15, then press Enter to put your change into effect. The tracking of your masthead should instantly change. Do you notice a difference? If not, be sure the masthead is highlighted, choose Edit ➤ Undo (⌘-Z), and repeat. It is important that you see a difference when kerning and tracking.

NOTE

Kerning and tracking values are very subjective. As a professional, you may prefer the look of certain kerned pair values over others, contrary to those depicted here.

After tracking, it is time to change specific kerning pairs in the masthead. Although changing the tracking cleaned up the range of characters, there are still areas needing slight modification. The specific character combinations you will work

251

with here, kern the *ic* character pair. To kern these follow the procedure outlined below:

1. Position and anchor the cursor between the *ic* character pair.

2. Alter the kern value field in the Measurements palette to read −5.

3. Press Enter to activate the kern.

NOTE

You probably see other bad kern areas within this area; feel free to practice you new skill in kerning wizardry.

Congratulations! You have successfully kerned and tracked the characters in the newsletter masthead. Save the revision copy, unless you don't want the changes to be made permanent. You can also save it under a different name through the Save As option (File ➤ Save As). Giving it a different name will ensure that your original is unchanged and that your new document is also saved.

TrueType and PostScript Fonts

MAC TRACKS   MAC TRACKS   MAC TRACKS   MAC TRACKS   MAC

TRACKS

Do you know the difference between a *font* and a *typeface*? To understand it, you must know that the history of typesetting goes back as far as around 250 B.C., when the Chinese used ceramic stamps pressed in clay. This eventually lead to inked characters, recorded in China by Pi Sheng in A.D. 1401. Johannes Gutenberg cast his first letters from a mixture of tin, antimony, and lead in A.D. 1441. These cast letters were called *movable type* because they could be removed, stored, and reused. It is also called *hot type*, *hand-set type*, or *cast type*.

NOTE

Hand-set and its associated machine-set metal type were the mainstays of the typesetting industry until only a few decades ago. Photographic type started to catch on in the 1960s and became commonplace in the 1970s. The last linecasting machine for metal type was produced in 1971.

Hand-set type makes a distinction between the cast character and the letter impression made when printed (see Figure 13.1). The complete collection of cast characters in one size and style is a *font*. The printed image or face of the font is the *typeface*.

TYPEFACES

Most typefaces have design variations of the original layout. For example, Helvetica has Helvetica Light, Helvetica Medium, Helvetica Bold, Helvetica Italic, etc. These variations of the same basic design are the *styles*. All styles together comprise the typeface *family*.

Electronic fonts of today share much of the terminology of their hot metal ancestors, but lack the physical attributes. This causes problems for many people starting in desktop publishing. They do not have the character to pick up and hold, they don't have the opportunity to see why "set solid" is called set solid (see Figure 13.2). They can't see the lead or copper strip placed between lines for spacing. In short, people working in the electronic typesetting industry today have a great disadvantage to overcome: lack of practical experience!

FIGURE 13.1

A representation of a metal type character, as used in hand-set typesetting

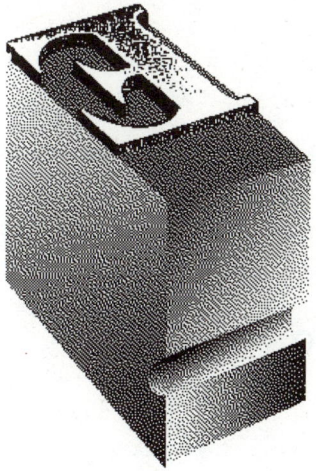

FIGURE 13.2

The leading in the left paragraph is set solid.

This is an example of text in paragraph format. This paragraph is set solid. That means that the leading equals the point size.

This is an example of text in paragraph format. This paragraph is set solid. That means that the leading equals the point size.

Today's electronic fonts are data stored on a disk or tape. These bits and bytes are a computer's blueprint, used to draw the face in very precise units (as small as 0.001-point increments). Capabilities of today's hardware and software blur the meanings of *font* and *typeface*, to the point where the two terms are interchangeable. However, if you use history as a guide, the definition of *font* is the computer data, and the output text is the *typeface*.

FONT CATEGORIES IN ELECTRONIC PUBLISHING

Specialists in the industry categorize electronic fonts in two distinct categories, *bitmapped* and *outline*. Bitmapped fonts are best identified as font software that enables the computer to create type images on the screen. Outline fonts are software applications that tell the printer how to form characters on the paper.

The highest resolution type will come from imagesetter output, especially at the high end of the resolution spectrum—nearly 3000 dots per inch. This is far better than the resolution you have on desktop laser printers at 300 dpi or your monitor at only 72 dpi. But things change, quickly. Read on.

BITMAPPED FONTS

Bitmapped fonts are sometimes called screen fonts; that is, they look better on the screen due to the monitor's 72 dpi resolution. When these are printed, the dot resolution does not improve. Figure 13.3 shows an enlargement of the bitmapped font character. It looks terrible! It looks just as bad in print. Bitmapped fonts are best used on the screen, not in the printer.

FIGURE 13.3
A representation of a bitmapped font character, enlarged to highlight the bits or pixel elements

These fonts have the following characteristics:

- Instructions to form characters on screen

- Require a lot of storage space on disk, compared to outline fonts

- Do not resize particularly well

- Primarily, but not exclusively, used as screen fonts

- Should be installed in all sizes you need to use (unless you have ATM—see *Adobe Type Manager* below)

- Are stored and moved in the Mac in files known as *suitcases*

- May be used for laser printers, but will show "jagged" edges (pixel rendition), improves somewhat with ATM

- Provides an information table with character widths, which allows variable width characters. This gives more true WYSIWYG.

OUTLINE FONTS

Outline fonts (also known as *vector*, *scalable* or *printer fonts*) are more precise and of higher quality, because they consist of a formula for the computer or printer to draw the character. See Figure 13.4 for a representation of an outline font character.

FIGURE 13.4

A representation of an outline font character. Outline fonts are usually, but not exclusively, used for output.

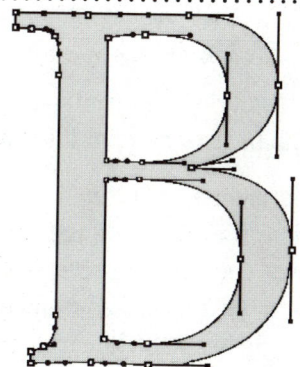

Outline fonts have the following characteristics:

- Mathematical formulations of the character shape using curves and lines

- Takes up less storage space on disk than bitmapped fonts

- Can be resized without degrading the character

- Are primarily, but not exclusively, for output to printer

- Are, in PostScript form, composed of Bézier curves

- Contain information about the size and shape of each character for the printer to use for output

- Allow you to print any typeface in any size, angle, and shade resolution available on the output printer, while maintaining clarity and precision

- May be used for screen display with ATM

OTHER VARIATIONS OF THE FONT DILEMMA

It may not be clear what type of font to use where, so here is a brief summary.

1. Bitmapped fonts belong on the screen only. Do not try to print with bitmapped fonts unless absolutely necessary.

2. Outline fonts are primarily for use on the printer. They send information to the printer when you print the document.

3. A new form of outline font from Apple (TrueType) allows both use on screen and in the printer. This may be the wave of the future, but now it is not widely accepted by the user community.

4. Adobe is countering TrueType with their own Multiple Master Font technology that will be used both for the screen and the printer.

From this information, the distinction between the technologies might seem clear: Bitmapped fonts for the screen and outline fonts for the printer. But that is not the way technology is moving, for several reasons. First, designers and typesetters have never been totally satisfied with onscreen font rendering because it is often not even close to the quality you can obtain in print. Competition in technology, being what it is, has brought about a new rivalry that may reshape the way type works.

NOTE

Remember, a language in "computerese" means a program that someone uses to communicate with. PostScript is a language that allows your computer to communicate to a printer. It tells the printer how to recreate your design on the paper using its internal laser as the drawing tool.

PostScript is a proprietary page description language from Adobe. It is currently the dominant language in output. Apple made the decision to get into the high resolution font business and introduced their TrueType font structure. TrueType is unique in that it is an outline font that can be used on the screen as well as for output print. Therefore, it does not have the limitations that bitmapped fonts have on the screen. Not to be outdone, Adobe, with their massive head start in this business, has taken steps to migrate PostScript into a new direction. PostScript's most recent development includes the use of what Adobe calls *Multiple Masters*. Here, a variety of custom typefaces can be generated from a single font file.

A standard PostScript printer font defines a single outline for each of its 256 characters. Each has a consistent weight, style, and width. Additional weights, styles and widths are available only on supplemental PostScript printer fonts. For example, Helvetica comes in regular, bold, and italic. To obtain Helvetica Thin, you have to buy another font specific to your needs. It cannot be redrawn from the original font through PostScript.

NOTE

A font's characteristics include its weight (light, black, bold, plain), character style (sans serif, serif, oblique), and width (condensed, regular, expanded).

Multiple Master fonts include *master designs*; that is, several font character definitions. Each master represents an extreme in weight, style, and width. A master forms a matrix, as shown in Figure 13.5.

FIGURE 13.5

A representation of a
Multiple Master design
matrix

Light condensed   Light oblique

Heavy condensed   Heavy oblique

A special built-in utility enables the user to create a custom typeface from these elements of the master design. Not only can you create a special typeface from this grid, but each Multiple Master may be best used for a specific size range of type. You could have one master best for 6–10 point type, another for 12–14, another for 14–24, and so on. This is essentially the way certain typesetting machine manufacturers dealt with the quality issue in earlier digital typesetting machines. They would digitize specific masters for a specific range of sizes. As the size range changes, the computer would shift to the next set of masters. In this way, the type designer is assured of quality in any size of type produced from the original artwork of the font.

As of this writing, Multiple Master fonts are not in widespread use. The prevalent system is the traditional PostScript fonts in Adobe PostScript Type 1 format. However, this business has a way of changing nearly overnight.

APPLE'S FONT STRATEGY

Advanced type capabilities is just one of the many factors separating the Mac from other computer platforms. The Mac allows users to see on the screen what is desired in print. These capabilities came in large part because of a technological partnership between Apple and Adobe. Early in the Macintosh evolution, Adobe PostScript Type 1 fonts were introduced. These quickly became a standard printer font in the industry.

In August 1991, Apple announced that System 7 would have Adobe PostScript Type 1 font rendering capabilities. They also indicated a willingness to work with Adobe for compatibility in future system enhancements.

Part of the strategic plan for System 7 is to extend the type capabilities of the operating system. In support of this, Apple introduced TrueType. This is a powerful font technology that addresses some of the limitations of bitmapped and outline fonts. It enables the user to have maximum legible type on screen and in print at any size. It works on a principle similar to outline fonts in PostScript in that it draws the character from a base formula. The difference is that with TrueType, the same font file is used for screen display and print output. This technology will serve as the foundation for new cross-platform typographic capabilities.

SYSTEM 7.X ENHANCEMENT

NOTE

Although many "power users" advocate trashing the TrueType fonts as soon as you load System 7, remember that one TrueType font file can replace several bitmapped files. It may be a cleaner solution!

System 7 handles print and display of TrueType at the core system level. This planning will enable future releases of System 7 to build on existing typographic capabilities. For example, an upcoming version of Mac System 7 will include the *Line Layout Manager*, a new typographic extension. This will enable all Macintosh applications to take advantage of such advanced type-manipulation techniques as kerning, tracking, and automatic ligatures. These features are currently only on specialized software applications such as QuarkXPress.

TRUETYPE BACKGROUND

In 1989, Apple announced at its annual developers conference that it was developing TrueType to be included with System 7. In the development of System 7, it had become clear that new strategies needed exploring that were not thought of when the Mac was introduced. Apple designed TrueType to help simplify font installation and management (see Figure 13.6). The goal to be compatible with every kind of printer and output device and to display and print high-quality type quickly was paramount. They wanted TrueType to be powerful and flexible enough to handle complexities of many world languages, not just the Roman alphabet. Finally, their goal was to design a type format to work on computer platforms other than Macintosh.

With the help and support of font vendors, Apple developed TrueType and shipped it in March 1991. It was capable of working in both System 6 and System 7. Currently, all System 7 software is shipped with a complement of TrueType fonts. Also, new laser printers are being introduced with TrueType abilities built in. Microsoft has licensed TrueType for use with their Windows operating system.

Chicago

FIGURE 13.6

The TrueType font icon is shown with several characters on its icon.

BITMAPPED VS. TRUETYPE FONTS

TrueType is an outline font technology. As described earlier, an outline font details all the characters as a series of mathematical lines and curves. PostScript uses Bézier curves for drawing the character, while TrueType uses a particular mathematical equation known as the quadratic curve. Quadratic curves are easy to compute and scale on the computer. TrueType enables conversion from other forms, such as the Bézier curves into quadratic curves, thus allowing type vendors to translate font libraries into TrueType format.

Because outline font information consists of mathematical formulas, it is easy for the computer to scale and reshape the font. Bitmapped fonts cannot be mathematically expanded or reduced without the character showing the "jaggies." To resize properly, you must install a specific bitmapped font for each type size you want to use.

NOTE

The Mac indicates which type sizes have been installed by showing them actually as outlines on the font size submenu.

In the early days of the Macintosh, there were only bitmapped fonts and Imagewriters (dot-matrix printers). Apple introduced the LaserWriter printer in 1985 and quickly found that the bitmapped technology was insufficient. The decision was to continue bitmapped fonts for screen display but allow laser printers to use the Adobe PostScript outline fonts. The LaserWriter contained its own outline version of the fonts displayed on the screen.

NOTE

Third-party accessory programs can be found through mail order houses, on-line services, etc., to translate TrueType from the Windows platform to the Mac and vice versa. The only thing different about the two is the extension of each file and how the respective platforms read and store the file, based on that extension. Transformation programs allow true cross-platform use of QuarkXPress with TrueType fonts.

Using outline font technology, printers were able to smoothly reproduce any font at any size. Meanwhile, Mac users were still working with design of bitmapped fonts on the screen. Resized bitmapped fonts distort so designers had difficulty seeing what they would get.

To counter these problems, Apple decided to create TrueType. Instead of addressing the deficiencies of bitmapped screen fonts only, Apple designed TrueType to work as both a screen and printer font. Furthermore, important program codes necessary to make TrueType function are made a part of the operating system. You don't have to have add-on files to place in specified folders to make fonts work. This gives high-quality, accurate, on-screen type display the same priority as it has for printed display. You can tell if there are any TrueType fonts in your system if the font icon has multiple characters.

HOW FONTS WORK

Both TrueType and PostScript fonts work in similar manner. They contain a instruction set that takes orders from the user. These orders consist of manipulations you give in the application; for example, you may want the type to be larger or narrower. Give the instruction and the font manipulates to obey. These instructions dictate the size, quality, and resolution of the final character. In PostScript, the character results in printed form. In TrueType, the form is both on screen and in print.

NOTE

Hinting is a programmer's method of telling the type designer how to place subtle differences in the type character. Fonts with hinting can have more manipulation by the type designer, compared to those without hinting.

These font formats provide type designers with *hinting* controls (see Figure 13.7). Hinting comes in high-level and low-level features that enable designers to control global characteristics such as the width of a character stem. This gives more control to the type designer to display the original design as intended.

Low-level hinting information is particularly important for displaying screen font characters. As you type, the Mac notes the font and style in use. It then refers to the TrueType outline for the chosen character and scales it to the correct point size. The Macintosh overlays a grid representing your Macintosh display monitor resolution and each cell in the grid. Hinting information is used to position pixels on the grid to fit the character outline as best as possible. The resulting pixels are turned black and the character appears on the screen (see Figure 13.5).

MIXING TYPE FORMATS

Multiple font formats can coexist in the Mac environment. You can use TrueType, bitmapped, and outline fonts all at the same time. Under System 7, the Macintosh follows a hierarchical order in determining what a character will look like on screen. Specifically, System 7 looks first to see if there is a bitmap that matches the font and size chosen. If none is found, it then looks for a TrueType version. If a TrueType version cannot be found, System 7 looks for an Adobe PostScript Type 1 font, stored on the hard disk and Adobe Type Manager (ATM). It uses ATM to convert the Type 1 outline format to a form it can display on the screen. If the Type 1 outline and ATM cannot be found, System 7 takes the next closest bitmap size and scales it for screen display.

NOTE

To ensure complete compatibility with System 6, System 7 ships with bitmaps for certain TrueType fonts installed. That's because TrueType versions of some standard LaserWriter fonts have slightly different widths than older bitmapped versions. In rare instances this could cause problems in line breaks and hyphenation. If you are not concerned about older documents reflowing under System 7, remove the bitmapped versions of the font.

FIGURE 13.7

To a type designer, the advantage of hinting allows them to customize a design for output. For everybody else, hinting means little but is required to make the laser type look good.

ADOBE TYPE MANAGER

A new technology called Adobe Type Manager (ATM) uses outline font info from printer fonts to create fonts on the screen. Without the need of each size having its own master, ATM allows outline fonts to be used as screen fonts. (This assumes you are using bitmapped and outline PostScript fonts, not TrueType.) Type sizes larger than twelve points are drastically enhanced in their screen appearance with ATM (see Figure 13.8).

NOTE

A master is the original design of the type character, as generated by the type designer. From this master the designer can create variations, such as larger or smaller sizes, condensed or bold type, etc. Think of it as something similar to a master mold.

The two primary advantages of ATM are:

▸ Screen representations of fonts can now be created using outline fonts, giving a much higher–quality look on the screen.

▸ Bitmapped fonts are needed only for reproducing special sizes under twelve points, drastically cutting font storage requirements.

ATM has the capability to use existing fonts in both bitmapped and outline format, in particular PostScript fonts. This has become very popular in view of the investment many have in PostScript font libraries.

FIGURE 13.8
Here is how screen fonts may appear with and without Adobe Type Manager (ATM) properly activated.

Quality

Quality

ENCRYPTION, FORMATS, AND MORE HINTING

It is difficult to make type look good in low-resolution situations. When outline fonts are scaled down, there are fewer pixels to draw the character. The same problem is true in low-resolution printers. When you get down to the point that the thickness of one pixel can make or break the look of your characters, you have inconsistent quality in type. Both TrueType and PostScript have *hints;* that is, algorithms that are part of the font and improve its ability to produce good-looking letters.

NOTE

There are Type 1, Type 2, and Type 3 formats. Types 1 and 3 are available to the general public. Type 2 was for certain proprietary purposes and never released for general public use. The difference between Type 1 and Type 3 is in the encryption capabilities. Type 1 format allows encryption, while Type 3 formats do not.

Encryption is the process used to protect certain code information in fonts and other computer files in general. Type 1 fonts are rarely encrypted any longer since Adobe released the font format in March 1990. Prior to that time, Type 1 font formats included the ability to allow encryption, thus hiding specific hint information. When hint information was encrypted, the key differences were kept from would-be software pirates. Designs remained intact and no copies were made. Competition forced Adobe to stop encryption techniques and open the market for everyone. This allows for a more open environment in the font technology and is one method to keep PostScript fonts popular in view of competition from TrueType.

WHICH IS BETTER, TRUETYPE OR POSTSCRIPT?

What factors determine which font format is better? It primarily boils down to cost, speed, and output quality. Cost factors deal with how much you have already spent on your existing type library, and how much has your service bureau already invested in theirs. You don't need any new hardware technology to utilize either Post-Script or TrueType; or do you? Sooner or later, everyone must upgrade his hardware. New printers are being built with both PostScript and TrueType capabilities. Currently, because PostScript is more popular, there are more PostScript printers on the market, but that should equal out as TrueType becomes more entrenched in the market. Therefore, the cost of new hardware and software seems not much of a determining factor.

What about speed? Which format draws faster on screen? Which one works faster in the output device? Well, both formats, TrueType and PostScript with ATM, perform poorly on slower processors. Don't bother with the older 68000 processor in machines such as the Mac Plus. Likewise, earlier PostScript printers are relatively slow. The primary factor in PostScript's slow acceptance in the typesetting market was speed. Original PostScript imagesetters moved at a glacial pace compared with the digital typesetters in use at the time. If not for the popularity of desktop publishing and advanced applications like QuarkXPress, the entire industry might not have taken off.

As for screen speed, the best thing you could do for either format is to use ATM's font cache. This places most font information in the quickest possible storage. On average, reports from various trade publications imply that PostScript with ATM draws characters on the screen faster than TrueType. However, since this is a function of the operating system, Apple's operating system, look for improvements in TrueType.

On the quality issue, both formats print to screen well, perhaps a bit too well. True-Type may have a tendency in certain situations to sacrifice type design to draw a better screen rendition. In general, quality of output is pretty much a draw. You have to make your own decision here.

NOTE

Talk to anyone using System 7 in the design field and chances are they will suggest, for now, to move all your new TrueType fonts into a safe-storage folder or simply to trash them. This saves you storage and you are no worse off with older bitmapped fonts already in your system.

The conclusion? In the short term, PostScript with ATM appears to have a slight edge. Not only do they have an established market with greater font selection, but they edge out TrueType in certain speed and quality issues. In the long term, True-Type is a cleaner solution. It provides one font for all sizes in both printer and screen formats. If you look at the history of improvements made in the Macintosh and its operating system, you've got to place a safe bet on TrueType.

MORE TYPOGRAPHIC MANEUVERS

To alter the amount of space between text and the border of its text box 280

use the Text Inset field option within the Text Specifications dialog box (Item ➤ Modify).

To edit selected text from the Measurements palette 282

simply highlight the value you wish to change, key in your replacement and press Enter or Return. In some cases, you manipulate arrows or choose from pop-up menus.

To ensure no surprises for document contents 282

anchor important items once you've settled on their final positions with the Lock option under the Item menu (⌘-L). Anchoring items will not prevent you from editing their contents. It only anchors the box, text or picture, containing these items. You can unlock and move it at any time. This command toggles to Unlock (⌘-L).

To specify the way lines and paragraphs stay together 282

choose Style ➤ Formats. The Paragraph Formats dialog box will appear. To keep selected paragraphs grouped with their successors, click on Keep with Next ¶.

There are typographic features of QuarkXPress that are not easily categorized under the word processing or typographic headings we've covered so far. This chapter encompasses typographic maneuvers for text boxes, paragraph controls, hyphenation, and other special timesaving features.

NOTE

The only place you can enter text in a QuarkXPress document is in a text box. You can key it in or import it from another source, but type will go only into a text box. Once the text is in the text box, you can edit it with the Content tool only.

MODIFYING A TEXT BOX

So far you have been shown how to use text within a text box, as well as how to import, export, color, and shade it, but do you really know how to manipulate that box yet? Here are some basics often overlooked when first starting the QuarkXPress document.

NOTE

Items created on a master page will become master items and will reflect on related document pages. Items created on a document page will show only on that document page.

CREATING AND RESIZING A TEXT BOX

To form a new or additional text box, select the Text Box tool. Click and drag to the opposite corner to form a text box. Release the mouse button. The exact size of the text box is not critical, since you can resize it at any time. You resize item boxes in one of three ways.

- Make manual changes through dragging the item's grab bars, a common Macintosh maneuver.

- Make precise changes in the Measurements palette.

- Make precise changes with Item ➤ Modify. Identify the text box and select Item ➤ Modify. This brings up the Text Box Specifications dialog box, an outstanding feature of QuarkXPress that enables you to edit numerical coordinates of the item.

Precision is typically down to three decimal places in many fields in the Text Box Specifications dialog box.

THE TEXT BOX SPECIFICATIONS DIALOG BOX

Depending on what item you identify, Item ➤ Modify brings up different dialog boxes. See Figure 14.1 for the various dialog boxes for each item type. You must be careful when identifying (clicking on) a specific item, so as to get its appropriate Specifications dialog box.

FIGURE 14.1

Each type of item (line, groups, picture box, text box) brings up a different Specifications dialog box, as shown here.

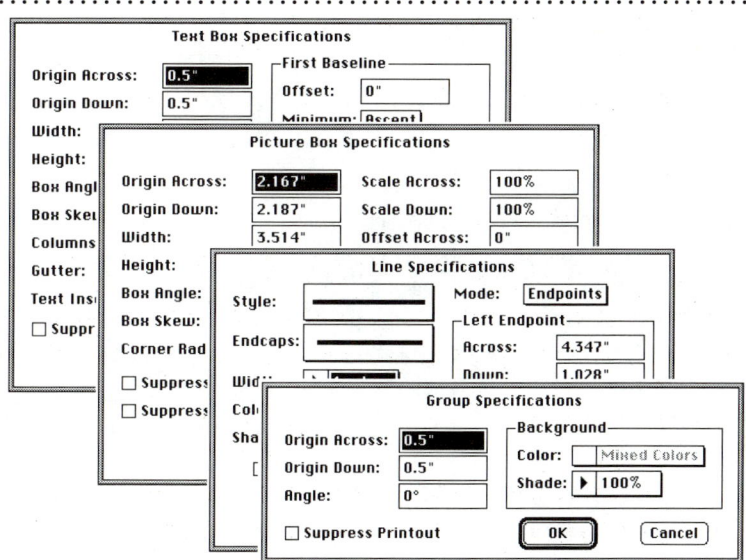

Select the text box and Item ➤ Modify to bring up a dialog box entitled *Text Box Specifications*. You can manipulate this text box and its contents in a variety of ways.

NOTE

A couple of handy tricks: first, to bring up the Text Box Specifications dialog, double-click on the text box with the Item tool. Furthermore, to turn the Content Tool into the Item tool, hold down the ⌘ key.

LOCATION AND SIZE VALUES

The first four fields in the dialog box deal with the placement and size of the item. The Origin Across and Origin Down values position the top-left corner of the text box, relative to the 0,0 ruler position. If the 0,0 ruler position changes, these values will automatically change also. The next two values are the Width and Height values. Typically the text box is a rectangle, whose dimensions are reflected here. Similar to other QuarkXPress dialog boxes, you can enter values in any combination of measurement systems and the program will translate them for you. In Figure 14.2, a value has been entered in the Origin Down box that is actually a hybrid of inches and points.

FIGURE 14.2

QuarkXPress will translate any measurement system combination (almost) that you throw at it. Here a combination of picas and points is placed in the Origin Down value. At right is the translation in inches.

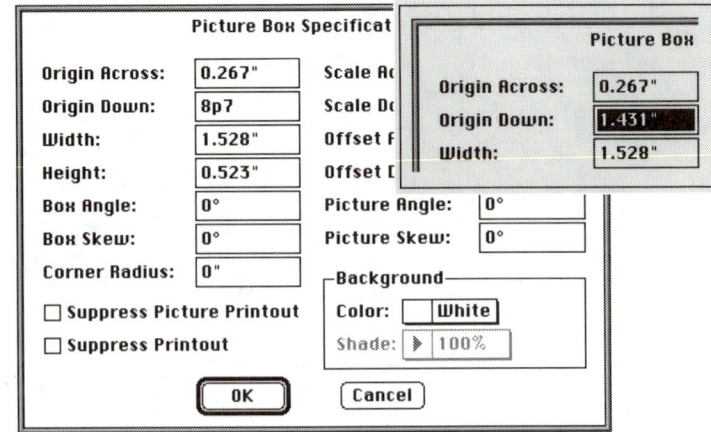

The Box Angle value is the rotation value of the text box. In QuarkXPress you can rotate the text box along with its contents a range of −360–360°, in increments as fine as 0.001°. The default rotation is counterclockwise. A positive number in the Box Angle value rotates the text box counterclockwise; a negative number rotates the text box clockwise. You can also rotate the text box manually using the Rotation tool or through the Rotation field on the Measurements palette.

TIP

If you want to make money, you must spend money. The best way to work with QuarkXPress is to spend your money on a fast Macintosh with a large monitor and high-resolution graphics card. Consider a 24-bit card as standard for high-quality graphics. Remember, QuarkXPress is a production tool. The rule of the game is that whoever gets production out quickest with the highest quality and lowest cost is the winner!

Another interesting feature of QuarkXPress's rotation capability is that you can edit rotated text. This advantage meets with mixed admiration, though. It does save time, in that you don't have to unrotate text or go to some dialog box to edit. In many cases, however, rotated text is difficult to read on screen, making fine detail editing cumbersome. This problem is mostly a function of your hardware. If you have a standard Macintosh arrangement, perhaps the resolution of the monitor and card are insufficient to read small type at an odd rotation angle.

Then there's the Box Skew field; this input field enables you to skew or distort the box. Your range of skew runs from -75 to +75 degrees.

COLUMNS AND THE GUTTER

The next two field values in the Text Box Specifications dialog box are for Columns and Gutter. These values are similar to the ones you set when creating a new document (in the New dialog box). Values in the New dialog box affect the entire document. In contrast, values in an active Text Box Specifications dialog box change only that item. You can have from 1 to 30 columns and the gutter value can range from 0.042″ to 4″.

TEXT INSET

The Text Inset value represents how much border or nonprinting space there will be from the edge of the text box to the type. This represents a buffer zone of sorts in that it assures your type will be a minimal distance from the edge. This setting is especially important when you shade the text box or place a border frame around it. Values for the Text Inset are usually in points but you can use other measurement systems. QuarkXPress will translate.

SUPPRESS PRINTOUT

Use this handy check box to prevent the contents in this particular Text Box item from printing. This options will not affect other items on the page. Apply Suppress Printout for occasions when you don't want printed text immediately. An example of this might be a text book where you want to have a student edition and have teachers' notes non-printing for the student. You can print out a distinct copy for the teacher's edition. Another occasion to use this option may be in an editorial situation when the editor wants to leave notes to the author, artist, etc., that you would not want to print. You may even want to highlight these notes in a color!

FIRST BASELINE

The First Baseline area of the dialog box controls where the paragraph will start. The Offset value represents the first line's starting location from the top of the text box. It takes only a positive range of values. You can start the measurement from the Ascending characters, Cap Height or Cap + Accent characters in the Minimum pop up menu.

. . . .

WARNING

Use caution when you apply a First Baseline value, as it may be affected by the Text Inset (the amount of space the text has on all four sides of a text box). These two variables, First Baseline and Text Inset may have a dramatic influence on each other if used simultaneously.

Cap Height is equal to the height of a zero (0) in the font of the largest character on the first line. Cap + Accent is that space *plus* the space needed for an accent mark *above* the Cap Height. Ascent is equal to the height of the ascenders (see Figure 14.3) in the font of the largest character on the first line of text.

VERTICAL ALIGNMENT

Vertical Alignment handles the alignment of text material within the text box. It works just as Vertical Alignment did when you explored it in *Chapter 8*. The Type pop-up menu enables you to specify the alignment: Top, Bottom, Centered, or Justified. Choose Justified and a value field appears for placing the inter-paragraph spacing (called Inter ¶ Max). This is a maximum spacing value between paragraphs as they align vertically to fill the text box. Values here range from 0″ to 15″.

BACKGROUND

The background color option shades the text box background, not the type itself, with the chosen color. You can pick colors from the existing document color palette. Edit this color palette through Edit ➤ Colors. Shades are represented in values of 10%, but you may key in your exact value in the field as necessary. The default color is white and has no shade available.

FIGURE 14.3
You use the First Baseline area to specify the location of your first baseline, in reference to the part of the type character.

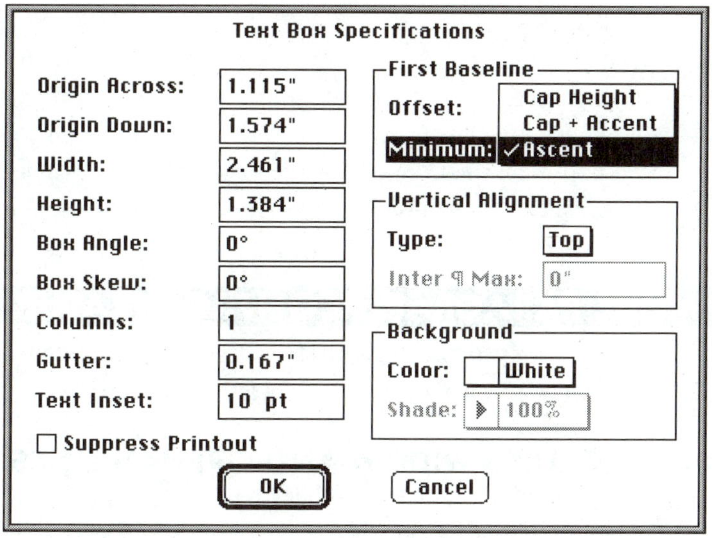

Text Box Specifications

Origin Across:	1.115"
Origin Down:	1.574"
Width:	2.461"
Height:	1.384"
Box Angle:	0°
Box Skew:	0°
Columns:	1
Gutter:	0.167"
Text Inset:	10 pt

☐ Suppress Printout

First Baseline
Offset: Cap Height / Cap + Accent
Minimum: ✓Ascent

Vertical Alignment
Type: Top
Inter ¶ Max: 0"

Background
Color: White
Shade: ▶ 100%

[OK] [Cancel]

THE MEASUREMENTS PALETTE FOR EDITING THE TEXT BOX

The Measurements palette is another way to position the text box. It includes values for position, size, rotation, and columns. The Measurement palette also has information on font, style, size, leading, and alignment. To edit the selected text box item from the Measurements palette simply highlight the value you wish to change, key in your replacement and press Enter or Return. In some cases, you manipulate arrows or choose from pop-up menus.

LOCKING AND UNLOCKING ITEMS

If you have placed an item on the document page and don't want it to move, you can lock it in position. This is handy when working on a complex layout where the slightest error would mean trouble. If you inadvertently click on an item to move it a pixel or two, it might destroy your layout.

NOTE

At times, relocation of an item is unwanted and inadvertent. To avoid accidental movement of an item, choose Item ➤ Lock (⌘-L). This fixes the item in position so you cannot move it. If you wish to move the item you must unlock it first.

To ensure no surprises once you've settled on their final positions, anchor important items with the Lock option under the Item menu (⌘-L). Anchoring items will not prevent you from editing their contents. It only anchors the box, text or picture, containing these items. You can unlock and move it at any time.

MORE PARAGRAPH CONTROL FEATURES

There are two more features for paragraph control you have yet to meet. These include widow and orphan control and initial caps.

CONTROLLING WIDOW AND ORPHAN LINES

First, you may want a refresher on just what widows and orphans are, typographically speaking. They are undesirable effects that fall at the end of a paragraph. A *widow* is a short line at the end of a paragraph, if less than one-third the line length. An *orphan* occurs when a widow is carried to the top of a column or page. You should avoid starting a page or column with a single or partial line; likewise, you should avoid beginning a new paragraph as the last line of a column or page. You can eliminate these typographic problems manually or use automated settings that help prevent widows and orphans from occurring in QuarkXPress.

To specify the way lines and paragraphs stay together, choose Style ➤ Formats. The Paragraph Formats dialog box will appear (see Figure 14.4). To keep selected paragraphs grouped with their successors, click on Keep with Next ¶.

WARNING

Use of automatic widow and orphan control in the Paragraph Formats dialog box could place entire paragraphs on the next page, leaving a gap in the previous page. This may present unwanted effects in vertical justification.

To keep all lines of a particular paragraph together (avoiding orphans and widows), check Keep lines Together, then click on All Lines in ¶. When you click All Lines in ¶ QuarkXPress treats the paragraph as an indivisible unit.

FIGURE 14.4

The Paragraph Formats dialog box is the same dialog box you encountered when working with style sheets.

Paragraph Formats

Left Indent: `0"`	Leading: `14 pt`
First Line: `0"`	Space Before: `0"`
Right Indent: `0"`	Space After: `0"`

☐ Lock to Baseline Grid ☐ Keep with Next ¶
☐ Drop Caps ☐ Keep Lines Together

Alignment: `Left`
H&J: `Standard`

[Apply]
[OK] [Cancel]

HOW TO CREATE THE AUTOMATIC DROP CAP

An *initial cap* is the first character or word of a paragraph enlarged to create a special visual effect. QuarkXPress enables you to create this effect several ways, including initial drop caps, initial cap styles, hanging caps, and raised caps.

You must begin by selecting the paragraphs for which you want an initial cap. Typically, you do this by placing the cursor within a single paragraph or highlighting a range of paragraphs.

The checkbox for initial caps is in the Paragraph Formats dialog box (Style ➤ Formats) as shown in Figure 14.4.

Click on Drop Caps and the dialog box changes to show your new choices. Check the Drop Caps option to identify from one to eight characters to alter. You can select the number of characters to drop as well as the number of lines to drop them. The value for line count must be between 2 and 8. You can also increase or decrease the size of a drop cap by highlighting and specifying a percentage in the Measurements palette (see Figure 14.5).

FIGURE 14.5

The default Drop Caps option in the Paragraph Formats dialog box gives the initial cap an outstanding look. Change the percentage in the Measurements palette to increase or decrease the size of the initial cap.

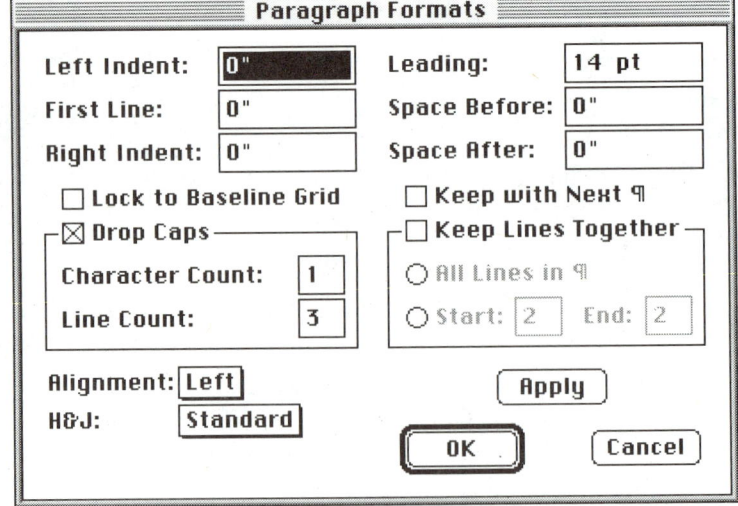

HYPHENATION AND JUSTIFICATION

Justification is a complex process whereby the computer determines how many characters will fit on the line. It takes into account the possibility that the last word on a line can be hyphenated. Regardless, a certain amount of extra (non-character space) remains. In justification, that extra space is distributed throughout the line, first between words and then between characters. If evenly distributed throughout the line, the text appears flush left and flush right (justified). This option usually requires hyphenation to work best. That is why the two are known together are *H & J*.

NOTE

You can include H & J specifications as part of a style sheet's paragraph format. Then you can apply specific H & J settings to various parts of your document as necessary.

SPECIFYING WORD AND CHARACTER SPACING RULES IN JUSTIFICATION

The way in which the program distributes extra space is governed by the settings in the Edit Hyphenation and Justification (H & J) dialog box (see Figure 14.6), which you can see by choosing Edit ➤ H&Js, choosing an H&J file, and clicking Edit. H & J works for the QuarkXPress user as an option regulating space between letters and words. You can regulate essentially three types of space between letters, and three types of space between words. These spaces include minimum, maximum and optimum. The H & J Edit dialog box enables you to place values in each—a minimum value, maximum value and optimum value. These values are stated in percentage. A normal value, as predetermined from the type designer, is 100%. Any variation of this is either below or above 100%, that is spacing less, is below 100%, while spacing more is over 100%. Other controls within this dialog box deal with hyphenation. You can control the number of lines in a row you will allow hyphenation or not. In most cases, the default values for the H & J specifications work fine, with no need to modify. However, if you want to fine-tune your text, here is another technique!

FIGURE 14.6

*The Edit Hyphenation
and Justification
dialog box*

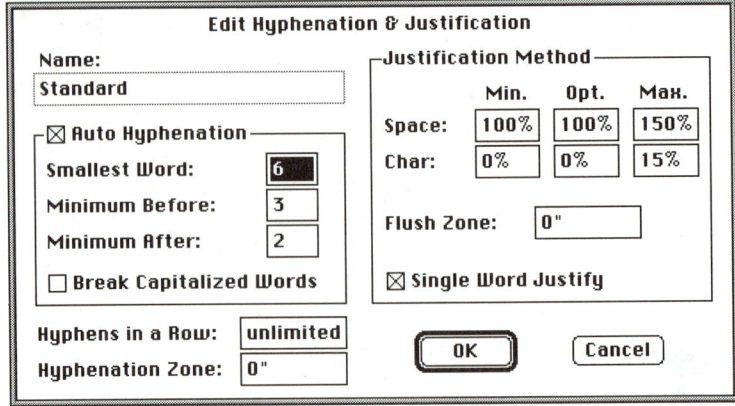

The Justification Method area of the dialog box allows you to specify minimum, optimum, and maximum values for both space and character. The justification process uses these values to determine where to add extra space. The minimum spacing value indicates the smallest amount of space allowed between characters or words. In order for the computer to get the best possible fit of characters on the line, it sometimes must squeeze words and characters together (or stretch them apart). The minimum value is the absolute smallest space you allow in this process, while the maximum value is the absolute largest space allowed between words or characters. These settings are expressed in percentages.

The optimum value is the best possible value for spacing. This is the most desirable because it is the most typographically correct.

H & J specifications for the QuarkXPress document are paragraph attributes. This means that you can apply one set of values to one paragraph and another set of values elsewhere. Different paragraphs may have different needs.

NOTE

QuarkXPress allows you to control word and character spacing in several ways. These include H & Js, kerning and tracking, standard kerning tables, and customized tracking tables.

THE FLUSH ZONE

This sounds ominous! The Flush Zone option enables you to specify the area within which the last word in the last line of a justified paragraph must fall to justify. If you were to enter, for example, a value of 1″ in the field, this would mandate that the line be within 1″ of the right indent margin for justification allowance. Otherwise, the text will default to flush left.

NOTE

Justification allowance is that zone at the end of the line that allows the computer to either place more text or consider justification with no more text on the line. If justification is appropriate, the extra (non-text) space on the line is distributed, first between words, then between characters, if necessary.

MULTIPLE HYPHENATION SPECIFICATIONS

The Edit Hyphenation and Justification dialog box also gives you a choice of automatic or manual hyphenation. Check the Auto Hyphenation option and you can specify values for the smallest word to hyphenate, minimum number of character before a hyphen, and the minimum number of characters after a hyphen. Leave this option unchecked to hyphenate manually. Also, you can control how many successive hyphenated lines your copy has.

WARNING

Although H & J follows preset rules for hyphenation for English, it is sometimes incorrect. Careful proofreading is always advised.

In the same dialog box, you also have control over the *hyphenation zone*. That is, you can determine where the hyphens are to be in the line. You may want to force-justify text up to a half inch from the end of the line, if so, place that value in the Hyphenation Zone field. This gives you more control over the text within that ½″ zone, countering inappropriate automated hyphenation.

NOTE

For good typography, do not hyphenate more than two lines in succession.

THE FIND AND CHANGE OPTION

If you have followed along in the book and tried each new feature as introduced, there's very little left, at least in the type manipulation area. Here is one holdout; it is use of the Find and Change feature. Use this for text replacement (search and replace) and, as an added bonus, can also change type attributes!

NOTE

The Find and Change feature is a standard Macintosh feature in every way; in fact, Claris' MacWrite II has the same dialog box and capability. So you may be familiar with its operation from other software.

A typical word processing feature that QuarkXPress incorporates is Find/Change. Select this by choosing Edit ➤ Find/Change or by using the keyboard shortcut ⌘-F (see Figure 14.7). As you would expect, Find/Change allows you to find a string of text with the options of matching the whole word or just part and of including case sensitivity. You can use this to search for a particular word or phrase without making changes or you can take advantage of the Change to area to replace the phrase with a new one. Click on Find Next and it will search forward through the document to find the information you seek.

USING ATTRIBUTES

Click on the Ignore Attributes option, and the dialog box opens to an array of text attributes for both Find and Change (see Figure 14.8). You can search and replace not only text, but also the font, size, and style. You can search for any or all of these attributes independently. Use this to search for only 12-point text in the document and replace it with ten point text; search for bold text and replace with italic. Any combination is acceptable.

FIGURE 14.7

The Find and Change dialog box

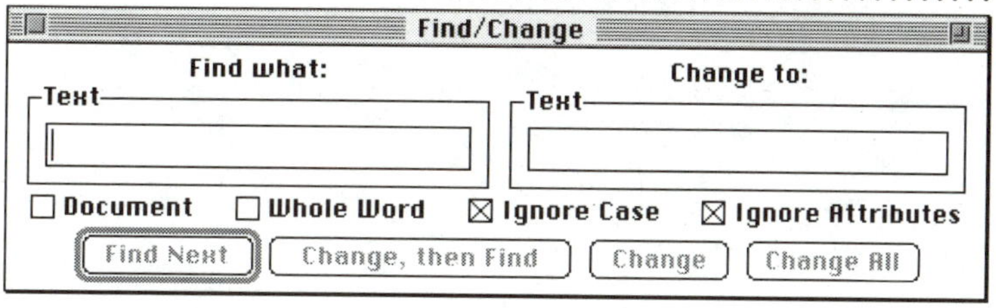

Find/Change

Find what:

Change to:

Text

Text

☐ Document   ☐ Whole Word   ☒ Ignore Case   ☒ Ignore Attributes

(Find Next)   (Change, then Find)   (Change)   (Change All)

FIGURE 14.8

The full Find/Change dialog box with attributes.

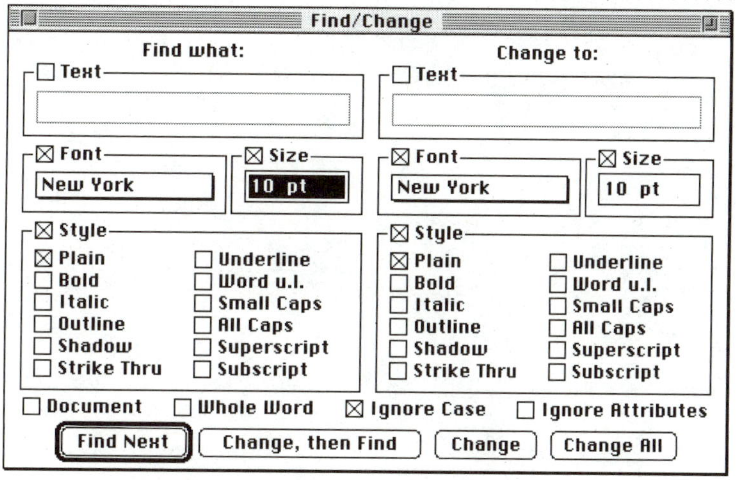

Find/Change

Find what:

Change to:

☐ Text

☐ Text

☒ Font   New York   ☒ Size   10 pt

☒ Font   New York   ☒ Size   10 pt

☒ Style
☒ Plain   ☐ Underline
☐ Bold   ☐ Word u.l.
☐ Italic   ☐ Small Caps
☐ Outline   ☐ All Caps
☐ Shadow   ☐ Superscript
☐ Strike Thru   ☐ Subscript

☒ Style
☒ Plain   ☐ Underline
☐ Bold   ☐ Word u.l.
☐ Italic   ☐ Small Caps
☐ Outline   ☐ All Caps
☐ Shadow   ☐ Superscript
☐ Strike Thru   ☐ Subscript

☐ Document   ☐ Whole Word   ☒ Ignore Case   ☐ Ignore Attributes

(Find Next)   (Change, then Find)   (Change)   (Change All)

TIP

When working on a situation involving text, use a shortcut of popular words in your keystroking. For example, in this book, the word QuarkXPress is used often. Rather than typing this repeatedly, the author used the code QX. After all input, Find/Change allowed a quick replacement of QX with QuarkXPress. That is also why you do not see the software referred to simply as Xpress!

Graphics and Pictures

V

MANIPULATING PICTURES AND GRAPHICS

To immediately resize the imported graphic   306

to fit the size of the picture box, key ⌘-Shift-F. If you don't like the result, immediately press ⌘-Z (Edit ➤ Undo)

To reposition the graphic element inside the picture box   306

use the Content tool. This tool changes the cursor to a hand icon when over a picture box. You should click on the picture with the hand icon and drag it as necessary. This does not change the size or aspect ratio of the picture; it only slides it around inside the picture box.

To rotate the picture within the box (while leaving the picture box unrotated)   309

use the Picture Angle field, in the Picture Specifications dialog box (Item ➤ Modify). You can rotate the picture in similar range as that of the box angle. Values range from −360° to 360° in 0.001° increments.

To print the picture box but not its contents   310

check the Suppress Picture Printout box, in the Picture Specifications dialog box (Item ➤ Modify). This option is a time-saver when dealing with complex graphic images, which can seem to take forever to image.

As stated earlier, QuarkXPress is centered around the concept of *items* (text boxes, picture boxes, lines, and groups). This section of the book discusses the picture box and its capabilities.

To use a graphic or picture element in QuarkXPress, you must first create a picture box in which to place that element. These picture boxes come in a variety of shapes, as do graphic elements. One common thread in all picture box shapes is that they must originate from the picture box tools on the Tools palette.

PICTURE BOXES IN QUARKXPRESS

All pictures, including charts and graphs, as well as the obvious photograph, help bring a page layout to life. They add emphasis and they communicate to the reader, often better than the surrounding text. QuarkXPress allows you to import a variety of picture formats including scans, paint, draw, and illustration graphics. After importing a graphic, you can resize, reposition, and manipulate it in several ways.

NOTE

An active picture box is one that you select then modify through Item ➤ Modify. You can only modify one box at a time (the active one).

THE TOOLS PALETTE AND PICTURE BOX CREATION TOOLS

To incorporate pictures or graphics, you must first create a picture box, since all pictures must be contained in a picture box. The way you create a picture box in QuarkXPress is to use one of the four picture box creation tools in the Tools palette.

NOTE

A polygon picture box must have at least three sides.

Each picture box tool has its own shape, because in most cases, pictures will rest within text; that is, text will flow around a picture item in some way. As these two items mix, there are considerations of *layering* and *runaround*, which are the focus of *Chapter 16*.

NOTE

To specify a corner radius for an active picture box, use the Corner Radius field of the Picture Box Specification dialog box (Item ➤ Modify). You can also use the corner radius icon in the Measurements palette.

To create any of the four picture box shapes, select the appropriate tool from the Tools palette (the rectangle, rounded corner rectangle or oval). Then click and drag (to the opposite corner) to create the picture box. Just as with text boxes, picture boxes can be resized or relocated manually or numerically. Do not be concerned with detail initially, because they can be resized and relocated at any time. The Polygon is a little different in approach. To create a polygon picture box, you have to select the tool then click on a location in the working area. Next, click on another area, completing one side of the polygon. Click on another location and you have two sides of the polygon. Continue this process for the number of polygon sides you need for your picture box, then finish up by clicking on your original point, the point where you started the polygon. There are four picture box shapes to choose from, the Rectangular Picture Box, the Rounded-corner Rectangular Picture Box, the Oval Picture Box, and the Polygon Picture Box (see Figure 15.1).

FIGURE 15.1
*You can draw any of
four picture box shapes:
a rectangle, a rounded
rectangle, an oval, or a
polygon.*

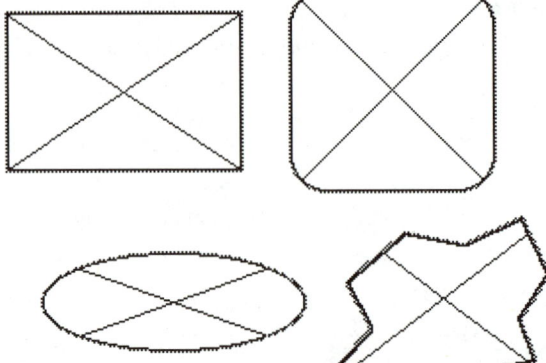

NOTE

*To draw a perfectly square or perfectly circular picture box, hold
down the Shift key as you draw or resize the graphic box.*

You can manipulate picture boxes in the following ways:

▶ Use the Item or Content tool to alter the box shape by clicking and dragging
the grab bar

▶ Move the box through click and drag of the Item tool (click on the body of
the box, not the grab bar handles)

▶ Reposition graphic or picture elements inside the box with the Content tool
(click on the element and drag, not on the grab bars)

▶ Rotate picture boxes using the Rotation tool (this works the same as with
text boxes)

▶ The Measurements palette gives information about location, size, and rotation of the box, which you can alter

▶ Select Item ➤ Modify for the Picture Box Specification dialog box and adjust
the settings to your liking

Hold down ⌘ and double-click with the Item or Content tool on an item box and the Specifications dialog box appears.

TYPES OF GRAPHICS AND FILE FORMATS

To help clarify your possibilities with QuarkXPress, it may be useful to know a little about graphics. There is a difference in file formats and the types of graphics that applications produce. A *file format* is the method or structure that the image data is recorded in. You can use the same file format for more than one kind of graphic image. The type of graphic (bitmapped or object oriented) determines quality of the picture.

TYPES OF GRAPHICS

There are two basic types of graphic images in use for the Macintosh. They are *bit-mapped* and *object oriented*. The bitmapped image is the older of the two types. It was the basis of the original Macintosh. Perhaps the easiest way to understand bitmapped is with the dot or pixel, as images appear on the computer screen. Each image consists of a series of dots or pixels used to paint the picture on the monitor. In bitmapped graphics, the dot-composed images are printed as dots on the page. Early in the desktop computer revolution, there were no laser printers and the dot-matrix printer was dominant. Bitmapped graphics print well in dot matrix, partly because the image was composed of dots. Also, people didn't expect terrific quality. Today, more sophisticated technology is used and bitmapped graphics show excellent dots. The problem is, now people have certain standards of quality and they don't want the dots. They want perfect images from the printer.

The object oriented graphic is higher quality, both onscreen and in print, because it draws from a series of mathematical algorithms composing the look of the image. When the graphic is resized, the algorithms recalculate the best look of the image. The output is near perfect, no "jaggies", especially on imagesetter output.

MANIPULATING
PICTURES AND GRAPHICS
. . . .

CH. 15

IMPORTING VARIOUS PICTURE FILE FORMATS

In QuarkXPress, you create a picture box, then you import a picture or graphic element from another file. This file is usually generated from another application outside QuarkXPress. You can use files from a variety of software types, including draw, paint, illustration, and scanned images. File formats compatible with QuarkXPress picture boxes include the following:

Bitmapped (PAINT)

TIFF and RIFF line art

TIFF and RIFF grayscale

TIFF color

PICT

Black-and-white Encapsulated PostScript (EPS)

Color EPS

Let's look at each of these in detail.

THE BITMAPPED (PAINT) FILE FORMAT

Paint programs create bitmapped images made of dots or screen pixels. These images are unique in that resized images appear to be larger bits, unlike other file formats in which the image as a whole enlarges. Bitmapped images are simply a collection of dots that compose the graphic image. These dots are pixels (picture elements) on your screen. Bitmapped paint images on the Mac are always at a resolution of 72 dots per inch, and cannot exceed an $8'' \times 10''$ page. They are the lowest resolution image for printing purposes. Programs such as MacPaint and SuperPaint create bitmapped images.

TIFF IMAGES

A popular file format for Mac and Non-Macintosh computers is *Tagged Image File Format* (TIFF). Like paint files, TIFF images are bitmapped, but they are resizable. They can be any size and have any resolution. Typically, scanned images are stored as TIFF images. TIFF images are commonly black-and-white or grayscale, but a few programs support color TIFF images.

NOTE

You can convert pictures when importing through keyboard commands. Hold down ⌘ while importing a TIFF grayscale to convert it to TIFF Line Art. To convert TIFF line art to TIFF grayscale, hold down the Option key during the import. Hold down ⌘ and import to convert TIFF Color to TIFF grayscale.

TIFF formats are a standard on many different computer platforms, but not all TIFF images produced on these different platforms are alike. IBM TIFF images differ slightly from Mac TIFF files, due to the different data storage conventions used by each computer; these must be converted when moving from one platform to another. Several programs that generate TIFF images include a conversion utility, which translates IBM to Mac and vice versa, a growing concern in cross-platform production.

TIFF images can be quite large. It is common, for example, for a full screen image in TIFF to take up nearly 900K on disk. It may be impractical to include in your document at that size. Therefore, QuarkXPress stores and displays TIFF images in the lower resolution PICT format. The higher resolution TIFF image must be accessible to QuarkXPress. The original TIFF file links with a lower resolution image in the document. To send documents with TIFF images to a service bureau, you must also include the original high-resolution TIFF file for the imagesetter. If you fail to do this, you will get a bitmapped image (lower resolution) of the picture.

THE RASTER IMAGE FILE FORMAT

Similar to TIFF, the *Raster Image File Format* (RIFF) is a high-resolution image format designed for quality output. TIFF and RIFF images print well on imagesetters, which use photographic paper and high-quality laser exposure, yielding "continuous" tones at nearly 3000 dpi. TIFF is more prevalent on the Mac than RIFF.

NOTE

Typically, TIFF and RIFF representations reproduce on the screen at 36 dots per inch (dpi). You can increase the screen resolution of the picture to 72 dpi by holding down the Shift key as you import the graphic.

PICT GRAPHICS

Object oriented graphics created by drawing or drafting programs store as *PICT* (not an acronym) files. Programs that generate the PICT format include computer aided drafting (CAD) and drawing programs such as MacDraw and Canvas. Some scanning programs also give the option of saving in PICT. PICT graphics show well on the newer Macintosh monitors.

Mathematical algorithms define the object oriented graphic. This helps define crisp, smooth lines with quality and precision. PICT graphics are among the best for line artwork. However, they are lower resolution and not suitable for demanding grayscale or color work.

ENCAPSULATED POSTSCRIPT GRAPHICS

PostScript files with a screen preview are *Encapsulated PostScript* (EPS) files. This is the higher level drawing file format used by such programs as Illustrator and Freehand. QuarkXPress also creates EPS files through File ➤ Save Page as EPS.

The EPS format, like TIFF, is equally popular in the Mac and IBM communities. In fact, the two platforms can exchange EPS files without conversion.

EPS files tend to be large. Therefore, a lower resolution representation of the image displays while high resolution data resides in an external file for output. EPS file names are shown in the QuarkXPress Picture Usage dialog box (Utilities ➤ Picture Usage).

OTHER FILE FORMATS

As cross-platform computer practices grow in various industries, you can expect to see new file formats. There are two ways to anticipate this probability. First, you should communicate with your clients and users of the "other" computer platform to see whether their software can store in a compatible form. If it cannot, then bring data in by disk, modem, network, etc. The second method is to find a translation program. These programs enable you to translate from one foreign file format to a more familiar one. In most cases, a file format can convert to another usable format. At times it may take a couple of translations, but you will prevail.

PICTURE MANIPULATION IN QUARKXPRESS

If you take the word "picture" to include all graphic images, QuarkXPress has a wide variety of methods for importing, storing, manipulating, and printing pictures. The previous section presented graphic descriptions; now you can bring them into play!

NOTE

Many people working with QuarkXPress speak of it with words like "having fun." Perhaps this is because it gives you the freedom to imagine better graphic solutions. It is a philosophical point, but imagination is an extension of the Macintosh philosophy.

IMPORTING PICTURES

As noted earlier, you can import pictures from a variety of file formats. To do this you must perform the following steps:

1. Make sure there is a graphic file available to import. It can be on file on a floppy disk, on your hard drive, on a network connection, or whatever, but it must be accessible.

2. Create a picture box with one of the four picture box creation tools from the Tools palette. The size and location of the box is not critical yet, since you can relocate or resize later.

3. Using the Content tool, click on the new picture box to select it. You can only import graphics when the Content tool is active and the picture box is selected (see Figure 15.2).

FIGURE 15.2
*Edit or import the pic-
ture box contents by
using the Content tool.*

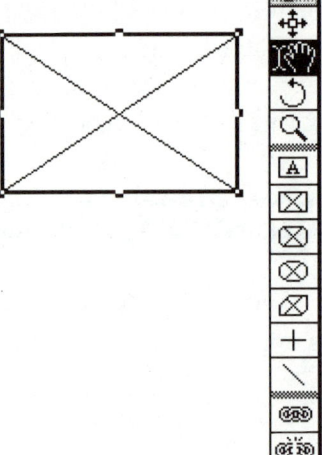

4. Select File ➤ Get Picture or simply use the keyboard equivalent ⌘-E. This
   brings you to a dialog box where you can choose the file to import (see Figure 15.3)

FIGURE 15.3
*The Get Picture dialog
box allows you to select
a picture file and see a
preview before import-
ing it.*

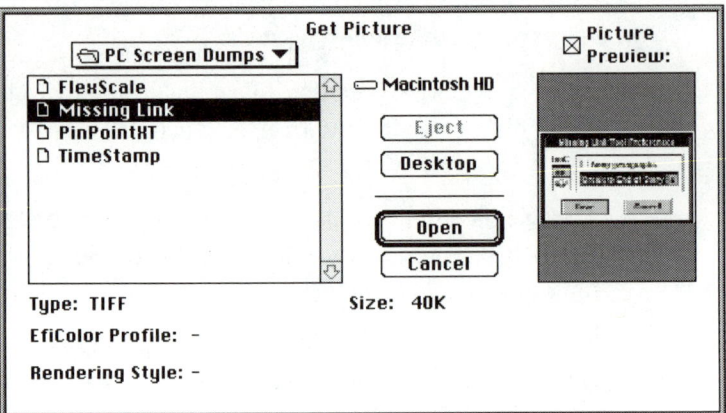

5. Search through the dialog box to locate the graphic file to import. Clicking on Preview presents a rough representation of the image.

6. Press Return or Enter or click on Open to import.

As your image imports there is a good chance that it isn't quite what you expected. Perhaps the screen image has low-resolution quality. That does not necessarily relate to print quality. Remember, there may be a linked high-resolution image tagged to that graphic box for printer purposes.

Another observation: The image and picture box have no apparent correlation in size or ratio. You may import a large picture into a small picture box, or a square picture into a rectangular box. Remember, when you created the picture box, its initial size and location weren't important. The size and positioning of both the picture and the picture box can be controlled independently of each other.

NOTE

If your picture box appears empty after import it probably means that a blank area of the graphic falls on the window area of your picture box. Try using ⌘-Shift-M to center the image in the middle of the picture box. This will start your manipulation of the graphic to fit it in the picture box.

Another situation that may arise is that of the image nearly or even completely missing the box "window." The fix for this is a simple adjustment of moving or resizing.

MODIFYING THE IMPORTED GRAPHIC AND PICTURE BOX

Once the image imports to the picture box, you can make modifications. Which one you change first depends on your layout and the graphic image. Here, you can take the approach of reshaping the box first, as the examples shown are too small for the existing picture box.

NOTE

*To immediately resize the imported graphic to fit the size of the
picture box, key ⌘-Shift-F. If you don't like the result, immediately
press ⌘-Z (Edit ▶ Undo).*

Figure 15.4 demonstrates how to enlarge the picture box manually. Use either the
Content tool or the Item tool to enlarge the box. Resizing the box will not distort
the image itself.

Other picture box controls are in the Measurements palette and the Picture Box
Specifications dialog box (discussed later in this chapter).

NOTE

*To reposition the graphic element inside the picture box, use the
Content tool. This tool changes the cursor to a hand icon when
over a picture box. You should click on the picture with the hand
icon and drag it as necessary. This does not change the size or
aspect ratio of the picture; it only slides it around inside the
picture box.*

Manual resizing of the picture box allows you a quick look at the box in relationship to the graphic it holds. As you can see in Figure 15.5, the box is much larger
than the graphic. The picture box will have to be resized, and perhaps the graphic
should also be resized. To adjust size of the box, again, drag grab bars until the
picture is "framed" to your satisfaction. To adjust the size of the graphic image,
use the Picture Box Specification dialog box.

FIGURE 15.4

*You can manually ex-
tend the picture box by
dragging one of the grab
bars.*

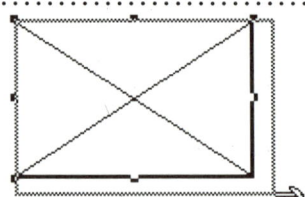

FIGURE 15.5

*After enlarging the pic-
ture box, you can view
the entire graphic
image.*

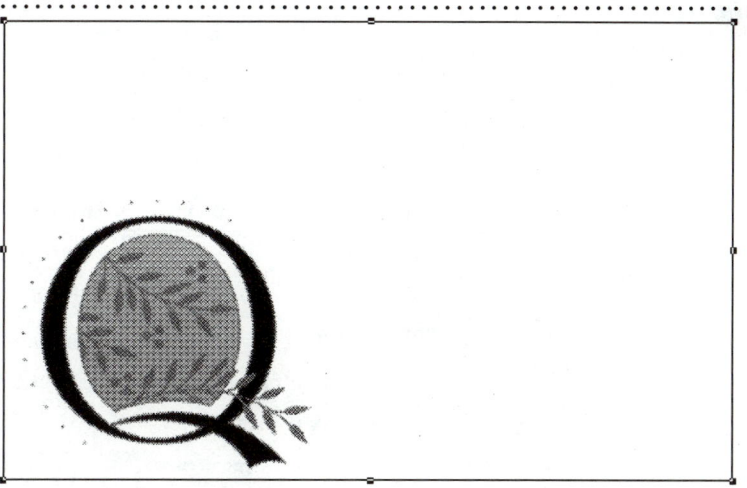

THE PICTURE BOX SPECIFICATIONS DIALOG BOX

Select the picture box and choose Item ➤ Modify for the Picture Box Specifications dialog box (see Figure 15.6). This dialog box is the most extensive area for
manipulating the picture box numerically. You could also use the Measurements
palette, but it is not as inclusive for all picture box values.

NOTE

*Oval and Polygon Picture boxes do not have the Corner Radius
field showing in the Picture Box Specifications dialog box.*

The first six fields on the left in the Picture Box Specifications dialog box have similar value areas to that of the Measurements palette. They tell the location (origin
down and origin across of the box), width and height, box angle, box skew, and
corner radius (if applicable). Changing any of these values will affect the picture
box accordingly.

Box Angle (rotation) values range from −360° to 360° in 0.001° increments. Corner Radius values range from 0″ to 2″. The Corner Radius field is not available for
oval or polygon boxes.

FIGURE 15.6

*The Picture Box Specifi-
cations dialog box*

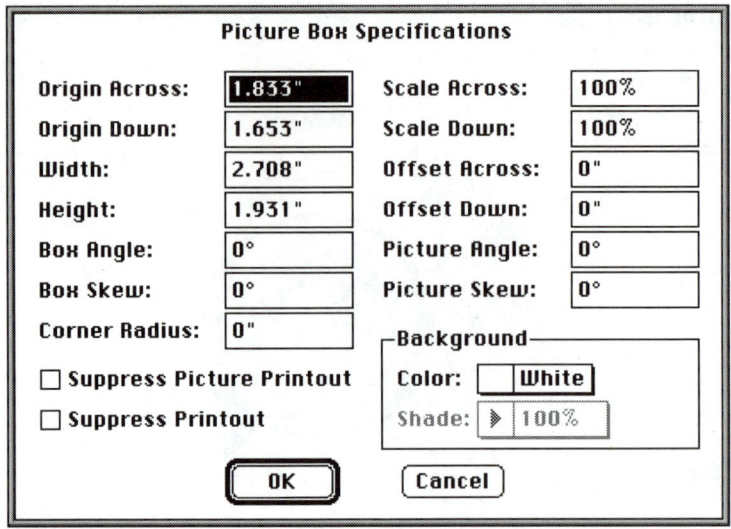

Picture Box Specifications

Origin Across:	1.833"	Scale Across:	100%
Origin Down:	1.653"	Scale Down:	100%
Width:	2.708"	Offset Across:	0"
Height:	1.931"	Offset Down:	0"
Box Angle:	0°	Picture Angle:	0°
Box Skew:	0°	Picture Skew:	0°
Corner Radius:	0"		

☐ Suppress Picture Printout

☐ Suppress Printout

Background
Color: White
Shade: ▶ 100%

[OK]   [Cancel]

NOTE

*Keeping the aspect ratio constant means that when the width of an
item changes in size, its length changes by the same percentage.
For example, if a 2" by 3" box were reduced 50%, both the width
and height would be reduced by 50%, leaving you with a 1" by
$1^1/_2$" box.*

In the second column of the Picture Box Specifications dialog box, you have scaling values. Scale Across modifies the graphic in a horizontal scale. Scale Down
modifies the graphic in a vertical field. Scale values for either field range from
10% to 1000% in 0.1% increments. You can maintain the same *aspect ratio* by
placing equal values in the Scale Across and Scale Down fields.

NOTE

Offset values are relative to the position of the box origin. They do not necessarily reflect measurements from the ruler or relative document location.

To numerically reposition the picture within the active picture box, use the Offset Across and Offset Down fields. A positive value in the Offset Across field moves the picture to the right; a negative value moves it to the left. In the Offset Down field, a positive value moves the picture down, while a negative value moves it up.

To rotate the picture within the box (while leaving the picture box unrotated), use the Picture Angle field. Values range from −360° to 360° in 0.001° increments.

You can slant the picture within the picture box by entering values within the Picture Skew field. Values for skew range from 75° to −75° in 0.001° increments. Positive values slant to the right and negative values slant the picture left (see Figure 15.7).

The Background option of the Picture Box Specifications dialog box enables you to apply color and shade to the picture box. Even if the picture is not in color, you can add background color through this area of the dialog box. Colors listed in the

FIGURE 15.7

These photos illustrate the various picture box manipulation techniques at work.

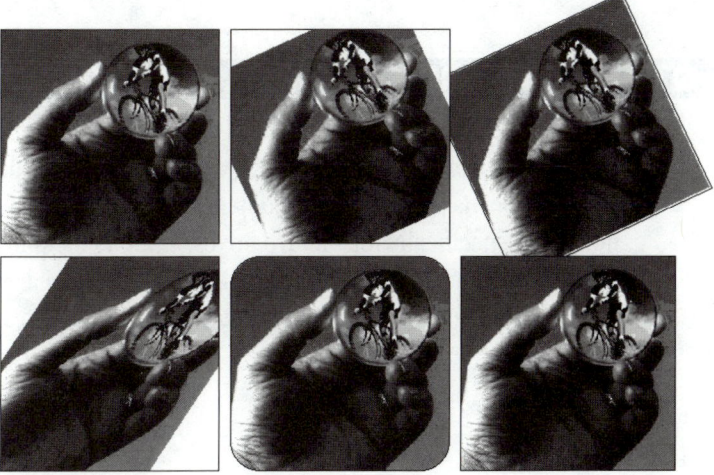

pop-up menu include those on the document's system palette. Add or edit using Edit ➤ Colors . (See *Chapter 17* for full details in this area.) Shade modification values range from 0% to 100% in 0.1% increments. You can choose from a pop-up menu or just type in the value.

To prevent an active picture box and its contents from printing, check the Suppress Printout option. To print the picture box but not its contents, check the Suppress Picture Printout box. These two options are time-savers when dealing with complex graphic images, which can seem to take forever to print.

NOTE

It is important to keep in mind that when the Item tool is selected, Cut, Copy and Paste, Past, Clear, and Delete all work on both the item and its contents. When the Content tool is selected, these commands work on the contents of the box alone.

Use the Item tool and Cut (Edit ➤ Cut) to remove an active picture box and its contents. Cut will place the removed item and its contents on the Clipboard. The Copy option, places a duplicate of the selected item and its contents on the Clipboard. Paste places a copy of the Clipboard's contents in the center of the current screen. Activate the picture box item with the Item tool, and the Clear option removes the item with its contents. Use the Content tool, and Clear removes only the contents of the item, leaving the picture box itself.

OTHER PICTURE CONTROL TECHNIQUES

Along with the manipulation methods mentioned, there are a few remaining techniques accessed from menus. These include the use of the Style menu items. When a picture box is active and the Content tool is selected, the Style menu takes on a new look, specifically for picture boxes. Options include addition of color and shade to the image; the ability to make a picture appear negative; contrast variables and screen choices for printing. *Chapters 17* and *18* cover these features in detail.

Combining Text and Graphics

- Text runaround options
- Picture Box item and other item runaround options
- Layers

To accomplish the best looking text item runaround   322

you have to employ a little *TLC*. You can provide this in a number of ways, including adjusting the runaround outset, the photo box size, etc.

To set runaround the easiest way for picture box items   323

use the Auto Image runaround mode. Auto Image is a runaround mode that is designed for picture box items. It cannot be applied to text box items. The idea behind Auto Image is that you can have QuarkXPress automatically determine where the type will run around your graphic.

To have more precise control over the runaround of text   324

select the Manual Image runaround mode.

There are two major areas of consideration when combining text and graphics: *runarounds* and *layering*. Runarounds refer to the effects you can get in QuarkXPress when you place an item (typically a picture items) in the middle of text. Layering involves organizing multiple items on top of one another on the document page. Each item takes up a new layer, like a tissue overlay over a mechanical layout. Each time an item is resized, moved, or changed in any way, it goes to the top of the stack. Layering can be somewhat frustrating for the beginner and can cause problems for anyone if not handled properly.

RUNAROUND TEXT AND GRAPHICS

QuarkXPress treats a *runaround*, or *text wrap*, as the way in which text flows with respect to items and pictures placed in front of the text. When you choose to run text around a picture there are variations to consider. You can elect to run text around the picture box perimeter or the frame; you may want to run text around the picture itself. In any event, there is an assortment of runaround variables that must be set. Variables can be selected for any item: picture box, text box, line, or group. The manner in which you combine these runaround variables determine your results.

NOTE

Think of Item mode with runarounds as being similar to oil and water. Pour oil in water and the water makes room for the oil; it does not mix with it. In a similar way, when you place a text or picture box over another text box, the text moves away, like water from the oil.

Usually you run text around either picture or text boxes. It is rare that you run text around lines or grouped items, although certain graphic designs may require it. QuarkXPress offers a variety of runaround techniques, including the categories of None, Item, Auto Image, and Manual Image. You'll find these options in the Runaround dialog box for an active item (Item ➤ Runaround), which is where you control most of the parameters of runarounds (see Figure 16.1).

TEXT BOX ITEMS WITH RUNAROUND MODE: ITEM

Item mode is the default runaround setting (see Figure 16.2). This option forces the text to wrap around the graphic object by a prescribed distance on all sides. If two text box items are involved, the text of one item box runs around the text of the newer text box item. As you create a text box, it is placed on the top layer of other elements in your design. Previous text may wrap around this new text element as if it were a picture box. The default offset value in the Item mode is 1 point on each side.

FIGURE 16.1

The Runaround dialog box for an active item

Runaround Specifications

Mode: | Item |

Top: | 1 pt | ☐ Invert

Left: | 1 pt |

Bottom: | 1 pt | (OK)

Right: | 1 pt | (Cancel)

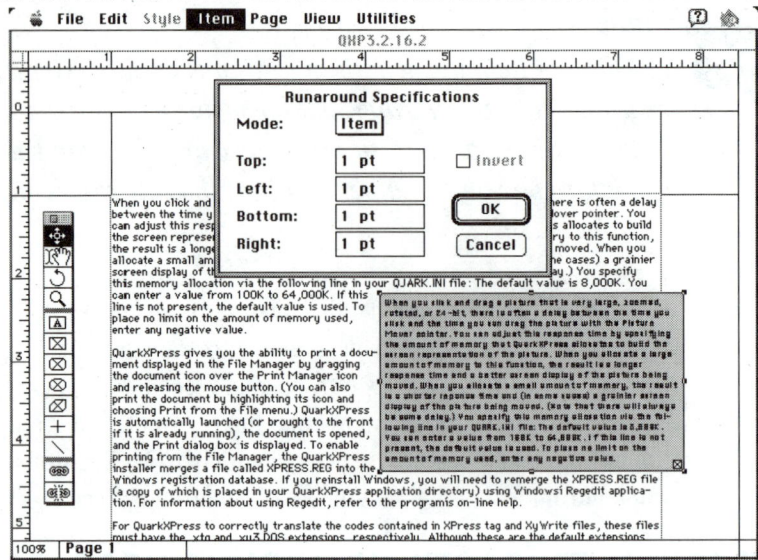

FIGURE 16.2

The smaller text box is placed on the larger. The smaller box is active and is in Item runaround mode.

NOTE

With text boxes, you have only the Item and None modes for runaround. With picture boxes, though, you can select from all four runaround options.

Here, a small text box is positioned over another text box. The active text box is shaded, with reduced type. Notice that the text in the larger box has moved out of the way to make room for the smaller one.

This is not perfect, however. The text on the left side of the big box is too close to the shaded box. The inset values are the same on all sides (one point), but there appears to be much less space on the left side. This results from additional space on the top and bottom from the line spacing of the large box. If QuarkXPress cannot entirely fit a line next to the runaround box, it moves the line somewhere else, leaving white space. This gives the appearance of leaving more space than was allocated. One way to cure this problem is to place more space on the left runaround side (see Figure 16.3). Note that the left value is the only one changed, but it is a more pleasing layout of two runaround items.

FIGURE 16.3

Placing more offset space on the side will give a pleasing runaround. Other manipulations help also, such as changed text inset values and justified alignment in this example.

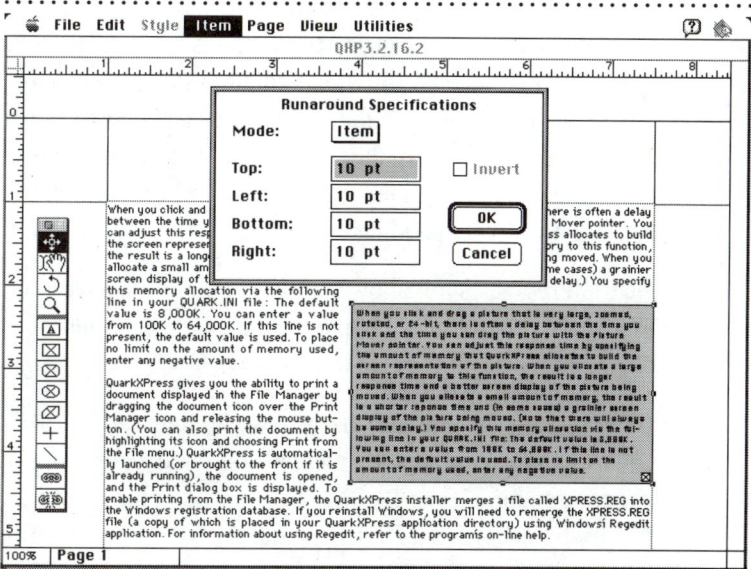

FIGURE 16.4

The three-sided runaround for single columns of type

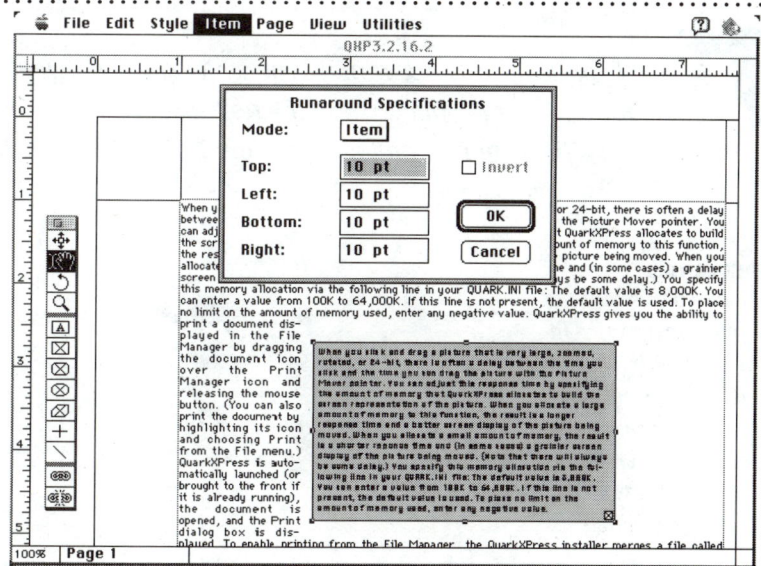

One runaround problem for many new users of QuarkXPress is that of the three-sided runaround (see Figure 16.4). This is not a glitch in the runaround; it was planned! Think about it: In a one-column layout, would you really want type broken up with a box item in the middle? No! The best way to handle four-sided runarounds is to have multiple columns, as discussed later in this chapter. The blank area in a three-sided runaround may be to the left or to the right of the runaround area, depending to how close your runaround item is to a given margin.

QuarkXPress does not allow you to design poor typographic conditions by using a four-sided runaround for single columns of text. When asked whether they would "fix" this condition they answered *no!*

Incorporating text and picture boxes with Item mode works much like text on text runarounds, except that the picture doesn't actually move out of the way; it is simply covered up. Figure 16.5 shows a text box placed over a picture box. The picture box contains a PICT item and does not displace. You should expect this result for any format of picture item.

TIP

If you want to place a non-type white space between the text and the text box perimeter, use the text inset field in the Type Specification Box dialog box (Item ➤ Modify or ⌘-M).

FIGURE 16.5
Picture boxes running around text work a little differently. The picture does not displace to make room for the text; rather, the text box just covers up a portion of the figure.

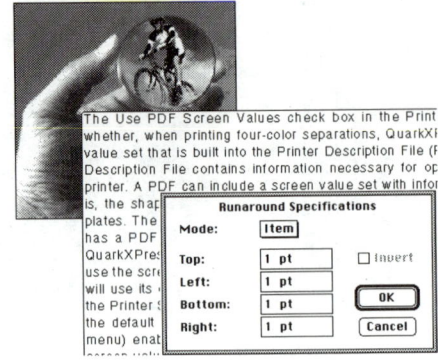

Notice that in Figure 16.5, the runaround values are 10 points on all sides. One problem you may encounter with runaround value is when a text box positions over a photograph, such as in the example. The picture does not break apart for runaround. Therefore, the runaround values chosen, such as in the example, are of little significance.

TEXT BOX ITEMS WITH RUNAROUND MODE: NONE

Perhaps the best way to understand the None runaround mode is to visualize the type (or graphic) being on clear acetate. The image appears with a transparent background, allowing you to see other "layers" or items beneath it. This can get quite confusing, if you see several layers at once.

Figure 16.6 demonstrates what happens to the small, shaded text box when it is placed on another text box and the runaround mode is changed to None. At first there doesn't appear to be much difference from previous examples, unless you had to read the larger box text!

FIGURE 16.6

When the runaround mode for the small, shaded text box is set to None, the larger text box becomes impossible to read, since the text continues "behind" the smaller runaround box.

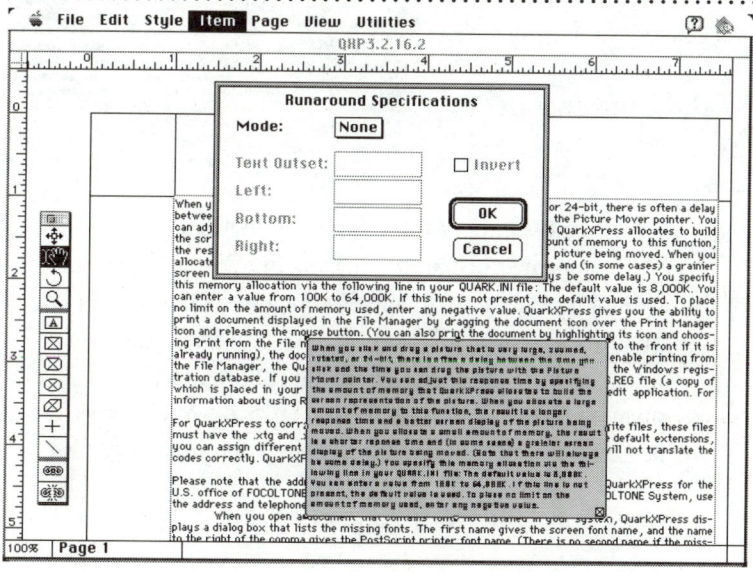

Because the example in Figure 16.6 is shaded, you cannot see the two layers simultaneously. Shading acts as an opaque coloring on the item. No shading or coloration would render the item background as transparent.

To demonstrate this, there is a third, non-shaded text box in Figure 16.7. This new text box is simply a headline reading *All Text Runarounds set to None…3 Layers are shown!* It appears to be transparent; you can see through the background to the type behind it. The text in the other two boxes does not move away from the new item, because it is set to None runaround mode. This can be either good or bad for your layout.

FIGURE 16.7

The third text box is set to the None runaround mode. You can see both text boxes "beneath" it.

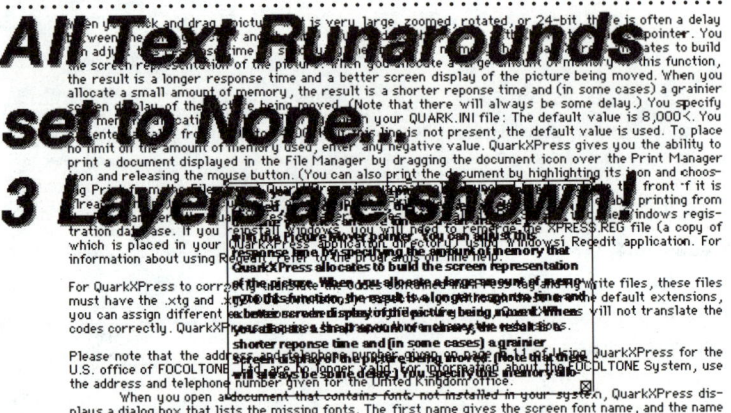

Figure 16.8 shows how the None mode works for several items. The unshaded text boxes appear transparent. The shaded box still appears to be opaque, and the text behind it is still unreadable. The picture is the bottom layer of this stack. Since the picture consists of all pixels in a PICT graphic, there is no background to have transparent. Therefore, setting the runaround to None for the graphic element is meaningless. If placed on the top layer it would completely cover the text beneath it. Layering can get to be a problem when working on a complex layout.

FIGURE 16.8

FIGURE 16.8

Using the None runaround mode with text over text items and over picture box items can lead to fairly complicated (and not always aesthetically pleasing!) layouts.

PICTURE BOX ITEMS SET TO RUNAROUND MODE: ITEM

In a manner similar to text boxes, picture boxes with the runaround mode set to Item (the default) disperse text "behind" them. In Figure 16.9, the example has a photo inside a picture box, placed in a two-column layout. The corners are rounded to demonstrate slight type wraps near the corners. Given that this is not a perfect square, a new field shows in the Runaround Specifications dialog box: *Text Outset*. This setting generally takes care of any odd shaped item box and treats all sides equally. Rounding the corners on this rectangular box makes it similar (at least to QuarkXPress) to an oval picture box.

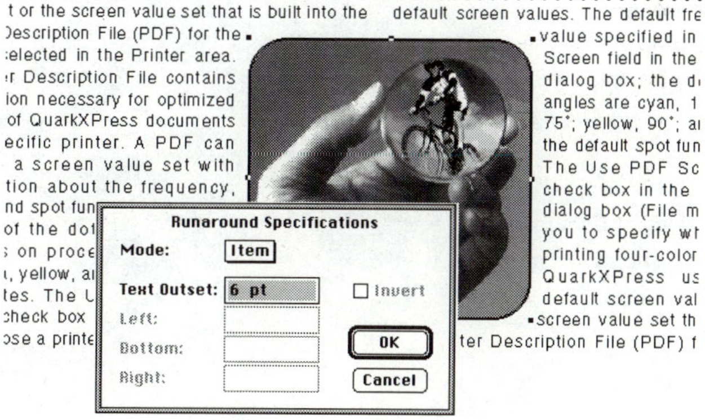

FIGURE 16.9

A graphic with the runaround mode set to Item is placed over two columns of type.

Runaround Specifications

Mode: Item

Text Outset: 6 pt   ☐ Invert

Left:

Bottom: [OK]

Right: [Cancel]

As you can see, with a text outset value of 10 points, there is a noticeable white border around the graphic restricting text flow. This is not good typography because some type lines need adjustment, some *TLC*. You can provide this in a number of ways, including adjusting the runaround outset, the photo box size, etc.

Notice too, that this is a two-column layout and the runaround appears to take place on all sides. The runaround is still a three-sided layout, but with two-columns it gives you the illusion of four sides. The type is readable in a two-column layout where it would not have been in a single column with similar runaround.

PICTURE BOX ITEMS SET TO RUNAROUND MODE: NONE

What do you think happens when you place a picture over text items and have the picture box set to None runaround mode? Right, you can't read the text. Maybe this is a problem, maybe not. Depends on the client, right?

In theory, placing a picture box (with Runaround: None) over a text box will simply make the picture background transparent. However, if you are truly working with a photograph, as in Figure 16.10, with no "background," None has no effect.

What if you were using a different graphic, a non-photo type? The results may be a bit different. Try it! What should happen when you place runaround to None is that the graphic background appears transparent. The graphic foreground is shown and appears as if on the top layer, over previous elements on the document page.

FIGURE 16.10

Placing a bitmapped graphic in a picture box with runaround mode set to None covers the text, because in a photo, there is no background that can be set to "transparent."

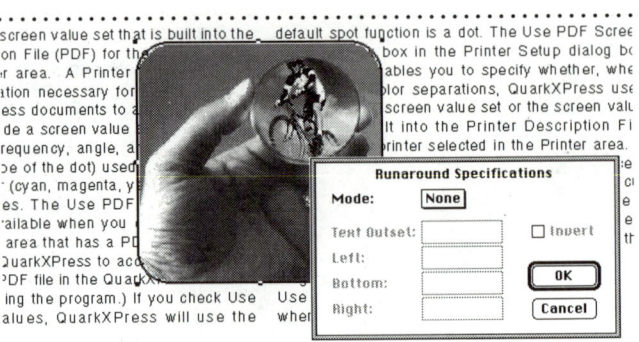

PICTURE BOX ITEMS SET TO RUNAROUND MODE: AUTO IMAGE

Auto Image is a runaround mode that is designed for picture box items. It cannot be applied to text box items. The idea behind Auto Image is that you can have QuarkXPress automatically determine where the type will run around your graphic. Simply place the runaround mode on Auto Image, set the text outset, and you're done! The only problem is that it doesn't do much for photographs. See Figure 16.11 for results in placing a photograph in a picture box set to Auto Image.

NOTE

In Item mode, the runaround goes around the item's box. In Auto Image or Manual Image mode, the runaround goes around the graphic, not the box. That is why Auto Image and Manual Image are available for picture boxes and not text boxes.

Auto Image is a bit improved in Figure 16.12. See how the text delicately wraps around the graphic image, not just the perimeter picture box. Okay, it doesn't look that great! A little *TLC* again? In the event that you have a picture box spread between two columns and you want the text to wrap tightly around it, change the alignment to *Justified* as shown in the example.

FIGURE 16.11

Auto image works for some graphics, but is not effective for photographs, such as in this example.

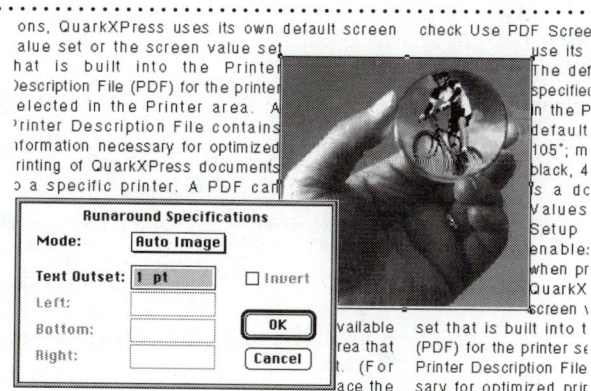

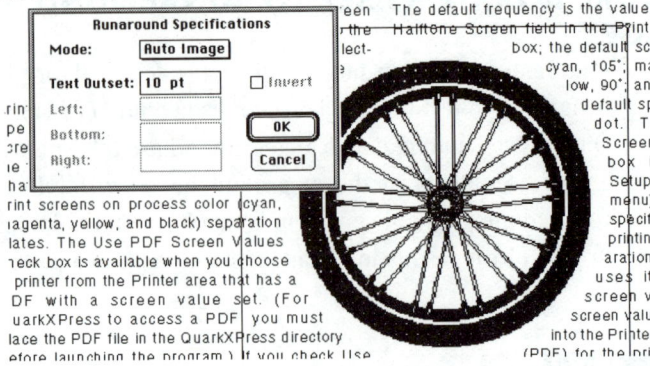

FIGURE 16.12
*Use of a picture box
item (non-photo) with
Auto Image mode of
runaround. Notice how
the text wraps around
the image itself rather
than the picture box
perimeter.*

PICTURE BOX ITEMS SET TO RUNAROUND MODE: MANUAL IMAGE

If you want something done right, you have to do it yourself. To have total control over your type, or at least as much as a computer allows, select the Manual Image runaround mode. This allows you to specify where the text will wrap around your graphic element. Figure 16.13 shows the example getting closer to acceptable, but not quite there yet!

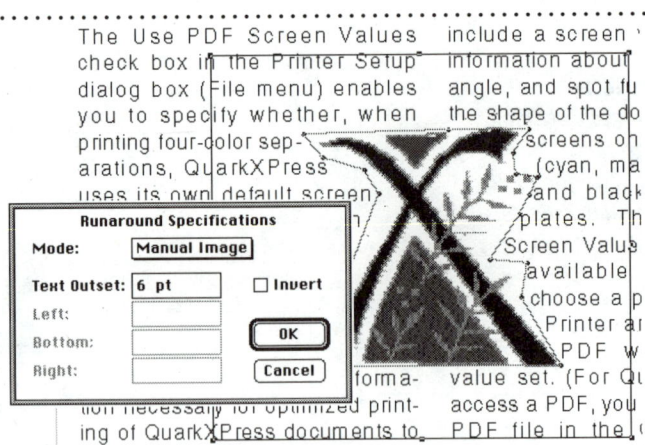

FIGURE 16.13
*To have more precise
control over the
runaround of text,
select the Manual
Image mode.*

A close-up view of Manual Image runaround mode shows that it places dozens of tiny grab handles around the graphic image or images within your picture box (see Figure 16.14). The type projects through the boundary of the picture box and is stopped by the new manual boundary around the picture (not the box). You can relocate these grab handles through click-and-drag. If no grab handles are available where you want one, hold down ⌘ and click on the outline; a new grab handle will appear, which you can relocate. **To** delete an unwanted grab handle, position the cursor over it, hold down ⌘, and click the mouse button.

TIP

Hold down the spacebar, and QuarkXPress will refrain from refreshing the screen while you manipulate grab handles. This can save a lot of waiting time.

INVERTING TEXT, AGAIN!

You were briefly introduced to the idea of inverting text earlier in the book. The concept is not well liked by many QuarkXPress users. Maybe because it is rather difficult to use effectively, or maybe it is rejected because type often looks bad when inverted.

FIGURE 16.14

A close-up of Manual Image runaround mode—use the grab handles for fine control on text runaround.

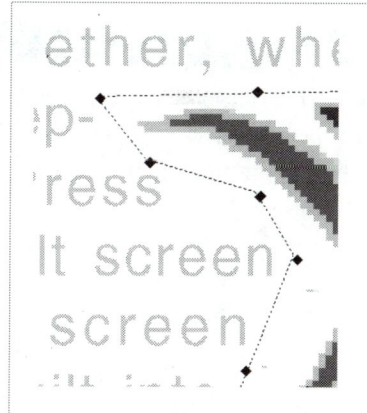

Since we are discussing runarounds, here is another quick look at inverting text to fill a graphic shape. Follow these steps:

1. Create a filled column of text, or better, two columns of text. The Invert appearance will look better if you make the text alignment *Justified* (Style ➤ Alignment ➤ Justified).

2. Create a picture box and import a graphic into it. Bring it in from some other source such as the Scrapbook, or import from a stored file.

3. Position and resize the picture box and graphic to where you want the inverted text to reside.

4. To have the text fill the shape of your graphic just imported, click on the picture box to make it active.

5. Select the Manual Runaround (Item ➤ Runaround).

6. Check the Invert option in the Runaround dialog box.

7. Click on OK, and voila! Your type takes the shape of the graphic. Unfortunately you can't see it because the graphic is blocking your view.

8. Click on the graphic with the Content tool and its picture box to activate it.

9. Press the Delete key to remove the graphic and see your text in its shape. The graphic should disappear, leaving you with a lot of type that may be difficult to read, in whatever shape your graphic was (see Figure 16.15). Enjoy!

LAYERING

As promised at the outset of this chapter, you were to have both runarounds and layering. For the most part, layering was introduced subtly through out the chapter; you really cannot function well in runarounds without it.

FIGURE 16.15

Inverting text to fill a graphic shape.

The Use PDF Screen Values check box in the Printer Setup dialog box (File menu) enables you to specify whether, when printing four-color separations, QuarkXPress uses its own default screen value set or the screen value set that is built into the Printer Description File (PDF) for the printer selected in the Printer area. A Printer Description File contains information necessary for optimized printing of QuarkXPress documents to a specific printer. A PDF can include a screen value set with information about the frequency, angle, and spot function (that is, the shape of the dot) used to print screens on process color (cyan, magenta, yellow, and black) separation plates. The Use PDF Screen Values check box is available when you choose a printer from the Printer area that has a PDF with a screen value set. (For QuarkXPress to access a PDF, you must place the PDF file in the QuarkXPress directory before launching the program.) If you

check Use PDF Screen Values, QuarkXPress will use the screen value set in the selected printer's PDF. If you do not check Use PDF Screen Values, QuarkXPress will use its own default screen values. The default frequency is the value specified in the Halftone Screen field in the Printer Setup dialog box; the default screen angles are cyan, 105°; magenta, 75°; yellow, 90°; and black, 45°; the default spot function is a dot. The Use PDF Screen Values check box in the Printer Setup dialog box (File menu) enables you to specify whether, when printing four-color separations, QuarkXPress uses its own default screen value set or the screen value set that is built into the Printer Description File (PDF) for the printer selected in the Printer area. A Printer Description File contains information necessary for optimized printing of QuarkXPress documents to a specific printer. A PDF can include a screen value

TIP

To select a particular layer, click on it while pressing the ⌘-Shift-Option keys. This allows you to jump systematically through each layer.

As items rest on the same geometric space in the layout, they take up layers. Each item created on the layout adds a layer. If Runaround is set to Item, the item is opaque and elements beneath it move out of the way. If on different layers, opaque objects block the view of items "beneath" them. One way to deal with this is to keep sending the item on the top layer to the back. The Item ➤ Send to Back and ➤ Bring to Front options help you relocate items on their respective layers.

As you have seen from the previous examples in this chapter, layering can affect the quality of your layout. It becomes even more important as you incorporate runarounds.

Color Concepts

17

In the world of color there are a few definitions that try to qualify or quantify the mysterious. Although experts use these terms, when all is said and done, color is left to the consumer. In the business of printing and publication, that consumer is often the client. You may have studied color as presented by historical experts—Maxwell, Munsell, or others who mapped out the strategy of color—but who is really the expert in print production? That's right, it is the client. Remember as you see new gadgets and techniques, color is not always the same, on all equipment, or to all people.

NOTE

Color will appear different on the monitor, on a proof, and on the final print. Don't be surprised if you design something in color and the print is different from what you expected.

THE MAKEUP OF COLOR

There are several historical figures and systems that artists and designers study to gain an understanding of color. Regardless of the system, there seems to be a trend in the vocabulary they use in describing the color system. Granted, these descriptions follow a variety of names, but they all seem to boil down to four areas. These color definitions include: *hue*, the qualitative value or richness of the color; *saturation*, the purity of the color; *chroma*, a relationship of color to levels of gray; and *brightness*, the light amount that is transmitted through a transparent color or reflected from an opaque color.

NOTE

Other names for hue include tone, tint, or tonality. Chroma may be called value or lightness.

Color comes in a variety of forms, including transmitted or reflected, additive, and subtractive. The problem you have in electronic prepress is that there is no international standard for color. Also, you have a variety of mechanisms interpreting color. These include color scanners, still video cameras, your monitor, the software application, your color printer or proofing system, imagesetters, and, of course, the printing press. Also, keep in mind that the biggest variable in color is the person operating the piece of equipment. In this business, it seems that no two people judge color alike, and if they do, their opinion differs from that of the client!

WARNING

Color means different things to different people. To avoid surprises, talk to your print sales representative before getting involved in color prepress work.

In the print production cycle there are the following variables that may affect color rendition:

- Incorrect screen tint values

- Register

- Wrong process color inks

- Press dot gain

- Pressmanship

- Paper color

- Run sequence

- Plate quality

- Press color control

- Color viewing conditions
- Press layout
- Condition of equipment

THE COLOR MODELS OF QUARKXPRESS

This chapter isn't going to be a "magic bullet" for your color problems, QuarkXPress has many practical color applications. QuarkXPress 3.2 currently supports nine color models in base form, (XTensions may add to these models). These color systems are Pantone, Pantone Process, Pantone ProSim, Pantone Uncoated, FocolTone, TruMatch, HSB, RGB, and CMYK.

PANTONE COLORS

Colors used on only a single item, area, or specific parts of the page, as opposed to throughout the page layout, are called *spot colors*. These are used to add emphasis or impact to your design without the huge expense of four-color printing. For example, you may want the banner of your newsletter to be printed in a color, while the rest of the document remains black and white. The color, if used properly, will add some communication impact to your newsletter.

NOTE

A process color is a color used as the basis for four color printing. Magenta, cyan, and yellow are process colors. These transparent inks, when used in the proper combinations, simulate full color for printing. Black is usually the fourth ink used in four-color printing although it is not considered a process color.

A popular color system often specified by graphic designers for spot color and multicolor print jobs is *Pantone*. This is a system of colors from Pantone, Inc., which is part of the overall system including the Pantone Matching System (PMS). A Pantone color can be specified as either a *spot color* or a *process color*. Traditionally, Pantone colors were available through color swatches that designers placed with their camera-ready artwork. This would be an indicator to the printer that the specified ink color is to match the given Pantone color swatch. New to QuarkXPress 3.2 is the inclusion of three more Pantone models, including Pantone Process, Pantone ProSim and Pantone Uncoated. These give more variations of color specifications to match the printed paper stock and ink combinations.

THE FOCOLTONE SYSTEM

A recent addition to QuarkXPress is the color model, FocolTone. It is a color system designed exclusively for process printing. The FocolTone colors represent all available process color combinations and can be reproduced as process tint percentages or single spot colors. FocolTone lists 763 color combinations. A complete reference set including swatch book and large format chart with CMYK screen percentages and mixing formulae are available from the company. See *Appendix A* for address information.

The concept behind FocolTone is that of a mixture intended to reproduce colors accurately regardless of printing conditions. The system's combination of colors, coupled with a software program for printers, compensate for a variety of printing problems. One major problem for the printer is *dot gain*. The software calculates for printer problems such as dot gain for standard paper and newsprint. It is available in both Mac and PC disk formats, provided directly to the printer for solutions to these special color problems.

THE TRUMATCH COLOR SYSTEM

One of the most promising color systems available in electronic publishing comes from TruMatch, Inc. It is quickly becoming the new standard in achieving predictable four color printing when the prepress work is handled by PostScript imagesetters.

The *TruMatch* system is the first to digitally match your screen color with your proofer color and a printer swatch. It enables you to compensate by adjusting the monitor, to find a lighter or darker color value, without having to change any of the color cast values (i.e., hue, saturation, chroma, or brightness). This gives a remarkable rendition of the color value through the precision of imagesetters and the ability to output screen percentages in of 1% increments.

An advantage of TruMatch is that you can output color separations at your local service bureau with digital accuracy. This gives the designer another option over traditional color separation techniques.

HSB COLOR

HSB is a color system invented by three physicists, Harry, Steve, and Bill, hence the name. Just kidding. They were really artists, not physicists! Actually, *HSB* is the old standby of hue, saturation, and brightness. These are three of those elusive quantifiers making color what it is today.

HSB is more popular with artists than designers or printers, in part because of the way they mix colors. HSB is more for the enjoyment of screen color and has little to do with printers colors of magenta, cyan, yellow, and black. In order for a printer to have proper separations, the HSB must translate to CMYK for separations.

RGB COLOR

Bill decided to strike out on his own, so he left the HSB group and formed the RGB color system. He called it that because he looked at it when finished and said to himself, "Real Good, Bill!"

If you believe that, there's no hope for you! Actually, the *RGB* color system is the one you probably see each time you look at a color monitor. It represents the colors of light in your cathode ray tube: red, green, and blue. In the spectra of light, red, green, and blue when mixed give the full color spectrum, or at least as much of the spectrum as your monitor will allow.

NOTE

No matter what color system you choose to select in QuarkXPress, chances are your monitor only uses only three colors, red, green and blue. You can't change physics by a menu selection.

RGB is known as an *additive* color system. When added together they make the appropriate colors of the total color spectrum available for use on your monitor. Mix equal percentages of red, green and blue on your screen and the result is *white*.

CMYK COLOR

CMYK represents the *subtractive* color system that printers use. *CMYK* is an acronym for cyan, magenta, yellow, and black. How *K* became black is anyone's guess!

Ink color is subtractive because it absorbs light. When the *primary colors* of cyan, magenta, and yellow are mixed together equally, they make black. *Secondary colors* are mixed from primary colors. Green is mixed from cyan and yellow; red is magenta and yellow, while magenta and cyan make blue.

EDITING AND CALIBRATING COLOR IN QUARKXPRESS

As mentioned, color is a rather subjective art. It has many variables as well as applications. Many of these variables come from the equipment you are using. To use QuarkXPress to the optimum, you should have 24-bit color through properly matched graphics card and monitor combination. This means you can pick from "millions" of colors. You may be able to get away with working with thousands of colors rather than millions, but sooner or later, you will find your system lacking.

NOTE

Default values and selections are those made when all documents are closed. Values and selections made with a document open typically are specific to that document and do not affect default (global) values.

One of the ways you can "control" color is through QuarkXPress's color edit capabilities. You can gain access to these through the Default Colors dialog box (Edit ➤ Colors). This is a color inventory of all current colors in QuarkXPress. From this dialog box, you may choose to add or edit colors through the Edit Color dialog box. If all documents are closed, the dialog box is called Default Colors (see Figure 17.1). These are colors that will appear in all documents.

FIGURE 17.1
*The Default Colors dia-
log box (Edit ➤ Colors).*

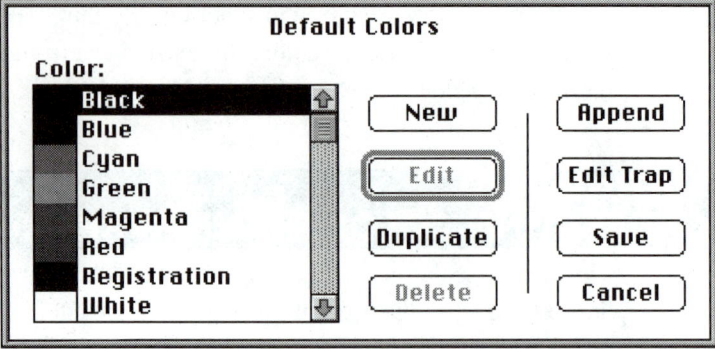

THE COLORS DIALOG BOX

The Default Colors dialog box appears when you select Edit ➤ Colors and no
documents are open (see Figure 17.2). It displays the active document or default
colors palette. You can perform the following through this dialog box:

▶ Edit an existing color from the palette

▶ Add a new color for the palette

▶ Duplicate a color from within the same color palette

▶ Delete a color from the palette

▶ Append colors from other QuarkXPress documents

▶ Specify trapping values for specific colors

▶ Save changes to the palette

▶ Cancel all activities and leave color unchanged

One of the options within the Edit Color dialog box is the ability to select and edit from a particular color system in QuarkXPress. Here, you can select from colors in one of the Pantone systems.

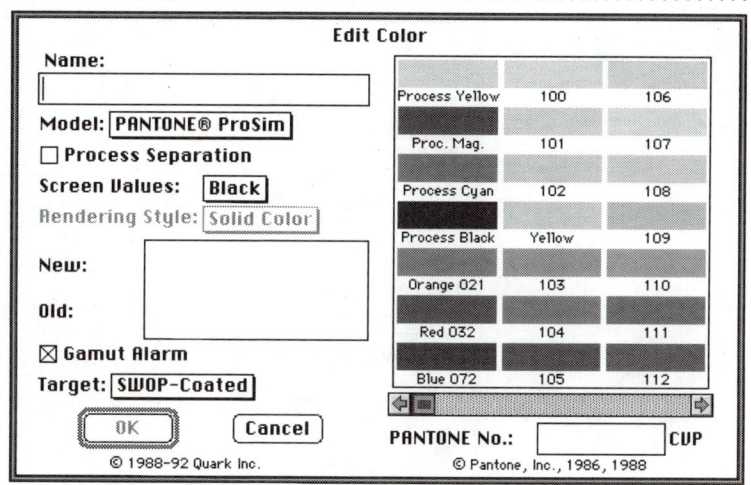

TIP

Dialog box changes, once made, cannot be undone like errors in your document. Make sure you are happy with your changes before you close the dialog box. When you want to save, click the Save button; to cancel and make no changes, click Cancel.

ADDING A NEW COLOR TO THE PALETTE

Clicking New brings the Edit Color dialog box. This enables you to select a new color in one of the many color models, as listed above. To choose a color system, select the pop-up menu in the Model field (see Figure 17.3).

Once a color model is selected, the dialog box changes to reflect the particular color chart or wheel for that model. Figure 17.4 illustrates all nine models and how the dialog box changes to enable you to select a color. In those models with a color wheel—RGB, HSB and CMYK—you can either select from the wheel or numerically key in your setting from the values below. To select a new color from the color wheel, click anywhere on the wheel. The color will be noted as a color swatch in the New field to the left of the wheel. You change the intensity of color by using the vertical scroll bar.

FIGURE 17.3

Select from one of the color models in the Edit Color dialog box.

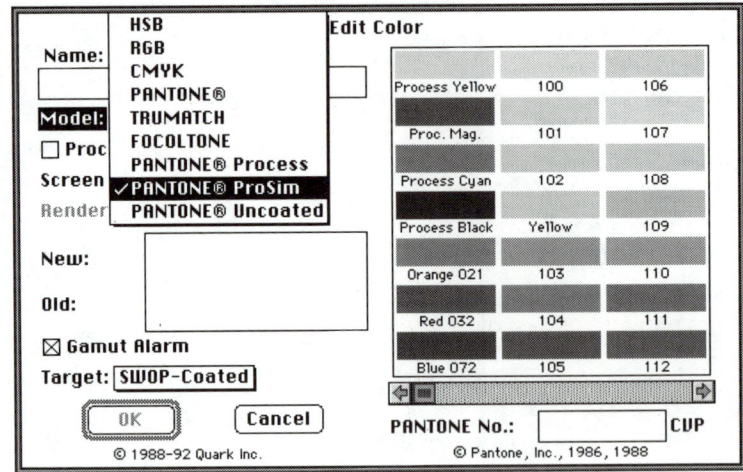

FIGURE 17.4

The CMYK option for selecting a new color. It uses the color wheel, numerical values or scroll bars to enable customization.

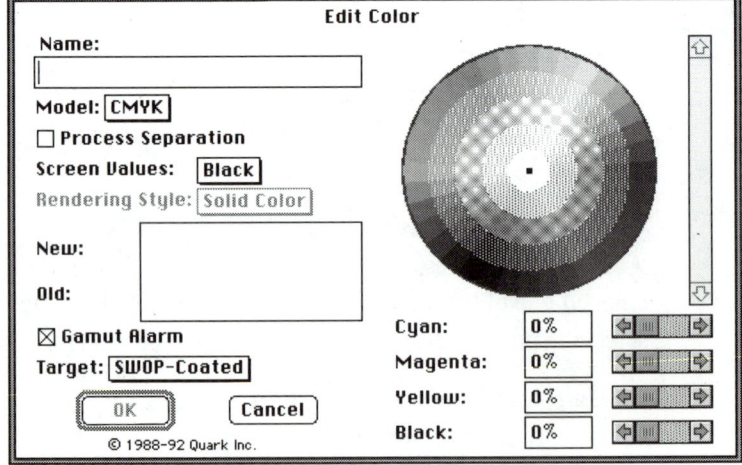

As you become more experienced in QuarkXPress, you will rely on numerical more than visual esthetics. If you select a color from the color wheel, jot a note as to its numerical value. This way you can recreate it without too much difficulty. If you lose the note, look up the value from any document, via the Append option, explained below.

Below the color wheel in the RGB, HSB, and CMYK models are numerical value fields (and horizontal scroll bars). As you change the color wheel, the appropriate numerical value changes in these fields. An alternative is to change the value and have the color wheel reflect its change. Alter the numerical field by typing in your new value or using the horizontal scroll bars.

Other options in this dialog box include Process Separation check box and the Screen Values pop up menu. Selecting the Process Separation check box instructs QuarkXPress to separate a color into cyan, magenta, yellow, and black plates when you click Make Separations in the Print dialog box (File ➤ Print). Leave unchecked and QuarkXPress will print the color as a spot color only. You select the plate to place this spot color within. To do this, select Separations in the Print dialog box; then from the submenu next to Separations, select the spot color (plate) to print.

The New, Edit, and Duplicate options in the Default Colors dialog box all appear to be identical. Be careful, they are not! You can easily change an existing color if you select the Edit button instead of New or Duplicate. It is too easy to make a mistake here and no Undo is available. Also beware of Delete; if you click this button, the color will be removed without warning.

Once all changes and options are acceptable, you can give it a file name in the Name field and press OK to apply. Your new color appears in the color palette inventory. If changes were made on the global (default) color palette, they can be seen in any document. If you made the changes in a specific document, they will apply to that document only.

EDITING IN THE DEFAULT COLORS DIALOG BOX

Edit is the default option within the Colors dialog box. That is, as you open the Colors dialog box, and select a color, pressing Enter or Return opens the Edit (Colors) dialog box.

Edit enables you to alter a color from your existing color palette. To properly use this option, first select (by clicking on) a color from the color palette shown in the Default Colors dialog box. Then press Enter or Return, or click on the Edit button. This leads you into the Edit Color dialog box again. All procedures are the same as indicated for the New option above. The only difference is that the color swatch will show both a new color choice and the original color (chosen in the previous dialog box). You can give this new color a name in the Name field. This works with all selectable colors *except* for standard selections of Registration, Black, Cyan, Magenta, White or Yellow. In Edit mode, the new name replaces the name of the color you chose to edit.

THE DUPLICATE OPTION IN THE DEFAULT COLORS DIALOG BOX

The Duplicate option works like those above, with the exception of the Name field. Immediately upon opening the Default Colors dialog box, select the color you wish to copy and click on the Duplicate option. A dialog box for Edit Color appears. In the name field, it reads *Copy of* your color name.

The Duplicate option is available so you can make subtle changes to existing colors while using them as a reference, keeping the original color unchanged. To remove a color from the color palette, identify the color and press the Delete option. The color disappears.

THE APPEND OPTION

The Append option enables you to import another document's color (from its color palette) to your active document's color palette. Click on this option and the Append Colors dialog box appears (see Figure 17.5). This is a "search through everything you've got to select a file" dialog box, which you probably have experienced on many Mac applications. Once you have selected the file, the Edit Colors dialog box appears and you select the color from that document's color palette to import.

FIGURE 17.5

The Append Colors dialog box appears when you select Append from the Default Colors dialog box.

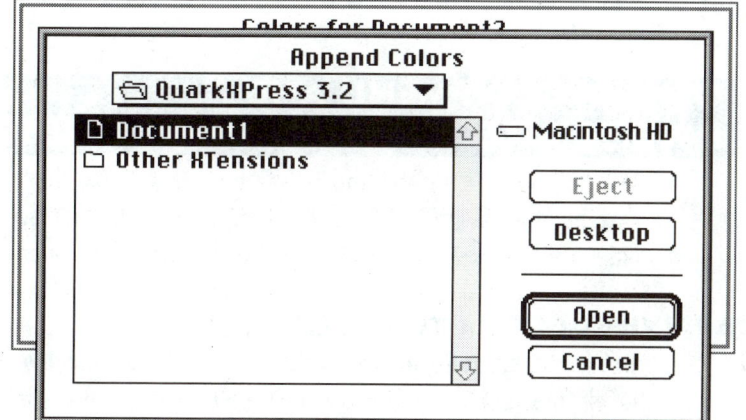

WARNING

Some people have a bad habit of adding colors to the palette for frivolous reasons; e.g., they might want to see their type in a blue pastel on a yellow background. Do not waste memory adding changes that are not essential to production. All these kind of changes slow processing and add to the activity of the program.

You might use this option when you are working on related documents and want to edit colors in certain documents, but not make them global options. Also, if you add a color to only a few documents, you save the memory overhead of bringing up the new colors in all documents, many of which might not use them.

THE EDIT TRAP OPTION

In the Edit Colors dialog box, you have the options of Save and Cancel. To enter your changes, click on *Save*. To cancel all activity and make no changes click on *Cancel*.

The Edit Trap option enables you to select from a variety of trapping options for color separation purposes. Further discussion of Trapping is presented in *Chapter 19*.

OTHER COLOR MENU AND PALETTE SELECTIONS IN QUARKXPRESS

In addition to the Colors and Edit Colors dialog box, there are other areas of color manipulation in QuarkXPress to identify. These include specific color menu and palette selections for items within the QuarkXPress document.

APPLYING COLOR TO A TEXT ITEM

You can apply color to a text item's foreground or background in a number of ways. One such method is through the menu selection for color.

You must first have an active text box in your document, preferably with text inside. Highlight the text with the Content tool (click-and-drag over the range of type characters). You will apply color only to the type characters here. This is foreground color in the text box item.

NOTE

Another way to alter colors is through use of the Colors palette. See the section on the Colors palette later in this chapter.

Once highlighted, select Style ➤ Color. This brings up the color palette for the document, including default colors for all documents (global). Change the color for your selected type range from the submenu color palette and it changes the color of the type in your document item. You may also use the same technique to apply Shade to type characters (Style ➤ Shade). You can shade in any color, including black. You may select a shade for this color as well (see Figure 17.6).

FIGURE 17.6

*You can select color and
shade combinations for
the text in a text item.*

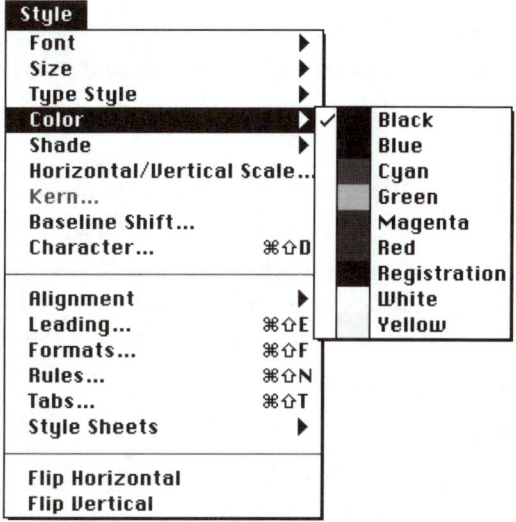

NOTE

*Two other ways to color the background of an item include use of
the Item ➤ Modify specifications dialog box and through the
Colors palette (View ➤ Show Colors).*

Here you can designate the background color of the document item from the assorted document colors or from the default (global) colors.

The background color of a text item can also be colored and shaded. To color and/or shade the background area of a selected text item, choose Item ➤ Modify for the Text Specifications dialog box. Using options within the dialog box, change colors and add shading percentages as desired.

ADDING COLOR AND SHADE TO PICTURE BOXES

Adding color to a picture box is similar to adding it to a text box. You can place color in the foreground or background. In picture boxes, however, a large determinant of color rendition is the type of graphic placed in the item box. Remember, you have a variety of formats to deal with here. Also, how the box is sized around the graphic has a lot to do with showing or not showing background color.

NOTE

PICT images will not allow changes in color, shade, or halftone screen value, as they are essentially "snapshots."

Many picture formats, i.e., bitmapped images, etc., in an active picture box item can have color manipulation. Click on a picture box item to make it active, and you can manipulate the foreground and background color and shade (see Figure 17.7). To alter the item's foreground color and shade, select the appropriate option from the Style menu (Style ➤ Color or Style ➤ Shade).

NOTE

Grouped items also have color and shade potential for the background only. You cannot color or shade the foreground of items that are grouped, but you can modify the background. Other manipulations for grouped items are similar to those for ungrouped items.

FIGURE 17.7

QuarkXPress enables you to color and shade certain graphic formats (Picture Items) through the Picture Box Specifications dialog box (Item ➤ Modify).

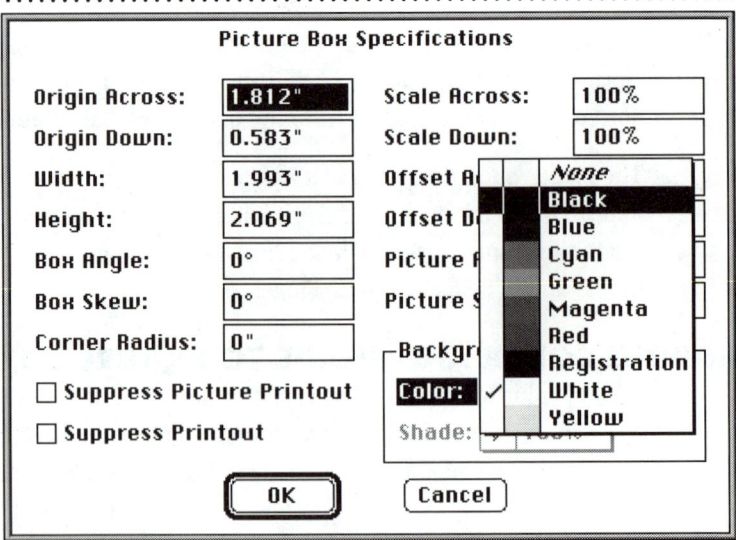

This gives the Picture Box Specifications dialog box. To alter background color for the picture box, select Item ➤ Modify and then choose either the Color or Shade option. Just as with text boxes, select the appropriate color and shade from the submenus as desired.

APPLYING COLOR TO LINES

Lines may not receive as much attention as text or picture boxes, but you can manipulate them in many ways. Draw a line with one of the line drawing tools, the Orthogonal Line tool or the Line tool.

An active line can be colored and shaded through the foreground only. This makes sense, because lines really have no background, since they are not contained in boxes. You can change a line's color and shade through the Style menu (see Figure 17.8) or through the Line Specifications dialog box (Item ➤ Modify).

The Line Specifications dialog box (Item ➤ Modify) enables you to modify the line, including its Color and Shade. Other modifications deal with line width, type, arrows, location, and rotation. Style menu selections also enable alterations to active line items for such choices as Color or Shade (Style ➤ Color, or Style ➤ Shade)—see Figure 17.9.

FIGURE 17.8

Menu options for a line item include color and shade applications

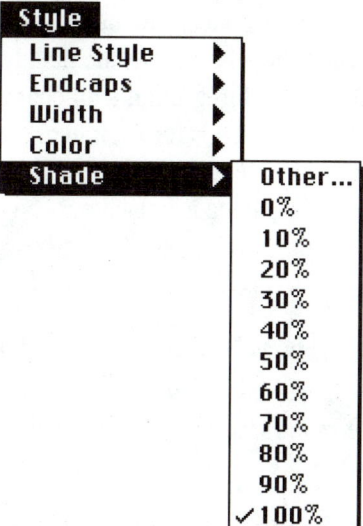

347

FIGURE 17.9

Alterations can be made to active line items through the Line Specifications dialog box, or directly through Style menu selections, as shown, for Color and Shade.

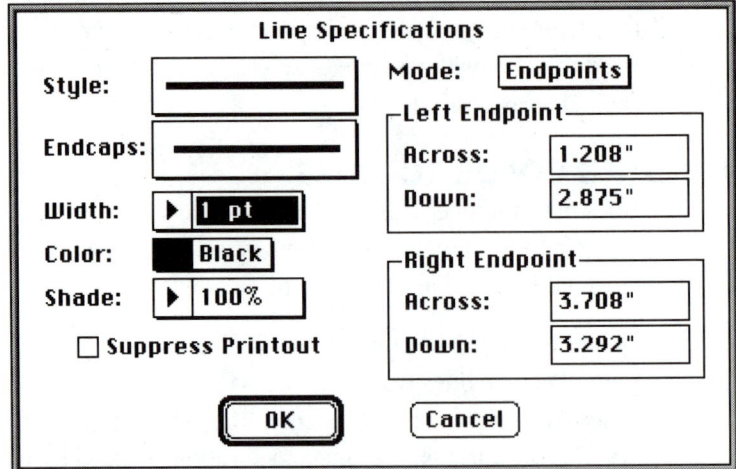

THE COLOR PALETTE

One of the palettes we haven't explored much is the Color palette (View ➤ Show Colors). Like other palettes, you may show hide, relocate, and resize it as needed.

The top part of the palette consists of a row of icons representing coloration and shade for the item frame, foreground, and background. In addition, there is a shade control (see Figure 17.10). As the item type changes, the foreground icon alters appropriately. The foreground icon changes to reflect the active item. Figure 17.10 indicates alternate icons for each item type. Icons not applicable, e.g., the background icon for line item, are dimmed. If nothing in your document is selected, the entire color palette is grayed out.

NOTE

The Solid blend is another type of blend, but it is not shown in Figure 17.11. You should experiment with the Solid blend and compare results with that of the Linear Blend style.

FIGURE 17.10

*The Color palette has
color selection, shade,
and blend capabilities.*

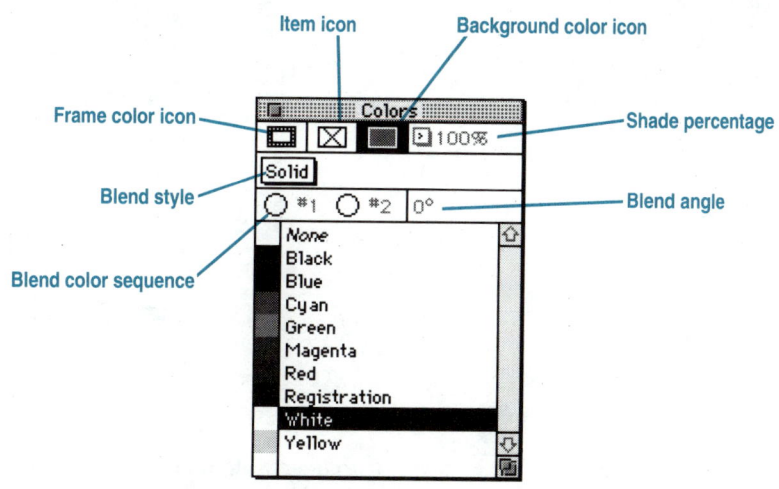

Item icon

Background color icon

Frame color icon

Shade percentage

Blend style

Blend angle

Blend color sequence

Another function of the Color palette is that of color blends. To create a blend from the choice of blend styles in the palette, (see Figure 17.11), follow these steps:

1. Create a text box and key in some text (modifying it if you like).

2. With the Colors palette showing and the text box active, click on the background icon.

3. Select a blend style from the pop-up submenu. QuarkXPress version 3.2 adds several new blend styles to the list.

4. Select the #1 button option to choose the first color in the blend.

5. Select the #2 button and choose a second color in the blend sequence.

6. Before executing your blend, you may also want to select an angle of rotation for the blend. To alter the rotation, highlight the angle degree value and overstrike with your desired change.

FIGURE 17.11

Blend options in version 3.2 are enhanced to give greater flexibility to your document.

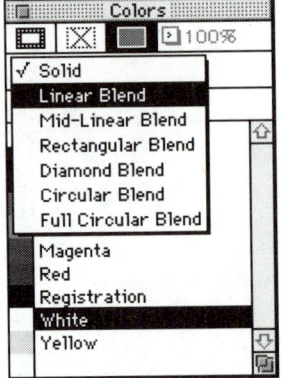

7. Click outside the text box to deactivate it and watch QuarkXPress perform the blend, (with rotation changes). The Color palette again dims as you click outside the text box, because nothing is selected for alteration.

Color palette applications can color the foreground, background, or frame of an item, or all three in combination. You can also apply shade values to any color chosen. The Color palette is one-stop shopping for all your color needs!

CONTRAST AND HALFTONE OF PICTURE BOXES

Two last manipulation areas, applicable only to picture boxes, are control over Contrast and Halftone. They were held back to incorporate in the Color Concepts of the book because they are manipulations similar in nature to color manipulation. You can also add these concepts with color for very interesting results as you will see in the examples.

CONTRAST POSSIBILITIES FOR PICTURE BOXES

Under the Style menu, you can manipulate various picture images for contrast, in particular, TIFF images. Your selections include rendering the image Negative (see Figure 17.12) and adjusting contrast to Normal, High, and Posterized (see Figure 17.13). You may also select Other Contrast to visit the Picture Contrast Specifications dialog box (see Figure 17.14).

FIGURE 17.12
*A picture box changed
to Negative*

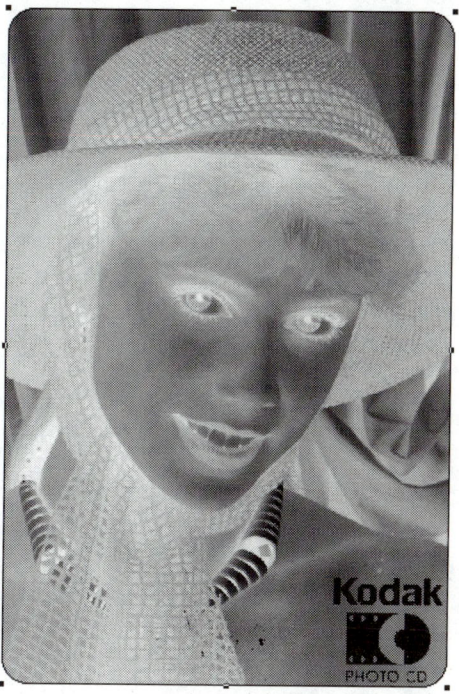

The tools in this dialog box are described here:

- The Hand tool moves the entire contrast curve on the graph.

- The Pencil tool makes freehand adjustments to the curve.

- The Line tool makes linear adjustments to the curve.

- The Posterizer tool places handles in the middle of the 10% increments of the curve. *Not* the same as the Posterizer Contrast tool.

- The Spike tool places handles on the 10% incremental marks on the curve.

FIGURE 17.13

The image shown with a Posterized option

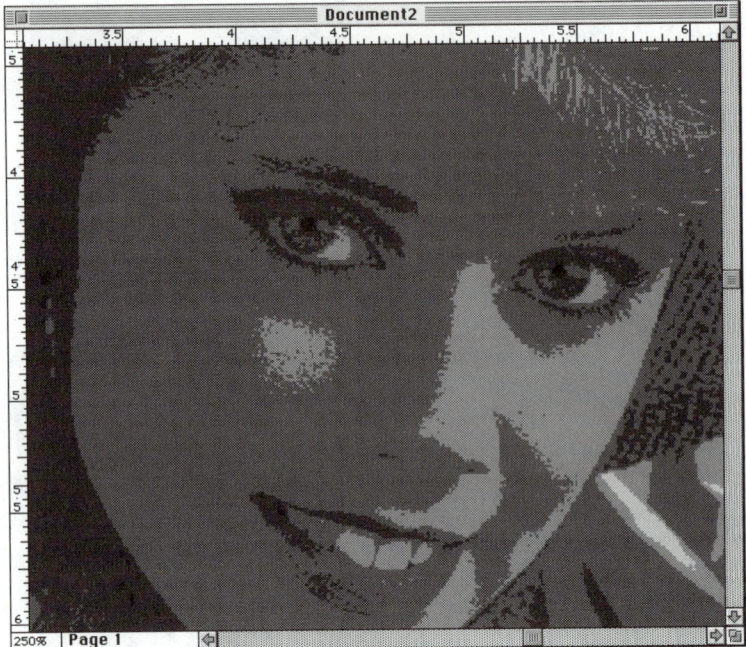

- The Normal Contrast tool resets the contrast to a normal 45° line.

- The High Contrast tool creates a curve with two levels: 0% and 100%.

- The Posterized Contrast tool creates a curve with six levels: 0%, 20%, 40%, 60%, 80%, and 100% contrast.

- The Inversion tool flips the image vertically.

When you activate a picture box containing a color bitmapped or TIFF image and choose Other Contrast, the Picture Contrast Specifications dialog box includes your choice of color model. You can modify contrast for an individual color component or a combination of color components for the selected model (see Figure 17. 15).

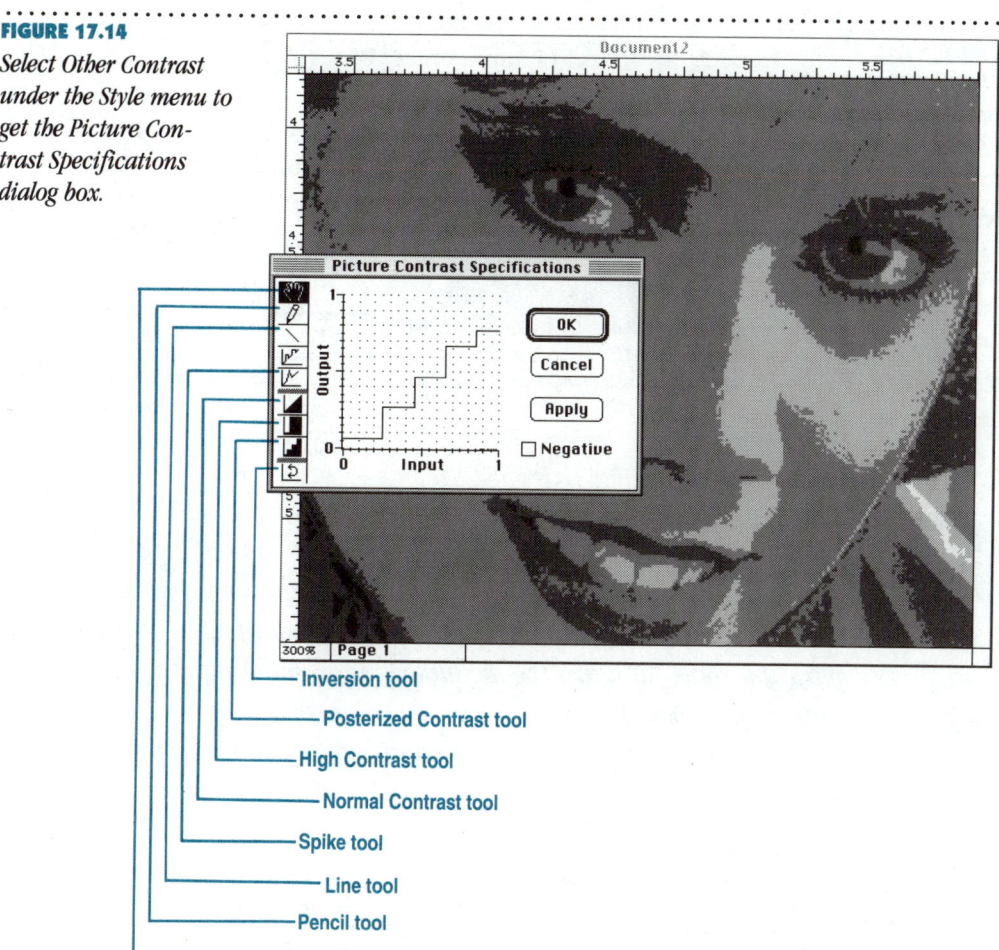

FIGURE 17.14

Select Other Contrast under the Style menu to get the Picture Contrast Specifications dialog box.

- Inversion tool
- Posterized Contrast tool
- High Contrast tool
- Normal Contrast tool
- Spike tool
- Line tool
- Pencil tool
- Hand tool

DEFINING HALFTONE SCREENS

Traditionally, the lithographic camera operator would have to photograph a continuous tone print using a contact screen to create a *halftone*. A halftone is an image consisting of a series of black-and-white dots of various sizes, that when printed, give the illusion of a continuous tone photograph. Since the press does not print with shades of gray, the only way to create the illusion of gray tones is through halftoning techniques.

FIGURE 17.15

The color and model options are shown in the Picture Contrast Specifications dialog box (for Color TIFF or Colored bitmap images). It enables you to alter contrast per color.

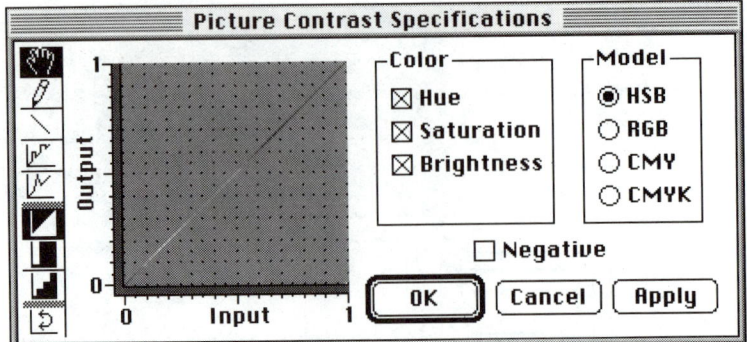

TIP

Talk to any professional designer working in the area of high resolution screen photographs in QuarkXPress and they may tell you that they still prefer to take photos out to the traditional color separation shop. Although the technology is growing rapidly, many designers feel they should not be in the color separation or halftone business; others are more qualified to deal with these areas.

QuarkXPress has halftone capabilities built in, so you can import a scanned TIFF, RIFF, or EPS image and apply your own halftone screen for imagesetter output. Standard screen choices are listed under the Style menu (see Figure 17.16). Standard screen choices include Normal Screen, 60—Line Line Screen/0°, 30—Line Line Screen/45°, and 20—Line Dot Screen/45°. There is a difference in the final appearance of each screened photograph. Different situations and design considerations determine your choice here.

WARNING

Check with your printing sales representative to see what kind of screen value would be best for the product you want to print. There are many variables to creating a good screened image, the least of which is probably how the image looks on your monitor. Don't judge halftone quality by what you see on the screen.

FIGURE 17.16

Standard Style menu commands include Normal Screen, 60—Line Line Screen/0°, 30—Line Line Screen/45°, and 20—Line Dot Screen/45°.

Picture Screening Specifications

┌─ **Halftone** ─────────────────────────

Screen: default **(lpi)**   **Angle:** 45°

┌─ **Pattern** ───────────────────────

◉ **Dot**   ○ **Line**   ○ **Ellipse**   ○ **Square**

○ **Ordered Dither**

☐ **Display Halftoning**   (**OK**)   (**Cancel**)

You may also wish to create a halftone screen from the custom area of the Style menu, the Other Screen (⌘-Shift-S). Figure 17.16 illustrates the Picture Screening Specifications dialog box. Here, you can specify the line frequency in lines per inch (lpi) and screen angle. Pattern "dot" choices include the traditional Dot, the Line, Ellipse, Square, and Ordered Dither. The Ordered Dither is not a traditional printer's halftone dot; rather it is a new method developed to print photographs with screens on low-resolution printers, such as your desktop laser printer. You should not submit this for print quality.

TIP

*Don't display the halftone on your screen as you work because it
simply takes more time for QuarkXPress to draw and takes away
from productivity.*

Also on this dialog box is a check box enabling you to display the halftone photo
on your screen as you work. Perhaps a handy feature if the client is standing over
your shoulder as you work, but rather useless otherwise.

USING THE EFICOLOR XTENSION

A color management system that is gaining in popularity in the "prepress" community is that of the EfiColor system. Quark has incorporated EfiColor in its QuarkX-
Press 3.2 program through the EfiColor XTension. If you implement this XTension,
it will alter some of the color manipulation and editing features previously described. Because the EfiColor XTension places a heavy burden on your computer's
RAM, many QuarkXPress professionals may choose not to implement it. Therefore,
both the indications of standard color manipulation and EfiColor are noted in this
chapter. The remaining information concentrates on application of the EfiColor
XTension in QuarkXPress 3.2.

COLOR MANAGEMENT SYSTEMS

Color management in electronic prepress helps simplify matching colors on various devices. It helps match color capabilities across several devices, including
scanners, monitors and proofing printers. Although there are others vying for
color management supremacy, including Kodak (ColorSense) and Apple (Col-
orSynch, part of the future QuickDraw GX), the industry is quickly adopting EFI
products. These EFI products include a color-management engine and output profiles that can be plugged into a variety of hardware/software applications. EFI's Cachet product has been extremely well received, praised for its excellence in color
manipulation. Now, similar technology is available in QuarkXPress through the Efi-
Color XTension.

ABOUT THE EFICOLOR XTENSION

Color management is a sticky problem, especially in today's progressive electronic prepress industry. Currently, there is little standardization in color perception from one scanner to another, from one monitor to another, or for any two different devices. For example, consider the scenario in which you scan a color photograph of your new red Porsche. By the time you see the image on your computer monitor, you may have worked with three different color variations of "red" for the car. First, the actual Porsche itself is a unique shade of red. Porsche calls it Guards Red and mixes it to an exact formula so that each Guards Red Porsche looks like the next. The photograph, when processed, has many variables for color, due to the shot lighting, film type, processing, enlargement paper type, and processing chemistry. Odds are against even the best photograph identically duplicating the full-color spectrum reflecting off your new Porsche in the summer sunlight. Hence, two representations of red. Now, digitizing this photograph with a scanner increases the odds that another shade or value of red will appear as the image projects on your monitor. Scanners and scanning software have their own set of variables and quality levels, dependent on many factors, including the computer. As you can see, each step involves another possible alteration on the "real" color. Imagine this theme taken to completion with color proofing, separations, plates, printing (with its many variables) and you'll understand how color can be quite an aggravation!

In an attempt to solve these color management problems, QuarkXPress has incorporated the EfiColor XTension. It is a color management system designed to let you specify a variety of colors in QuarkXPress and render them to match capabilities of the output printer. Ideally, this match is performed by having a precise EfiColor Profile matching your computer monitor and the specific color output or proofing device.

The EfiColor XTension, when installed in QuarkXPress enables you to:

▸ Match or calibrate colors on your monitor with the color output device you use for proofing.

▸ Find the acceptable, printable colors of supported color printers (the XTension flags colors that overstep the capabilities of the proof printer).

> ♦ Include colors in your designed proof, rather than simulations, yielding the *for-position-only* or FPO graphic.

> ♦ Betters your chances of doing high-color separations correctly, directly from QuarkXPress.

WHAT THE EFICOLOR XTENSION CAN'T DO

The EfiColor XTension is intended to be used for calibrating various colors across "platforms," rather than as a retouching or image-correction program. You cannot change spot colors or pixels in a photograph with EfiColor XTension. There are other software programs better suited to these forms of alteration, such as Cachet from EFI.

NOTE

Designing with color demands clear and continuous communication between client, designer, color specialists (scanner/proof operator) and the printer. Remember, each member of the production team has her own interpretation and expectations. To avoid confusion, communicate!

AN ATTEMPT TO SIMPLIFY THE COMPLEX

The documentation given with QuarkXPress regarding the EfiColor XTension readily admits that color is a complex issue. There are many aspects to color theory and application that venture far beyond the scope of this book as well. Therefore, an attempt is made here to simplify color management and the EfiColor XTension. Certainly, the combination of QuarkXPress and EfiColor capabilities give the professional a "no-limits" capability in electronic prepress, surpassing any manual!

In attempting to deliver fundamentals, an overview of the EfiColor XTension capabilities is presented in this chapter. Use this as a foundation to build upon, enhancing your skills in color management.

DISPLAY "ACCURATE" COLOR ON YOUR MONITOR

This text assumes that you have properly installed and configured QuarkXPress to use the EfiColor XTension. The first step to consider is that of adjusting or calibrating your monitor. This involves selecting your monitor from selection options in the Application Preferences dialog box (Edit ➤ Preferences ➤ Application). In the Display Correction pop-up menu, select your monitor from the listings (see Figure 17.17). If your monitor is not listed, contact EFI to obtain the proper profile for your equipment.

FIGURE 17.17
Select your monitor type from a list of profiles in the EfiColor Preferences dialog box. If your monitor is not shown, contact EFI to purchase the proper profile.

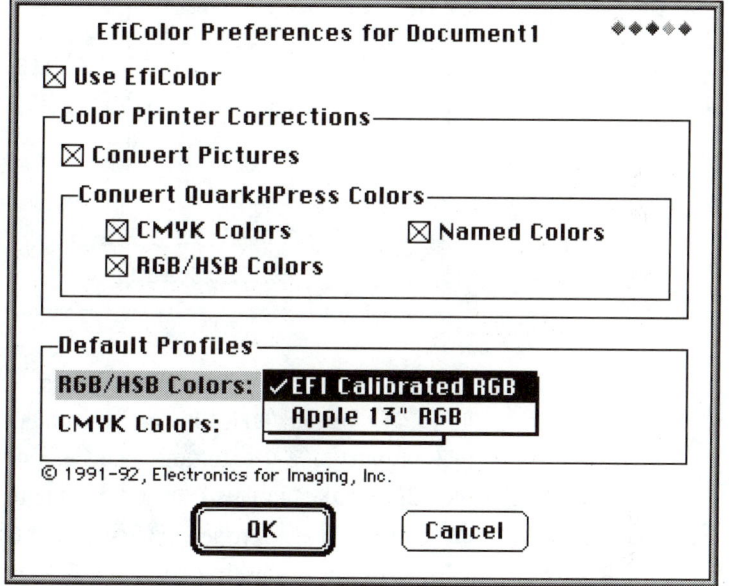

TIP

To maximize use of the EfiColor XTension and color management systems, you must have a calibrated monitor and appropriate software. Most standard color monitors, unless otherwise noted will not have this capability.

MANAGING COLOR FOR IMPORTED PICTURES

The EfiColor XTension adds EfiColor Profile and Rendering Style pop-up menus to the QuarkXPress Get Picture dialog box (File ➤ Get Picture) when properly installed. These new options give more control when importing pictures, converting their color information to fit within the range your printer can output (see Figure 17.18).

FIGURE 17.18

When using the EfiColor XTension to import pictures, you can tag a profile and rendering style to match your needs.

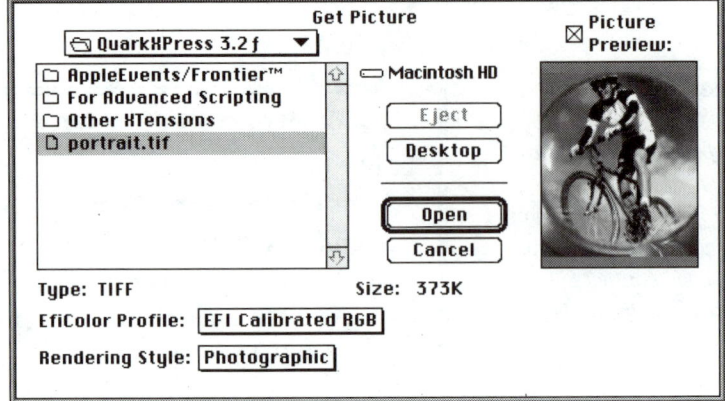

Images altered by EFI's Cachet program may have tags or information in the new Metric Color Tag (MCT) format. TIFF, EPS, or DCS images manipulated in Cachet or others that may support MCT are automatically assigned an EfiColor profile that defines their color. This makes the MCT-tagged file a natural for importing to QuarkXPress, through EfiColor XTension. EPS or DCS picture files import with unchangeable colors, however, as EfiColor XTension does not convert colors in these formats.

PICT and TIFF files without MCT tags are assigned a default profile when imported, based on whether they are RGB or CMYK pictures. Profiles for these formats can be changed upon import.

To import a picture using the EfiColor XTension, activate a picture box with the Content Tool and choose Get Picture from the File menu. Select the picture to import in the dialog box as you normally would when importing a graphic image. Next, select a profile from the EfiColor Profile pop-up menu matching the color space for the picture. Select the default profile if you aren't sure of the proper profile for your picture. If the profile shows an underline, the picture is already tagged with a profile by the EfiColor XTension. A grayed-out profile indicates a missing or improperly installed profile.

After selecting the appropriate picture and profile for import, select a rendering style. The pop-up menu, Rendering Style in the same Get Picture dialog box enables you to choose when importing continuous tone pictures. Pick Solid Color when exact color matching is critical—e.g., Pantone colors. Click Open to import the graphic into the active picture box.

When using EfiColor XTension for importing color pictures, it is recommended that you keep to the following formats:

- PICT—the native Macintosh picture format that specifies colors in RGB values. PICT files have limited resolution and the format is suited only to basic charts or graphs with simple geometric elements.

- RGB TIFF—a tagged image file format specified in red, green and blue values. Standard TIFFs are often RGB TIFFs;

- CMYK TIFF—an alternative to the RGB TIFF; these formats are indicated in the printer's colors: cyan, magenta, yellow, and black. These images are often used in color separation, destined for the printing press.

COLOR
CONCEPTS
....

CH. 17

▶ EPS—Encapsulated Postscript files are text files defining a picture through PostScript commands. EPS images are among the highest quality, but are often much larger in file size than alternative file formats. EPS files contain a PICT preview to display a representation of the photo on the screen when importing (as shown on the Picture Preview box of the QuarkXPress Get Picture dialog box). Illustration programs such as Freehand and Illustrator save pictures in this format.

▶ DCS—Desktop Color Separation is an enhancement to the EPS definition of pictures. It also contains a PICT preview, like EPS. There are several manipulations you can make to DCS files, including color-correction, screen angles, retouching, dot function, and transfer functions. Instead of one file, however, the DCS 1.0 picture has five, one for the main file with a PICT preview and four other files, one each for the cyan, magenta, yellow, and black EPS separation plates. A DCS 2.0 file is a single file format including main file information for the image as well as separation plate information;

▶ OPI—Open Prepress Interface formats are used typically with high-end color separation scanners, such as Crossfield or Scitex machines. OPI specifies five files—a main file including a low-resolution TIFF for placement and manipulation in QuarkXPress documents, and four separation files. These separation files often reside in a separate OPI server, not connected to the QuarkXPress document. Typically, the photograph is scanned at a color separation house or service bureau and the designer gets the low-resolution TIFF file on disk to manipulate in QuarkXPress. When needed for separations, the original separation files are electronically altered to match those alterations used by the QuarkXPress professional.

EFICOLOR PREFERENCES

The EfiColor Preferences dialog box (Edit ➤ Preferences ➤EfiColor) is available to control color models, conversions, and default configurations (see Figure 17.19). CMYK, RGB/HSB, or named colors can be altered in QuarkXPress; EPS, DCS, and OPI images cannot, due to their multi-file formats.

FIGURE 17.19

The EfiColor Preferences dialog box allows alteration to Color Printer corrections and Default settings. You may also disable the EfiColor XTension from this dialog box.

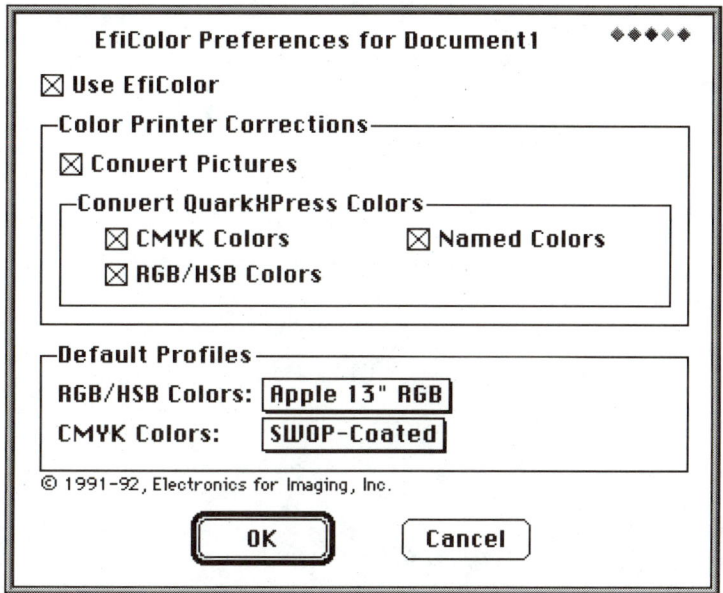

Settings altered in the EfiColor Preferences dialog box without a document open means that subsequent documents opened will inherit the new settings. If a document is open, alterations to the dialog box affect only that document. Each open document can have different EfiColor settings.

In addition to enabling or disabling EfiColor, there are two other areas in the EfiColor Preferences dialog box, Color Printer Corrections, and Default Profiles. The Color Printer Corrections allow you, through check boxes, to convert a picture's colors in imported CMYK and RGB files.

Settings in the EfiColor Preference dialog box also affect spot colors, depending on the type of color proof, composite (one full-color page from a color printer), or separation plates (four separation plates, representing magenta, cyan, yellow and black printers). This list details whether the EfiColor XTension converts colors for various combinations of formats, options, and color types.

ITEM	COLOR TYPE	CONVERTS SEPARATION	CONVERTS COMPOSITE
If you check Convert Pictures			
PICT	8- and 24-bit	Yes	Yes
TIFF	RGB	Yes	Yes
	Colorized Grayscale	Yes	Yes
	Grayscale	No	No
	CMYK	Yes	Yes
EPS/DCS/OPI		No	Converts only if the preview is printed.
If you check RGB/HSB Colors			
RGB	Process	Yes	Yes
	Spot	No	Yes
If you check CMYK colors			
CMYK	Process	Yes	Yes
	Spot	No	Yes
If you check Named Colors (PANTONE, FOLCOLTONE, TRUMATCH)			
Named Color	Process	Yes	Yes
	Spot	No	Yes

The Default Profiles allow selection of RGB/HSB or CMYK color monitor profiles. Alternative monitor profiles, if any, are listed in pop-up menus.

Chosen default profiles convert QuarkXPress colors when you print. The EfiColor XTension uses RGB/HSB Colors as default for colors you create in the RGB and

HSB color models or CMYK Colors as default for colors you create in the CMYK color model. Changes in the default alter output results of your document.

If you change profiles for default and the command is dimmed in the pop-up menu, the profile is missing from that computer. Remember, you may be using more than one computer for your document: yours, and that at the service bureau. So if this occurs, quit QuarkXPress and properly install the missing profile.

Default profile names are listed in the EfiColor Preferences dialog box and also show in the Get Picture dialog box (File ➤ Get Picture). If an RGB picture selected for import does not have a tagged profile, the default RGB/HSB profile applies; similarly, untagged CMYK pictures use the default CMYK profile.

To avoid color conversion when printing CMYK percentages created in QuarkXPress, select your final output device as the default CMYK profile in the EfiColor Preferences dialog box.

ADDING AND EDITING COLORS

While using the EfiColor XTension, the Edit Color dialog box allows you to better define process separations and colors "out-of-gamut" for your chosen printer. You need to specify the printer in the Gamut Alarm's Target pop-up menu (see Figure 17.20).

FIGURE 17.20

Select a target printer profile from the Edit Color dialog box. Notice in this example, the gamut is limited on the color wheel and chosen colors are "out-of-gamut."

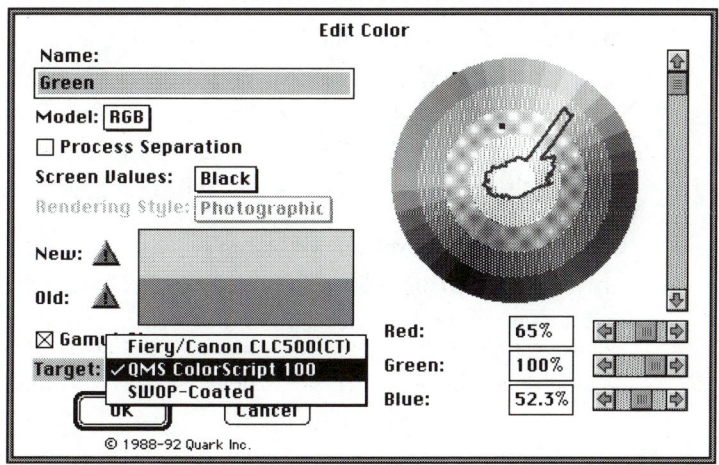

© 1988-92 Quark Inc.

TIP

You cannot edit the process colors cyan, magenta, yellow, or black in QuarkXPress. White is also unavailable for edit.

EfiColor XTension provides an outline of the color gamut (range of available colors for the chosen profile) superimposed over the color wheel if you choose RGB, HSB, or CMYK color models. Colors outside the outline are out-of-gamut. The color wheel in this dialog, however, is a two-dimensional representation of a three-dimensional space. In reality, color is mapped in three-dimensional values—remember, you were warned of color complexities! If you see a triangle with an exclamation point inside, placed next to the New or Old color selected, this indicates that it is out-of-gamut (see Figure 17.21).

FIGURE 17.21
The out-of-gamut warning

CONTROLLING THE ENVIRONMENT

Quark and EFI have teamed up to give you the best possible system available for matching color from one device to another, but the true test of color is from your point of view. As a QuarkXPress professional, only you can judge to see if the color you have worked with on the monitor, the proof, and final printout all match. Environments surrounding color inspection are critical. Lighting is a major consideration when analyzing the document on the monitor, the proof and press sheet. Color professionals often have a special light box or room in which to view proofs, allowing them to exactly control light and color spectrums surrounding the proof.

Colors displayed on your monitor can be affected by a number of factors—least of which is the exterior lighting in the room where you work. Is there any reflected light that may alter your perception of the color rendition on the screen? Are there any windows, allowing natural sunlight in the room? Natural sunlight differs in spectrum from fluorescent lighting, incandescent lighting, and so forth.

Color is an extremely difficult concept to understand and control, but you can begin with simply manipulating your environmental lighting.

OUTPUTTING DOCUMENTS

VI

POSTSCRIPT PRINTING

 **TRACKS   MAC TRACKS   MAC TRACKS   MAC TRACKS   MAC**

Today, the accepted standard page description language in desktop and electronic publishing is *PostScript* software from Adobe Systems Incorporated. It is in use by more than 240 products from over 40 manufacturers. This product, perhaps more than any other, has revolutionized prepress technology.

WHAT IS POSTSCRIPT?

PostScript is the name of a computer language that describes how pages image on output devices. It can describe any page, and any element on the page. This was an advancement over previous typesetting machines, or non-laser machines that could output only alphanumeric characters. The laser allows programs such as PostScript to draw any image on the page. The PostScript language is communicated by applications such as QuarkXPress when they want to tell a printer or imagesetter what to draw.

PostScript is not the only page description language. It is the most popular, though, because it outshines other languages in capability and versatility. It includes provisions for using outline typefaces and halftone images.

The Macintosh hardware and operating system (the print manager in particular) are not optimized for producing PostScript quickly. Tim Gill of Quark, Inc. suggests the following: (1) Use a dedicated machine to handle printing when possible, (2) connect the printing computer directly to the printer with no others on the network, (3) use Ethernet rather than Appletalk, (4) Avoid placing EPS and TIFF files in the document on the network server, (5) scan grayscale and color images at a resolution just over twice the final output resolution, (6) scan line art at resolutions lower than final output, and (7) remove all INITs not needed in your Mac. Obtain further information on this from the QuarkXPress Users International or directly from Quark, Inc.

One of the most convenient aspects of PostScript is that the typical user does not have to be a programmer to take advantage of its power. Instead, applications make intelligent decisions, based on user input, and place the appropriate Post-Script commands into action. These commands generate from a special part of the application software called a *driver*. This software driver program runs over 55 PostScript printers and imagesetters shipping today.

POSTSCRIPT AS AN INTERPRETER

The PostScript Interpreter, a program residing usually in the printer, receives Post-Script language signals from the application. A variety of configurations for the interpreter are available including dedicated PostScript interpreter boards within a connected computer, a special PostScript interpreter board placed in the printer or imagesetter, or a separate stand-alone box containing the interpreter connected to the printer (see The Raster Image Processor).

NOTE

Although imagesetters are capable of setting quality at 2540 dots per inch (dpi), they may be set by the operator for lower quality. Visually, few people can tell a quality difference between 1400 dpi and 2540 dpi. Imagesetters that output type at nearly 1400 dpi run twice as fast as those at 2540 dpi. Productivity!

Regardless of its physical makeup, the interpreter receives signals from the application and constructs a representation of the page to draw in the laser printer. While printing, it takes into account the capabilities of the output machine. The output machine can range in quality from the desktop laser printer at 300 dots per inch (dpi) to a 2540 dpi imagesetter. The interpreter outputs the desired page according to the machine's maximum quality standards (as set by the user).

THE RASTER IMAGE PROCESSOR (RIP)

Often, the interpreter program resides on a circuit board or cartridge inside the output machine. Some imagesetters have an external interpreter inside a Raster Image Processor (RIP). It may be an external box or an attached computer. The RIP is often what determines the speed of output.

RIP technology is extremely fast-paced in its evolution. It also is the most problematic of the PostScript system. If any problems occur in image output, most often they originate in the RIP. Many people are perplexed with RIP technology because it is relatively new and constantly changing. No one has had years of experience with any particular RIP.

A key component in the imagesetter RIP is the hard disk drive. It performs a variety of functions for page description. It involves inputting, manipulating, and storing a great deal of data. It is common for a color file to have 30 to 35 Mb of material. Efficiency is extremely critical in data loads of this size.

In addition, the hard disk stores the PostScript Interpreter software, printer fonts, and font cache, and on some RIPs, a screen cache. The hard disk with its PostScript interpreter is the center of all this data. Managing the data requires efficiency and working toward more efficient systems keeps companies competitive in the Imagesetter/RIP business.

As you keep abreast of changes, the most widely publicized are the new RIPs. They are part of an extremely fast moving technology, changing nearly every day.

POSTSCRIPT LEVEL 1 AND LEVEL 2

The page description language as described in this chapter is known as *PostScript Level 1*, or more simply just PostScript. It has been a powerful description language, and if Adobe has its way, will continue to dominate. To keep above the competition and evolve PostScript Level 1, Adobe has introduced *PostScript Level 2*. It involves more efficient ways to describe the appearance of a page. These include improved font switching, text composition, compressed image transmission, and better caching of the text and graphics that describe the appearance of forms and patterns. A powerful upgrade strategy is that any page you can print on a PostScript Level 2 printer can print or display on the current installed base of PostScript products. You can seamlessly integrate the newest PostScript printers and imagesetters.

POSTSCRIPT LEVEL 2

PostScript Level 2 extends the boundaries of Level 1. It incorporates several PostScript language enhancements made over the last few years, such as color printing, Japanese language printing, and Display PostScript. Level 2 products include support for:

- The cyan, magenta, yellow, and black (CMYK) color model

- Color images (RGB and CMYK)

- Non-roman character sets and encodings (Japanese, Chinese, etc.)

- Optimized text and graphics operators from the Display PostScript system

- Forms and form caching

- Patterns and pattern caching

- Device-independent color

- Data compression and decompression filters

- Improved halftoning algorithms for color separations

- Improved memory management

- Resources management

- Improved support for printer-specific features.

NOTE

When products list as Roman and Non-Roman, these designations refer to the alphabet style. For example, the Roman alphabet, as used in the United States, differs from Kanji characters used in Asia.

WHAT KIND OF PRODUCTS USE POSTSCRIPT?

There are several products using PostScript; these are classified in distinct categories. Products that might enhance your business's output include:

- Black-and-white printers: Roman and Non-Roman

- Color printers: Roman and Non-Roman

- Film recorders

- Imagesetters/typesetters: Roman and Non-Roman

- Stand-alone RIPs: Roman and Non-Roman

- Software RIPs

For a complete list of these and other products and more information on Post-Script, contact Adobe Systems Incorporated (see *Appendix A*).

PRINTING CAPABILITIES OF QUARKXPRESS

Typically, the QuarkXPress user will prepare documents for printing for one of two categories of output: the laser printer or the imagesetter. There are a few distinct steps to perform in preparing documents for these.

PREPARING YOUR DOCUMENT FOR LASER PRINTING

Although QuarkXPress is a production tool in print publication, you may use it as a short-run communication tool in the office environment. For this, imagesetting output is inappropriate. Rather, the best way to produce the "quality" of communique appropriate is through the desktop laser printer. These come in a variety of quality standards ranging from 300 dpi black-and-white to over 1000 dpi. Some machines print in color or grayscale, and some non-laser machines can accept PostScript output. You can use any of these devices to proof your work before sending it to an imagesetter, or in many cases, to produce the end product.

THE CHOOSER

The first area to check is that of the Chooser, under the Apple menu. It is important to double-check, because if it is incorrectly set up, your document won't print. Make sure you have a proper connection to the printer and set AppleTalk to either Active or Inactive. You may also have to use this dialog box to select from different printers, and network zones. See your Macintosh manuals for a complete description on printing and the Chooser dialog box.

TIP

If you do not have enough memory for complex document printing in background, turn Background Printing off in the Chooser. This ties up your computer. Look on the bright side; at least you are constantly aware of document status.

THE PAGE SETUP DIALOG BOX

To print the document, you must perform a few preparatory steps. Save the finished document on the hard disk, floppy disk, or network for later retrieval. Then select File ➤ Page Setup to get the Page Setup dialog box. This dialog box allows you to specify the printer you have connected as well as to control various output features (see Figure 18.1).

FIGURE 18.1
*The Page Setup dialog
box enables you to se-
lect the printer and
various options for
output.*

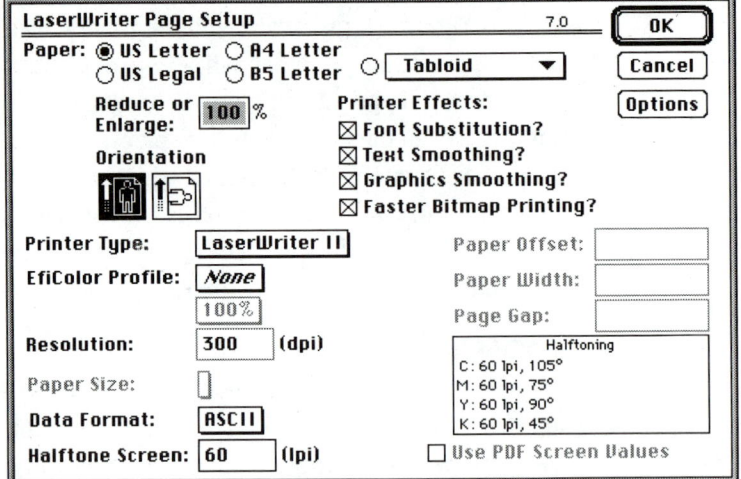

TIP

*Remember to save early and often. Before printing and before
closing the document, save it! You will find that electronic
publishing is not yet an exact science; an ounce of prevention is
worth a pound of cure.*

One key area in the Page Setup dialog box is the selection of printer types. QuarkX-
Press enables you to print on a variety of output machines, many of which are in
the pop-up menu in Figure 18.2. If your printer is not listed, try alternate printers.
Often printers with different names have the same tech specs as the ones listed. If
you still have no luck, contact Quark and they can suggest an another solution.

FIGURE 18.2

The pop-up menu in the Page Setup dialog box lists several output printers.

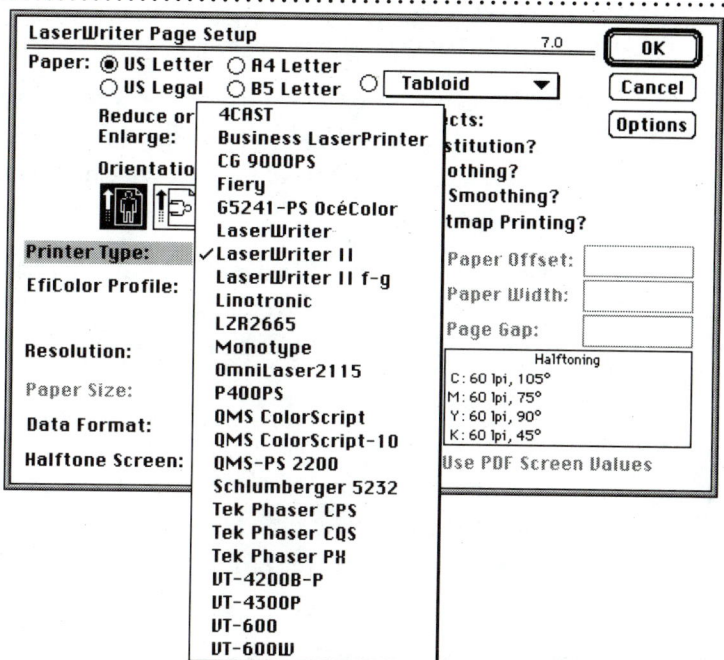

> **NOTE**
>
> *There is a difference between lines per inch (lpi) and dots per inch (dpi). Lines per inch is an older judgment of quality for the printer industry. It represents the coarseness or refinement of the halftone screen. Newsprint prints on about 85 lpi. On the opposite end, fine, high gloss paper such as on annual reports may require 200 lpi screen quality. In dots per inch, 300 is near the low end and 2540 is imagesetter quality.*

Also, this dialog box allows you to select from a variety of halftone options and color profiles. This enables you to best match your printer type, getting the optimum quality output. For the typical table top laser printer you can stick with the basic default values; i.e., 60 lines per inch (lpi). This is acceptable quality for a

POSTSCRIPT
PRINTING
....

CH. 18

laser printer. Higher resolution may be wasted on a 300 dpi printer. As you select other printers, the values may change according to their specifications.

Another option, new to 3.2; is the Data Format. You have now an option of submitting data in ASCII or Binary format from this dialog box. Check with your printer's output options, or service bureau for the most efficient method of outgoing data for your purposes.

You see other information fields dimmed because they apply to imagesetters or other film recorders. Select one of these "printers" and the options become pertinent, showing in black. When you have finished making your selections, click OK.

NOTE

Several of these options in the Page Setup as well as Print dialog boxes may have special uses with color output. Look at Chapter 19 for more information on color applications and printing.

IMAGESETTER SETTINGS

Preparing a document for printing on an imagesetter is very similar to preparing a document for printing to any other laser printer until you reach the Page Setup dialog box (see Figure 18.3). Once chosen, the imagesetter will open other field values, as shown. Check with your service bureau. If you have an imagesetter in your company, check the manufacturer's manual for that machine.

TIP

If you want the high quality output of an imagesetter but don't own one, contact a service bureau. Service bureaus, also called typesetting shops, will output your document from stored floppy disk to the imagesetter. Call first for information on page options for their equipment.

FIGURE 18.3

Choose an imagesetter from Printer Type and you have a new assortment of fields to fill. Check with your service bureau or imagesetter manual for specifications on their machine.

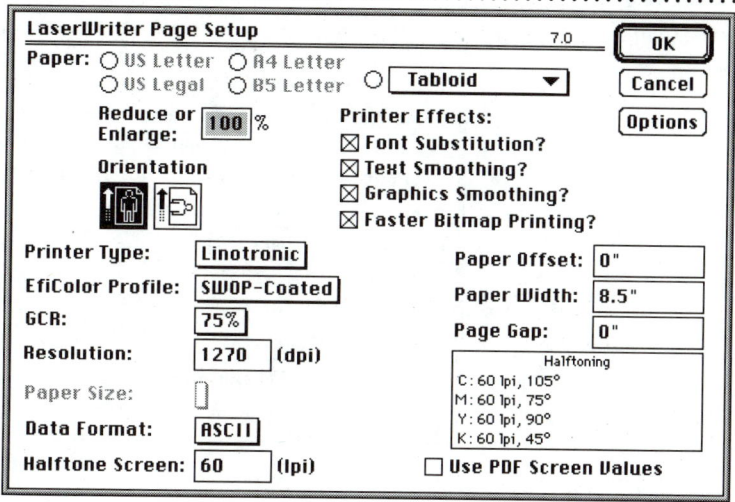

THE PRINT DIALOG BOX

The somewhat familiar, Macintosh Print dialog box (File ➤ Print or ⌘-P) contains new options in QuarkXPress 3.2, including:

Page Sequence

Output

Tiling

Separation

Registration

Collate

Spreads

All other options in the Print dialog box are endemic to Macintosh printing, for the most part, or were QuarkXPress options familiar in earlier versions. However, the order and placement of some options have changed in version 3.2. These include such QuarkXPress staples as the Calibrated Output, Include Blank Pages, Print Colors as Grays, and OPI (see Figure 18.4).

FIGURE 18.4

*Some QuarkXPress
staples*

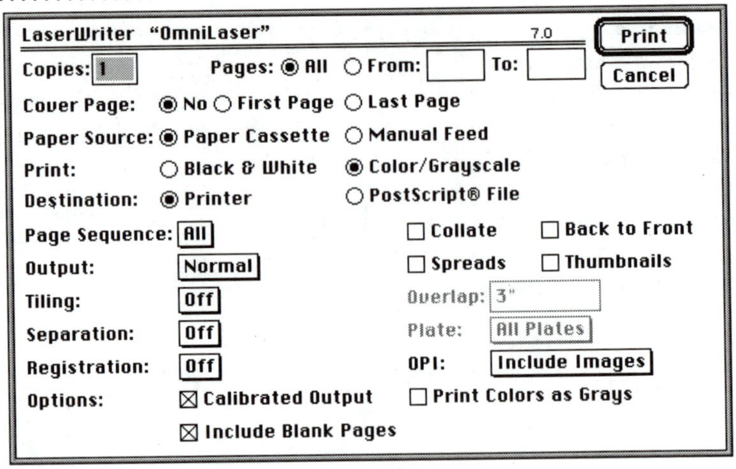

PRINT TO DISK

Before System 7, you had to know a special trick to save your document as a Post-
Script file; i.e., to print to disk. You had to send the document to print and immediately hold down ⌘-F This worked on system 6.x only with Finder, not with
MultiFinder. System 7 makes it easy; there is now an option right in the Print dialog box in the Destination area.

The default is Printer, but if you click on PostScript File, the document will be converted to a PostScript file and stored on disk. Actually, when you click on the Post-
Script File option, the Print button changes to Save. Click on Save and a new dialog
box appears (see Figure 18.5). Save the document to the location you want. You
can rename the file or allow the program to do so for you; it will sequentially
name the saved documents *PostScript 1*, *PostScript 2*, and so on. This is a System 7
feature and may not be available if you are running System 6.X with QuarkXPress.

OUTPUT OPTIONS IN THE PRINT DIALOG BOX

Output options define the printed look of your document. The *Normal*, *Rough*,
and *Thumbnails* options of earlier QuarkXPress Print dialog boxes have changed
to reflect user needs and improved equipment. These options are now offered in a
low, medium and high resolution of the product (see Figure 18.6). While the
thumbnail option is still available, you have to select it from a check box outside of
the Output pop-up options.

FIGURE 18.5

A new dialog box appears in System 7 if you choose to save your document to a Post-Script File.

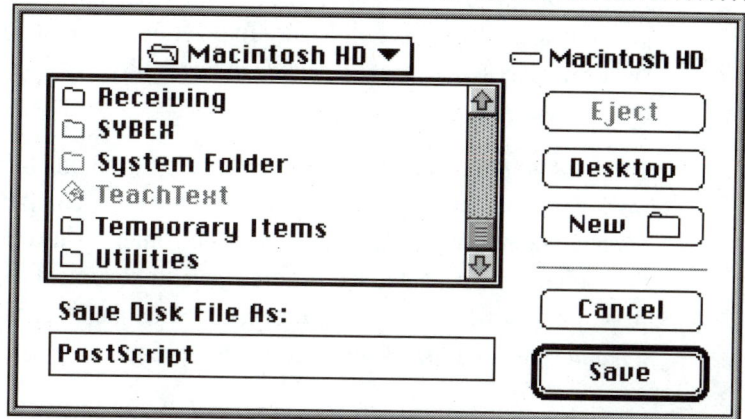

TIP

Use the Odd and Even options for your document to print on both sides of the paper. Run the job on Odd Pages, then take the stack, flip it and run through it again, checking Even Pages. It takes a little practice to get the system down, but you can put together great dummy publications or one-of-a-kind reports this way.

FIGURE 18.6

The new Output options in the Print dialog box, reflect both the user work style and evolving equipment quality.

The *All*, *Odd*, and *Even* options (Page Sequence) do what they imply. To print all pages in sequence, select All Pages. To print only odd numbered pages (usually right side pages in a spread), pick Odd Pages. Even Pages are for left facing pages of a spread.

The *Back to Front* option is handy for moving from one printer to another. Today's work environment may force you to move from one computer to another. Consequently, you may work on several styles of printers. This option saves the aggravation of having to reshuffle the papers when all document pages print first to last page. Use it with *Collate* to help sort sequential pages. *Spreads* allows you to print left and right hand pages together as one spread.

One interesting feature is that of the *Blank Pages* option. At first, it may not seem very intelligent to pay for printing blank pages at a service bureau. Before the document goes to the service bureau you may want to make that dummy, using the desktop laser printer. But this option allows you to keep your sanity when creating a comprehensive layout.

NOTE

Many QuarkXPress users feel more comfortable with their own form of registration and trim marks. They choose to draw their own marks, rather than use those in the software. Also, at the last QUI conference some people noted that the registration marks were off one pixel, which was not acceptable in their work.

Select the popup menu option **On**, in the *Registration* option and your document will print with trim and registration marks. You have the option of placing these marks on center or off center.

WARNING

Check with your service bureau or printer to see what setting they suggest in OPI.

The OPI options are also relatively new (introduced in version 3.1). This pop-up menu allows you to specify the way pictures and Open Prepress Interface (OPI) comments are output. The choice depends on which way you plan to output the document and on whether you have high-resolution files with pictures in the document. OPI is available only when you select a PostScript device in the Chooser. Options include *Omit Tiff*, *Omit TIFF & EPS*, and *Include Images*.

Omit TIFF & EPS suppresses the printout of images in both the TIFF and EPS picture format. OPI comments for both formats are in the output data. You should choose this option when going out to a device that replaces TIFF and EPS comments with those of higher resolution images. Sending PostScript images to color separation devices like a Scitex or Crossfield will require replacing low-resolution images with high-resolution ones.

Omit TIFF suppresses the printout of TIFF pictures but TIFF OPI comments remain in the output data. EPS pictures print normally, but EPS OPI comments are not included. Choose this option when outputting to an OPI system that replaces TIFF pictures (most systems use this method).

Include Images prints pictures in TIFF and EPS formats as usual. OPI comments are included for TIFF but not EPS data. If the high-resolution image is not found, the system will default to using the associated PICT image in substitution.

The *Calibrated Output* is a helpful feature, especially for those QuarkXPress users striving for quality output. To use the calibrated settings built into QuarkXPress for most printers, check this option. Unchecked, the output matches other noncalibrated applications. The default is checked.

You can print *master pages,* as of version 3.1. If a master page displays in the document window, all controls in the Page Setup dialog box are available and all controls in the Print dialog box are available, except *All, From*, and *To. When a facing page master displays, both pages print.*

Hold down the Shift key as you click Print in the Print dialog box and you will have an information box show with Print Status. It gives you progress in printing, including information on Page number, what plate is currently imaging in CMYK separations, what tile is processing in tiled document printing and what file is in use for pictures.

PRINTING FOR COLOR

FEATURING

▶ Color input

▶ Color systems

▶ Trapping in QuarkXPress

Printing for color is perhaps the most controversial aspect of electronic publishing. For years, the work was divided among many experts: the typesetting shop set type; the artist generated the artwork; photographers photographed; camera operators converted it all to film, etc. Now you are in the midst of a one-stop prepress software environment capable of manipulating virtually all prepress specializations from one workstation.

Although QuarkXPress is on the leading edge in color capabilities, people are still reluctant to jump into color. Some professionals take the approach that color separation is a specialty best left to the color separation shop. It involves years of experience and expensive equipment to perform properly. Others see this new desktop technology as the stepping stone to one-man (or one-woman) prepress; there is no need to pay hundreds of dollars to separation specialists for a QuarkXPress job you can output at the local service bureau.

As electronic publishing software gains in sophistication and equipment becomes more powerful, it becomes a natural evolution to have desktop programs perform high level color work. This causes a dilemma for the typical user of software like QuarkXPress. That is, if the hardware and software can handle the job, why can't the people? Often, graphic designers and art directors are caught in the middle between art and craftsmanship. They are artistic in their creative designs and layouts, while the craftsmanship comes from a skilled technician operating a camera or printing press. Now, they must go into unfamiliar and uncomfortable territories to stay competitive. To maintain today, you have to have multiple skills. The designer must not only know type, page layout and communications skills, they now must also master the computer! The computer programs they face daily necessitate high skill levels in a wide variety of disciplines including photography and retouching, lithographic camera work, stripping and color separation. Programs such as

QuarkXPress make it an absolute priority to master these skills, if one is to stay competitive today. Most designers and artists are overwhelmed with the challenge, while printers feel challenged by new prepress tools. The dilemma continues! Can a desktop publishing program do it all?

This chapter attempts to just lay it on the line, presenting QuarkXPress in its base form. Certain XTensions can launch QuarkXPress into another realm in color, but, that's another chapter—*Chapter 20* to be exact!

GETTING COLOR INTO THE SYSTEM

There are several ways of getting color into your QuarkXPress document. These depend on what type of color image you need. Color ranges from *spot color* (single colors in a specific area or areas of the document page) to full color photography. The simplest way to deal with color in QuarkXPress is to use the techniques introduced in this book for applying color to your layout. This may include changing type to a specific color, or applying color and shade to item boxes or frames. If you need to import more complex work, such as a scanned piece of artwork or a photograph, there are a few alternatives.

BRINGING COLOR IN WITH A DESKTOP SCANNER

One of the most common tools to import color images incorporates the *desktop* or *flatbed* scanner. Scanner technology, like all other computer technology, has emerged fairly recently for the electronic publishing field. Anyone who started in this five years ago may have a collection of table-top scanners, from the original page scanners that frequently "ate" the copy, to flatbed black-and-white, color, grayscale, and now 24-bit scanners. Technology is moving at a frantic pace. Fortunately, the cost of desktop equipment is relatively low compared with traditional printers' equipment.

Desktop scanner costs range from a few hundred dollars for hand-held scanners to a few thousand dollars for medium quality, 24-bit color scanners. For a few thousand dollars more (nearly fifteen thousand more), you can get into the high level of desktop scanners. Naturally, the lower costing machines are more prevalent.

These machines all scan on a flat bed, so you can place the artwork or photograph over a glass, similar to making a photocopy. Appropriate software in the computer operates and manipulates the scan. Once the image is in the computer, you can manipulate the image through the scanning software or through certain photo retouching software packages or XTensions (see *Chapter 20* on XTensions).

There is another type of scanner to consider if you are in the market. The *slide scanner*, is also popular, although not so much as the flatbed style. With this device you scan a 35-mm photographic slide and alter the image with photo retouching software. There is something about transmitted light that has an edge over reflected light for scanner quality. The slide scanners were early in the market and have a quality edge over flatbed scanners.

A third kind of scanner, gaining momentum in the marketplace is the *drum scanner*. It looks like a shrunken color separation scanner that may be in the printer's shop, and in theory it works like the printer's more expensive equipment. To operate, you mount a color film transparency, or print on a glass drum or tube. A mechanism inside transmits light and analyzes every particle of the image as the drum rotates around at a high rate of speed. This digitizes the information and stores it on the computer for analysis and manipulation. The entire unit rests on a desktop. Desktop drum scanners have an input resolution of up to 4000 dpi.

Technology is changing so quickly that you must do your own investigating into price and quality. What may be the best quality or emerging standard today may be outdated next year. The best way to keep abreast of technological advances is to attend trade shows and conferences whenever possible. You should also subscribe to trade journals and magazines.

CAPTURED VIDEO AND STILL VIDEO

Another method of color image input is through the technology of video. Video comes to desktop publishing in two basic styles: *captured* video and *still* video.

Captured video uses a video card and software inside your computer. This video card has connections to a video tape player and/or camcorder. As you play the tape, the software controls a utility that can capture one of the video frames (similarly for live video). The software then digitizes the captured image, making it suitable for manipulation like any other color image. Motion video captures have a tendency, as of this writing, to be of lower quality than still video captures, due to their scan-line capability. This may change if high-definition television (HDTV) becomes a standard.

Still video is somewhat similar to captured video. In still video, you use the same video capture board and software. You can directly connect the configured computer to a still video camera and/or a still video player (with record and play capabilities).

The still video camera resembles a traditional hand held 35-mm camera for film. You place a tiny floppy disk in the camera, though, rather than film. The image is stored on the floppy disk. Cameras range from rather inexpensive (a few hundred dollars) to extremely expensive (several thousand dollars) with complete interchangeable lenses from such well-knowns as Canon and Nikon. Naturally, the more expensive cameras have greater scan resolution. These cameras also have an external player—a video disk player you connect to the computer's video capture card.

These still video cameras are remarkable. You can even connect them to a telephone modem and transmit digital image. In Operation: Desert Storm, the military used these cameras to record images and send the pictures back to Washington for analysis the same day. This helped with daily strategy in the war.

MORE ON COLOR COMPUTER EQUIPMENT

What does it take to run color on your desktop? The answer is, money! To be properly equipped and competitive in this market today, you should plan to spend from $20,000 to $30,000. Costs include a quality scanner or scanners, a souped-up computer, and a color printer or proofing device.

TIP

Buy lotsa memory! If you intend to work with color, you're in the big leagues. You need the right tools to make it work. You should have a fast computer; at this writing a Quadra-style machine is best. It should have a minimum of 8 Mb of RAM, a large hard drive, and a removable cartridge drive. And while you've got the checkbook out, buy a 24-bit color graphics board with a two page high-resolution monitor.

All too often, people see the false potential for jumping into the desktop publishing market by looking at clone prices in the newspaper. They think that desktop computers and software can do it all. For the price of a clone and a software application, they think they can do everything that a troop of prepress craftsmen can. Obviously, it doesn't work like that.

THE COMPUTER

Since you already have a general idea on color input devices, as described above, you can jump ahead to the computer. This may be more appropriately named the "color workstation." There are several companies marketing packaged systems that they call color workstations. The packages include all necessary hardware, storage, and software to be in this business.

If you want to build a system yourself you can do it through standard computer equipment and peripherals. Start with a solid computer platform, such as a Macintosh that you can expand later. For example, the IIcx and IIci machines can upgrade to the Quadra line. Since it is the philosophy of Apple and other computer manufacturers to update their computer lines once or twice a year, it is inappropriate to quote specific model recommendations in this book. So generically, you want to obtain a fast computer, with potential for upgrade.

This fast computer should also have a high RAM memory potential. You should install a minimum of 8 Mb of memory, much more if you want to get serious about color. It is not uncommon for people working in this field to have 20, 32, or even 64 Mb of RAM memory in their systems. Today, with the 32mb memory modules, you can install up to 128 Mb RAM in high-end Macs (must be the John D. Rockefeller model). Remember, an uncompressed, high-resolution color picture may consume about 8 Mb of memory. You also have the advantage of using virtual memory in System 7, but reading and writing to a hard disk drive is much slower than using RAM memory.

TIP

In shopping for removable storage systems, check with your service bureau. If you are sending large files to the service bureau for color separation, it makes sense to purchase the same style of unit they use.

To store the large files you'll undoubtedly be using, you should also have a large hard disk, accompanied by a removable cartridge or disk system. Most service bureaus support the Syquest style of removable 44 or 88 Mb cartridges at this time. However, there are emerging technologies of optical disk and cartridge systems storing in excess of a gigabyte (1000 Mb) of material.

To see the high quality image on your computer, you need a monitor and graphics card capable of 24-bit quality, the highest available today. The ideal setup is to buy this configuration with a two-page monitor, or perhaps two monitors. In QuarkXPress, you may find it more productive to have a standard monitor (Apple 14″ RGB) to the side of your document layout monitor. This standard monitor could then house all your palettes. Two graphics cards in a Mac enable you to use two monitors; you can switch from one monitor to another with a sweep of the cursor.

PREPARING FOR COLOR OUTPUT WITH QUARKXPRESS

Along with the color capabilities outlined in the previous two chapters, QuarkX-Press excels in desktop publishing in an area called *trapping*. What is this mysterious concept so new to electronic publishing? Basically, it is manipulating the colors of objects so that there will not be too little or too much overlap of two colors side by side.

TRAPPING WITH DESKTOP COMPUTER TECHNOLOGY

Here is a good prank to play on your local printer. Call your print sales rep and say you have a color job prepared on the computer, complete with separations and trapping. Insist on highest quality and quick turn around. If your printer is like most you will hear dead silence on the other end of the line.

Generally, computer-prepared color has not been well received by the production community. Primarily, it has a bad track record because of calls like the one described above. Printers say that only about 5% of all color composed on the desktop computer is correctly done. Designers skilled in graphic layout have tried color separation and trapping fundamentals through an inexpensive computer program. True, today's programs can perform great work, but like anything else, skill makes the product as much as the tool. If you don't know about stripping, camera work, and separations, you probably will be out of your element in electronic separation and trapping.

But what the heck, maybe it is getting foolproof! QuarkXPress and its many XTension developers would like you to do separations on the computer. So now we get to the capabilities of separation, and more specifically in this chapter, trapping, in QuarkXPress.

WHAT EXACTLY IS TRAPPING ANYWAY?

Just what is trapping and why is it so controversial on the desktop computer? Trapping is a manipulation process in color work that overcomes the limitations of printing with the transparent inks that are, for the most part, used in process color printing. It is the combination of those transparencies that give the color spectrum for full-color printing. If you want a specific color to highlight, you may choose to have it print alone on the paper, not to overlap. As Figure 19.1 depicts, if you hold back ink in certain areas, such as for the type characters, then fill with a different colored ink, registration has to be perfect! Anything less is blatantly recognized as an error in printing. Printers hate this because it makes them look bad, even if it is the person doing the prepress work (i.e., *you*) who is in error. A certain amount of press misregister is attributable to paper shrinkage, plate misalignment or other reasons. Proper trapping hides this due to a precise overlap that barely covers where the two colors meet.

NOTE

Registration is when each color image in the multi-color printing process is in exact alignment and position, relative to other colors of the print. In four-color work, cyan, magenta, yellow and black must be in exact position printed on the same sheet of paper to give full-color printing properly. Printers use the registration mark target (circle with lines crossing) to help align each color as it prints on the press.

FIGURE 19.1

Using shades instead of colors (because the book is not printed in color), the illustration shows trapping problems.

TRAPPING OPTIONS AND CORRECTIONS

There are three options in trapping: traditional, high-end, and desktop. Printers and prepress shops often must originate or duplicate (repair) separations and traps made by desktop publishers. This is nothing new. These people have been in that business since day one. The biggest frustration they have is redoing someone else's work—usually the desktop designer's.

In traditional shops, printers may ask clients to go back and correct faulty traps (although it's highly unlikely they will succeed the second time) or they can correct it themselves. Most often they opt for the latter because they know how to control quality.

NOTE

Outline type was generated through choke and spread techniques on the camera before the font was available on phototype.

In a traditional trap, the printer (lithographic camera operator or stripper) creates create *chokes* and *spreads*. These are trapping terms meaning to enlarge the size of specific colored image areas, slightly, to meet and overlap the next color they touch (spread) or reduce them slightly (choke). This is a technique that has been around for decades.

A popular way to hide the white paper when two colors meet is to spread or choke colors so that they overlay slightly. When adjacent colors have a slight overlap of the proper amount, they give the optical illusion of just touching and help hide misregistration. Other names for chokes and spreads include *shrinks* and *grips* and *fatties* and *thinnies*.

Another form of trapping is through high-end equipment. These machines are laser scanner systems costing up to a million dollars. These systems can be deadly accurate, as well as perform a variety of special effects. Ask an owner of one of these systems if your $700 Mac software can trap as well as his equipment!

Most printers would rather generate their own traps from the start. So if you plan to work with a particular printer, camera operator or color separator, talk to them first before blindly plowing ahead. If you decide that traditional and high-end color separation aren't appropriate for your needs, you may want to consider color separation and trapping on the desktop computer. The following section gives an overview trapping potential in QuarkXPress.

TRAPPING WITH QUARKXPRESS

If you decide that traditional and high-end color separation are not appropriate for your needs, you may want to consider color separation and trapping on the desktop computer. This section gives an overview trapping potential in QuarkXPress.

TIP

Some colors are more difficult to trap to than others; for example, gold is difficult. Good communication with your printer during the job preparation can help you avoid generating unprintable areas. A little planning goes far.

To print the colors you have in your QuarkXPress document, a printing plate is made for each spot or process color separation. When multiple plates (inks) are used on a press job, each one has to print in perfect registration. If not, in places where one ink meets another, a thin white line (the white of the paper) will show through. This is undesirable!

To deal with trapping problems in QuarkXPress, select Edit ➤ Colors. The Colors dialog box displays (see Figure 19.2). Remember, if you are in a document, the Colors for *document* dialog box is specific to colors in that document. If you are not in a document, default or global changes will occur as you change color attributes in the Colors dialog box.

FIGURE 19.2

*The Colors for docu-
ment dialog box (Edit
➤ Colors) has a button
for Edit Trap.*

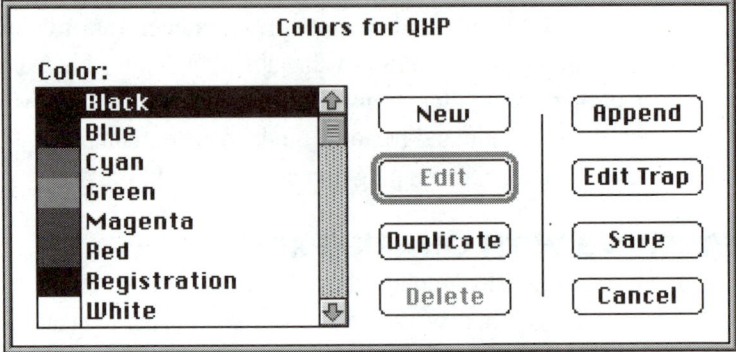

NOTE

*There are three types of trapping in QuarkXPress: automatic, color-
specific, and custom.*

Highlight a color you wish to trap and click on the *Edit Trap* button. This takes
you to another dialog box, the Trap Specifications for *color* dialog box (where
color is your specified color). As shown in Figure 19.3, the Trap Specifications dialog box allows you to pick the color your chosen color will trap to. It spreads to
the background color you select here. If, for example, yellow type is to appear
over a blue background, you would have selected Edit Trap for Yellow; on the Trap
Specifications dialog box, your color (background) choice would be Blue.

NOTE

*A foreground color (also known as an object color) can trap
relative to its background color in two ways: (1) Spreads—the
color item enlarges slightly to overlap the background color; (2)
Chokes—the area of the background where the object should go
(called the knockout area) reduces slightly so that the background
color overlaps the foreground color.*

FIGURE 19.3

The Trap Specifications dialog box for your chosen color to trap to the background color.

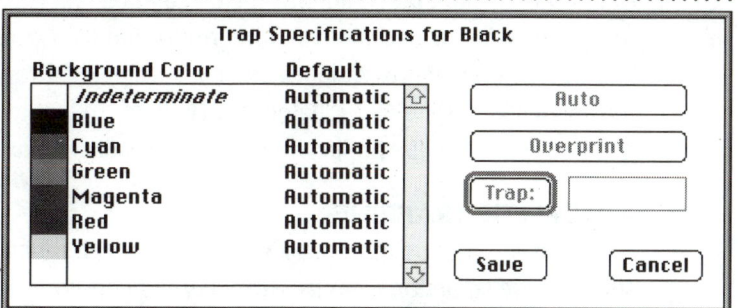

Once you select the background color to trap toward, you can apply the trap in an automatic or manual technique. The preferred method is manual, because of the control you have over trap values. In QuarkXPress, you select manual by typing in a trapping value, thereby creating one uniform spread or choke around the colored object. Certain problems may arise when objects protrude slightly out of the background area. Other problems may occur where there are more than three colors involved (see Figure 19.4). Trapping is meant to have one color work with another (two colors); when you have three or more colors, the formula gets rather complex and confusing.

FIGURE 19.4

You may have trapping problems when odd overlaps or odd color combinations occur.

QuarkXPress' automatic trapping, the default method, is based on the relative *lu-minance* (value or darkness) of foreground and background colors. You can specify how QuarkXPress applies automatic trapping through the Trap options in the Application Preferences dialog box (Edit ➤ Preferences ➤ Application). Figure 19.5 illustrates the Application Preferences dialog box.

AUTOMATIC TRAPPING

To specify the method that QuarkXPress uses to determine the trapping relationship, choose an option from the *Auto Method* pop-up menu in the Trapping Preferences dialog box. *Absolute* traps the value in the *Auto Amount* field, according to the darker foreground or background color. The background color chokes by Auto Amount if the foreground color is darker; it spreads if the foreground color is lighter.

Choose *Proportional* to trap using a fraction of the value in the Auto Amount field. This is based on the difference between luminance of the color. The formula is:

Auto Amount x (foreground color darkness—background color darkness)

The background color chokes by the resulting amount if the foreground object color is darker; the foreground color spreads by the amount if the object color is lighter.

. . . .
FIGURE 19.5
The Trapping Prefer-ences dialog box

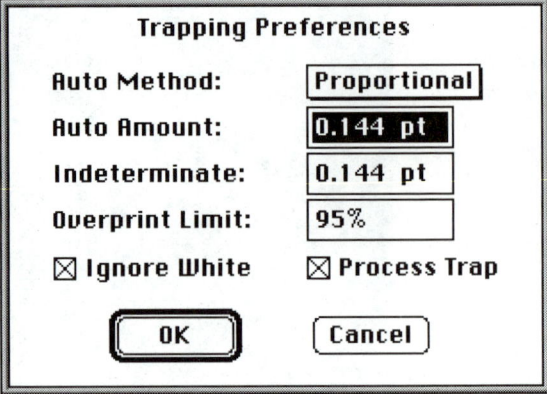

To control the amount of automatic choke applied, (Auto Amount + or Auto Amount −), enter a value between 0 and 36 pt, in increments as fine as 0.001 pt in the Auto Amount value field. You can also enter the word *overprint*, which results in foreground and background colors with an Auto relationship.

The *Indeterminate* value controls the amount of trap applied to objects in front of multiple-color or conflicting trap-relationship backgrounds. Values should range from −36 pt to 36 pt., in increments as fine as 0.001 pt. You may also type *overprint* in the field. This results in foreground colors with Auto relationship to the Indeterminate background color.

The Overprint Limit option enables you to specify a shade above or below which an object color will overprint its background, enter a value between 0% and 100%, in increments as fine as 0.1% The value entered here affects black when black is an object color set to Auto in the Trap Specifications dialog box. It also affects any object color specified Overprint as the color-specific trapping relationship in this dialog box.

Check *Ignore White* to specify that an object in front of multiple backgrounds (including white), not take white into account while trapping. Unchecked, all items overprint a white background color. Overprint is considered an infinite choke. If an object (foreground) color is in front of both a white background and background color as specified to spread, it will trap to the Indeterminate color.

THE PROCESS TRAP OPTION OF THE TRAPPING PREFERENCES DIALOG BOX

Check the Process Trap option to have QuarkXPress trap process separation plates individually when a page contains overlapping process colors. QuarkXPress compares the darkness of each process component of the foreground (object) color relative to its background color darkness. So if, for example, two shades of magenta are compared, then like comparisons are made for the other printer separation plates, yellow, cyan and black.

Check Process Trap with overlapping process colors and an *absolute* trapping relationship and QuarkXPress divides the absolute value in half and applies it to the darker component of each plate. This provides a smoother trap while providing the same area of overlap.

If touching process colors have *proportional* automatic trapping, the amount of trap is determined by multiplying the Auto Amount value (specified in the Trapping Preferences dialog box) by the difference in darkness between the object color and the background color. This trap value then applies as explained above for colors with *absolute* trapping relationships.

COLOR	OBJECT	BACK-GROUND	ABSOLUTE TRAP	PROPORTIONAL TRAP
C	70%	30%	+1/2 trap amount	Auto Amount (70%–30%)/2
M	30%	50%	−1/2 trap amount	Auto Amount (30%–50%)/2
Y	70%	80%	−1/2 trap amount	Auto Amount (70%–80%)/2
K	20%	15%	+1/2 trap amount	Auto Amount (20%–15%)/2

When Process Trap is unchecked, QuarkXPress traps all process components equally using the trapping value associated with the object color relative to the background color.

NOTE

When Process Trap is checked, trapping values in the dialog box may not be implemented as you expect when you print process separations: the trap value specified will be divided among plates. To trap text, pictures, and items as they were in earlier QuarkXPress versions, uncheck Process Trap.

COLOR-SPECIFIC TRAPPING IN QUARKXPRESS

To specify trapping values for specific objects relative to specific colored backgrounds, use the Colors dialog box (Edit ➤ Colors). Select the color to trap as the foreground or object color, and click the Edit Trap button. The Trap Specifications dialog box displays. The Default column lists trap values for each color, as defined in the Trapping Preferences dialog box. Overprint indicates that the object color (with an applied shade greater than that specified in the Overprint limit field of the Trapping Preferences dialog box) will not be knocked out of the background color's separation plate. A numeric value indicates a custom Trap value.

NOTE

For small text (less than or equal to 24 points) and small objects (dimensions less than or equal to 10 points), QuarkXPress attempts to preserve the object shape during process trapping. It does this by disallowing spreads or chokes when the object's shape would be compromised. QuarkXPress does this by comparing the darkness of the object on each plate to the darkness of its entire background and only spreading if the darkness of that plate is less than or equal to half the darkness of its background. Conversely, choking will only occur when the background plate component is less than or equal to half the darkness of the object.

NOTE

A term describing a background with multiple colors in QuarkXPress is Indeterminate color. A color picture would be an example of Indeterminate color because of its multi-color background. QuarkXPress traps foreground colors to a specified background color in an Indeterminate color environment.

To specify trapping between the selected foreground color and the background color, select from one of the background colors listed. To select more than one background color, hold down the Shift key while clicking on background color names to select. The Auto, Overprint, and Trap buttons become active.

Specify auto trapping between the foreground color and selected background color(s) by clicking on Auto.

To ensure that applied foreground color items are not knocked out of the selected background color's separation plate, click Overprint. Only object colors with an applied shade greater than that specified in the Overprint Limit field of the Trapping Preferences dialog box will overprint.

To specify a trap value between the foreground color and selected background color(s), enter a value in the Trap field and click Trap. Enter values from −36 pt to 36 pt, in increments as fine as 0.001 pt. A negative trap value chokes the object color's knockout area on the background color's separation plate; a positive value spreads object colors so they overlap the background color.

THE TRAP INFORMATION PALETTE

The Show/Hide Trap Information command under the View menu displays a palette you can use to specify trapping relationships for adjacent colors on an object-by-object basis. Bring up the Trap Information palette as you would any other palette listed under the View menu. Then move it and close it also as you do other palettes. See Figure 19.6 for a representation of the Trap Information palette.

The Trap Information palette consists of pop-up menu areas that vary, depending on the type of active item involved. They display six options for trapping color applied to the active item to its background color or adjacent color. The palette also enables you to trap text or a picture to its background color, or trap a frame to its background color. Options include Default, Overprint, Knockout, Auto Amount (+), Auto Amount (−), and Custom.

The *Default* option enables you to trap the current active object color against its background. The trap value is displayed in the field to the right of the pop-up menu.

Select *Auto* to trap determined by the Auto Amount and Auto Method settings in the Trapping Preference dialog box.

FIGURE 19.6
*The Trap Information
palette (View ➤ Show
Trap Information)*

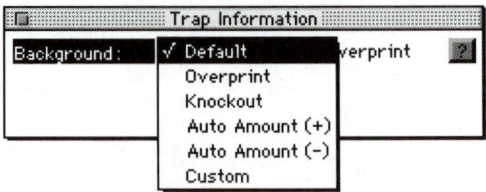

The *Overprint* option is chosen if you want to specify the current object color not knock out of its background. This allows the foreground color to print over the background color directly and may yield unexpected results if the printer uses typical transparent inks. Choosing Overprint overrides the *Overprint Limit* value entered in the Trapping Preference dialog box.

To specify the current object color knock out of its background color (printing on the white paper, rather than the background color ink), with no trapping, choose *Knockout*.

Select the *Auto Amount* (+) or (−) options to select a spread or choke preference. Choose Auto Amount (+) for the value displayed to the right of the pop-up menu is positive, indicating that the object color will be *spread*. If you choose Auto Amount (−), the value displayed to the right of the pop-up menu is negative, indicating that the background color will be choked.

Specify your own trapping value for an active item by choosing *Custom* from the pop-up menu. Enter a value in the field to the right of the pop-up menu from −36 pt to 36pt in increments as fine as .001-point.

Information is available by clicking and holding on the question mark button. This is a type of on-line help built into this palette. To close the information window, release the mouse button.

PRINTING A COLOR DOCUMENT

Like everything else, there are a variety of ways to do a color print of your document. You might want to buy a color printer for around $10,000. There are two basic varieties. First, there is the *thermal wax transfer*; this takes colored wax sheets and bakes each color image down on the page, e.g., yellow, magenta, cyan, and black. Currently this takes about a minute per color. This means that a letter-size document with full color will proof in about four minutes. The cost and speed of production prevent this from being much more than a proofing system at this time.

 **NOTE**

Rendering color on the computer monitor differs from rendition color on the proof. And both are different from color on the printed paper. An absolute must when doing prepress work for color printing is to have a proof made after the film is run in the imagesetter. Buy a Chromalin or some comparable high quality proof. Average price for the proof is about $50.

Another type of machine used more often for photographic rendition is the *dye sublimation* printer. Originally intended as an output device for still video, it can be used to print document pages. However, output size is more in line with photographic paper standards than for printing paper standard sizes. For example, you can print a dye sublimation print in 8″× 10″, but not 8½× 11″. This may change as the dye sublimation printer gains wider acceptance in the desktop market.

These methods provide the designer and client with comprehensive layouts or proofs of the layout. They are nowhere near accurate enough to provide a color separation proof. This must be done using output negative film in more traditional methods. There are a variety of techniques used here also such as ColorKey, Matchkey, and Chromalin. These tend to be more accurate than the color printer proof, but they still take some imagination compared with color on the printed page. This type of proof is more the standard in the industry than other techniques mentioned.

The ultimate color proof always has been and always will be the *press proof*. This is a proof that is run on the press, using the exact negatives, printing plates, inks, and paper used for the job. This is also the most expensive kind of proof, for obvious reasons.

THE EFICOLOR XTENSION IN PRINTING

The EfiColor XTension can have a profound impact on color printing and the methods you use to send the document for output. Specifically, you can calibrate your document's color for output in a PostScript or QuickDraw environment.

PREPARING TO PRINT A POSTSCRIPT DOCUMENT

The EfiColor XTension enables proper color management for both PostScript output devices and QuickDraw output devices (those using Apple's proprietary output language). To prepare a document for PostScript output, select the printer from Chooser, under the Apple menu. Then, open the Page Setup dialog box (File ➤ Page Setup). The EfiColor XTension adds two pop-up menus in the Page Setup dialog box. These enable you to select the EfiColor profile and, for color separation profiles, the percentage of Gray Component Replacement (GCR).

Gray Component Replacement (GCR) is a technique used by printers to compensate for ink impurities. Theoretically, combining the yellow, magenta and cyan inks will yield black. In reality, they combine to form a muddy color. To counter this, the printer removes a percentage of each color substituting it with pure black ink. This reduces the amount of ink necessary for proper page coverage, reduces cost, and produces a richer look.

Since GCR applies only to a color separation setup in QuarkXPress, it works only when you select a separation profile in the Page Setup dialog box (e.g., SWOP-Coated). The percentage represents the amount of gray component (based on your document color applications) replaced by black ink. Your choice may have a significant effect on the document's printed color appearance.

WARNING

"You want to do what?" Selecting GCR may be risky if you are an experienced printer. A great deal of practice (combined with taking your printer out to lunch) may eventually yield the results you want. You can do it, but be careful!

After activating your document (you can't print a document without its being open, unless it was saved with the "print to file" option checked), open the Page Setup dialog box. In this dialog box, change any field or pop-up menu to the setting desired, including the Printer Type. Next, choose a profile from the EfiColor Profile pop-up menu (e.g., SWOP-Coated). *SWOP* is a paper term meaning Specifications for Web Offset Publications. Select *None* if none is available.

TIP

If there is no appropriate profile for your printer or offset process, choose the None option. This disables the EfiColor XTension color conversion for printing.

If a color profile is available, the GCR (Gray Component Replacement) percentage pop-up menu becomes active. Select your percentage value for this field.

NOTE

For many printer color profiles, the GCR menu is activated, but the value is hard set at 100%. For some black-and-white printers, selecting an EfiColor profile leaves the GCR menu off.

Depending on the printer selection, the check box (near the lower-right corner of the Page Setup dialog box) has a different label. If the printer choice is a color printer, the check box shows *Use EfiColor Screen Values*. Check this option to ensure documents make use of profile-specific screen angles; unchecked, the QuarkXPress default screen angles are active.

If you have a black-and-white, low-resolution printer or an imagesetter chosen, the check box reads *Use PDF Screen Values*. Check this option to ensure proper output with available screen angles in the Printer Description File (PDF). Left unchecked, QuarkXPress applies default screen angles.

After you've checked all other fields and pop-up menus, click OK. Finally, open the Print dialog box (File ➤ Print). Make necessary changes, then click OK to close the dialog box. Your document should then begin processing for the selected output device.

PREPARING TO PRINT ON A QUICKDRAW DEVICE

Contrary to popular belief, not all Macintosh output is PostScript-driven. Adobe's PostScript page description language dominates the electronic publishing industry, but there are alternatives, including *QuickDraw*, from Apple. The EfiColor XTension allows QuickDraw output with the proper profile. Contact EFI for information about obtaining a profile if necessary.

NOTE

Contact EFI (Electronics for Imaging) at 415-742-3400 for additional profiles. Pricing typically ranges from $129 to $329 for each profile.

To prepare for QuickDraw printing, begin by opening the document. Select the appropriate QuickDraw device (printer) from the Chooser under the Apple menu. (Not all output devices are printers; some may be film recorders, imagesetters, etc., hence the moniker, *device*). Next, choose Page Setup (File ➤ Page Setup). Make appropriate selections in the dialog box for page orientation, scaling, etc. Select the appropriate profile in the EfiColor Profile pop-up menu. After all necessary alterations, click on OK to accept and close the dialog box.

Page Setup dialog box options (for QuickDraw) are intuitive, in typical Mac style so you shouldn't have any trouble. However, various output devices may have different options showing in the Page Setup dialog box. If you need assistance, use the dialog box's online help or check the manuals.

TIP

To obtain matching color, any special effects you choose must be the same as those specified on the EfiColor Profile Reference Card. The Reference Card is available with your new QuarkXPress 3.2 and EfiColor XTension manuals, or may be supplied when you order a new EfiColor Profile from EFI.

Finally, to print on a QuickDraw device, choose Print from the File menu. Make appropriate modifications in the Printer dialog box. Click OK and send the document to print.

THE MISSING PROFILES ALERT

If you try to print without an appropriate profile (in either PostScript or Quick-Draw) the Missing Profiles alert box appears (see Figure 19.7). It shows the options to List Profiles, Cancel or OK. To bypass the Missing Profiles dialog box click OK. The EfiColor XTension will print using default values specified in the EfiColor Preferences dialog box.

FIGURE 19.7

The Missing Profiles alert appears when you try to print without an appropriate profile.

Select the List Profiles option and a Missing Profiles dialog box appears listing profiles with their associated objects and status. Objects include such things as pictures, RGB/HSB colors, and CMYK colors. Choose a profile whose object is Pictures to replace profiles for all pictures at once or on a picture-by-picture basis. Pick a profile whose object is RGB/HSB or CMYK and you can replace profiles for all QuarkXPress colors defined in those chosen models.

To replace a profile for *all* pictures, select a profile whose object is pictures; then click Replace All. A small dialog box appears giving you the option of changing rendering styles for all pictures or the EfiColor Profile.

Substitute profiles for *individual* pictures from the Missing Profiles dialog box by selecting (clicking on) the profile to alter. Click the Show First button to display the first picture with a missing profile. Click Replace. Select a profile from the EfiColor Profile pop-up menu and click OK. Click Show Next to display the next picture; repeat the process until all pictures display and alterations complete.

NOTE

Holding down the Option key while clicking the Show Next in the Missing Profiles dialog box changes Show Next to Show First.

Use similar techniques, as just described to alter profiles for objects in the RGB/HSB or CMYK colors. Highlight the profile assigned to the color model you want to change, click Replace All; choose a profile from the EfiColor Profile pop-up menu and click OK. After necessary profile alterations, click OK to close the Missing Profiles dialog box.

YOUR CAPSTONE DOCUMENT

Now, that you are in the final chapters of this book, it's time to introduce your Capstone document. Similar in fashion to your first QuarkXPress document in *Chapter 1*, you will have the opportunity here to work through a comprehensive document. This exercise incorporates many of the features and tricks introduced throughout the last eighteen chapters, plus a few not introduced until now.

This project is your *Capstone Document*, for lack of a more descriptive title. The project consists of a document with four pages incorporating text, graphic and line items (see Figure 19.8).

You will position most items on the Document pages, but the automatic page number should appear on a Master page. The *Capstone Document* incorporates a wide variety of QuarkXPress features, from basic to advanced; including the following:

- Alteration of preferences (Application, General, EfiColor)
- Creation and utilization of a Library palette
- Multiple column layouts
- Importing of text and pictures
- Manipulation of colors and shades

FIGURE 19.8
*A representation of the
Capstone document in
its facing pages format.*

- Flip (horizontal or vertical) of text and graphics
- Incorporation of the Cool Blends XTension
- Vertical justification of text
- Layering
- Runaround options
- Manipulation of horizontal and vertical scale for text
- Drop cap and other format manipulations for text
- Image manipulation across a two-page spread
- Manual integration of text box items
- Linking of text items
- Framing
- Automatic page numbering
- Auto save
- Auto backup
- EfiColor Profiles
- Adding new colors to the QuarkXPress system palette
- Creating new pages through the Document Layout palette
- Automatic trapping
- Color proofing and color separation

The project will have twelve steps:

Step 1: Planning Your Project

Step 2: Creating a New Document

Step 3: Creating a New Library (Palette)

Step 4: Stocking the Library via the New Document

Step 5: Creating Linked Text Boxes

Step 6: Positioning Automatic Page Numbers

Step 7: Importing Generic Text

Step 8: Changing Text Attributes

Step 9: Importing and Altering Library Graphics

Step 10: Creating and Manipulating the QuickRelease Banner (Front and Back Pages)

Step 11: Including New Colors and Blends

Step 12: Gathering the Document for Printing

To properly participate in this exercise, you have to treat it in somewhat of a "cookbook-style" fashion. The "ingredients" you will need may vary from those illustrated here, but generic copies are acceptable, (you're learning how to apply features here). So before you begin, locate the following:

▶ Text Files—you need two or three text files from a word processor. You can save these text files in their native formats. (For this exercise, it doesn't matter what the text says because you are practicing technique only). The word processor file format should match one of those in the XTensions list. Remember, while in QuarkXPress, you can hold Option down and choose Apple ➤ About QuarkXPress to look at the QuarkXPress Environment and see the installed XTensions in your system. Text files saved as ASCII or generic text will work fine here also.

▶ Graphic Files—the Capstone Document uses primarily TIFF and EPS file formats; but use whatever format you want, as long as you understand its strengths and weaknesses in the document.

▶ Cool Blends XTension—this is a new addition in QuarkXPress 3.2.

▶ EfiColor XTension—this exercise requires use of the EfiColor XTension. If you haven't enough memory currently to run this, run out and get some more. We'll wait for you!

▶ A dye sublimation color printer—well, OK, if you don't have one of these, don't run out and buy it. A $20,000 expenditure may not really be necessary. Let's just skip the color proof thing for the Capstone Document! You may find it helpful though to have a standard black-and-white laser printer attached to your Macintosh.

Once you have these elements of your document (sans the dye sub), place all files in a folder you can easily gain access to, such as on the desktop. Label it *Capstone Folder* (see Figure 19.9).

FIGURE 19.9

Keep it on the desktop during your project for quick reference.

Capstone Folder

Step 1: Planning Your Project

Carefully planning the project document prior to execution is extremely important. Read that again. CAREFULLY PLANNING THE PROJECT DOCUMENT PRIOR TO EXECUTION IS EXTREMELY IMPORTANT! You should have all elements planned, down to the point size, scale, color, and placement that you will use.

In the printing industry there is a phrase that says "There's never enough time to do it right, but always time to do it over!" This is why there is only an average of 3% profit margin in this industry. In today's highly competitive electronic publishing industry, you must do better.

To give you an edge on this document, you can see a thumbnail sketch of the completed Capstone Document back in Figure 19.8. You should try to create a similar document, using graphic elements available in your system.

What's the first thing to do when designing a new two-dimensional communication, such as a QuarkXPress document? You should get to know your customer and the intended audience of the communique. You must know the customer, because graphic design is a psychic business. You must be able to read someone else's mind and please them with your design. A customer's litany must include the words "just design something and make it look good" or "I don't know what I want, but I'll know it when I see it!" Next, you must determine the best communication for the selected audience. These are details you probably work with every day, so skip to the good stuff, your Capstone Document. It is largely predetermined for you so the client and customer considerations are not necessary here. You can concentrate on technique!

The Capstone Document depicted here contains the following specifications:

- Four (facing) pages in the document, page size is a standard US Letter ($8\frac{1}{2}\times11''$).

- Typefaces used are Avant Garde for banners.

- Type specs for the first banner: page 1 includes 123.83 point size; −10 tracking with specific added kerning areas; center alignment within the text item. The mirror image banner consists of the same type specs, but with a flipped image in a 20% black color. The "banner" on page 4 has been manipulated to fit the space, as shown.

- All items, unless otherwise noted, are set to Runaround None.

- The first story (text file) for page 1 consists of approximately 200 words (greeking is used here for placement). The story on linked text items spanning pages 2–3 contain approximately 730 words. Page 4 has a story of around 300 words This information is given so you can gauge your dummy copy size for insertion.

- The graphics used include those identified through the Picture Usage dialog box (Utility ➤ Picture Usage). See Figure 19.10 for a representation. Note, it is important here to collect a copy of all graphic files into a single folder so that output later will be correct. Files that are moved or not readily linked to your document's picture items are classified as Missing. You can update their locations (links) through this dialog box.

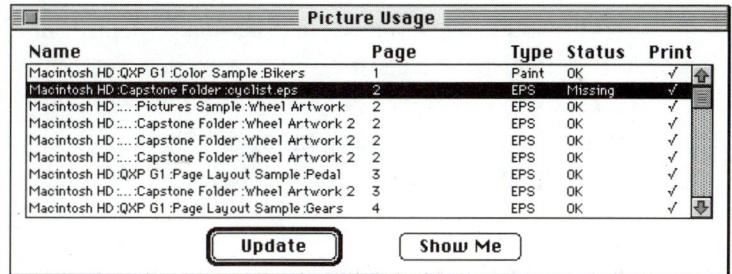

FIGURE 19.10
The Picture Usage dialog box shows an on-going record of what files are used.

- Colors added to the QuarkXPress color palette include two new CMYK combinations, named appropriate to their mixture, e.g., 15—10—20—0 and 38—65—40—0. It may be easier to add these colors to the palette before beginning the following procedural steps for the Capstone Document.

- EfiColor Profile usage is set as shown in the Profile Usage dialog box (Utilities ➤ Profile Usage). See Figure 19.11.

- The 27 lines on page 1 consist of a one-point weight, rotated 45 degrees with a step and repeat combination of 1 pica vertical, 1 pica horizontal.

FIGURE 19.11
The Profile Usage keeps track of your pictures and their associated color profiles.

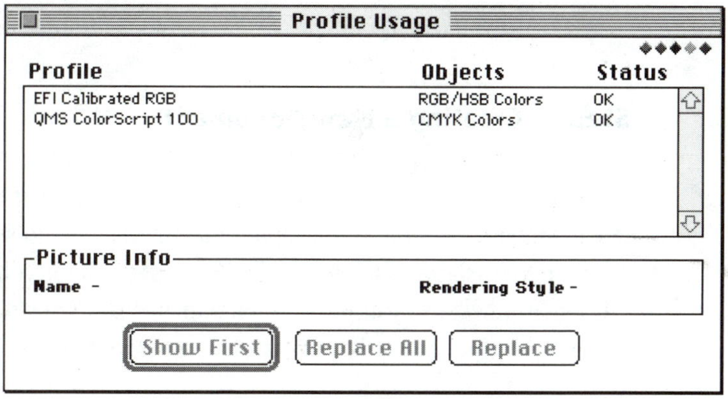

```
☐▒▒▒▒▒▒▒▒▒▒▒ Profile Usage ▒▒▒▒▒▒▒▒▒▒
                                            ◆◆◆◆◆
Profile                    Objects        Status
EFI Calibrated RGB         RGB/HSB Colors   OK      ⬆
QMS ColorScript 100        CMYK Colors      OK



                                                   ⬇
┌─Picture Info──────────────────────────────────┐
│ Name  -                     Rendering Style  - │
└────────────────────────────────────────────────┘
      ( Show First )  ( Replace All )  ( Replace )
```

BUILDING THE NEW DOCUMENT AND CAPSTONE LIBRARY

To storehouse items, you will take advantage of the QuarkXPress library palette. This is, in essence, a separate file. Once open, it acts like any other floating palette in that it can be moved and resized. The library can be used to store items, whether text, line, picture, or grouped. It is handy because, unlike the import feature (Get Text/Picture), it allows you to store, see, and label each item.

You place items into the Library from a QuarkXPress document. It does not allow you to simply import files; rather, you copy items from an active QuarkXPress document, then paste them into the Library. In our example, it may not seem like a proper use of time to import graphics into the Capstone Document, just to cut them for pasting into the Library, but think of the process. If you were to use the library items repeatedly, through other documents, it would be a good use of your time; for now, it remains only an exercise, so you can experience the process.

NOTE

Throughout the book, creating a new document has simply been noted as File ➤ New. QuarkXPress 3.2 differs slightly in this area by adding a pop-up menu in the File ➤ New selection. This pop-up menu includes your options of creating a new document or a new library. It has been assumed that you, as an experienced Macintosh user, would select the correct choice.

Step 2: Creating a New Document

Start by launching QuarkXPress (with EfiColor XTensions properly installed). Create a new document (File ➤ New). QuarkXPress 3.2 has altered the File/New Document area to show a pop-up menu enabling you to select either a New Document or a New Library to create. Throughout the book it has simply been noted as File ➤ New because you were, when appropriate, creating new documents, not libraries. Here again, you should create a *New Document*.

Although it sounds a bit out of sequence, you will use this new document as a "tool" to identify items for placement in the library, and later, for the final Capstone Document. In this way, the library will be stocked with items you may use in future documents, at least that is the rationale behind the Library.

Alter the New document dialog box to the following specifications: standard US Letter, facing pages with (inch) margins 1.25 inside, 0.75 outside, 0.75 top, 0.75 bottom, two columns with a gutter of 0.167 inches and the automatic text box is NOT checked (off). This will give a document that will allow a larger margin on the inside, for binding or hole punching. Press Enter.

Immediately upon opening the newly created document, save it in the Capstone Folder, under the name *Capstone Document*. The new Auto Save feature of QuarkXPress 3.2 will then save your document periodically and you don't have to worry too much about it. Once saved, you can activate the Auto Save feature through the Application Preferences dialog box (Edit ➤ Preferences ➤ Application).

The Application Preferences dialog box includes Auto Save as well as other new options. Check the Auto Save option to make it active (see Figure 19.12). Then, select the time you wish the auto save to work, the default is every five minutes, but you can change that by overstriking a new number in the field.

FIGURE 19.12

You may want to take advantage of the new Auto Save, Auto Backup, and Auto Library Save features in the Application Preferences dialog box (Edit ➤ Preferences ➤ Application).

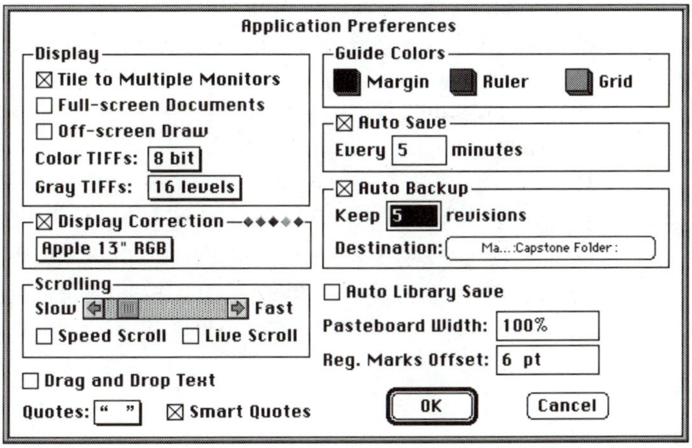

You may also wish to check the Auto Backup box in this Application Preferences dialog. Checked, it saves a backup file of your document at the time interval and location of your choice. Automatic Backup files are given the same name but a numerical suffix is added indicating the saved sequence. You may want to save these in a temporary area that you can easily trash later because they do take up space and aren't self-destructing files.

Other options in the Application Preference dialog box you should check (turn on) for the Capstone Document include Auto Library Save, Drag and Drop Text, Smart Quotes, and Display (EfiColor) Correction. The Auto Library prevents you from closing a document and not saving items placed in the library palette, which is a file unto itself needing to be saved. Smart Quotes converts word processing quotes, looking like inch marks, to typesetting quotes with a left opening set and a right closing set. Drag and Drop Text is a new feature for 3.2 that emulates other software applications so you can highlight a text string with the mouse and drag it to another location. At the new location you release the mouse button and the item moves there. The new Drag and Drop feature takes a bit of practice.

The Display Correction option shows a pop-up menu with either the Apple 13″ RGB or EFI Calibrated monitor as default. You should obtain, if necessary, and install the proper profile as described in *Chapter 17*. Once installed, your monitor's name becomes an option in this pop-up menu. Change it to read your monitor's profile for proper EfiColor XTension capabilities.

Additional elements of the Application Preference dialog box are not critical to operations for your use. Briefly, they include options to alter scrolling, picture rendering or drawing speeds, pasteboard size (that area outside your document page) and register marks offset. Leaving these to their default settings is OK here. Time to move on!

Next, open the EfiColor Preference dialog box (Edit ➤ Preferences ➤ EfiColor). Change the profile to match your monitor. Alter the output only if you have that expensive dye sub color proofer and the profile is listed; otherwise, leave it at the default value. Press Enter to accept the new changes and close to close the dialog box.

Open the General Preferences dialog box (Edit ➤ Preferences ➤ General). Make changes to the Guides and Item Coordinates. Guides is typically set in default to BE-HIND, which is a mystery. Why would anybody want a guideline they couldn't see? Changing it to FRONT enables you to see the guide line when you drag it from the ruler. Item Coordinates is changed here because the Capstone Document is a facing page spread (by choosing the Page option in the Item Coordinates area of the General Preferences dialog box).

For now, no other changes in preference selections are necessary. You can always change preferences while working on a document without having to save or worry about losing your project.

Step 3: Creating a New Library (Palette)

Prior to QuarkXPress 3.2, the Library was a floating palette available under the Utilities menu. This was the "black sheep" palette, as all others were selected or hidden from the View menu. Now, the Library palette has been removed from all menu show/hide options. The Library floating palette is now a full-fledged file that you must create and open from the File menu (File ➤ New ➤ Library). Once open, it can remain open in tandem with other QuarkXPress documents.

NOTE

The Library palette, although a self-contained file, acts like other floating palettes including the capability to remain in the same size and location if you quit QuarkXPress. Once you again launch QuarkXPress, the Library will be showing in exactly the same size and location it was last left. Once closed, you must open it from the File menu, as you would any other file. This enables you to have several library "files" rather than just one large library.

Functionally, you use the Library as a storage area for saved items you wish to call up frequently. You place items in the Library from the Mac's Clipboard. Click on a document item to activate it, then Copy (Edit ➤ Copy or keyboard equivalent) or Cut (Edit ➤ Cut or keyboard equivalent) it. Click on the library palette to activate it and Paste the recorded item in "work area" of the Library. You can then label it alphanumerically and use this as a reference as well as the visual check. You are now going to create a new Library for the Capstone Document.

Step 4: Stocking the Library via the New Document

First, you should already have the original document, Capstone Document, still open, as instructed in Step 2 above. Use this to create and modify an item(s) to place into the library. Start by creating a new picture item. Draw it large enough to comfortably house the graphic you want to import. Don't be concerned about exact size yet, as you can do some editing once the graphic is imported.

Next, you want to change to the Content Tool, activate the picture box item (show grab bars), and choose Get Picture (File ➤ Get Picture). Search out the file you want to import from your presaved inventory in the Capstone Folder. The example shown in Figure 19.13 shows a wheel taken from the QuarkXPress tutorial files. This EPS file imports easily, showing a PICT representation of the wheel. After importing the graphic, resize the picture item to be a tighter fit around the graphic. A simple way to resize the item is to click and drag on the bottom-right grab bar. This moves the boundaries of the item but does not affect the contents of the item.

FIGURE 19.13

The wheel artwork was used in its original form as well as altered in Adobe Illustrator for the Capstone Document.

To save this item with the resized perimeter, change to the Item tool, then click on the item to make it active. Select Cut from the Menu, keyboard, or command key sequence; this takes it from the screen to the Clipboard. Then, click on the library workspace to activate the library and Paste the clipboard item in position (bracketing pointers indicate a slot ready to paste into). It will show up as a thumbnail sketch of the original.

You can label the new library picture by double-clicking on the thumbnail. This brings up a dialog box enabling you to "name" the item. You may select a descriptive or categorical name. Labels can be used to screen items in the library. For example, you may want to have a library for transportation only. In this library you have pictures categorized, by label, of bicycles, automobiles, buses, etc. Selecting the label option allows you to show only the selection(s) you wish to see by category (see Figure 19.14).

Repeat the processes described above until you have all your picture items in the library (in this case only a few items are necessary). If you wanted to jump ahead

FIGURE 19.14

The Library enables you to save and classify items by name as well as through the thumbnail sketch.

to Step 10, the banners could even be stored as Library items, after manipulation. The Library can store any type of item, not just pictures. Once your items are archived you can then "begin" to work on the main document.

Step 5: Creating Linked Text Boxes

Actually, text boxes are linked on all pages except page 1, so you can start there. When the new document was created, the option for an automatic text box was intentionally NOT checked. This is because you will be working some manipulation of text around graphic items that requires full control of each column. An automatic text box would allow text to flow into two columns but would limit your control. On page 1 an automatic text box would force you to start copy in column 1. By manually placing a new text item inside the boundary of column 2 you can start the copy as desired.

Start by selecting the Text Box creation tool from the tool palette. (Hint: looks like a text character inside a box.) Next, click and drag to form the text box. Don't worry about the size or location. Rather, make sure the Measurements palette is showing (if not, select from View ➤ Show Measurements). Next, change the specifications (in the Measurements palette) of this new text item to match the following: X=4.519, Y=4.222, W=2.963, H=5.778. Type will be Bookman, 10 point, with Auto leading. As you may have guessed, these specifications come from looking at the product after design. You don't really have to be right on the mark for some of these, but if you use the Snap to Guides option (View ➤ Snap to Guides), it will help.

Next, create similar text item boxes to fit each column of the facing pages, page 2 and page 3. After each is constructed, use the Link tool and click on the first text box, column 1 of page 2. This activates the text box item; next click on the next column of that page. An arrow will show signifying where text will flow from column 1 (it will resume at the top of column 2). Select the Link tool again, click on column 2 to activate then click on column 3 (first column in page 3). This links those two columns. Repeat the linking process for column 3 to column 4. After you have all four columns linked on this two-page spread, then go to page 4.

Page 4 also has two manually inserted text box items (one in each column). Create and link these two columns together. Do not link them to any other columns or pages. When concluded you should have constructed and linked (where appropriate) a total of seven columns in the four-page document.

If you have a document with several pages it may be more efficient to create and link text boxes on the Master Page(s). Since this is only a four-page layout, working on the document page is acceptable. However, if you were setting up the layout on a master page, you could also include automatic page numbering.

Step 6: Positioning Automatic Page Numbers

To place an automatic page number on a document, the best place to do it is on the Master Page(s). Go to the Master Page of your Capstone Document. Remember, you can use the Document Layout palette or simply choose Master page from the Page menu (Page ➤ Display ➤ M1-Master 1).

Since you chose to create the new document with facing pages, the master consists of two pages in the layout, a left master and a right master, named L-M1-Master 1 and R-M1-Master 1.

Create a new text box for your automatic page number, on the left master page. The new box should have the following specifications on the Measurements palette: X=0.065, Y=8.021, W=0.949, H=0.653, Centered, Avant Garde, 24 point. The text you insert will be the designation for an automatic continuing page (Command-3). The copy placed by this code will look like a less-than sign, a pound sign, and a greater-than sign, but will change to the appropriate page number on your document pages.

After you have keyed in the proper key combination for the page number, highlight it for further manipulation. Use the content tool to highlight the text and change its Vertical Scale. Select Horizontal/Vertical Scale from the Style menu. In the dialog box, click on the pop-up menu to select the Vertical option (as opposed to Horizontal). Change the figure to 150% for a vertical stretch of the characters. Vertical scale is a new feature in QuarkXPress 3.2.

Since you have this text item and its contents all set up, duplicate it through the Step and Repeat feature. Set the horizontal step to 16 inches, vertical to 0 inches, and have one repeat. This will place another page number on the right master page, opposite the one you just manipulated on the left master.

That's all you need for these master pages. Now change back to the Document pages to import text.

Step 7: Importing Generic Text

As indicated prior, this exercise stresses features and techniques, therefore, the text files used are of little consequence. Use any text, as long as you can properly import and edit it as specified.

Starting with page 1, select the content tool and click on the single text item in column two. Once active, choose the Get Text option located in the File menu. Locate and import the copy you have set aside for this area. The text will flow into your designated text box item. If the file is properly sized, the amount of text is nearly equal to the room you have established for the text item. You can make some adjustments as necessary.

Next, go to the first column of page 2 and repeat the text import process, bringing in the proper text file large enough to adequately cover the columns. If the text is too little to fill all four columns, don't worry. Several lines of text will be displaced through Runaround once you bring in your graphic items.

Finally import text for columns on page 4. Use the same technique as just described above. Once text is imported for all pages, you can fine tune.

Step 8: Change Text Attributes

You have to start out manipulating text by changing the font, size, style, etc. as needed. Chances are that you don't have the specified font and size, i.e. Bookman 12 point, already in your text, so you can change it now. You could do this by starting at page 1. Activate the text box with the content tool and highlight all the copy; change the font and size accordingly; repeat for the story on pages 2–3, and page 4. But, please don't bother with this tedium!

The easiest way to change type attributes for this example is through the Font Usage option under the Utilities menu. This dialog box has information on all your font uses and allow you to alter them as needed (see Figure 19.15). Make alterations here to change type attributes to Bookman, 10 point, or whatever font you have that is close to Bookman.

FIGURE 19.15

The Font Usage dialog box (Utilities ➤ Font Usage) enables you to selectively alter font characteristics for the entire document.

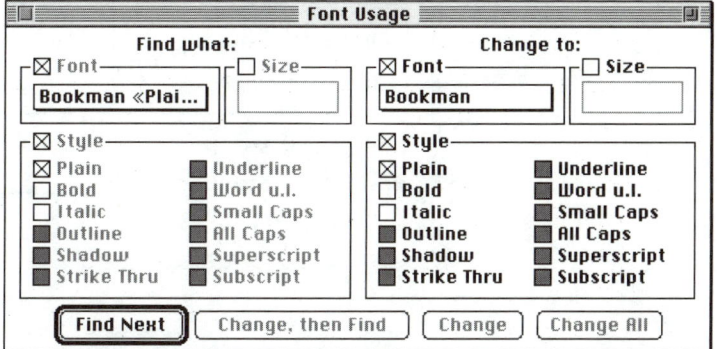

Next, you want to manipulate the Format for each story. Since they are three independent stories, unlinked, you must repeat this for each. Starting with the story on page 1, highlight it using the Content Tool. Then, select Formats under the Style menu. Alter the formats dialog box in the of First Line (0.3) and Space After (0.042) areas. This will give an automatic paragraph indentation of the first line as well as kick just about three points in after each paragraph to help differentiate them. If you have already included paragraph first-line indents, take them out. (It's more fun this way!)

The first line of the story has a Drop Cap with no indentation. This paragraph will have to be highlighted by itself and the Format dialog box altered for only that copy. Change the Format dialog box for the first paragraph only so that the First Line (indent) is set at 0, for no indent. Then click on the Drop Cap check box to enable the first character to be a drop-cap style (see Figure 19.16). This style of manipulation will be repeated a few more times throughout the document.

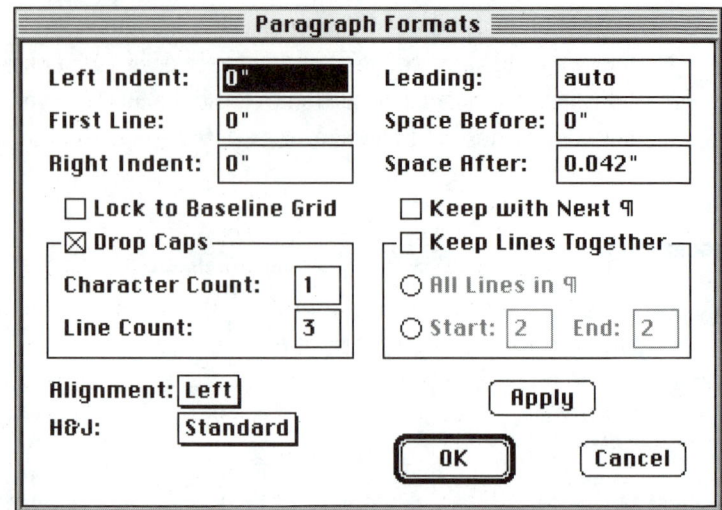

The final manipulation you want to perform for the first story deals with Vertical Justification. A common problem when dealing with columns and pages is that of getting all text to end at the bottom of each column and page for a uniform look. If you are a traditionalist, you're thinking X-ACTO knife about now, right? Well, throw that knife away, carefully. You can now vertically justify, right in the software.

All you have to do to specify vertical justification is highlight the copy, then through the Item Modify dialog box (Item ➤ Modify), select the Vertical Alignment option. A pop-up menu with several options enables you to select if you want the paragraph text to favor a top, center, bottom, or justified alignment in the column. Additionally, you can specify the variable-spacing maximum distance placed between paragraphs in the column. You can insert any number using any measurement system; i.e. 0p3 for zero picas, three points, even though the default measurement system is in inches. QuarkXPress will convert it for you.

In similar manner to the procedures to alter the remaining document text, place occasional Drop Caps as you think a story may warrant. Work on making the columns all in proper alignment across the top and bottom for uniformity.

Step 9: Importing and Altering Library Graphic Items

Now that most of the copy is squared away, you are ready for a few graphic items. Start with page 1 again. Change to the Rectangle Picture Box tool. Click and Drag to form a blank picture box item. You will recognize a picture (graphic) box item by the X appearing in the box, drawn from corner to opposite corner. Text box items do not have the X.

Here, you are somewhat on your own. Since you may not have the same graphic elements, you must designate how big the picture item must be to import the graphic available. A quick way of going is to draw the graphic box practically full screen. Then after importing the picture, you can quickly move the grab bars to a better, proportionate location and size. To resize the contents of the item after import, you can either alter the width and height from the picture's Item Specifications dialog box (Item ➤ Specifications) or hold the ⌘ key down while you click and drag a grab bar.

In the Capstone Document, all graphic items are on *document pages*. There are no graphic elements on *master pages*, although this is also a design option you may want to investigate. On page 1 the graphic consists of the two bicyclists. The graphic used was a PICT format, which allows you to color the picture itself, independent of the picture item background. Other graphics, such as the EPS and TIFF files used are unchangeable in QuarkXPress color. For such files, you can color only the picture item box, not the item contents; they remain as they were imported. If you need to retouch formats such as these, use another software program such as Cachet or Photoshop, then import! (Page 1 also includes an "empty" picture item colored with a diamond-shaped blend; this will be described shortly. For now, just ignore the blended rectangle and focus on picture and graphic elements).

Page 2 includes the wheel artwork (top left corner) and modifications of this artwork distributed throughout several locations on the two-page spread. The smaller and lighter colored wheel artworks have been modified in Adobe Illustrator to allow for a light color fill. This light color enables you to successfully read type characters on top of the graphic image. Several of the graphic images sent with QuarkXPress tutorial disks over the past several revisions have been originated in

Illustrator and saved as EPS files. You can modify them if you wish to work with other layouts if you have a software program that will allow alterations.

Also on the two-page spread are the graphic images of a bicycler and a pedal. The three dominant graphics; i.e. wheel artwork, bicycler, and pedal are all placed on the page and manipulated with a Manual Runaround (Item ➤ Runaround). You will have to experiment with the graphic files in your document for runaround modifications. At times some fairly sophisticated fine-tuning is necessary to get the type to run around the graphic images properly. Remember, as you place a runaround graphic over text, the text will move out of the way, causing it to flow further down the text item column (and link to the next text item in linked-text situations).

Notice on the spread of pages 2 and 3 that graphics can be placed in such a way that they can bleed off the page. A certain amount of this works, but the portion off the page is still calculated and slows down the QuarkXPress output, so try to keep it to a minimum. Additionally, the bicycler, as shown in Figure 19.17 is spread across pages 2 and 3. This spread will be separated automatically when the QuarkXPress document prints; proper alignment will be maintained.

FIGURE 19.17

This represents a two-page spread in the Capstone Document.

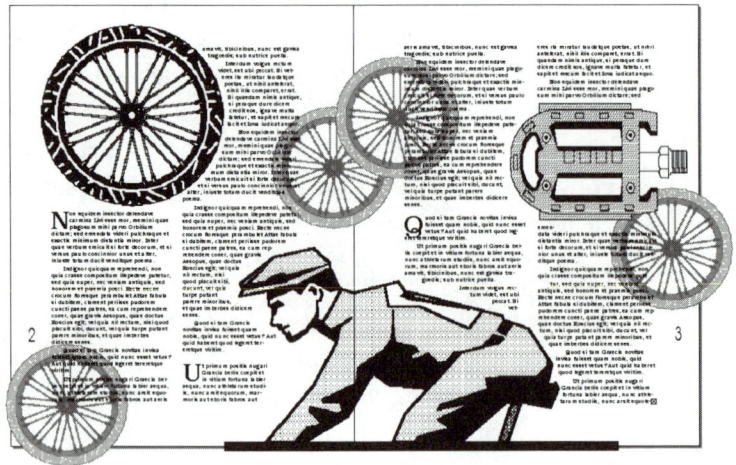

Page 4 of the example Capstone Document involves more complex use of graphic and text elements. The graphic elements on page 4 include the photograph and a gear drawing. These work with the linked text items and a "banner" in such a way that runarounds and layers are tricky. For now you should just include a photo and make sure the Runaround (Item ➤ Runaround) is set to Item. Place a value of runaround in each field as necessary. Your first value for each runaround side will probably not be the best. You can come back and alter this later after you see how the text will look running around the picture.

Next, frame the picture, using any of the colors in the color palette, frame styles, and thicknesses (Item ➤ Frame). Position the picture where you want, resizing both the item and its contents as necessary.

NOTE

A way to alter both the item and its contents at the same time is through holding the Option key down while dragging on a grab bar. To maintain a square (or circular) format while reshaping, also hold down the shift key.

The Gear is another EPS file, when placed on the page, a PICT image appears. Manipulate this image by choosing a Manual Runaround (Item ➤ Runaround). Then adjust the specific runaround sections as necessary. An automatic runaround may give you a somewhat similar appearance but is not controllable, therefore a manual runaround is preferred.

If you choose to have one graphic (gears) overlap another slightly (picture), then it's best to manipulate the layering of all three elements; i.e. the text items, the photo item, and the gear item (see Figure 19.18). Multiple items raise the possibility of frustration when working with the QuarkXPress layering features. Since you cannot specify which layer an item is to move to in QuarkXPress, other than front and back, patience is a must!

FIGURE 19.18
*Page 4 of the Capstone
Document involves some
tricky runaround and
layering manipulation.*

TIP

*Don't try to work with complex QuarkXPress layers after several
cups of coffee. It is one of the most frustrating features available
in the program.*

You still have the "banner" to add to page 4, so don't worry about exact layering or runaround on that page until all elements are present. Manipulation of the banners (page 1 and page 4) is next.

Step 10: Creating and Manipulating the QuickRelease Banner (Front and Back)

The Banners, both on page 1 as well as its misdirected cousin on page 4, come from the same text box item (see Figure 19.19). These text boxes start as a single text box item, created for the nameplate "QuickRelease." As indicated in the specifications above, first, you create the text box item, then alter its shape and location. Key in the QuickRelease text. Then, modify font, size, style, color, alignment, etc. until you have it the way you want. Finally, change Runaround to *None* to avoid interference with other page items.

After the initial QuickRelease nameplate is created, duplicate it to form a second text item. This is the name that will appear mirrored to the original. Click on the new nameplate to activate it, then select the Mirror feature (Style ➤ Flip Vertical). This mirroring feature is new to QuarkXPress 3.2 and can be accessed through the menu or from new mirroring arrows in the Measurements palette (see Figure 19.20).

After you flip (mirror) the duplicated text box, edit as necessary and relocate under the original banner. Remember to make both Runaround—None, otherwise you will not be able to move them close enough for the design.

Finally, activate the original QuickRelease text item with the Item tool. Duplicate it again for inclusion on the last page. Once it is duplicated, drag it down, or over to your page 4. Manipulate it for Runaround—None also, if necessary. Alter color and shade as necessary then resize to resemble the text in page 4 (see Figure 19.19). To alter the text box quickly for proper fit, use the new QuarkXPress 3.2 feature for interactive text resizing. To resize the text and its text box, hold down the ⌘ key while dragging one of the grab handles on the text box. The point size (and Automatic leading, if applicable) will resize horizontally or vertically, depending on how you modify the text box. This is a great feature that allows more spontaneous page layout design than was previously available in QuarkXPress.

FIGURE 19.19
Page 1 of the Capstone Document involves complex trapping that may be beyond standard QuarkXPress capabilities.

....

FIGURE 19.20
Flip arrows are new to the QuarkXPress measurements palettes.

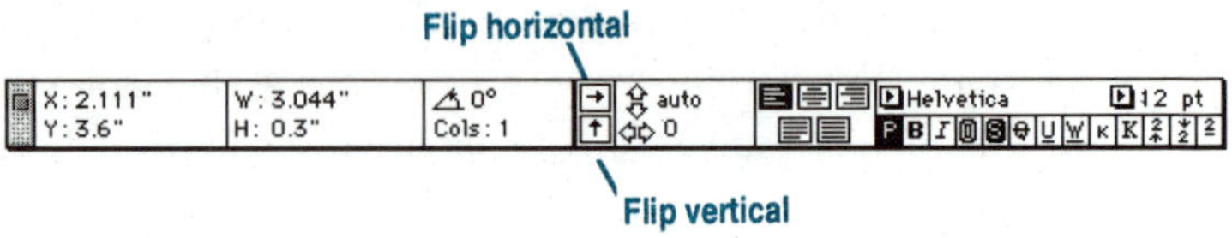

While working on elements of the page 4 design you may begin to feel frustration while layering the elements. One trick to use, (and its used here), is to break down certain text columns, into smaller text columns. In the given example, column 2's text is broken into about four smaller text items. In this way, you can more easily manage specific runarounds, localize them as it were. Plus, if each text box item is linked, through proper use of the Link Tool (Tools Palette), you can move them around as much as you need and the text flows accordingly.

Step 11: Including New Colors and Blends

The new colors you may want to add to the QuarkXPress document palette can be done at almost any stage of the document. Many consider this a preparatory step and suggest color manipulation be made prior to new items in the document. Either way, you have to add new colors to the color palette (Edit ➤ Colors) if you wish to use them on items in the Capstone Document.

In the example, two new colors were "mixed" from the CMYK color scheme. Their proper mixture is indicated in the specifications given at the outset of this project. Colors were applied to areas of pages 1 and 4 only. The inside spread of pages 2 and 3 remain standard black-and-white fare, although you could have some interesting combinations using your new color mixes on the proper paper stock.

On page 4, the color is simply applied to the QuickRelease banner. It is screened out lightly (Style ➤ Shade) so that only 20% of the color shows. The combination of a light color and shading lighten the type to the desired contrast for layering as shown.

The complexity of colors come on page 1. There, a new graphic box is created to bleed over the left half of the document page. Then, using the new Cool Blends XTension of QuarkXPress 3.2, a Diamond Blend pattern is chosen through the Colors Palette. You can practice with various results, including screen and angle for your blends. QuarkXPress allows a bleed comfortably, so feel free to do so to manipulate the blend pattern as desired. In this case, the design needed a diamond bleed specifically in the center of the left half of the page (the open area), where the bicyclers would be showing movement toward.

Once you have "colorized," runaround, layered, and resized all items in the document, you are ready to send it to output. Before you do that you should know that the Capstone Document, as designed in this exercise, is specifically created to be an almost impossible task for QuarkXPress to print properly. Professionals have been proclaiming that excellent color separation results with proper trapping can only be obtained through high-end equipment. Quark and EFI, through this version of QuarkXPress and EfiColor XTensions, claim that you can perform high quality color work now in the electronic publishing environment. You be the judge. You may even want to take a copy of the document created to your local service bureau for color separations and proofs to compare traditional with QuarkXPress color capabilities. Specifically, when you output the document, look for good trapping where there are three layers of elements, such as on the front page, near the banner overprint (on the blend). This is very difficult to automate and may well be the definitive test of QuarkXPress color capabilities.

Step 12: Gathering the Document for Printing

Printing a document is easy, right? You just go to File and select Print. Automation! Don't you just love it? Well, if you want good results in QuarkXPress, there's a bit more to it than that. First, with a good backup copy already saved. You can prepare for output by "Collecting" the document's various parts.

You cannot output a high quality document at the service bureau without sending along files of all the elements with the document. Remember, earlier how the formats of EPS and such were explained? Each picture you use in the QuarkXPress document, unless a low-resolution PICT or PAINT file has associated files that accompany it. You must send not only the QuarkXPress document file, but also the picture or graphic files used in you document's design. For example, most graphics used in the Capstone Document were originally EPS files, with the exception of the photograph used on page 4. These EPS files consist of a total of five parts, the low resolution PICT file that you see on the screen, as well as a Cyan file, Magenta file, Yellow file, and a Black printer file. These obviously are designed for color separation use.

The pictures you use in a document must be "linked" to the original files. If not, QuarkXPress will notify you that the original file is missing, through the Pictures Usage (Utilities ➤ Picture Usage) dialog box. If missing, it gives you an opportunity to re-establish the link.

In addition to graphic files, a common headache for service bureaus is when clients send jobs in with unknown fonts. Most service bureaus tend to stay with the brand name font suppliers and shy away from the $5.00 fonts that may be advertised in the back of trade magazines. If you aren't using a font from a reputable font dealer; i.e. Linotype, Adobe, Agfa, etc., there may be a problem in printing your document.

To circumvent all these problems in identification, Quark has included what was previously a supplemental XTension into its base 3.2 software. This feature asks you to "gather" elements of your document. This new feature in QuarkXPress is called "Collect for Output" and is located under the File menu. Specifically, it enables you to save all document information and associated graphics necessary for a service bureau to successfully output your job. It will not save the associated fonts, however, for obvious copyright violations. Therefore it is imperative that you match your font needs with those the service provider has available.

As you choose Collect for Output, QuarkXPress creates a *Report* file containing information about your document. It also copies the document, graphic files and the *Report* file into a folder for delivery to your service bureau.

The report file contains the information about the document:

- Document name, date, total pages, width, and height

- Version of QuarkXPress and file size

- Required XTensions for your document

- Active XTensions

- Fonts used

- Graphics used, including the size, angle, skew, path name, type, fonts in EPS, and location within the document

- H & J Specifications

- Colors created and information to reproduce custom colors

- Trapping information

- Color plates required for each page

• Resolution of pictures scanned or saved

Take this information to the service bureau and let them have at it! You may have direct access to a color proofer or imagesetter for the document. If so, then you have to properly set up the Print dialog box options for output. In any event, you are done with the Capstone Document. Congratulations! You have come a long way from the simple page document in *Chapter 1*. You deserve a lot of credit, so take the rest of the day off!

XChange and XTensions

To quickly prepare a job for the service bureau   454

install the XTention *Magpie*, from Show-Ads Omega Group.

To gain the ability to move items through layers   456

you should get the XTension called *LayerManager*. It enables you to move elements up or down as little as one level at a time, all with a simple click of the mouse.

To change your QuarkXPress program into a professional keyliner   498

install the XTension called Keyliner from Datastream Imaging Systems, Inc. This program turns your desktop computer into a professional stripping station, which can build page geometry from conventional art boards and documents.

Tensions are the focus of QuarkXPress expansion. They are add-on programs that enables you to enhance custom features of the QuarkXPress application, tailoring it to your individual needs. These add-on programs allow you to continually keep current in features that help make your business remain competitive.

WHAT ARE XTENSIONS?

QuarkXTensions technology lets you add software *modules* to expand the features and capabilities of QuarkXPress for specialized publishing tasks. Common applications include links to databases, pagination systems, automation of common processes, special color-separation tools, and scanner drivers. Using QuarkXPress as the core of a publishing system and strengthening its capabilities with XTensions is a cost-effective way to solve complex publishing problems.

WHERE DO XTENSIONS COME FROM?

Like the application QuarkXPress, some XTensions come directly from specialists at Quark. However, independent and group developers from all parts of the world also write XTensions. People are writing and releasing XTension modules faster than the information can reach the QuarkXPress user. That is why QuarkXPress users around the world rely on the premier XTension clearinghouse, *XChange*. This company provides the QuarkXPress user base with quality XTension modules in a one-stop shopping environment. All XTensions listed in this book are available through XChange and suggested prices appear at the end of this chapter to give you an idea of relative costs. Prices are subject to change, and new XTensions emerge frequently; check with XChange for a complete list of their inventory.

HOW TO REACH XCHANGE

Contact XChange by telephone, fax, or through one of the major online services:

Sales: (800) 788-7557

Sales (outside the continental U.S.): (303) 229-0656

FAX: 303-229-9773

Developer Relations: (303) 225-2484

CompuServe: 75300,2336

AppleLink: W.Buckingham

America OnLine: XChange.CO

XChange OnLine is the product information, suggestion, and correspondence link. Their staff monitors the DTP Vendor Forum on CompuServe (GODTPVEN) daily and try to respond to requests for information within 24 hours. In addition, members of the XTension of the Month Club get access to a private library of XTension demos, updates, and more. CompuServe offers a special sign-up bonus to new members registered through XChange. See *Appendix A* for more details on CompuServe.

NOTE

XTensions, their descriptions, actions, screen designs, prices, XChange, CompuServe and any other service or product mentioned here are subject to change without notice. The volatility of this marketplace incurs several mergers and closures which may affect the availability of products or services mentioned in this book.

OTHER SERVICES AND PRODUCTS

XChange is expanding rapidly, offering more services and products than just their initial listing of XTensions for QuarkXPress. One concept they appear to work diligently upon is keeping the customer, you, abreast of all changes in this area. They offer a variety of methods to get you involved, including the Disk of the Month program, an ongoing newsletter and a membership arrangement with pricing incentives. In the event that you do not see the XTension to suit your needs here, you should contact XChange. They keep a ear to the ground when it comes to emerging XTensions and can also direct you to custom XTension developers if needed.

X3—THE QUARKXPRESS XPERTS XCHANGE

XChange presents the QuarkXPress XPerts XChange—the way to stay up to date on what's happening in the world of Quark XTensions. Each month members will receive a package containing:

- The Disk of the month, with a free XTension, demo versions of new or existing XTensions, and other neat software.

- A newsletter with information about soon-to-be-released XTensions, reviews of products written by professionals who use them every day, and tips from the pros on how to get the most from QuarkXPress and XTensions.

- Special members-only pricing on featured XTension products.

New members of the QuarkXPress XPerts XChange receive:

- A FREE X3 T-shirt!

- Beta test-site consideration for new XTension products.

- A special membership discount to CompuServe. You'll get free sign-up and a $15.00 introductory usage credit to explore the XChange section and CompuServe's other offerings.

- More special offers throughout the year.

XTENSIONS FOR MACINTOSH

This chapter includes descriptions of all XTensions available through XChange. The number of XTensions increases, however, with each product catalog XChange publishes. To keep current, contact XChange and request they add your name to the mailing list. XTensions list as somewhat related products and loosely by functionality; e.g., Design, Production, Editorial, etc. However, you should examine each section because several XTensions are difficult to pigeonhole in only one classification. A price list is noted at the end of the chapter. These prices are, as with most list prices, subject to change. International pricing and site-license pricing must be negotiated directly with the developer or with XChange.

INPOSITION

(DK & A) The once time-consuming task of imposition ordering has just become vastly easier, thanks to INposition. This revolutionary XTension is the missing link in the electronic pre-press process: it does both signature creation and book building, and it enables you to impose your entire publication on any PostScript imagesetter. INposition allows you to create signatures from any existing QuarkXPress document, giving you total freedom and control over the book being imposed.

INposition will meet your complete press and bindery needs, because all signature variables are user-definable. For example, you can set cut-and-fold marks, as well as make adjustments for creep-across pages. And with INposition you can create and store several different book styles, and retrieve them later for automatically imposing your QuarkXPress documents into a book.

Set press sheet and layout styles to suit your needs; you have total control over numbering as well as signature configuration. INposition will work for you, whether you opt for saddle stitch or perfect bound. Control bindery needs like grind, creep, page bleed, and cross-over bleeds and create publications of nearly any size and dimension.

COLORCHANGE

(Vision's Edge, Inc.) The ColorChange dialog box utilizes QuarkXPress's familiar find/change interface. Users can check how colors are used in a document and then change them based on specific type of usage. Even shading percentages can be changed document-wide with a click of the mouse. The utility allows you to segregate color changes to text, frames, background, and picture colors. Features:

▸ Selectively search and replace each occurrence of the colors.

▸ Change all occurrences of a color at once.

▸ Option to search and replace text, picture, background and frame colors.

▸ Lists the colors that are currently used in the document.

> Displays how each color is used.

> Ability to search and replace shades.

COLOR USAGE

(Vision's Edge, Inc.) This utility from Vision's Edge lists the colors in a given document in a dialog box that indicates where and how the color is used. Colors are sorted by page number, with additional information on whether process separation is selected for the color. Color Usage shows background or line color, frame color, picture color, and text character color. When you select a color from the dialog list, the RGB and CMYK values as well as a screen display sample of the color are shown.

SPECTRESEPS QX

(PrePress Technologies) A Color Separation XTension from Pre-Press Technologies, Inc. SpectreSeps QX lets you make high-quality color separations of QuarkXPress documents, including continuous-tone images. Includes sophisticated control over color-correction and separation parameters, and lets you use custom halftone screening information as well. Never again will a QuarkXPress pages need to be stripped conventionally. Features:

> Separations of color TIFF and PICT2 images.

> Brightness, contrast, color saturation, and sharpening control.

> Custom halftone screen angles and frequencies.

> Paper/Press setting for undercolor removal (UCR) and dot gain compensation.

> Accepts color correction, unsharp masking, and gray balance parameters from other applications.

> DCS compatible.

SPECTRESCAN QX

(PrePress Technologies) SpectreScan QX lets you make scans from within QuarkXPress, using any of the most popular desktop scanners, in black and white, grayscale, or color. You can make color corrections to a low-resolution preview scan, then scan a high-resolution corrected image into an active picture box or directly to disk as a 1-, 8-, or 24-bit TIFF file. Capturing a high-quality image onto a QuarkXPress page has never been easier. Features:

- Brightness, contrast, color saturation, and sharpening control.

- Auto-import of scanned image into picture box.

- Includes SpectreDrivers for Microtek MSF-600Zs and La Cie scanners.

Additional SpectreDrivers available for Nikon LS-3500; Sharp JX-300, JX-450, and JX-600; Howtek Scanmaster, Scanmaster II, and Scanmaster 3; Imapro QCS-35, QCS-450i, and QCS-120; Imapro QCS-600 and QCS-1200; Microtek MTS-1850S; Eikonix 1412 and 1435; and Spectre5000 and Spectre35.

TABLEWORKS 2

(NPath, Inc.) Tableworks gives you all the professional table-making features you'll need to create and edit any type of table as part of your QuarkXPress document. Tableworks makes tables entirely out of standard QuarkXPress objects, such as text boxes and rules, so you have full use of all QuarkXPress formatting and typographic controls when editing tables. For text cells, use multiple paragraphs of any style, any sort of horizontal or vertical justification, text and background color, frame style, and rotation. For picture cells, use any graphic format supported by QuarkXPress.

Create tables with any structure by straddling or dividing cells. You can resize rows or columns visually with the mouse, or to exact specifications; even the most complex tables are adjusted automatically to all changes. Tables can be fit exactly to text contents, with precise control over gutters or individual cell spacing. Add custom rules to your table, and they will be adjusted to all size changes. Import text in any format supported by QuarkXPress or exported from popular spreadsheet or word-processing programs. Turn global style settings for shading and lines on or off, in any combination. Make multipage tables with column header replication.

With the 2.0 release, Tableworks offers an even richer array of features than before, within a new unified and powerful interface. A single palette controls most row or column layout settings. A new template library feature lets you easily replicate your favorite tables with all customized changes. And now very-large table support is available, for large regular data sets.

TEXTLINKER

(Npath Software, Inc.) This newly released XTension from Npath Software, Inc. adds System 7 Publish/Subscribe capability for text to QuarkXPress. Publish/Subscribe is a powerful feature of System 7, allowing data to be "linked" between documents and different applications. With TextLinker, you can "Publish" text from your QuarkXPress document, to be used in other documents, or "Subscribe" to text from other documents. The documents you link to can be other QuarkXPress documents or documents produced by any other applications that support Publish/Subscribe, such as Microsoft Word and Excel.

TextLinker is easy to use and follows the guidelines for standard Publish/Subscribe support. When you modify a Publisher, all its Subscribers can be manually or automatically updated. You can also make a Publisher out of any selected text in a document. Simply highlight the text and use the standard Publisher dialog box to specify the name of an Edition file.

Additionally, users can optionally Subscribe to text formatting as well as the text itself, with the ability to change font, font size, or other format attributes of the Publisher. The changes are automatically duplicated in Subscribers. As an added bonus, when used with TableWorks (also from Npath), users can Publish or Subscribe to entire tables.

COLORMANAGER

(CompuSense) ColorManager weaves power and simplicity into a "must have" XTension if you do any color work with QuarkXPress. This program allows you to identify, control and easily manipulate any color used within your document. It provides a tool that makes the production of any color job less arduous and more efficient in terms of money and time.

ColorManager allows users to search and replace colors easily. Colors can be replaced whether they are found in text, lines, frames, or backgrounds and users have the option to specify what percentage shade the resulting color should be. More importantly, you can optionally specify what percentage shade of a specified color to look for when searching. This XTension allows you to implement global changes of all color occurrences or individual occurrences of a color. The Process Separation toggle for all colors in your document can be checked and set in an easily attainable manner.

ColorManager's interface adds an item (Color) to the menu bar with various selections. The first option, Color Usage, allows users to search for, replace, and manipulate colors in their current document. Custom and process colors used in high-resolution EPS files are tracked using the EPSF Usage feature. It allows users to locate, select, and open the EPS file you want to check. A preview of the graphic is also available. For custom colors that appear in the EPS file, you can determine if that color already exists in the current document. If it doesn't, you can create it from within ColorManager.

The EPSF Report option will provide users with a printed report of all EPS files in a selected document, listing for each the custom colors contained within. It presents a dialog box similar to that found in QuarkXPress when you create a new document. It allows you to specify the report's name, page size, and the position of its margin guides. You can specify whether the report should be printed immediately after it has been compiled, or saved for examination later.

The final two features included are the Screen Angles and File Mover options. The Screen Angles option allows users to specify custom CMYK screen angles to four decimal points for printing. Finally, the File Mover feature enables you to save a file to any destination disk or folder. The file and all its linked files will be transferred to the specified location.

COLORSNAP 32+

(Computer Friends) ColorSnap 32+ is a 24-bit, frame capture board. Files are captured in 24-bit color but can be stored in a variety of formats. They have taken particular care to enhance the quality of the image captured. Images can be printed in full color using a thermal or a color ink jet-printer, or they can be color-separated. They can also be printed on a common LaserWriter. The ColorSnap 32+ XTension is a hardware/software combination. The board is installed in any nubus slot, and is System 7- and QuickTime-compatible (waiting for the day when you can play movies in QuarkXPress...).

The ColorSnap 32+ application software is installed into your Mac. The XTension is installed in the same folder as QuarkXPress. Connect the input of the ColorSnap 32+ board to a camera, camcorder, still video camera, recorder, etc., and you are ready to import pictures into any graphic box in a QuarkXPress document. ColorSnap 32+ comes with a picture data base, so you can archive your images and preview them in "thumbnail" format. Click on the thumbnail and the image fills the whole screen. FastCompress compacts images to a fraction of the original size in less than ten seconds.

MAGPIE

(Show-Ads Omega Group) Magpie is a QuarkXPress XTension that allows the user to quickly and easily archive or prepare a job for delivery to a service bureau. By examining the original QuarkXPress document, Magpie determines which fonts and high-resolution graphic files are required by the document, makes a copy of those elements in a new "job" folder, and places a copy of the original document in that folder as well. This folder can be placed on a floppy disk or removable cartridge for delivery to a service bureau.

Depending on the requirements of the job as specified by the user, Magpie will also use Disk Doubler to compress all of the required files for delivery to a bureau via modem. In addition, this XTension will create a report of the fonts and graphic files a document uses and whether or not they were available for inclusion in the job folder.

CURSORPOS

(Kytek, Inc.) CursorPos provides users with a floating palette to continuously display the position of the cursor. When the cursor is located in a text box, the Cursor-Pos palette will display the horizontal and vertical position of the cursor in the current horizontal and vertical units of your document. The position is continually updated as you move the cursor through the text.

The X popup menu in the palette allows you to indicate that the cursor horizontal displacement be measured from the text inset of the left edge of the current text box, from the left margin of the page or from the left edge of the page.

The Y popup menu in the palette allows users to indicate that the position of the baseline of the cursor line be measured from the top of the current text box, from the top margin of the page or from the top of the page. Both features allow for easy comparison between locations in different boxes that are located at different positions on the page.

FCS TABLEMAKER

(F.C.S., S.A.) FCS TableMaker is a collection of functions designed to facilitate the production of simple tables of data in QuarkXPress. Though succinct in function, FCS TableMaker provides a large portion of the functionality needed by most users. The XTension includes functions for building gridlines, establishing an exact centerpoint on a page, building a grid of either text or graphics boxes, and several tab functions. TableMaker also contains a function for creating grouped sets of horizontal and vertical rules, using the default rule style set for the orthogonal line tool in the QuarkXPress tool palette. Additionally, "Create Style Sheet" will define a new text style with the name you select, and apply all tab settings built in TableMaker.

GRAPHXCHANGE

(Equilibrium) GraphXChange is the perfect utility for anyone who needs to import "alien" graphic formats into QuarkXPress. This XTension will allow you to read in graphics file formats not previously supported by QuarkXPress. These documents can then be printed in your document, eliminating the need to translate the graphics with another application.

GraphXChange supports many file formats, though no guarantee can be made that the XTension supports all versions of each format. Supported file formats include the following:

PCX

PIC (Lotus 1-2-3)

TIF (PC)

MSP

EPS (PC)

RGB

LBM

TGA

IMG (GEM)

WPG

LAYERMANAGER

(a lowly apprentice production) Whatever your QuarkXPress requirements are, from newsletters to magazine design, the LayerManager is sure to make the time spent dealing with QuarkXPress elements much more efficient. And as you know, doing more in QuarkXPress means more boxes, more lines, and more time spent moving between them.

LayerManager is a non-obtrusive palette smaller then QuarkXPress's own measurements palette, but don't let the size fool you! LayerManager comes equipped with the ability to move elements up or down even one level at a time, all with a simple click of the mouse. No longer will you have to stop what you're doing and navigate your way up and into the menus just to bring an element forward, or send one back a few levels. The LayerManager will allow you to numerically specify which level you want an element to be placed on. And, of course, the LayerManager tells you how many elements are on the current spread.

The LayerManager also will allow you tag elements that should always be at the top or the bottom levels, or even just near the top or the bottom, and again with a simple click of the mouse, the elements tagged will be moved to their preset locations. If you work with QuarkXPress, then consider the LayerManager a must!

SXETCH PAD

(Datastream Imaging Systems, Inc.) SXetch Pad is the XTension that Quark users have been waiting for! SXetch Pad allows users to illustrate in QuarkXPress. Because SXetch Pad is an XTension, it incorporates many of the excellent modification features of QuarkXPress such as fills, X/Y position, line weight, and text runaround. This has two advantages. First, by making use of QuarkXPress's powerful command structure, the program runs with greater effectiveness and efficiency. Second, it substantially reduces the amount of training needed to become proficient with the software. In short, knowledgeable QuarkXPress users should find themselves productive with SXetch Pad almost immediately.

Another great feature of SXetch Pad is trapping. Graphics imported into QuarkX-Press often cause unpredictable, hard to fix, trapping problems because they come from stand-alone illustration packages which have limited or no spread and choke options. Developed with this specific problem in mind, SXetch Pad utilizes the native trapping features of QuarkXPress. Illustrations created with SXetch Pad are just as easy to trap as any QuarkXPress object. Features:

- Convert type to outline form and fill with a Multicolor blend.

- Type on a curved path.

- Illustration exported as an EPS file.

- Use TIFF or PICT file as a template for easy tracing.

- One Step Multicolor Blend (spot or process colors).

- Bézier-controlled curved lines, open or closed.

SXetch Pad will be available on the PC platform by the second quarter of 1993.

COMBS XT

(Durrant Software Limited) Combs XT Lets you quickly and easily add data *combs* to your QuarkXPress layouts. Combs are those convenient to use, but impossible to create, grids for facilitating completion of forms and applications.

Combs XT makes this otherwise tedious process of creating data combs simple and painless. Combs may be constructed in several different styles—open, box, cage, underline, top closed, and bottom closed. Each of these styles can be edited and modified to meet the most demanding design specification.

Any designer who needs to create any type of data entry form will love this XTension.

TYPEMASTER

(Sparking Mad Software) This XTension from Sparking Mad Software offers QuarkXPress users the chance to manipulate type the way they've always wanted to do it—by clicking and dragging it to the right position. The interface couldn't be easier or more intuitive. Highlight the text you want to work on with the content tool, and select TypeMaster... from the Utilities menu.

The selected text will appear in a floating palette capable of delivering an 800% magnification. Adjust the view to an appropriate working scale, and indicate with check boxes whether you want to kern, baseline shift, or both. Make adjustments by clicking and dragging on desired characters. If you've selected only kerning, characters will remain on the baseline, allowing only a right-to-left adjustment. Baseline shift permits you to drag the character up or down off the baseline. Selecting both functions allows the character to be freely moved in all directions.

But wait…there's more. Holding the Option key while dragging a character causes the type to be horizontally scaled larger or smaller. Holding the Shift key and the Option key allows you to proportionally scale the character visually. The Copy Kerning checkbox allows you to effortlessly duplicate your kerning pair adjustments across your selection. With the Export box checked, TypeMaster will copy the new kerning information to the font's kerning pairs. TypeMaster is a great tool for both typographers interested in the highest quality kerning possible, and for designers who like to manipulate type for display effects.

DESIGN TOOLS

(Integrated Software, Inc.) A collection of quality XTensions for design professionals:

CELLER "step and repeat" creates a grid of boxes identical to the original. "Divide and repeat" creates a grid of boxes inside the frame of the original box.

STARBURST creates many different starburst shapes and sizes quickly and easily.

AUTOSAVE saves your documents at user-specified intervals.

PICTURE SCALE provides a powerful yet easy way to scale pictures and picture boxes, both proportionally and anamorphically. Scales the picture box and its contents simultaneously! Lets you fit your image to the box, or the box to the image.

SHADOW creates a drop shadow effect for any box, applying the color and shade of your choice.

NUDGE moves a box or its picture contents in user-defined increments. Also nudges a group of boxes!

SKEW can skew a text or picture box, as well as its contents.

JOB FOLDER identifies all text and image files on your layout page, then copies them into a single folder. Great for service bureau work!

DOCUMENT REPORT produces detailed reports on graphics, style sheets, and text elements, EPS fonts and EPS colors, and much more. Essential for checking your layouts for fonts, images, and colors before sending them to your favorite printer!

NAVIGATOR XT

(Vision's Edge, Inc.) Here's another great XTension to help you sail through your QuarkXPress document. Navigator XT presents a palette that allows you to navigate through a QuarkXPress document effortlessly. The palette offers a thumbnail view of the page or spread. Clicking on a point in the thumbnail immediately takes you to that point on the document page. This can be invaluable when working on documents with layers or when the document is magnified.

Besides simplifying access to specific points on a page, Navigator XT also makes it easy to move between pages in a document. Three arrow buttons quickly move you to the previous page, next page, or any page via a pop-up of all pages in the document. This utility is unobtrusive as well, because the palette can be quickly opened at any location by pressing ⌘-Control and clicking at the point.

PICTURE TOOLS

(Vision's Edge, Inc.) Vision's Edge has created another utility—Picture Tools— with a variety of enhancements for working with pictures. Features include:

Picture Suppression—performed via a dialog that lists all pictures in the document. Users can set the suppression by selecting a picture in the list and then setting the picture or box suppress check boxes. The suppression for every picture can be set using a global command.

Global Greeking contains a user-definable command key for toggling picture greeking. Individual Picture Greeking is the third feature added to QuarkXPress using this XTension. Individual greeking allows you to greek a single picture while leaving others ungreeked. This is useful when working with really large pictures.

Size Box to Picture quickly resizes the picture box to fit the picture. The box can be resized to fit the current picture scale or it can enlarge the picture to 100%

and then resize the box to the picture. No other XTension makes working with pictures in QuarkXPress easier!

FILEMANAGER

(CompuSense) File Manager allows users to easily label, categorize, search for, move and otherwise control all their QuarkXPress documents.

The FileManager XTension is a powerful, yet simple to use, add-on software module for QuarkXPress. It is an essential tool for administering your QuarkXPress documents, either on stand-alone or networked Macintoshes. It provides a valuable tool to help any QuarkXPress user who creates many documents of non-standard sizes as well as anyone who needs to transfer her documents to different locations such as service bureaus. Features include:

▶ The ability to create a new document allowing the user to choose the page size from one of the many pre-defined standard page sets.

▶ Allows the user to create and maintain their own libraries of non-standard, commonly-used page sizes and other page parameters.

▶ The File Mover… option allows you to select a file and specify a destination disk or folder where you want to copy the file. The file and all its linked files will be transferred.

▶ The Font Mover… option allows you to select a file and specify a destination disk and or folder where you want to copy the fonts that are used in the file. All screen and printer fonts that can be located will be transferred.

▶ When moving or copying a file, the user may select to also move the QuarkXPress Preferences file and the fonts at the same time.

▶ An Error Log can be maintained of all screen and printer fonts that could not be located or moved.

▶ The Document Manager is a high-performance publication tool that provides management and tracking capabilities for all your QuarkXPress documents.

▶ The user can create a header file for each document with information about the creator, the project the document belongs to, creation and last modification dates, as well as the revision status of the file.

- It is possible to modify the header files at any time.

- The user can specify defaults as to what the Creator and Project name in the header file will contain. It is also possible to define the number and names of the various revision status elements that a document can have.

- The Document search utility provides high speed searching for files based on document name and/or document header data.

ELECTRONIC BORDER TAPE AND ELECTRONIC BORDER TAPE, TOO!

(ShadeTree Marketing, Inc.) *Electronic Border Tape* is a collection of 101 decorative borders and frames for the QuarkXPress power user. They're great for certificates, ads, brochures, flyers, manuals, direct mailers, and many other documents.

The designs from EBT will give your work a polished, professional look. They range from simple and elegant to fancy and flashy, and some are just visual fun. Of course, there are designs appropriate for all the major holidays. The ease of using EBT is just a mouse click away.

EBT Frame Mover ships with every package of Electronic Border Tape so you can create new frames in the future and move frames in and out of your frames data/preferences file.

EBT Too! is the sequel collection of 100 decorative borders and frames. The designs from EBT Too! include sports, animals, southwestern designs, holiday borders, and party frames. EBT Too! was designed just for fun and is the perfect complement to any electronic frames library.

RESIZE XT 2.0

(Vision's Edge, Inc.) If you've ever had to laboriously scale each element of a layout to fit a new format, you know how much time such a project can consume. Just realigning all the items to maintain the aspect ratio of the original layout can be unbelievably cumbersome.

Resize XT 2.0 allows all the elements of a group, which could include all the contents of a page or spread, to be scaled from 20 to 400% of the original size. Just check off the attributes you wish to be scaled in the Resize XT dialog under

Item...Scale Boxes. Resize XT also adds a new tool to the tool palette. The Resize Tool is the alternate way to resize groups of boxes.

To use the Resize Tool, select the group to be resized and then click on the Resize Tool in the tool palette. Handles appear around the edges of the group. Drag a side or corner handle and release it when the group is the desired width. The Resize XT dialog box appears with the Scale % value already calculated for the size change indicated with the Resize Tool. At this point, set the appropriate Scale Attributes and click Scale to resize the group. Life is good again.

SETSKEW

(XTend) SetSkew addresses a concern heard from many QuarkXPress users; the need to import unique text effects created outside of QuarkXPress has been eliminated. Importing graphics and other effects usually poses no problems, provided no editing needs to be performed. However, when editing is necessary, users face prospects such as files that are missing or modified, screen previews that lack the true fidelity of the original graphic, or the inconvenience of having to open several applications besides QuarkXPress.

SetSkew allows users to create these unique text effects directly within QuarkXPress by skewing text boxes. This is accomplished by rotating the vertical axis +/− 75° around the horizontal axis. This feature is akin to XPress's built-in ability to skew graphic boxes. By combining the power of SetSkew and the normal palette of QuarkXPress tools, effects never before possible are now attainable. All text within the skewed text box remains totally editable. Users may modify character attributes such as typeface, size, horizontal scaling, kerning/tracking, baseline shift, etc. The paragraph formatting commands such as Formats..., Rules..., and Tabs... remain in effect as well.

Skewed text boxes maintain their link to other text boxes and may be viewed by any QuarkXPress user. Frames that encompass a text box preserve the correct angle of skew. In addition, SetSkew may be applied to any existing or newly-created document.

ALIAS

(Reseaux) Alias is a customizable typographic correction tool that adds multiple "search and replace" capabilities to QuarkXPress. Multiple target and replacement strings can be defined (optionally with text attributes) and saved as "tables."

"Special" (PC control characters) or characters not usually available on all keyboards can be inserted into the strings by a simple click. Whole sets of search and replace operations can be executed in one step, much more quickly and easily than in the original search and replace function. Uses include typographical correction, conversion of PC text files, filtering of downloaded text files, implementation of professional ligatures, and copy correction. Alias 2.0 offers users the capability of a multi-string search and replace across selected text, boxes, or entire documents. The search and replace can also be accomplished during import.

ANCHORBOX

(Alphalogic) AnchorBox is an XTension for QuarkXPress that enhances Quark's anchored box capabilities. Normally only single boxes can be "anchored" into the text of a Quark document. AnchorBox allows grouped objects to be positioned in the text. Once a group of boxes or a single box has been anchored using Anchor-Box, it will move with the flow of the text but it can also be dragged around as if it were a free box. Boxes can be unanchored via a menu or simply by dragging them out of the parent box. Thus one has all the same control as with normal anchored boxes, plus the feel of direct manipulation.

AUTOLIB

(Vision's Edge, Inc.) Have you ever wanted to create a library of the artwork that you use in QuarkXPress, but you don't have the time to import each file into a library? Now there is an easier way. Using AutoLib, you can quickly create graphics libraries by selecting the folder of graphics. AutoLib does the rest. The XTension creates the new library, inserts the graphics from the selected folder into it, and saves the new library when it's done. After AutoLib has created the new library, it can be renamed and moved to another folder if desired.

The AutoLib interface consists of a special file dialog box. This dialog box allows you to navigate to the folder that contains the graphics for the library. The Select button uses the current folder to build a new QuarkXPress library. AutoLib imports any graphic that QuarkXPress can currently import.

DEFAULT SETTINGS 2.0

(a lowly apprentice production) This popular XTension has been enhanced for use with newer QuarkXPress versions. All of its previous features are still available, allowing you to customize your version of QuarkXPress. You can control the appearance of windows, palettes, and dialog boxes, as well as customize the way TIFF images are displayed. Also, this XTension enables you greater control over default measurements and units for such areas as leading, font size, text inset, trapping, and more. Sets of default settings can now be stored and retrieved quickly. Without having to reenter all the desired values, you can have multiple sets representing your different needs.

Also built into this version is a/iCu, the XTension that keeps a watchful eye on most everything you do. Features include:

‣ Enhanced interaction with QuarkXPress.

‣ Enhanced printing features.

‣ Customized TIFF-image handling.

‣ Enhance the look of the interface, set scrolling to be interactive, enhance the speed at which your document is redrawn.

‣ Set the default unit of measurement for those items not affected by QuarkXPress's own default units.

DOUBLESAVE

(TechnoDesign) Save on! With this new product, also from TechnoDesign, an extra backup of your document is created after a standard save command. This extra copy can be stored anywhere, even on a fileserver. The DoubleSave XTension has been developed for those who require saving their documents locally, as well as an archived copy on their fileserver.

Normally this procedure requires users to navigate through several folders/volumes in order to correctly place the documents for storage. This method leads to errors, and often users will forego it altogether because of its complexity.

When the DoubleSave XTension is active, the folder for backup needs to be selected only once per document. The name of the backup folder is saved with the document. The cost of losing one document can more than pay for this great XTension!

GRID LAYOUT

(J. Michael Marriner) The Grid Layout 1.1 XTension creates uniform snap-to guides for easy alignment of design elements. Choose the number of columns and rows in your layout grid, type in the numbers, and the guides appear. Grids will start at the edge of the page or margins, and can apply to a single page or across page spreads.

Color can be specified to distinguish grid lines from margin lines or other guides, but the grid does not print. This version now has optional horizontal and vertical gutters (space between grid units) of any width. Once created, grids follow a document, so they won't be "lost" if the file is opened by somebody who doesn't own this handy tool. Grid Layout 1.1 was developed by J. Michael Marriner and Robert Schwalbe.

GRIDLOCK

(Mousedown Productions) GridLock adds an option to the Utilities menu that brings up a dialog box into which you can put exact numerical definitions for gridline positions—including multiples. For instance, you can enter 10*75 for 75 guides at 10-point offsets. GridLock guides can be a different color from those applied by hand, and can be locked and saved in sets.

PRINTIT

(a lowly apprentice production) This XTension not only permits users to designate multiple pages for saving as EPS files, or to save a selected text or picture box as an EPS, but actually allows for defining a printable area of the page by dragging a marquee around the desired elements.

PrintIT adds a new tool to the QuarkXPress tool palette, the Marquee Tool. When you need to print or save parts of a page as EPS files, simply drag the Marquee Tool around the required area. PrintIT shows you a preview of the upcoming print job, then either prints the job or creates an EPS file of the page(s). Incredibly intuitive, and a major time saver.

LOGICAL XTENSIONS I

(Alphalogic) Logical XTensions I is a bundle of two utilities: Crop Marks and In-Case Tools. Crop Marks provides a considerably more flexible system of creating and manipulating crop marks than those provided by Quark. Text Tools provides a set of tools for manipulating the case of text runs.

CROP MARKS

The existing crop mark facility within QuarkXPress is restricted to automatically placing crop marks around the document as a whole. The Logical XTensions Crop Marks utility allows the operator to place crop marks around the currently selected box, or set of boxes on a document with a single command. The eight crop marks will mark the corners of the smallest rectangle that encloses a set of boxes. The crop marks are completely accurate and are produced in a fraction of the time that it would take to create them by hand.

INCASE TOOLS

InCase Tools provides a set of commands to change the case of a selected run of text. It provides commands to convert a run of text into uppercase, lowercase, or to capitalize the first character of each word within the run. This is particularly useful in situations where the text for a given document is submitted entirely in uppercase and converting the text would otherwise require re-keying. There is an "undo" facility provided on all the text commands.

LOGICAL XTENSIONS II

(Alphalogic) Kern-Ease is an XTension for Quark QuarkXPress that enables the operator to have a very precise control over the kerning of any selection of text. The XTension provides a manual kerning palette which allows the operator to add or remove kerning to a selection of text as easily as tracking. Unlike tracking, using Kern-Ease to change the kerning of a run of text does not destroy the kerning inherent in the font—rather it adds a specified kern to that which naturally exists within the font. Kern-Ease allows the kerning to be added to a run in increments of one, ten, twenty, or to be removed entirely.

LTD_XS

(Trias) This XTension is a managing editor's dream. With LTD_XS, you decide which functions within the QuarkXPress interface will be available to users. Text-editing functions can be restricted to editors, and manipulation of graphics available only to designers or production personnel.

Using an administrator utility, indicate which menu items you would like to remain available, and which you would like locked off. Install the XTension on the user's machine and launch QuarkXPress. Those items which are unavailable appear grayed out in the menus. That's all there is to it!

MASTERMENUS

(Vision's Edge, Inc.) MasterMenus from Vision's Edge provides an easy way for you to have commonly used menu items as close as a mouse click on a user-customizable palette. The MasterMenus preferences dialog provides a quick, intuitive interface for the user to add or remove menu items from the palette.

Horizontal and vertical scroll bars allow you to scroll through the menus to find the commands you desire, and a popup menu allows you to quickly target a specified item. Select the item, click "add," and you've customized your palette! Even the width of the palette is user-definable.

You also have the choice over what a QuarkXPress menu item is named in the MasterMenu palette. The MasterMenus palette is what you make of it.

MIMIC

(Mediamatic) Mimic is an efficient tool for duplicating box and text specifications quickly. Useful for applying many characteristics at once, Mimic can transmit background color, text style and formatting information, frame color and size, and box size attributes—all with the click of a mouse.

Users who build classified ads, labels, or any other box-intensive layout work will benefit from Mimic. The XTension even transmits multiple text formats line by line. Mimic is indispensable to users who do repetitive formatting. You can even shift-select multiple items and Mimic all their attributes at once.

467

**XCHANGE
AND XTENSIONS**
· ·

CH. 20

ONTAP

(Mousedown Productions) OnTap is for QuarkXPress users who like keyboard shortcuts. The XTension gives you the ability to assign easy-to-remember keystrokes to fifty or so QuarkXPress menu commands. It adds an option to the Utilities menu that brings up a scrolling list of functions and commands normally accessed only by mouse or pull-down menus. Any key combination can be assigned to these functions.

OnTap is roughly equivalent to a macro utility, though easier and faster to use. Commands are executed entirely within QuarkXPress, and the XTension uses the familiar QuarkXPress user interface to assign or change keyboard equivalents. And OnTap features handy commands previously unavailable, such as selecting an entire sentence, selecting contiguous style sheet use, making case changes, and many more.

NUDGEIT

(a lowly apprentice production) This new XTension from lowly apprentice productions allows the user to define and apply custom nudge amounts from a floating palette. Increments can be specified to 0.001-point accuracy. Nudging may be applied either from the palette or the arrow/cursor keys, and can affect any item or box and its contents.

As with QuarkXPress's normal nudge feature, the tool selected determines what moves when you press a nudge key. When in the item tool, a box and its contents moves the prescribed amount. Nudging while in the Contents Tool nudges a graphic within its box. If in a text box, it moves the cursor the nudge amount. Pressing the option key as you activate a nudge key permits nudging in a tenth of the specified amount.

PROPUBLISHER

(Epic Publishing Solutions) ProPublisher provides extended features for QuarkXPress, utilizing extended keyboards. You now have use of the F5 through F15 keys to perform QuarkXPress functions. ProPublisher includes a custom extended keyboard template for ease of use and quick reference for commonly used keyboard shortcuts, plus the ProPublisher XTension to QuarkXPress. The speed of publishing with QuarkXPress is greatly enhanced, the learning time is minimal, and proficiency is superb with ProPublisher. The following are the predefined keys (recall that F1–F4 are Macintosh-assigned keys):

F5—Creates a text box on the page and automatically opens the Text Box Specifications dialog box.

F6—Creates a picture box on the page and automatically opens the Picture Box Specifications dialog box.

F7—Sends a selected item to the back.

F8—Brings a selected item to the front.

F9—Brings up a special dialog box allowing you to create a document of any size with border, color, frame, type, and fill.

F10—Brings up the Specifications dialog box for a selected item.

F11—Brings up the Frame Specifications dialog box.

F12—Brings up the Space/Align Items dialog box.

F13—Brings up the Print dialog box.

F14—Makes an item transparent.

F15—Brings up the Library dialog box.

RELINK

(North Atlantic Publishing Systems, Inc.) Have you ever had a series of linked boxes all laid out in QuarkXPress, filled them with text, and then decided to switch the order of the text boxes…only to discover that you have to go back and use the Link Tool to relink the boxes in their new order? With North Atlantic Publishing System's Relink XTension, you can automatically reflow the text in the proper order for your new design.

THE MISSING LINK

(Vision's Edge, Inc.) This XTension deserves commendation! How often have you wished you could "freeze" the links in a text chain to facilitate special editing, drag-copying from document to document, or placement in a library?

Your wish is granted, and then some. The Missing Link adds a new preference dialog box, accessed via the Unlink Tool. Here the user decides if The Missing Link unlinks the original text boxes, duplicates them in position, or duplicates and offsets them.

Also included with The Missing Link is the ability to link text boxes/chains that already contain text to other boxes/chains that contain text. The user has the option of telling The Missing Link to keep paragraphs intact as it creates the link between boxes. And single or multiple text boxes can even be broken out of a text chain to create new text chains, without disturbing the rest of the chain.

VIEWIT

(a lowly apprentice production) Are you tired of wasting time scrolling from page to page, changing views and switching between documents? ViewIT is a new XTension that will assist you in managing the way you look at a document so you can spend more time working on the document instead of navigating around various views. Features include:

- The ability to quickly arrange windows using various window resizing schemes.

- The ability to automatically save and recall a window's position whenever you save or open a document.

- A Hide/Show menu that allows individual documents to be hidden/shown.

- A popup document menu.

- An easily accessible "go to page" menu.

- A user definable view menu—you decide which viewing scales are best for you.

VISION'S EDGE UTILITY PACK

(Vision's Edge, Inc.) This utility pack includes several XTensions—a palette to open and close other palettes, a palette for setting vertical text alignment and text insets, and a popup menu that allows document preferences to be stored and accessed when creating a new document. Opening palettes at desired locations and closing them again is as simple as clicking a button. The top six icons on the Palette Manager represent the six built-in QuarkXPress palettes. Palette Manager supports most XTension palettes as well, listing the first three letters of their names.

The Insets & Align Palette allows the user to set different text inset values for the top, bottom, left, and right sides of a text box. The palette also provides ready access to the vertical paragraph alignment setting through a popup menu on the right side of the palette.

Nouveau adds a feature to the QuarkXPress New dialog: a popup menu which can store new document page preferences. Instead of entering the same margins, column settings, or odd paper sizes over and over again, the user can save them once and then select the setting whenever it is needed.

TRUPACK

(Durrant Software Limited) TruPack is made up of two XTensions that enhance existing functions in QuarkXPress. TruNew replaces the standard QuarkXPress New… dialog box with a much improved version adding several new options.

QuarkXPress provides five standard page sizes and one Other. With TruNew, those five standard sizes can be redefined. Just hold down the option key and click on any of the standard page size radio buttons. A new dialog box appears that lets you change the name and page size associated with that button. Any page size can be used in landscape format by just checking the TruNew Landscape checkbox.

QuarkXPress will not print crop marks or registration marks independently. TruNew provides two check boxes which specify whether the document should print with crop marks, registration marks, both, or neither. The TruNew dialog box also lets you choose your first page number and number of pages you want your document to contain. You may also start a new document on any page number—even left-hand pages.

TruLock enhances the standard QuarkXPress item lock function, which doesn't lock the contents of text or picture boxes. When TruLock has been installed, holding down the option key changes the standard Lock menu item to TruLock. When a box has been TruLocked, the contents tool cannot be selected while the TruLocked box is selected.

XNOTES

(Vision's Edge, Inc.) This XTension permits the user to assign electronic Post-Its to an QuarkXPress document, or to individual items within that document. These notes can be up to 2,550 characters each, and are hidden away within the document until needed. They can be used for a multitude of tasks, from editing or commenting layouts to giving explicit instructions on an element-by-element basis to your service bureau.

The XNotes palette provides easy access to all the controls for creating, editing, deleting, assigning and viewing the notes. Preferences let the user determine what happens when a document containing notes is opened. Choices include an alert sound or the automatic opening of the XNotes palette as the document is opened. In addition, all notes within a document may be printed in a report format, or globally deleted with a single command. The palette can even be specified to align under the element referenced by the currently displayed note.

Included with the XTension is a read-only version of XNotes which may be freely distributed. This permits anyone using QuarkXPress to view and print the notes (but does not allow editing of them) without possessing the full XTension.

XTENSION MANAGER

(DK & A) This is the XTension every QuarkXPress user should have. This powerful tool lets you enable and disable XTensions when launching QuarkXPress. No longer will you have to shuffle XTensions in and out of your application folder. XTension Manager will take care of this mundane housekeeping for you. Plus, XTension Manager lets you load XTensions from other machines or from network servers.

The Manager is easy to use—when QuarkXPress is loading, hold down the shift key and you will be presented with the dialog box below. Simply check the XTensions you want to load and uncheck the ones you don't; the Manager takes care of the rest.

Let the XTension Manager take the hassle out of XTension file management. Once you try the XTension Manager, you will agree that it is the single most-needed XTension for QuarkXPress.

XTENSION SAMPLER

(XChange) XChange now offers eight free and shareware XTensions on one diskette. They run the gamut from incredibly useful to just plain fun. The diskette includes:

ASave/Stamp: This XTension allows the user to set a predetermined interval for automatic saving.

Bureau Express: Works in conjunction with BureauMaster to automatically log in files sent to a service bureau through modem.

Color Prefs: Sets the various dialog boxes, page guides, and other interface elements to your favorite color.

FlashEdit: Prepares a cover report for service bureau output.

SetInset: Allows the user to specify different text insets for the left, right, bottom, and top of a text box.

SetSnap: Allows the user to set the distance for the Snap to Guides command.

Sounds: Adds sounds to QuarkXPress functions—useless, annoying, and fun.

TypesettingMarks XT: Corrects common typography problems, including the removal of extra spaces, the replacement of inch and feet marks with "smart quotes," and automatic replacement of characters that support ligatures.

THE GATHERER

(Managing Editor Software, Inc.) This XTension from Managing Editor Software, Inc. functions as a Finder-like runsheet (document item list) in QuarkXPress, bypassing the standard QuarkXPress import interface to allow users to quickly select and drag text and graphic files into a QuarkXPress document. The Gatherer not only facilitates locating the files you need, it remembers what you've already placed, and where.

Setup is a snap. The Gatherer shows up under the View menu, and appears on screen as a floating palette. The user creates a series of text and/or graphic Gather Sets, each of which can contain a variable number of folders located anywhere on the network. This means you can set up drop folders locally or remotely for all pertinent stories and graphics. And you can set up as many Gather Sets as you need for different projects. The cumulative contents of the specified Gather Set are displayed in a scrollable list that displays information about the file type and its modification date. Any file can then be dragged out of the Gatherer palette, precisely positioned on a page with a crosshair and dragged out to the size you need using a number of options. For text files, after defining box-creation coordinates, you can specify the number of columns and Gatherer will construct the box. If you wish to place text in an existing text box, ⌘-drag the text file over the appropriate position, and the text will flow into the selected text box/chain.

Graphic files are positioned much the same way, but the user is given the option before the graphic is imported of scaling the graphic to the box's dimensions, scaling the box to precisely enclose the graphic at 100% scale, or maintaining the aspect ratio and scaling the graphic either based on the horizontal or vertical dimension of the box. Graphic files can also be ⌘-dragged to an existing picture box, with all of the above options available during import.

Items that have been placed are displayed in the palette with a red line through the file name. To locate an item in an QuarkXPress document, double-click on the item name you wish to locate. You will be scrolled to the document's box automatically. To remove a file, select the name of the file you want removed and choose Remove from Document from the Do menu in the Gatherer palette. And there are a number of keyboard shortcuts and options build into the Gatherer to guide and alert you to potential errors.

STYLIST

(Reseaux) It's back! After a six month hiatus, this timesaving XTension is available again. Stylist is a small floating palette that offers fast access to style sheets and allows users to apply a style to the current text selection. The name of the current style sheet in use is continuously updated in the small, unobtrusive palette. Entire style sheets or just the character-based attributes of a style sheet can be applied by clicking in the palette, or through keyboard equivalents.

COPYSET

(Vision's Edge, Inc.) CopySet from Vision's Edge helps QuarkXPress users find and correct overset and underset text boxes. CopySet includes a palette that lists overset and underset text boxes for the active document, allowing the user to determine how much text is affected in each story, and giving the user the option of naming the individual text boxes for easy identification in complex documents.

The palette displays the amount overset/underset in a choice of three measures: character count, line count, and in default measurement system units. The amount of text required for a box to be considered underset is user definable in either default measurement increments or in lines. By using the trim command, a text box can be shortened or lengthened to accommodate the text it contains with the click of the mouse.

Overset text can be viewed and edited by selecting the edit command or clicking on the overset text icon in a text box. This creates an editing text box of the same column width adjacent to the overset box, and gives the user the ability to work with text that would otherwise be unavailable beyond the overset mark. These editing boxes can all be closed via a menu command, or the user can elect to save the document with the editing boxes intact for future work. CopySet also includes a feature that counts lines, words, and characters in a selected story and indicates whether the story is overset.

DASHES

(CompuSense) The Dashes XTension provides high quality Hyphenation for your QuarkXPress text. It's aim and purpose is to provide a tool that improves the appearance and readability of a user's page by inserting hyphens which are inconspicuous, so as not to disturb the flow of meaning in the story.

The internal hyphenation code that is used in this XTension has been licensed from Circle Noetic Services, thus you are guaranteed to receive the same high standard of hyphen breaks, as is provided by their renowned Dashes DA.

▶ Allows you to insert discretionary hyphens into a selection of text, the current text box, or the complete document.

▶ When inserting hyphens, the Auto Hyphenation Rules that you specify from within QuarkXPress (Edit ➤ H&Js) are fully obeyed.

▶ Allows you to remove discretionary hyphens from a selection of text, the current text box, or the complete document.

- If you are unhappy with the way the XTension hyphenates a word, you can enter it into your own Dashes exception dictionary.

- Each Dashes hyphen has a stylistic ranking associated with it. This allows you to exclude hyphens that are not up to the stylistic quality you specify.

- Allows you to import and export hyphenation exception lists into and out of the XTension.

- Will correctly hyphenate words that contain ligatures.

- All the hyphens inserted are stored as discretionary hyphens within the document, thus the document will not reflow due to hyphenation exceptions, when opened or printed on another machine.

- Will correctly hyphenate the document, regardless of the System or Program language.

- Dashes XTension is a linguistically based algorithm. It puts in over 99% of the possible hyphens with over 99% accuracy in all the languages offered.

COPYSPECS

(Frank Kubin) Makes it easy to copy and paste type specs anywhere within a paragraph. Special *List* function lets you select sections of text anywhere in your document and change the specs of all sections simultaneously. Similar to using a style sheet but it works on text anywhere within a paragraph. Features:

- Interface Floating palette with pop-up menus and ⌘-key equivalents.

- Copy Specs copies the text attributes of the current selection.

- Paste Specs sets the text attributes of the current selection to the attributes copied.

- Add Selection To List adds the current selection of text to a list of text areas allowing for simultaneous attribute changing.

- Paste Specs To List applies the copied text attributes to all text areas currently on the list and does an "Update List."

- Update List will delete from the list any selections that no longer exist or that are in boxes that have been edited.

▶ Cut Last Sel from List deletes the last added selection for undoing a previous "add."

▶ Clear List clears the list for starting a new one.

INDEXTENSION

(Future Publishing, Ltd.) Another product from Future Publishing, IndeXTension provides a quick and easy utility for creating simple indexes in QuarkXPress.

Using refined text technology in QuarkXPress, IndeXTension allows you to quickly "mark" words or phrases using a menu selection or keyboard command. You can generate index listings for general phrases which do not form part of the text, but are a general theme. Index markers can be turned off and on for convenience and accuracy of line endings.

The XTension then generates an index list, which may be formatted with any combination of QuarkXPress character styles. You can automatically eliminate duplicate entries, and indexes may be combined from multiple documents into one index.

FACEIT

(a lowly apprentice production) True character-based style sheets are now available for QuarkXPress! faceIT allows you to set up special faceIT styles which will affect only the character attributes of a selected range of text. Now you can change the attributes of text embedded inside paragraphs without changing the entire paragraph. All standard QuarkXPress character attributes can be set with faceIT, including font, size, color, style, tracking, and horizontal scale. Use familiar QuarkXPress dialog boxes to create, edit, or delete faceIT styles. Change the character specification of any faceIT style, and the changes will be applied to any text to which that style has been set. Changes may be either global or affect only your current document.

The faceIT palette also contains handy pull-down menus to set your favorite local character style attributes without affecting either the QuarkXPress or faceIT style sheets.

LINE COUNT XT (LCXT)

(Kytek, Inc.) LcXT provides a convenient way to estimate the line count of a range of text based on the character count of the range.

The LcXT Options dialog box allows you to specify the number of characters which constitutes a line, whether to include hidden text in the character count, and whether to include overflow text in the character count.

Character count may be specified in fractional units so as to provide a more accurate estimate of line count. The option to exclude overflow text from the character count allows you to Select All and be sure that only the visible text is included in the character count.

When the palette shown above is visible it will display the character count (CC), characters per line as set in the options dialog (CPL), and the estimated line count (LC) whenever a range of text is selected. The estimated line count is calculated by dividing the character count into the characters per line.

OVERMATTER

(The Last Word) For displaying all overmatter associated with individual or a linked chain of text boxes. Suitable for all users.

Cuts and changes made in the original text box are reflected in the OverMatter window. A word and line count is provided and the window content is automatically updated as different text boxes are selected. This is a floating scalable window, not a temporary text box. Allows the editor to view overmatter in font and size of choice.

OVERSET!

(North Atlantic Publishing Systems, Inc.) Overset!, an XTension to QuarkXPress, saves you time fitting text to boxes. When you click on an overset mark within a text box, Overset! creates a temporary text box which allows you to view overset copy. You can then edit your copy or adjust your text box size in order to get the fit you want. The temporary text box will disappear when the text fits. If there is no actual copy, the temporary text box will turn on and off, signaling you that the overset mark is due to a return. When a document is stored, the temporary text box is automatically removed. Now you can get to an exact fit with ease!

QXEDIT

(Baseview Products, Inc.) QXEdit allows you to "lift" blocks of text from the QuarkXPress screen for quick editing in a larger, more readable format.

QXEdit works by creating a window into which the text of selected blocks can be placed. Most text style attributes, such as bold and italic, will be displayed in the window, along with line and paragraph justification. Other attributes, such as style sheet, font, and point size, are displayed in a palette similar to the Quark measurements palette.

The special text editing window can be opened and closed on demand. Style attributes in this window can be applied and saved back to Quark. Text flow is much easier to manage, because the window contains only text.

The QXEdit display window can be customized by the user. You select the display font and size, the size of the window, and where it is placed on the screen. A dialog box, which prompts you to save or discard changes from the editing window to Quark, can be enabled or disabled. When disabled, all changes are automatically saved.

This new, modestly priced QuarkXTension from Baseview will significantly enhance the productivity of your staff and contribute to your publication's editorial quality.

SPELLBOUND

(CompuSense) The SpellBound spell checker XTension enables you to check the spelling of a single word, of an active story, of an entire document, or of the text on master pages. It provides the following functionality and features not found in the internal QuarkXPress spellchecker.

- Allows multiple auxiliary dictionaries (up to five) to be open at any one time.

- Provides for an exception dictionary. This is useful if you wish to implement house styles to ensure words are always spelt in a certain manner; e.g., *disk* instead of *disc*.

- Detects capitalization errors; i.e., will flag a word such as *mexico* as wrong, and correctly suggest *Mexico*.

- Uses a comprehensive, phonetically-based algorithm when looking for alternative spellings to words.

- Has a more precise definition of word boundaries. This allows you to spell-check words such as Ph.D. and QuarkXPress.

- Allows you to use the spell checker as a "guesser"; you may interactively type in your guess and do a Lookup on this. This same feature allows you to highlight portions of compound words and get spelling suggestions on the constituent words.

- Distinguishes between words with the same spelling but different capitalization. When replacing a misspelled word, you may chose only to replace words with the same capitalization as the present word, or all occurrences.

- Gives you the choice of *casting* capitalization of the replacement word to that of the original or not.

- Allows you to edit any of the open auxiliary or exception dictionaries, while doing a spell check.

- Allows you to enter non-alphabetic characters into the auxiliary or exception dictionaries. Note: If nonstandard characters are entered into an English auxiliary dictionary, then this dictionary cannot be used with the Internal QuarkXPress Spell checker.

- Will spell-check words that contain *fi* or *fl* ligatures.

SHORTLINE ELIMINATOR (SEXT)

(Kytek, Inc.) SeXT detects and corrects paragraphs with short last lines. You may specify what constitutes a short last line in terms of character count and/or a hyphenated last word.

You control how the tracking of the paragraph may be altered to eliminate the short last line. You specify the tracking steps and the minimum and maximum tracking values to apply, relative to the default tracking you indicate.

You indicate whether you prefer all tight tracking values to be tried first (Tight), all loose tracking values to be tried first (Loose), or alternate loose/tight tracking (Loose Tie) or alternate tight/loose tracking (Tight Tie).

When a paragraph with a short last line is detected, SeXT adjusts the paragraph tracking to eliminate it. For example, if you specify alternate tight/loose and a step value of 0.2 (em) it will first tighten by 0.2, then loosen by 0.2, then tighten by 0.4 and so forth until the short last line is gone.

SeXT reports the tracking value of all paragraphs modified. It also notes all paragraphs with short last lines that could not be fixed within the given parameters.

The tracking step may be as fine as $\frac{1}{200,000}$ em if necessary. This allows you to make subtle changes to the paragraph spacing to achieve the elimination of short last paragraph lines.

SOFTCUTS

(The Last Word) For comparing "before and after" edited copy in a single text box or a chain of linked text boxes. Suitable for those involved in publishing and the legal profession who need to view all alterations to copy.

Recalls the text as originally appeared in the last "saved" version and shows subsequent amendments. Deleted type is shown as struck-through characters and inserted copy is shown as underlined.

SONAR BOOKENDS

(Virginia Systems, Inc.) With Sonar Bookends, anyone can easily make an index and table of contents for a QuarkXPress document in a matter of minutes. Product highlights:

- Automatic indexing of keywords. An index consisting of all words can be made in seconds. Common words or unimportant words can be automatically eliminated.

- Indexing of word/phrase lists. An index can be made of a user-supplied list of words and phrases.

- Support for multiple-level indexes. Hierarchical indexes are supported with an unlimited number of levels.

- Flexible formatting. Page numbers can be separated with either commas or tabs. Chapter references can also be included in the index.

▸ Index can be printed or saved. The index can be printed directly or brought back into QuarkXPress for further editing.

SONAR TOC

(Virginia Systems, Inc.) Sonar TOC extends Sonar Bookends' indexing and table of contents creation capabilities through the use of style sheets. Product highlights:

▸ Fast and easy table of contents generation. Simply tell Sonar TOC which style sheets are for headers, subheaders, sub-subheaders, etc., and Sonar TOC will produce a multilevel table of contents in seconds.

▸ Table of contents supports multiple sections. The page numbers in the table of contents appear just as they do at the bottom of each page in the document, including Roman numerals and prefix information.

▸ Indexing made even easier. Anything marked using style sheets can be passed directly to Sonar Bookends for indexing. This feature is especially useful when indexing a catalog.

STORY EDITOR

(The Last Word) For copy editing text chains with word-processing functions. Especially suitable for writers, copy editors, and fact checkers.

Provides a floating scalable interactive window, which allows editors to create and edit text in the font and size of their choice, whilst the original document retains the actual styles required. When editing is complete the changes may be applied to the original document by clicking an apply button.

TEXT TOOLS

(Vision's Edge, Inc.) The TeXT Tools XTension contains four utilities for altering or saving text. The first function allows you to skew text boxes. The second and third functions convert uppercase letters to lowercase. The fourth function exports all of the text in a document to a single file.

SKEW TEXT BOXES

Skews a text box to any angle between −90° and 90°.

QUICK LOWERCASE

Quickly converts uppercase letters to lowercase while leaving all text attributes alone.

EXTENDED LOWERCASE

An advanced uppercase to lowercase converter. Features:

- Optional small caps style.

- Change selected text or entire document.

- Option to change only entirely uppercase words.

EXPORT ALL TEXT

Exports all the text in a document to a single file. Features:

- Exports in top-to-bottom and left-to-right order.

- Can output using style tags or pure ASCII.

THESAURUS REX

(Vision's Edge, Inc.) The Thesaurus Rex XTension allows you to find the right word for your thought without taking your hands off the keyboard or your eyes off the screen. Just place the cursor anywhere in the word you want to look up and open the thesaurus. A window with a list of synonyms from the 220,000-word thesaurus will appear. Select the synonym you want, then select the Replace button. The new word replaces the old word in the document. Of course, you can choose to leave the original word in your document, using Thesaurus Rex to check spelling and meaning.

You can use Thesaurus Rex to look up synonyms for any word displayed in the synonym window. By repeatedly using the Look Up button, you can explore the richness of the English language right at your keyboard.

Thesaurus Rex adds variety and spice to your writing, while increasing your productivity and enjoyment.

XT_EDIT

(Trias) This great new product from Trias is actually a stand-alone text editor designed to work exclusively with QuarkXPress's powerful typographical features, and is an XTension that brings the preformatted and styled text into QuarkXPress via the Get Text dialog.

The editor offers the user the ability to enter text quickly, without waiting for QuarkXPress to draw the entered text or reflow the page to accommodate it. XT_Edit also accepts ACSII output from other systems, performing an automatic search and replace of odd characters or placeholders during import. This can greatly facilitate moving text files from one platform to another.

XT_Edit supports setting styles to be translated into the appropriate QuarkXPress style sheets, as well as local character-based formatting. There are also special keyboard or menu commands for inserting column breaks and thin, en, em and non-breaking spaces. The editor has a built-in search and replace function for text strings, as well as an online macro maker for frequently used words or phrases. XT_Edit even prints galleys, including the invisibles.

XSTYLE

(em software, inc.) Xstyle is the accelerator for QuarkXPress style use and reporting. The XTension greatly simplifies and accelerates the use of QuarkXPress style sheets and character and paragraph settings, whether you're an "XPress demon" or an enthusiastic beginner.

Xstyle provides easy, continual access to many character, paragraph, and style sheet settings previously accessible only via a cumbersome series of menu selections and deeply nested dialog boxes.

Xstyle adds three new floating palettes: Character (font, size, color, shade, horizontal scale, and baseline shift), Paragraph (paragraph style, left margin, first line indent, right margin, space above, and space below), and Style Sheet Editor (including all character properties and the most common paragraph properties).

Xstyle was designed with the serious keyboard user in mind, and provides "mouse-free" ways to change character, paragraph, and style sheet settings. For example, each palette has a user-assignable "hot key" that takes you directly from editing text into the first field with one keystroke. Numerous other shortcuts provide much greater efficiency than navigating through the morass of QuarkXPress submenus.

Xstyle goes well beyond QuarkXPress's style palette, providing easy multiple-level "undo" of style sheet changes, application of just the character settings from a style to the current selection, individual style copying between documents, easy cross-document style comparison, the ability to restore one or all settings of a style from its parent style, and much more.

Xstyle 1.5 produces style reports on all style sheets for the current document or on selected documents in "batch mode." Xstyle's reports are completely configurable both in content and in appearance, resulting in an ordinary QuarkXPress document that can be printed or saved.

Xstyle is risk-free. Xstyle comes with an outstanding manual and em's usual 60-day, money-back guarantee of satisfaction.

SCITEX PRECISION TOOLS

(Scitex) Scitex Precision Tools consist of four XTensions for creating electronic mechanicals quickly and accurately.

SCITEX ALIGN & MEASURE

Choosing Align from the Align & Measure palette enables you to align the top of a picture box with a text baseline, or center a line on a box, or a box on a page. Align any two points vertically, horizontally, or both. Specify alignment points as selection handles or center points of boxes or lines, as text baselines, or as any point on a page. You can also align two points by an offset amount.

Ever need to measure the width of a serif, or the distance between a text baseline and the top of a page? Choosing Measure from the Scitex Align & Measure palette enables you to quickly determine the distance between any two points on a page—including item selection handles, center points, and text baselines. The points' coordinates are displayed, along with the vertical, horizontal, and straight-line distance between them, and the angle of the straight-line distance. Clicking Show displays the measurement points you specify.

SCITEX ZOOM

When you need a closer look, use the Scitex Zoom palette to enlarge a selected area of the page to views ranging from 400% to 1600%. Simply specify the view you want, drag the selection marquee onto the page, and the selected area appears in the palette's window. Used with Scitex Align & Measure, Scitex Zoom is a powerful tool for fine tuning production details such as alignment and serif weights.

SCITEX LOCK

Scitex Lock enables you to globally lock text boxes, picture boxes, lines, or any combination of the three. Locked items cannot be moved accidentally with the Item tool, but they can be moved using the QuarkXPress Measurement palette or Modify command. The contents of locked items can also be locked. Scitex Lock protects text from designers and designs from editors!

SCITEX NUDGE

With Scitex Nudge, you can move a selected item in user-definable increments. Scitex Nudge works with Scitex Zoom, so you can nudge an item displayed at 1600% for highly accurate placement.

SCITEX FRACTIONS

(Scitex) Scitex Fractions enables you to fine-tune the appearance of fractions. You can specify numerators and denominators of up to three characters and independently adjust the size, position, and kerning of the numerator, denominator, and divisor.

SCITEX GRIDS & GUIDES

(Scitex) Scitex Grids & Guides is a powerful set of tools for creating and editing grids and guides. You can define guides one at a time, specifying their numerical coordinates, color, and the view at which they appear.

Create complex grids quickly and accurately by specifying a start point, end point, and the number of, or distance between, guides. Grids can be copied and pasted between a document's pages, and saved and imported from other documents.

By clicking on a guide, you can edit it or center it between any pair of guides. You can also define guides along, or offset from, the edges of a text or picture box.

Guides To Item allows you to quickly and precisely place a guide along any or all sides of a text or picture box.

SCITEX IMAGE TOOLS

(Scitex) Scitex Image Tools includes four XTensions for working with pictures and graphic elements.

SCITEX BLENDS

With Scitex Blends, you can create straight-line or radial blends of up to 14 colors. You can specify CMYK colors or pick them from the document's color palette, control the blend rate between pairs of colors (linear or logarithmic), and draw blend paths at any angle. When sent to a PostScript RIP, Scitex Blends produces standard PostScript-quality blends. When sent to a Scitex RIP, Scitex Blends generates Scitex degrades with "noise" to eliminate banding.

SCITEX SILHOUETTES

With Scitex Silhouettes, you can quickly silhouette a picture using straight-line or smooth-cut techniques. Scitex Silhouette may be used for comps, and, depending on image complexity and quality requirements, for production masks as well. In a Scitex production workflow, Scitex Silhouettes can be used for automatic mask substitution—the automatic swapping of the Scitex silhouette for a high-resolution mask cut on a Scitex production system.

SCITEX PICTURE SCALING

Have you memorized all the keyboard shortcuts for "live" picture scaling? With the Scitex Picture Scaling palette, you can scale a picture interactively in 1%, 10%, or continuous increments, and center or fit a picture within its picture box—without entering numbers in palettes or dialog boxes, or remembering keyboard shortcuts.

SCITEX QUICK PROOF

Ever get tired of waiting for EPS and TIFF images to print? When you need a quick look at an image-intensive document, use Scitex Quick Proof. This XTension prints the smaller PICT screen previews of EPS and TIFF images, giving you a fast proof with 72-dpi images in position. No need to suppress the printout of individual pictures one at a time—and then guess where the pictures should be when you look at the proof!

SCITEX DOCUMENT REPORTS

(Scitex) Scitex Document Reports enables you to extract information from a QuarkXPress document and prepare a report. You can choose from over three dozen document attributes on which to report, including page geometry, style sheets (character, format, tabs, rules), fonts (and fonts in imported graphics), text boxes, picture boxes, pictures, colors, and trapping. You can sort this information by page, by layer (with the Scitex Layers XTension), or for the entire document.

You can save, print, or export reports for use in other applications, and save the formats of frequently-used reports.

SCITEX LAYERS

(Scitex) Scitex Layers enables you to create and name up to 31 layers for viewing and printing. You can show or hide layers, and print only visible layers. Use Scitex Layers to organize electronic mechanicals with revisions or foreign-language versions, or just separate different elements for more efficient viewing and proofing.

DINGBATS

(Adept Solutions) Rather than accessing dingbats through the tedious Keycaps utility, just open the Dingbat palette, and select the character desired. Choose an element from the Dingbat palette to replace a character in the desired text, and it will retain the character's size and attributes. The procedure may also be reversed.

EASYTYPE

(Artemis Systems) This new XTension from Artemis Systems displays a small floating palette containing 36 characters from the extended ASCII set. EasyType allows the user to define sets of frequently used characters and save the configurations for use on other documents. You can select which characters are displayed in your palette and enter them into your document by simply clicking on the symbol in the palette. The selected character appears wherever the cursor is located or replaces any selected text.

EasyType displays the characters in either the font selected, or ASCII format. This XTension is a must for writers and editors in constant need of the extended character set, but who don't want to waste valuable time accessing it.

KERNING PALETTE

(Clearface) The Kerning Palette is a quick, intuitive kerning table editor. It will save you hours of repetitive labor creating the kern pairs necessary for high quality typography. It gives you control over character spacing that formerly required dedicated programs—without ever leaving QuarkXPress.

Because you stay in QuarkXPress, you can work on live copy in real documents. See changes to line breaks and copy fit instantly. View pairs in true context. Solve kerning problems once on an actual job, and they stay solved in the next one. You don't have to go anywhere to open font files, or type in pairs—just point and click, and access kerning values from a convenient floating palette. The tables you create can also be universally applied to font suitcase files system wide, so they'll be used by any program that supports automatic kerning.

The Kerning Palette allows you to define the units you want to work with, in any fraction of an em space. It allows you to view the contents of your QuarkXPress Preferences file, and add or delete kerning tables quickly and easily. Export tables to a variety of formats, including text files. Create a suitcase with all the fonts from the current document, or any other combination of fonts you choose.

ACCENTMASTER

(Linographic) AccentMaster is an indispensable utility for those setting body text in European languages. Some European and Baltic alphabets contain characters that have accents and other figures which do not normally appear in English-language text. AccentMaster gives users the ability to set foreign styled accents, umlauts, and other special characters otherwise impossible to place with QuarkXPress.

AccentMaster includes two special fonts—one serif and one sans serif—that contain special characters for printing text in frequently used European and Baltic languages within QuarkXPress.

AGENCYFIT, VOLUMES 1 AND 2

(Monotype, Inc.) Dissatisfied with the kerning pairs that ship with your Adobe and Monotype fonts? Tune your type with AgencyFIT from Monotype Typography. AgencyFIT was created by Monotype and PDR, the esteemed New York advertising typesetters. AgencyFIT consists of Macintosh screen fonts with over 1200 kerning pairs per font. All the popular Adobe and Monotype fonts have been meticulously kerned "tight not touching" to reduce the manual kerning required to achieve optimal typography results in QuarkXPress.

AgencyFIT Volume 1 contains 65 kerned screen fonts. AgencyFIT Volume 2 contains an additional 250 kerned fonts.

XACTHEIGHT

(Artemis Systems) This new XTension is a must for designers and other QuarkXPress users who need to produce headline and display text to a precise visual size. XactHeight allows type sizes to be specified by stating the visual height of capital letters or of the lowercase x-height.

The user may select from two operating modes. Palette mode provides a small, unobtrusive palette which continuously tracks and displays the visual height of the characters at the cursor position and also features convenient "up" and "down" buttons to interactively increase or decrease the type size. Dialog mode, for the more occasional user, opens a dialog box on demand and includes a handy Apply button.

Both modes allow measurements to be displayed and entered in millimeters, points, or inches, regardless of the units set in QuarkXPress Preferences.

INSERTSPACE

(XTend) InsertSpace provides a means for "justifying" multiple blocks of text on a line. This is accomplished by distributing the leftover white space at one or more locations within the line. This ability is commonly found only on today's dedicated typesetting systems. In a fraction of the time InsertSpace provides results that are more accurate than those achieved manually Users maintain full editing capabilities and the ability to modify up to 21 blocks of text when using InsertSpace.

InsertSpace improves many tab setting functions and aids in the creation of headers and footers. The ability to build tables from data that has been imported from spreadsheet or database files may now be automated as well.

PROTABSXT

(Software XTensions) ProTabsXT adds enhances QuarkXPress with professional typesetting capabilities once only available to traditional typesetting shops. This XTension lets you break the 20-tab barrier, straddle and balance columns, and more:

- Automatically calculates the widths of tab columns and gutters to ensure alignment and fit.

- Allows automatic calculation of fixed and variable-width columns.

- Allows alignment of column heads over the longest column line.

- Straddles text across any or all columns and gutters.

- Automatically generates vertical and horizontal rules across all combinations of columns, gutters, and rows.

- Autovert… command generates automatic vertical rules.

- Tab Style sheets allow you to save your settings for use in future documents.

Tables are entirely self-contained, and can be moved, resized, cut or pasted. Columns and rules will automatically be recalculated based on the new available areas.

Since ProTabs constructs its own combination of columns and gutters within its own user-defined box, the number of available columns is twice Quark's maximum of 20.

ProTabs returns the precision tabular control familiar to typesetting professionals on much more expensive dedicated typesetting systems.

VJ

(Trias) Do you frequently find yourself being asked to fill out underset or squeeze overset text into QuarkXPress text boxes or linked story chains? VJ (for Vertical Justification) makes the tedious job of copyfitting a breeze. Based on parameters that you define, this XTension examines the selected text box/chain and determines what it can change to make it fit. The options for VJ include:

- Adding or subtracting interparagraph space.
- Adding or subtracting leading.
- Tracking the text either in or out.
- Increasing or decreasing the horizontal scale.

The limits which VJ uses to make these adjustments are defined by you, and can be very minute. You can even choose not to use one or more of the options.

XTENSIONS FROM QUARK, INC.

(Quark, Inc.) These disks include all the free XTensions Quark, Inc. has released for QuarkXPress. Freebies are just the beginning:

Features Plus—create fractions and prices, convert between measurements on screen, remove manual kerning, and choose alternate em spaces.

Network Connection—allows users to exchange pictures, text, and messages across a network from within QuarkXPress.

Calibration—lets users compensate for screen tint inaccuracies when outputting to various printers.

Bob—adds Go-to-page, Line Check Utility for undesirable typographic elements, and Color-Swatch Drag, which permits users to click and drag colors from the Colors palette and apply them to text or picture box backgrounds, frames, and lines.

Color Sets—adds three Pantone color matching systems to QuarkXPress 3.1: Pantone Process Colors, Pantone ProSim, and Pantone Uncoated.

WordPerfect Filter—lets users import files created in WordPerfect 2.0 and later.

Son of Bob—adds additional interface enhancements, including command key view scaling, and the ability to use multiplication and division in any numeric entry field.

PageMaker Import Filter—lets users import Aldus PageMaker 4.0 and 4.2 documents in QuarkXPress.

Cool Blends—expands the linear feature in QuarkXPress 3.1's Colors palette to let users create any of six one- or two-color blend patterns for box backgrounds.

Multiple Masters Utility—supports Adobe Inc.'s new font technology in three ways: it creates Multiple Master instances for documents as they are opened with QuarkXPress, in addition to instances for EPS files as they are printed. It also gives you access to the Multiple Master Font creator dialog from within QuarkXPress.

XMATH

(York Graphics, Inc.) XMath is a professional mathematical typography enhancement available for QuarkXPress that enables users to build complex equations right in a QuarkXPress document. And since XMath is an XTension, you can take advantage of all the functionality of QuarkXPress.

Users can easily convert equations created using standard keyboard entries into math text—the program handles all the necessary font changes to get math signs and symbols from the correct fonts without manual font changes or tedious coding. XMath's rich set of features enable users to:

- Make simple text strings into buildup fractions.

- Typeset matrices.

- Compose roots, radicals, limits, and integrals.

- Change characters (such as parentheses, brackets, braces) to upsize.

- Insert math signs, symbols, and Greek characters into text anywhere in a document.

For complex equations, XMath uses Adobe's Mathematical Pi font, available from XChange.)

XTABLE

(York Graphics, Inc.) XTable is a professional table composition tool for QuarkX-Press. And since XTable is an XTension, users can take advantage of all the functionality afforded by QuarkXPress when setting type that is destined to be made into a table. XTable will calculate the tab stops, indentations, etc. to compose the table to the user's specifications. XTable features include:

▸ Control column and gutter widths.

▸ Set straddle heads and control how they are positioned over the columns they straddle.

▸ Automatically align horizontal paragraph rules with type.

▸ Specify text alignment in columns, and align type on special points within each of the columns.

▸ Change the positioning in the column of any data in the table—operations are allowed on any "cell," line, or column.

MATHABLE

(York Graphics, Inc.) Mathable is an integrated typographic enhancement for QuarkXPress that combines the features of York's XMath and XTable XTensions. Mathable has all the features of XMath and XTable, and allows users to create tables of equations and math problems for technical journals and exercise sections of textbooks. Features include:

▸ Make simple text strings into buildup fractions.

▸ Typeset matrices.

▸ Compose roots, radicals, limits, and integrals.

▸ Change characters (such as parentheses, brackets, braces) to upsize.

▸ Insert math signs, symbols, and Greek characters into text anywhere in a document.

▸ Control column and gutter widths.

▸ Set straddle heads and control how they are positioned over the columns they straddle.

▸ Automatically align horizontal paragraph rules with type.

▸ Specify text alignment in columns, and align type on special points within each of the columns.

> ▸ Change the positioning in the column of any data in the table—operations are allowed on any "cell," line, or column.

(For complex equations, Mathable uses Adobe's Mathematical Pi font, available from XChange—see below.)

MATHEMATICAL PI

(Adobe Systems, Inc.) Mathematical Pi contains six families of mathematical characters, and includes Greek letters, symbols, special parentheses, braces and brackets, and mathematical signs. With this font installed, XMath and Mathable XTensions from York Graphics automatically typeset complex mathematical equations, fractions, summations, roots, radicals, and integrals.

XCHAR!

(Schnittstelle) XChar! gives you a faster and more convenient way to insert special characters into your text! Special characters are already available from the Key Caps DA or by pressing the appropriate keyboard letter while holding down one or more of the Shift, Option, Control, or ⌘ keys. Pressing ⌘-9 or selecting XChar! from the Utilities menu displays a neatly arranged chart showing all the special characters from any available font. Select a character by clicking on it once, and an enlarged version appears in the upper-right corner of the table. Double-clicking on the character—or pressing the Insert button—inserts the desired special character in the desired font at your current cursor position, leaving surrounding characters unchanged.

QUARKPRINT

(Quark, Inc.) The Printing Productivity Tool for Power Users

Print Job—This feature of QuarkPrint saves time and reduces the probability of printing related errors by letting you save and apply frequently used settings from the Print and Page Setup dialog boxes. You can also specify custom CMYK screen angles and frequencies and print non sequential pages and ranges.

Document Statistics—Now you can print a list of all elements in a QuarkXPress document—even if the document is closed. No more guessing about formats, fonts, or other critical unknown elements in a document.

Print Area—Ever want to print a portion of a page? With this feature you can now drag out a box to print page elements for faster editing and proofing.

Printer Calibration—This feature allows you adjust screen output to compensate for dot gain on various printers—especially useful for color separations.

BACKTRACK

(DPN) BackTrack solves the problem of managing multiple iterations! Install this XTension and you have precise control over when, where and how your documents are saved. This is not just an auto-save mechanism. Instead of performing a normal save function, you can set BackTrack to keep as many iterations (versions of your document) on disk as necessary. The XTension automatically deletes the oldest copies from your backup folder.

The obvious advantage—even if a file becomes corrupted, you'll have another copy of recent vintage on hand. You get to decide how much time will elapse between versions and how long BackTrack will wait to backup during periods of keyboard/mouse inactivity. Via preferences, you decide whether the XTension prompts you when it creates an iteration or runs transparently in the background.

XSIZE

(Schnittstelle) XSize has been especially designed for the professional positioning of picture data. With this module, the size and the sector of a picture can be chosen depending on the selected QuarkXPress picture box. Magazines and other publications that require close cooperation between layout and picture processing will find XSize most useful.

XSize works with any QuarkXPress-compatible formats for picture data, including, TIFF, EPSF, PICT, and PAINT.

ADMEASURE

(GreyStone Computer Management Systems) This powerful tool is a must for those who work with co-op advertisements. When building ad pages, it's important to charge the correct amount for the proportion of space occupied by each vendor. AdMeasure calculates the amount of co-op dollars to charge each vendor based on your production cost estimates. You can have several publications with different close dates all accounted individually.

AdMeasure is simple to use—first, your administrator creates your vendor list. Next, you simply drag a marquee around any area, and assign it to a vendor. Ad-Measure compiles a report of all vendors and totals their proportional share of the cost of the publication. Common areas can be designated, so your vendors are always charged the correct amount.

ADPRO

(Alphalogic) AdPro is a mini-application that works within QuarkXPress as a QuarkXTension. It provides automatic "Pro-ing"—proportional size calculations—of a given set of advertisements. A publisher who wishes to produce an advertisement for a client typically has to produce a set of different sizes for each publication in which the ad will be placed. In such a situation the use of scaling and a float within acceptable tolerances makes it possible to prepare a significantly lower number of advertisements than would otherwise be required. With only a few planned insertions, it is possible, though laborious, to calculate a small set of advertisements by hand. Manually choosing the optimum number and scale of masters for a wide insertion is almost impossible without AdPro.

AdPro allows the operator to specify a list of all the different sizes required, together with the float and scaling factor that is acceptable for each set. AdPro then calculates the optimal set of Masters that will satisfy the production run.

EXPOSE

(Vision's Edge, Inc.) Here's another great XTension from Vision's Edge, Inc. With Expose, creating a catalog of graphic files is simple. Your catalog can look just like you want it to, because you build a QuarkXPress master page which will be used for each page of the catalog. Through the Expose preferences, choose whether to include the full path name, the date the graphic was most recently modified, the file size, the file type (EPS, Paint, Pict, TIFF, RIFF, or Scitex CT) and fonts imbedded in any EPS files. You may also optionally elect to have the graphic scaled to fit the box in the catalog.

Tell Expose where to find the graphics for the catalog and this XTension imports all graphics in the designated folder or folders, adding the information requested through the preferences dialog box. You have a catalog of your graphics in a fraction of the time it would take to create manually. If you've got volumes of graphic files you would like catalogued, let Expose do the work for you!

FCSLOCK

(F.C.S., S.A.) FCSLock is a QuarkXPress XTension designed specifically for large QuarkXPress installations. This XTension will allow an administrator to disable any feature of QuarkXPress so that other users will not be able to modify certain aspects of QuarkXPress documents. FCSLock can disable any menu item of QuarkXPress, the measurements palette, or any creation tool.

Every time you startup QuarkXPress with FCSLock installed QuarkXPress will operate in "Locked" mode. If the operator does not know the password, he will not be able to unlock the program. Only the administrator will be able to unlock and reconfigure FCSLock.

KEYLINER

(DataStream Imaging Systems, Inc.) Keyliner is a professional stripping station XTension that allows QuarkXPress users to input graphic elements and build page geometry from conventional art boards and documents. These QuarkXPress documents can be formatted quickly and precisely. Keyliner supports all QuarkXPress features.

Keyliner is designed to be used with a digitizing tablet. It is accurate to within 0.001″, depending on the digitizing tablet you use and the tolerance you select. Projects that used to take hours, can now be done in minutes using Keyliner! Features:

- Keyliner works independent of the Macintosh screen—so it's more accurate.

- Keyliner includes features found in high-end CAD systems.

- Keyliner Tools

STEP & FLEX-IT

(DataStream Imaging Systems, Inc.) Most Macintosh pre-press systems are geared toward the preparation of film for offset lithography. As a result, flexographic printers often find that there are key features missing from desktop systems. This means that additional steps frequently must be taken to get film ready for plate making. This can involve time-consuming manual camera work or expensive flexographic pre-press systems that move the process out of the economic range of Mac desktop publishing packages.

Now there is a cost-effective way to create film using QuarkXPress that comes out of the imagesetter ready to go to plate. It's called Step & Flex-It—a new XTension from DataStream Imaging Systems developed in conjunction with some of the industry's leading flexographic printers.

Step & Flex-It performs specialized functions, such as automatic compensation for plate distortion, label bleed, and step-and-repeat, which effectively customize QuarkXPress for the needs of flexography. It brings to QuarkXPress all the features needed to make flexographic film quickly and economically.

FLEXSCALE

(Vision's Edge, Inc.) Another new XTension from Vision's Edge, this utility allows a document to be scaled when output to a printer. Vertical and horizontal scaling percentages can be assigned independent from one another to create rudimentary flexography. The document can be scaled between 50% and 150% vertically and horizontally. To activate this XTension, the user simply holds down the option key while selecting the Print command. Then, the desired scaling percentages are entered into the FlexScale dialog box. The scaling percentages are accurate to two decimal places; i.e., 102.87%. After selecting the Print button, the printing process continues normally except that the output is scaled.

SCANNING PARAMETERS

(The Last Word) For those who need to provide values for enlargement, reduction, or rotation of images imported into an QuarkXPress page. Scanning Parameters is especially suitable for those working in production departments of magazines and newspapers, as it provides essential information about the placement of all your positionals.

The XTension will print out a text list, a layout with keylines or a layout with low-res positionals. From this the scanner operator can obtain all the necessary information for scan size, crop, rotation, etc., without having to repeatedly refer to

QuarkXPress and making manual notes. A real labor-saver and checkpoint for documents with high-res graphics.

QTOOLS

(Baseview) QTools is an inexpensive pagination and layout tool that can greatly simplify newspaper composition. QTools customizes the Quark environment for newspaper publishing. The program offers an array of features that streamline copy management, story paste-up and layout, and page composition.

Pages can be quickly composed with pre-defined templates that set up banners, boxes, headline and text formats. The templates are easily defined through the "Build Template" feature. The "Paste with Style" command allows you pull in text and formats of stories composed in Baseview's NewsEdit program or other text editing programs utilizing QuarkXPress Tags.11.

▶ A range of fitting tools makes it easy to automatically square off columns and feather text between lines—all within spacing parameters set by the user.

▶ A text overflow box displays the part of the story that doesn't fit into the current box.

▶ A jump page feature can automatically break stories between pages, adding jump tags automatically.

▶ A set of box flow options attaches an unfinished story to a box. Story editing can continue after the page has been composed.

▶ QTools can be customized to allow users to set up paths to folders and stories and set up text/box sizing options.

QTools provides many time-saving utilities not found in off-the-shelf versions of Quark. This powerful package can save time and energy in the newsroom, allowing editors to focus on the editorial content of the news. If you're using Quark to compose your newspaper, then you need QTools!

QSPOOL

(Baseview) QSpool adds high-speed document spooling to QuarkXPress. Users can place a Quark or NewsEdit document in a specified folder—typically one that resides on the network file server. QSpool continually scans the folder looking for documents to print. If it finds a QuarkXPress document, QSpool opens it, prints it, and deletes it. If it finds a NewsEdit document, QSpool creates a template according to the specifications embedded in the file. QSpool flows text into the template, prints the document, and then deletes the text and template file from the folder— or moves it to a "Done" folder. QSpool gives every user the power of QuarkXPress without the cost.

- Spools QuarkXPress documents to the printer, freeing up the computer for other tasks.

- Prints QuarkXPress quality galleys right from NewsEdit.

- Will handle QuarkXPress documents with pictures.

- Can handle color separations using QTools.

Stories are off the screen in seconds, freeing the computer for other tasks. Composers and editors don't have to wait for stories to print, and can spend their time more productively.

LOGX

(Vision's Edge, Inc.) Do you have volumes of QuarkXPress documents? Would you like to be able to tell what fonts or graphics are used in those documents without having to manually open each file and check? LogX can quickly gather this information for you. LogX is a cataloging program that provides an easy way to create catalogs of QuarkXPress documents. Catalogs can be made that describe a single document, a folder of documents, or even all of the QuarkXPress documents on a single drive. Report information can include:

- The full path name of the document

- The date the document was last modified

- The names of graphics in the document, their types, and the date each was last modified

- The names of imported stories included in the document, their types, and the date each was last modified

XCHANGE
AND XTENSIONS
∙∙∙

CH. 20

⬧ Fonts used in the document

⬧ The selected printer setup for the document

Once LogX processes a report, the report can be printed out or shown on the screen. Onscreen, the report shows the attributes of one document at a time.

PAGESHOT

(Vision's Edge, Inc.) PageShot allows users to select multiple, non-contiguous pages for saving as EPS files. Pages can be saved in color, B&W, and with or without OPI information. Users can also elect to save only a specified area of a specific page or pages by entering top, left, height, and width coordinates—PageShot EPS can be created that actually captures information up to 72 points outside the printable area of the page.

PageShot can also save a specific text or graphic box as the boundary by which a PageShot EPS is defined. Any contents of the box or any page elements partially or fully visible through the box (if it has a background of none) are included in the EPS.

PICTUREMANAGER

(CompuSense) The PictureManager XTension is a must for any QuarkXPress user who works with graphics in her documents. It incorporates a comprehensive credits management utility that allows you to create caption boxes for graphics with ease. It also has an automatic picture updating facility. This module will search through user-specified volumes or folders anywhere on the network for missing and modified files and will update all as required. Other features of the XTension help to streamline tedious graphic related production tasks from the initial importing of the picture to finally delivering the document to a service bureau.

The user can specify all the necessary Credit Defaults… that will be applied to the caption text box that is created for a graphic. These include text attributes, style sheets, caption frame and background options, caption positioning options relative to the graphic, including distance and orientation as well as default text for the caption. When a caption is created for a graphic, it is automatically sized and placed in the desired location. Any attributes of an individual caption box or text can be easily edited.

The File Mover... option allows you to select a file and specify a destination disk and or folder where you want to copy the file. The file and all its linked files (Including DCS files if required) will be transferred. When moving or copying a file, the user may select to also move the QuarkXPress Preferences file and other required auxiliary files at the same time.

The Auto Updater is a high-performance search utility that will search through predefined volumes or folders for missing or modified graphics and optionally update them. The user can completely control the process by specifying default search paths and/or update options.

Using the Picture Manager greeking can be easily turned on and off for all or individual picture boxes. It is also possible to suppress the printout of picture boxes or just the pictures on a global or individual basis. And this utility can be used to invert pictures for negatives.

The Picture group utility provides high-speed searching for graphics based on document names and types. The resultant batch of files is displayed in a floating palette. Any file can be dragged from the list and precisely placed in any open document.

CROPS + REGISTRATIONS

(Publishing Solutions, Inc.) This great new XTension from Publishing Solutions, Inc. adds professional, multiple crops and registration marks to any QuarkXPress page element or group. Just draw a picture box that crops your layout the way you wish, and tell C&R to do the rest. You'll instantly have high quality crops, registrations and CMYK indicators. And there is no limit to the number of crops/registrations on an QuarkXPress page. This long-awaited XTension is available now.

FCSPRINT

(F.C.S., S.A.) From the developers of FCS TableMaker comes this new XTension created specifically for service bureaus. FCSPrint will automatically set all the options of the Setup and Print dialog boxes to save as much film as possible and to avoid ever-costly human errors. Service bureaus who have been testing this product for over a year report incredible savings in time and errors.

The operator needs only to specify the resolution, screen ruling and type of job (e.g., RC Paper, film, film with separations, or color proof) and this XTension does the rest! The job will always be sent to the printer at the best orientation and with all the correct settings (emulsion side, crop marks, etc). This XTension even warns you on small page jobs to switch to a smaller film width to save you money, or just to let you know that the job does not fit the larger film width.

When printing separations, users have the option of automatically changing all the spot colors to separation colors with one click of the mouse. Even better, FCSPrint may be completely and easily customized with the use of the ResEdit template included with the purchase. ResEdit allows editing of all the settings by typing into clearly labeled fields, and no hacking in hexadecimal is required.

PRINTER'S SPREADS

(Corder Associates, Inc.) This XTension was created to aid printers and desktop publishers in composing saddlestitched publications, allowing the user to quickly convert QuarkXPress documents from reader's spread format to printer's spread format. QuarkXPress–compatible as well, it converts all automatic page numbers to their textual representation. After the pages have been ordered in reader's spread format, this utility can optionally move the elements of every page to allow for creep. The creep measurement is user-definable in points.

BLENDBUILDER

(XTend, Inc.) Blending new colors from within QuarkXPress during the design or production process is not always an easy task. That task becomes even more difficult when you must complement existing colors that are based on different color matching systems. XTend introduces BlendBuilder, an XTension that performs this chore for you. BlendBuilder provides the tools that allow you to experiment with more options and ensures results that are far more accurate than those derived by hand. Tightly integrated with the QuarkXPress user-interface, BlendBuilder allows users to add colors to their current document or the QuarkXPress application directly.

New colors are added by specifying two base colors, the number of blends preferred, and a color model to base the blends on. Users may blend colors based on the HSB, RGB, or CMYK color models to achieve unique results.

A preview feature allows users to view the colors before they are added to the document, as well as offering them the ability to compare that color with its two base colors. Support for colors based on the HSB, RGB, CMYK, PANTONE, TRU-MATCH, and FOCOLTONE color matching systems is included. In addition, users who have installed the Colors Sets file may choose from the PANTONE Process, PANTONE ProSim, and PANTONE Uncoated color matching systems.

UTILITYPAK II

(XTend, Inc.) UtilityPak II consists of three XTensions that enhance the user-interface and productivity of QuarkXPress. This collection of XTensions, which no QuarkXPress user should be without, includes:

OverHang—gives users the ability to adjust the height of the pasteboard along the top and bottom edges of a page or spread.

GuideHider—gives QuarkXPress users the ability to specify user-defined keyboard commands for the Show Guides, Show Baseline Grid, and Snap to Guides menu items. Never again will you have to fumble through the View menu to invoke these favorite commands.

SelectIt—allows users to deselect and reselect active items with a user-defined keyboard command. This feature will prove beneficial to individuals who frequently work in magnified views and find themselves forced to zoom out in order to deselect active items.

IMPRESS

(XTend) ImPress automates the task of stripping QuarkXPress pages into signatures. ImPress automatically imposes pages into a variety of standard signature arrangements; including sheetwise, work-and-turn, and work-and-tumble. All positioning and rotation of pages is handled automatically in a separate document, leaving your original document intact. Full editing capabilities are maintained in your original document, allowing the "ImPressed" document to be saved to disk or printed using the various print options available from within QuarkXPress.

Capable of handling very complex signatures, ImPress remains quite simple to operate. All variables, such as style of signature, output device, and collation method (saddle-stitched/perfect-bound) are presented in one easy-to-view dialog box. Users requiring control over page creep (shingling) and bleed values, as well as fold and trim tolerances, may set these values directly.

ImPress not only creates signatures, but also reduces media costs by efficiently ganging multiple pages on a single signature. This feature will appeal to user who don't require ImPress's powerful imposition function.

ImPress is available in several versions so that users may purchase only what they currently require and upgrade later.

TIMESTAMP

(Vision's Edge, Inc.) The TimeStamp XTension allows the user to apply unlimited time stamps to any document. Automatically updated whenever the document is saved, the time stamps allow the user to easily and accurately determine when a document was last revised. Features:

- Unlimited time stamps per document.

- Time stamps are automatically updated with every save.

- Five different date formats, with the flexibility to alter many aspects of each format.

- Ability to include the time along with the date.

- Ability to include the chooser name in any time stamp.

- TimeStamp frames can be placed on master pages to allow quick time-stamping of all pages.

XAMINER

(Alphalogic) Xaminer is a "stand-alone" desk accessory that allows users to determine the graphics and fonts that are directly or indirectly in a document without having to launch QuarkXPress. It displays "at-a-glance" whether the correct screen and printer fonts are installed and whether the required graphics are available. It will be of particular interest to bureau, design studios, and power-users of QuarkXPress.

As a desk accessory, Xaminer launches quickly and has a very low memory over-head. It can be used concurrently with any program independent of MultiFinder or System 7. It saves the user from having to launch QuarkXPress, having the text re-flowed if the correct fonts are not present, and provides the user with all the font and graphic related information in a single list that can be saved as a disk file or printed as required. In addition to checking QuarkXPress documents, Xaminer is able to check Encapsulated PostScript Files (EPSF) directly and provide a list of the fonts that they use.

PINPOINT XT

(Cheshire Group) If you've ever had PostScript errors at print time (!), this XTen-sion is for you. PinPoint XT reports any printing error that occurs while a Post-Script file is running on a PostScript or PostScript-compatible output device. PinPoint XT provides: a display that shows what was processing prior to the error, the error type, offending command, and current position on page using QuarkX-Press coordinates. Included with the program is a complete error dictionary that defines all possible PostScript printing errors, explains their causes, and shows how to solve them.

PRINTAREA

(XTend, Inc.) PrintArea provides a feature that has been unavailable through most QuarkXPress revisions, that is, the ability to print specific items or a portion of a page. This feature proves invaluable during the process of designing and proofing a document. Changes to a document are made more efficiently by not burdening the user with the overhead required in printing entire pages.

Users specify the area they wish to print by selecting one or more items and letting Print Area determine the X/Y coordinates for them automatically, or by entering the X/Y coordinates into the PrintArea dialog box directly. Of course, these dimen-sions may be changed at any time. PrintArea works equally well with all item types including text boxes, picture boxes, and lines; as well as grouped or multiple-se-lected items. Support is also provided for items that "bleed" off the page. Users who require the advanced printing options of QuarkXPress will find that Print Area fully supports the standard QuarkXPress Print dialog.

SETINSET II

(XTend, Inc.) SetInset II permits a user to specify text inset values for QuarkXPress text boxes. The text inset value is the distance between the edge of the text box and the text within. Modifications to the text inset value were previously limited to one value for all sides of a text box. Augmenting the text box formatting capabilities found in QuarkXPress, SetInset II allows the user to design pages with much more flexibility when used in conjunction with existing features such as text indent, vertical justification, and tabs. SetInset II allows the user to enter a value using the measurement unit of their choice and offers decimal precision similar to that found in QuarkXPress.

Recently updated, SetInset II is now implemented as a moveable dialog box and includes an Apply feature. Keyboard commands allow the user to access the SetInset II dialog or apply user-defined inset values (in increments of 1/10x, 1x, 10x) directly to the active text box.

AUTOXTRACT

(Vision's Edge, Inc.) AutoXTract is an XTension that scans preselected folders for QuarkXPress documents, opens the documents, and exports all of the text from those documents to a user-selected folder as a text file. The text stories are exported in order from left to right and from top to bottom. With AutoXTract, it becomes easy to set up an archiving routine that will run automatically. This XTension allows the user to choose when the text files will be automatically exported. The files can be processed as often as every minute, or they can even be set to process once every twenty-four hours. It also allows the user to run the text to be exported manually at any time.

AutoXTract lets the user choose which folders to scan for files and uses a user-designated folder for output. The file name for the output can be controlled, as well, and AutoXTract can be set to add an extension to the end of each exported text file for easier identification.

With AutoXTract, it's easy to set up a text extracting routine that requires no operator. Set the preferences and let AutoXTract archive your QuarkXPress documents for you!

LOGICAL XTENSIONS V (DATA PIPELINE)

(Alphalogic) Data Pipeline is a text file database utility that allows a Quark user to insert multiple records of information into an QuarkXPress document, with automatic formatting. The source is a text file with user-configurable delimiters for records and fields. Each field can be assigned a different font, size, and style. The first field of each record becomes the unique identifier of that record. After choosing the database file and setting up a format the Quark user can simply type in the unique identifier of a record and issue a menu command to have the text inserted. Multiple datafiles can be configured and held as well as multiple formats. The text file would normally be exported from a conventional database and placed on the operator's machine or local server for production use.

WORDPERFECT DOS FILTER

(DPN) The WordPerfect DOS XTension enables users to import documents created in WordPerfect DOS versions 4.2 and 5.1 directly into a QuarkXPress document, without the use of additional conversion software.

The XTension also enables style tags in the WordPerfect document to be converted directly to the appropriate QuarkXPress style information during import. If a Macintosh is equipped with an FDHD floppy disk drive, and has a PC file recognition utility installed (i.e., DOS-Mounter), the WordPerfect files can imported directly. Alternatively, if the WordPerfect files are stored on an AFP server visible to both Macs and PCs (i.e., a Novell server), direct import can take place without any additional software.

MS WORD DOS FILTER

(DPN) The MS Word DOS XTension enables users to import the text from MS Word DOS documents, including the character specifications. All MS Word DOS text with default character settings will be translated to the user's default QuarkXPress style. Other character specifications in text are supported by a user configurable mapping of the MS Word DOS characters to the appropriate Macintosh font. Paragraph specifications are translated to QuarkXPress style sheets with the inclusion of a new style sheet tag that can be placed in an MS Word DOS style tag.

If a Macintosh is equipped with an FDHD floppy disk drive, and has a PC file recognition utility installed (i.e., DOS-Mounter), the MS Word DOS files can imported directly. Alternatively, if the MS Word DOS files are stored on an AFP server visible to both Macs and PCs (i.e., a Novell server), direct import can take place without any additional software.

WANG WP/PC FILTER

(DPN) The Wang WP/PC XTension enables users to import Wang WP/PC documents directly into a QuarkXPress document, without using any additional conversion software. The XTension also enables the user to include style tags in the Wang WP/PC document and convert these directly to appropriate QuarkXPress layout specifications.

If a Macintosh is equipped with an FDHD floppy disk drive, and has a PC file recognition utility installed (i.e., DOS-Mounter), the Wang WP/PC files can imported directly. Alternatively, if the Wang WP/PC files are stored on an AFP server visible to both Macs and PCs (i.e., a Novell server), direct import can take place without any additional software.

THE PERFECT XTENSION

(TechnoDesign) The Perfect XTension from TechnoDesign enables you to import text created in WordPerfect (versions 2.0 and 2.1) into QuarkXPress documents quickly and easily. TechnoDesign created the XTension in consultation with a large number of QuarkXPress users who regularly import sizable amounts of text created in word processors.

With The Perfect XTension, the style sheet in the QuarkXPress document uses the same names as those created in WordPerfect. This allows WordPerfect users to compose text using style-sheet names well suited for word processing, without needing to know the details of the QuarkXPress style sheet. In addition, all of the character specifications of the WordPerfect text are retained in QuarkXPress.

The software also enables you to include style tags (e.g., <B> for bold, <I> for italics) in the WordPerfect text that are translated to the appropriate formats when imported into QuarkXPress. WordPerfect page-layout information is removed during the conversion.

PRESSMARKS

(Vision's Edge, Inc.) Until PressMarks, users had to be content with QuarkXPress's default crop and registration marks, and the default plate information generated by QuarkXPress during output. These consist of a fixed-size and placement set of crop marks, a fixed-design registration mark, and a fixed-position text slug indicating the file name, time of output, and plate color. PressMarks changes all of that.

The basic concept behind PressMarks is the combination of a predesigned printer's elements template with each document page at output time. This keeps the printer's elements off the QuarkXPress page until they are needed during output, reducing file size and screen redraw time. The PressMarks Preferences dialog shown allows the user to design any number of custom templates. These templates provide a design environment for placing printer's elements in the printable area surrounding the QuarkXPress page. Any template can be assigned the role of default template for all documents, or specific templates can be assigned at any time in the production process.

PressMarks ships with over thirty different PostScript printer's elements, including vertical and horizontal CMYK and grayscale calibration bars, a choice of over a dozen different registration marks, targets and compounds. Elements that will automatically update based on the particular file the template is associated with include document name, full path name, date and time, plate name, and page number. And if that's not enough, PressMarks includes the ability to place two custom text strings and up to six custom EPS files in any template. That's how the XChange logo can coexist peacefully with the other elements in the above illustration. There's even an element for QuarkXPress's default text slug!

Elements are placed on a template in one of three ways from the scrollable Item List. Double-clicking, selecting and pressing ⌘-I and selecting and clicking the Add Item button all add an element to a template. Once on the template, elements can positioned either by dragging them to their proper location, or by numerically specifying x and y coordinates. They can also be nudged in one point increments with the arrow keys. Crop marks are optional, unlike the normal QuarkXPress crops, with user-definable offsets and widths. They can also be specified to print as crosshair crops or standard crops. Bleed marks and a safety zone check box can also be added with user-specified offsets.

PressMarks is activated by selecting Use PressMarks under the File menu. The XTension then runs transparently in the background until print time. Then when Registration Marks is checked in the QuarkXPress Print... dialog box, the template is applied during output. PressMarks can be used to facilitate better tracking of film and paper output or maybe just to put a corporate logo on every proof sent to important clients. Either way, this XTension provides some much-needed functionality in an area where everyone else has missed the mark.

XDATA

(em software, inc.) Xdata 2.0 is the best-selling XTension that brings the full typographic power of QuarkXPress to bear on all your data-driven repetitive publishing tasks: catalogues, directories, form letters, financial summaries, labels, simple tables, lists of all sorts, and more.

Xdata automatically formats data exported from your Macintosh or PC database and spreadsheet applications, freeing you from tedious manual formatting. Join Fortune, Business Week, and The New York Times in automating your publishing with Xdata.

Using Xdata is a simple three-step process:

1. Sort and export data from your favorite database or spreadsheet application, such as FileMaker Pro, Excel, 4th Dimension. Xdata accepts any ASCII-format text in comma- or tab-delimited format.

2. Create your "prototype" document—as simple as building a mail-merge template in your favorite word processor, but giving you all the text-formatting features in QuarkXPress.

3. Select "Import From File..." from the Xdata menu, select the appropriate data file, and press "Start." Xdata does the rest, automatically applying all your character style formatting to the data is it flows into place in your prototype.

Xdata is easy enough for the novice to create form letters, yet powerful enough to automate nearly any database publishing task. Powerful conditional statements let you create sophisticated prototypes that apply different formats to a field based on its value, produce a page break or major heading when a field changes from the previous record, or select one of several paragraphs in a form letter based on the value of a field. And Xdata 2.0 supports tagged fields on import, so the entire QuarkXPress Tags language is available for even tighter text-formatting control.

Xdata 2.0 imports graphics, too. Xdata supports any number of anchored picture boxes in a record template. A simple HyperTalk-like scripting language command takes the pathname of a picture (any type supported by QuarkXPress) from one of your data fields, and imports it into the proper box.

Xdata 2.0 even creates running headers and footers—very useful for directory or catalogue creation. Xdata will automatically place any field of the first or last record on a spread as a header or footer.

Xdata is risk-free, and comes complete with an superb manual, several tutorials, many useful templates, and an unconditional 60-day, money-back satisfaction guarantee.

XTAGS

(em software, inc.) Xtags supports the full QuarkXPress Tags language, plus several major enhancements designed for data publishing, classified ad building, and input code translation.

Anchored text and graphic box creation. Xtags enables you to create and fill anchored text and graphics boxes in-line with the tagged text, controlling all properties of the anchored boxes with appropriate tag parameters. You can fill a text box with further tagged text of any sort, and can fill a graphics box with a picture of any type supported by QuarkXPress.

Input code translation. Xtags lets you apply string substitutions to the input text. These substitutions can be as simple as character replacement, or as complex as foreign front-end coding translation. User-defined substitution tables can be invoked at any point in the input stream.

Master page selection. Xtags lets you choose the master spread to be applied to the text at a given point in the text stream, including whether the first or last such application on a given page obtains. With this facility, you can build documents with layouts driven by your input text.

Error reporting. Unlike QuarkXPress Tags, which simply stops at the first error, Xtags has an optional facility for reporting on each error as it is encountered, outputting a brief error message directly in-line at the point of each error.

Guarantee of satisfaction. Xtags, like all em software, inc. products, comes with a 60-day, money-back guarantee.

PICTURE REUNION

(DK&A) Picture Reunion is a QuarkXPress XTension that automates the linking of picture files when they are reported missing. You can search for files in a folder, folders, or a even a whole volume.

The Picture Reunion main dialog is very similar to the QuarkXPress Picture Usage dialog located under the Utilities menu in that you can view picture file name, the page it resides on, the type of file and its status. However, Picture Reunion adds the functionality to select a volume or folder to automatically search for missing files and link them if they are found. In addition, you can save the picture file list to an ASCII text file and then import the file into QuarkXPress to print.

XMACRO

(Schnittstelle) XMacro enables the user to structurally capture data from foreign systems. Simply, shortkeys are given for the recording of the data, which XMacro automatically translates into user-defined XTag syntax. XMacro inserts the converted text directly into a selected QuarkXPress text box.

The conversion tables can be saved individually and are thus available for any repetitive tasks the user wishes to perform. Apart from its conversion control characters, XMacro can also translate additional characters of foreign systems. The shortkeys for the capturing can be defined freely. XMacro works with ASCII files. XMacro adaptations to specific requirements of clients are possible on request.

AD DIRECTOR

(Managing Editor Software, Inc.) Ad Director is a full-featured, automated advertising dummying program that builds runsheets, electronic dummies, and provides an accurate overview of where your ads are at any time. Dummying (positioning advertisements) a publication used to be a time-consuming process that would take production and advertising managers hours or days to complete. Ad Director takes your list of advertisements and places them in your publication in seconds.

Advertisement runsheets (lists of ads and their specifications) can be imported from most of the popular business system applications like Layout 8000. Once the ad specs are in Ad Director, you can place them manually using a drag and drop interface or let Ad Director place your ads automatically, based on information you set up in advance. Your publication's ad/edit ratio, reverse and coupon considerations, request pages, zone allowances, pickups, and dozens of other criteria are taken into account as Ad Director positions the ads on appropriate pages.

Once you've finessed the layout, the information can be exported back to your business system application, opened in Page Director (see next page) or imported directly into QuarkXPress with all the page geometry created automatically, ready for import of live ads. Features include:

‣ The ability to assign and lock color availability, ad position, and open pages.

‣ Complete reporting functions, including printout of the layout as it appears on screen.

‣ The ability to color code your ads for easy identification.

‣ Automatic placement of ads by ad type, zone, etc. across the entire publication or a range of pages.

‣ Assignment of advertising space to a page by issue ad/edit ratio, specific ratio, or a defined ad size (modulars).

And with the new Forms Manager edition of Ad Director, assignment and management of specific forms (signatures) within a publication is a snap. Call XChange for more information.

PAGE DIRECTOR

(Managing Editor Software, Inc.) Page Director is a publication management and production system, encompassing everything from organizing the various page elements, to sizing content, to configuring color and paginating the layout. And Page Director allows for multiple users to work on different pages or sections, with the ability to merge all the documents into one issue.

One of Page Director's great strengths is the built-in Gatherer function. You tell Page Director where on your hard drive or network to look for specific types of files. Page Director segregates page elements into Copy, Graphics, and Ads, and permits search for and automatic collection of files by their creator applications. You teach Page Director what to do with specific items, and the program will assign attributes to Copy, Ads, and Graphics as it gathers them. Page Director measures text files automatically based on assigned style attributes, then Size Updater lets you tinker with copy counts and the size of graphics to ensure a tight, professional fit. Once the files are gathered, they are available for placement on the page from the Item Editor—just click and drag. And because you're working only with geometry placeholders on Page Director pages, moving in and around your documents is unbelievably quick.

The Item Sorter allows you to organize the Item Editor by applying three levels of sorting, while the Relator function permits the loose grouping of elements; i.e., a story, a sidebar and related graphics, so nothing gets left behind. If you do manage to lose an element, Item Finder permits quick exhaustive searches to retrieve it. Locating a placed element on any Page Director page is as easy as double-clicking—the program takes you immediately to the object in question.

And once all the elements are in place, import your Page Director layout into QuarkXPress with the special XTension provided. Your stories, graphics, folios, cutlines, credits, jumps, etc. will be automatically built and imported at lightning speed. Other features include:

- The ability to add and clear multiple items from pages and to allow Page Director to choose element positioning for you.

- Complete report capability, including reports for color, comments and run of publication.

- The ability to view Page Director pages as copy lists, as statistics, as graphs or flagged according to color availability.

- Libraries for oft-used elements.

- The ability to import Xywrite files automatically.

- Automatic alignment and justification of page elements.

- Precise and easy interactive cropping of graphics.

PRICES

Following are prices for all the XTensions listed in this chapter. Site license pricing is available for all products. Call XChange for more information. All prices are in U.S. currency.

NOTE

Certain restrictions and disclaimers apply to each product or service noted here; contact the appropriate vendor for details.

PRODUCT	PRICE
AccentMaster	99.00
Ad Director	5,995.00
Ad Measure	179.00
AdPro	995.00
Agency Fit Vol I	79.00
Agency Fit Vol II	179.00
Alias	189.00
AnchorBox	179.00
AutoLib	195.00
AutoPage II	Call for current pricing
AutoSave	49.00
AutoXTract	200.00
BackTrack	79.00
BlendBuilder	79.00
Celler	99.00
Color Change	79.00

PRODUCT	PRICE
Color Usage	30.00
ColorManager	149.00
ColorSnap 32+	995.00
Combs XT	99.00
CopySet	129.00
CopySpecs	50.00
Crops & Registrations	69.00
CursorPos	59.00
Dashes	200.00
Dashes & Spellbound Combo Pack	300.00
Default Settings 2.0	39.00
Demo Pak	25.00
Dingbats	50.00
Document Report	149.00
Doublesave	79.00
EasyType	69.00
Electronic Border Tape	149.00
EBT TOO	149.00
Expose	99.00
faceIt	99.00
FCS Lock	195.00
FCS Print	195.00
FCS Tablemaker	95.00
FileManager	149.00
FlexScale	59.00
Gatherer	149.00
GraphXChange	149.00
Grid Layout	24.95

PRODUCT	PRICE
GridLock	59.00
ImPress	249.00
IndeXTension	99.00
INposition	1,750.00
InsertSpace	49.00
Job Folder	99.00
Kerning Palette	195.00
KeyLiner	2,500.00
LayerManager	79.00
LineCount XT	89.00
Logical XTensions I	79.00
Logical XTensions II	119.00
Logical XTensions V	199.00
LogX	89.00
LTD XS	225.00
Magpie	99.00
MasterMenus	69.00
Mathable	499.00
Mathematical Pi Font	179.00
Mimic	99.00
Missing Link	69.00
MS Word DOS Filter	295.00
Navigator XT	65.00
OnTap	79.00
OverMatter	95.00
Overset!	69.00
Pageshot	89.00
Page Director	1,895.00
Passport	2,495.00

PRODUCT	PRICE
Perfect XT	165.00
PictureManager	199.00
Picture Reunion	79.00
Picture Tools	69.00
PinPointXT	79.50
PressMarks	299.00
PrintArea	79.00
Printer's Spreads	179.00
PrintIt	79.00
ProPublisher	75.00
ProTabs	249.00
QSpool	695.00
QTools	195.00
QuarkPrint	195.00
QuarkXPress 3.1 (Mac & PC)	569.00
QXEdit	149.00
ReLink	129.00
Resize XT	99.00
Scanning Parameters	450.00
Scitex Document Reports	149.00
Scitex Fractions	69.00
Scitex Grids & Guides	99.00
Scitex Image Tools	199.00
Scitex Layers	99.00
Scitex Precision Tools	199.00
SetInset II	29.00
SetSkew	49.00

PRODUCT	PRICE
Shadow	49.00
Shortline Eliminator	99.00
Skew	49.00
SoftCuts	295.00
Sonar Bookends	129.95
Sonar TOC	99.00
SpectreScan QX	295.00
SpectreSeps QX	495.00
SpellBound	200.00
Starburst	49.00
Step & Flex It	1,500.00
Story Editor	165.00
Stylist	89.00
SXetch Pad	229.00
Tableworks 2.0	299.00
Tableworks ShortCut	119.00
TeXT Tools	59.00
TextLinker	89.00
Thesaurus Rex	69.00
TimeStamp	49.00
TruMatch	85.00
TruPack	99.00
TypeMaster	99.00
ViewIT	79.00
Vision's Edge Utility Pack	79.00
VJ	199.00
Wang WP/PC Filter	395.00
WordPerfect DOS Filter	295.00
XactHeight	99.00

PRODUCT	PRICE
Xaminer	150.00
XChar!	79.00
Xdata 2.0	299.00
XMacro!	225.00
XMath	399.00
XNotes	60.00
X3-QuarkXPress XPert's XChange	99.00
XSize!	169.00
Xstyle	79.00
XTable	299.00
Xtags	299.00
Xtags 10-Pak	995.00
XT_Edit	199.00
XTension Manager	69.95
XTension Sampler	25.00

APPENDICES

QuarkXPress Products

here are several areas from which to draw resources, including trade organizations, software developers, hardware manufacturers, etc. The appendix offers a few of the more important contacts for further document processing in QuarkXPress.

POSTSCRIPT PRODUCTS

The following companies manufacture hardware or software that use the Adobe PostScript page description language.

Adobe Systems Incorporated
1585 Charleston Road
P.O. Box 7900
Mountain View, CA 94039-7900
(415) 961-4400

Agfa Corporation
200 Ballardvale Street
Wilmington, MA 01887
(508) 658-5600

Agfa Corporation Business Imaging Systems
One Ramland Road
Orangeburg, NY 10962-2693
(800) 288-4039
(914) 365-0190

Agfa-Gevaert N.V.
Septestraat 27
B-2510 Mortsel
Belgium
32-3-444-2111

Agfa-Gevaert Japan, Ltd.
8-1, Higashiyama, 3-chome
Meguro-ku
Tokyo 153
Japan
81-3-5704-3071

Apple Canada, Incorporated
7495 Birchmount Road
Markham, L3R 5G2 Ontario
Canada
(416) 477-5800

Apple Computer, Incorporated
20525 Mariani Avenue
Cupertino, CA 95014
 (800) 538-9696

Apple Computer Europe
Le Wilson 2, Cedex 60
80, Avenue du President Wilson
F-92058 Paris la Defense
France
33-1-4901-4901

Apple Computer Japan, Inc.
25 Mori Building 24F
1-4-30 Roppongi
Minato-ku
Tokyo 106
Japan
81-3-3224-7000

AST Research Incorporated
16215 Alton Parkway
P.O. Box 19658
Irvine, CA 92713-9658
(714) 727-4141

Autologic
1050 Rancho Conejo Boulevard
Newsbury Park, CA 91320
(805) 498-9611

Berthold AG
Stammhaus Berlin
Teltowkanalstrasse 1-4
D-1000 Berlin 46
49-30-7795-116

Birmy Graphics Corporation
255 East Drive
Suite H
Melbourne, FL 32904
(407) 768-6766

Cactus
17 Industrial Road
Fairfield, NY 07004
(201) 575-8810

Canon, Inc.
Shinjuku Dai-ichi Semei Building
7-1 Nishi-Shinjuku 2-chome
Tokyo 163
Japan
81-3-3348-2121

Canon USA
One Canon Plaza
Lake Success, NY 11042-1113
(516) 488-6700

Dataproducts Australia
Pacific View Business Park
Unit 2/10 Rodborough Road
French's Forest, NSW 2086
Australia

Dataproducts Corporation
6200 Canoga Avenue
Woodland Hills, CA 91367
(818) 887-8000

Dataproducts Limited
Clonshaugh Industrial Estate
Dublin 17
Ireland
353-1-474-855

Diconix
3100 Research Boulevard
P.O. Box 3100
Dayton, OH 45420
(513) 259-3100

Digital Equipment Corporation
146 Main Street
Maynard, MA 01754-2571
(800) DEC-INFO
(800) 343-4040

Digital Equipment Corporation
Sunshine 60 Building, 55th Floor
1-1 Higashi-Ikebukuro 3-chome
Toshima-ku
Tokyo 170
Japan
81-3-3989-7212

Digital F/X
755 Ravendale Drive
Mountain View, CA 94043
(415) 961-2800

Eastman Kodak Company
343 State Street
Rochester, NY 14650
(800) 242-2424

E.I. du Ponte de Numours
600 Eagle Run Road
Newark, DE 19714-6099
(302) 774-1000

Electronics for Imaging, Inc.
950 Elm Avenue 300
San Bruno, CA 94066
(415) 742-3400

Epson America, Inc.
20770 Madrona Avenue
Torrance, CA 90503
(800) 289-3776

Epson Europe B.V.
Prof. J.H. Bavincklaan 5
NL-1183 AT Amstelveen
The Netherlands
31-20-5475-222

Fujitsu America, Inc.
3055 Orchard Drive
San Jose, CA 95134-2022
(408) 432-1300
(800) 626-4686

Fujitsu Limited
Marunouchi Center Building
6-1 Marunouchi 1-chome
Chiyoda-ku
Tokyo 100
Japan
81-3-3216-3211

GCC Technologies
580 Winter Street
Waltham, MA 02154
(800) 422-7777
(617) 890-0880

Gestetner Lasers Pty Limited
12 Rodborough Road
French's Forest, NSW 2086
Australia
61-2-975-0555

Hewlett-Packard
11311 Chinden Boulevard
P.O. Box 15
Boise, ID 83707-0015
(208) 323-6000

Hewlett-Packard GmbH
Herrenberger Strasse 130
D-7030 Böblingen

Germany
49-7031-140

International Business Machines
US Marketing and Services
 Dept. 805
900 King Street
Rye Brook, NY 10573
(800) IBM-2468

International Business Machines (Europe)
Tour Pascal-La Defense 7 Sud
Cedex 40
F-92075 Paris La Defense
France
33-1-4767-6000

Lexmark International, Inc.
740 New Circle Road
Lexington, KY 40511
(606) 232-2000

Linotype-Hell AG
Mergenthaler Allee 55-75
D-6236 Eschborn bei
Frankfurt
Germany
49-6196-980

Linotype-Hell Company
425 Oser Avenue
Hauppauge, NY 11788
(513) 434-2000

529

Linotype-Hell Limited
Bath Road, Cheltenham
Gloucestershire, GL53 7LR
United Kingdom
44-242-222-333

Mannesmann Scangraphic GmbH
Rissener Strasse 112-114
D-2000 Wedel/Hamburg
Germany
49-4103-801-106

The Monotype Corporation plc
Salfords, Redhill
Surrey, RH1 5JP
England
44-737-768-644

Monotype Incorporated
2500 Brickvale Avenue
Elk Grove Village, IL 60007
(708) 350-5600

NEC Corporation
33-1, Shiba 5-chome
 Minato-ku
Tokyo 108
Japan
81-3-3454-1111

NEC Technologies, Inc.
1414 Massachusetts Avenue
Boxborough, MA 01719
(800) 343-4418

NEC GmgH
Klausenberger Strasse 4
D-8000 Munchen 80
Germany
49-89-93-0060

Oce Graphics France S.A.
1, rue Jean Lemoine-B.P. 113
F-94003 Creteil Cedex
France
33-1-4898-8000

Oki Electric Industry Co, Ltd.
7-12 Toranomon 1-chome
Minato-ku
Tokyo 105
Japan
81-3-3501-3351

Oki Europe Limited
347/353 Chiswick High Road
London, W4 4HS
United Kingdom
44-81-742-2001

Okidata
532 Fellowship Road
Mt. Laurel, NJ 08054
(800) OKI-DATA

Optronics
An Integraph Division
7 Stuart Road
Chelmsford, MA 01824
(508) 256-4511

Panasonic Communication & Systems Co.
Computer Products Division
Two Panasonic Way
Secaucus, NJ 07094
(800) 447-4700

Panasonic Europe Limited
Panasonic House
Willoughby Road
Bracknell
Berkshire, RG124FP
United Kingdom
44-344-853-901

QMS, Incorporated
1 Magnum Pass
Mobile, AL 36618
(205) 633-4300

QMS Eastern Hemisphere Operations
117 Boulevard Magenta
F-75010 Paris
France
33-1-4526-0193

QMS Japan KK
4-3-7 Babadori
Utsunomiya
Tochigi
Japan 320
81-286-27-1185

Ricoh Company Limited
15-5 Minami Aoyama 1-chome
Minato-ku
Tokyo 107
Japan
81-3-3479-2905

Ricoh Corporation
Peripheral Products Division
3001 Orchard Parkway
San Jose, CA 95134
(408) 432-8800

Ricoh Europe B.V.
Hansa Allee 201
D-4000 Dusseldorf 11
Germany
49-211-528-50

Scitex America Corporation
8 Oak Park Drive
Bedford, MA 01730
(617) 275-5150

Scitex Corporation, Ltd.
P.O. Box 330
46103 Herzlia B
Israel
972-52-529222

Scitex Europe S.A.
Avenue Louise 120
B-1050 Brussels
Belgium
32-2-642-1511

Silicon Graphics Incorporated
2011 N. Shoreline Boulevard
Mountain View, CA 94039-7311
(415) 960-1980

Silicon Graphics GmbH
18, Avenue Louis Casai
CH-1209 Geneva
Switzerland
41-22-798-75-25

Texas Instruments, Incorporated
Peripheral Products Division
P.O. Box 202230
Austin, TX 78720-2230
(800) 527-3500

Texas Instruments
Manton Lane
Bedford, MK41 7PA
United Kingdom
44-234-270-111

Tektronix
26600 SW Parkway
Wilsonville, OR 97070
(800) 835-6100

Tektronix Europe Limited
Fourth Avenue
Globe Park
Marlow, Bucks SL7 1YD
United Kingdom
44-628-486-000

Varityper
11 Mt. Pleasant Avenue
East Hanover, NJ 07936
(800) 631-8134

Volt Autologic Ltd.
Alban Park, Hatfield Road
St. Albans
Hertfordshire, AL4 OJJ
England
44-727-834-132

Wang Laboratories, Inc.
One Industrial Avenue
Lowell, MA 01851
(508) 459-5000

Xerox Corporation
800 Long Ridge Drive
Stamford, CT 06904
(203) 968-3378

XTENSION DEVELOPMENT

In order to contact a private developer of XTensions or to request information on how you can become a registered XTension developer, contact:

United States Developer Desk

Quark, Inc.
1800 Grant Street
Denver, CO 80203
303-377-6327 fax
AppleLink D1590

International QuarkXTension Developer Desk

Q.S.S.
Kilbarry House
Dublin Hill
Cork, Ireland
021-300171 fax
AppleLink D2351

COMPUSERVE

The CompuServe Information Service offers a group of basic services for a standard monthly fee of $7.95. Services outside this group of basic services are offered on a pay-as-you-go basis and referred to as *extended* services.

Reading electronic mail from all incoming sources (except Internet) is free. Also, up to sixty three-page electronic mail messages can be sent free each month.

Perhaps the most important information for those in electronic publishing is found in electronic forums. These forums bring together thousands of members sharing ideas and information about careers, hobbies, health, lifestyles, computer technology, etc. CompuServe has a desktop publishing forum available giving you outstanding information in this field. You can also download freeware and shareware XTensions, fonts and other software programs through CompuServe. If you want to ask a manufacturer directly about a product, chances are they have an address on CompuServe. More than 180 software and hardware companies provide support for their products through online forums.

To find out more call a customer service representative at (614) 457-8650 or write to CompuServe Corporate Headquarters, 5000 Arlington Centre Boulevard, P.O.Box 20212, Columbus, OH 43220.

APP. A

ORGANIZATIONS

There are many trade organizations—both local and international—that may be helpful to your efforts in desktop publishing. Two such organizations that you should put on your *Must Join* list are:

QuarkXPress Users International
P.O. Box 170
Salem, NH 03079
(608) 898-2822
603-898-3393 fax

Typographers International Association (TIA)
2233 Wisconsin Avenue, NW
Suite 235
Washington, DC 20007
USA
(202) 965-3400
202-965-3522 fax

QuarkXPress
Library

This appendix is a gallery of important and commonly used QuarkXPress elements. It includes palettes, menus, and dialog boxes.

THE QUARKXPRESS ENVIRONMENT

The main elements of the QuarkXPress environment are contained in the document window (shown in Figure B.1). These include:

Ruler origin box: Enables you to reposition and reset the ruler origin.

Close box: Use to close the current window.

Document name: Tells the name of the file.

Title bar: Click and drag to move the document window

Zoom box: Click to shrink or enlarge the window.

Pasteboard: A nonprinting work area surrounding pages.

Scroll bars/boxes/arrows: The position of the scroll boxes within the scroll bars indicates the position of the document page(s) within the document window. You can click the arrows or in the bar, or drag the box, to move about in the document.

Size box: Use to reduce or enlarge the window to a specific size.

Page number indicator: Displays the number of the page currently displayed in the document window.

View Percent field: Indicates the magnification or reduction of the page view. Enter values in this field from 10% to 400%. Press the Return key to implement the value you enter.

Ruler origin: The point at which the rulers measure 0 across and 0 down.

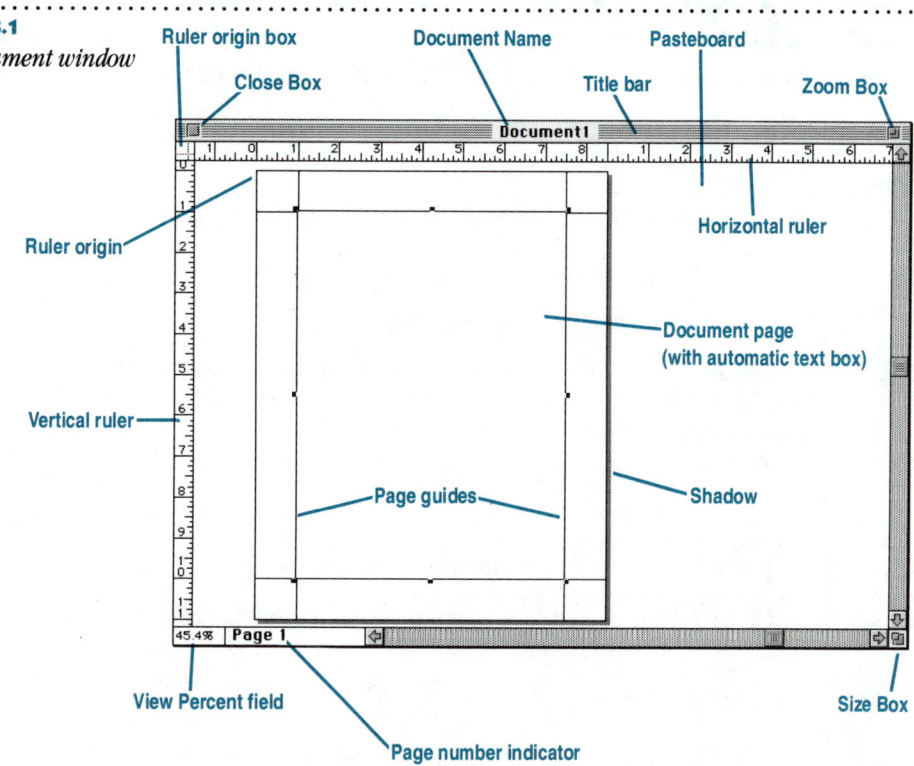

Page guides: Nonprinting lines that indicate a page's margins and columns. (Page guides are dotted lines on black-and-white and grayscale monitors.)

Vertical ruler: shows distance down.

Horizontal ruler: shows distance across.

Document page: This is where you place the item boxes that will make up your page layout.

Shadow: Indicates the border between the pasteboard and the page.

Automatic text box: The text box that QuarkXPress places on the first page of the document if you select the Automatic Text Box option in the New dialog box (File ➤ New).

THE PALETTES

QuarkXPress includes seven "floating" palettes (that means you can click and drag to move them wherever you want) that you can either hide or show from the View menu.

THE TOOL PALETTE

The Tool palette (shown in Figure B.2) includes the following:

Item tool: Enables you to move, group, ungroup, cut, copy, and paste items (text boxes, picture boxes, lines, and groups).

Content tool: Enables you to import, edit, cut, copy, paste, and modify box contents (text and pictures).

Rotation tool: Enables you to rotate items manually.

Zoom tool: Enables you to reduce or enlarge the view in your document window.

Text Box tool: Enables you to create a new text box.

Rectangle Picture Box tool: Enables you to create rectangular picture boxes.

FIGURE B.2

The Tool palette

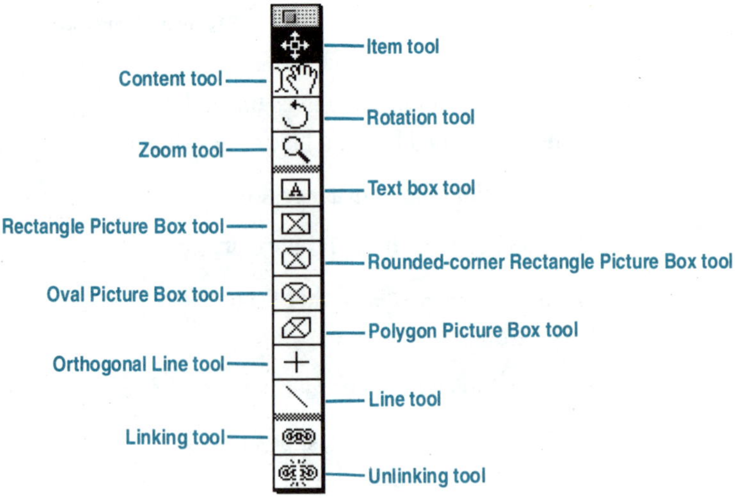

Rounded-corner Rectangle Picture Box tool: Enables you to create rectangular picture boxes with rounded corners.

Oval Picture Box tool: Enables you to create oval and circular picture boxes.

Polygon Picture Box tool: Enables you to create polygon picture boxes. (A polygon is a shape with three or more sides.)

Orthogonal Line tool: Enables you to create horizontal and vertical lines.

Line tool: Enables you to create lines of any angle.

Linking tool: Enables you to create text chains to flow text from text box to text box.

Unlinking tool: Enables you to break links between text boxes.

THE DOCUMENT LAYOUT PALETTE

The Document Layout palette (View ➤ Show Document Layout), shown in Figure B.3, enables you to create, name, delete, arrange, and apply master pages;

FIGURE B.3

The Document Layout palette

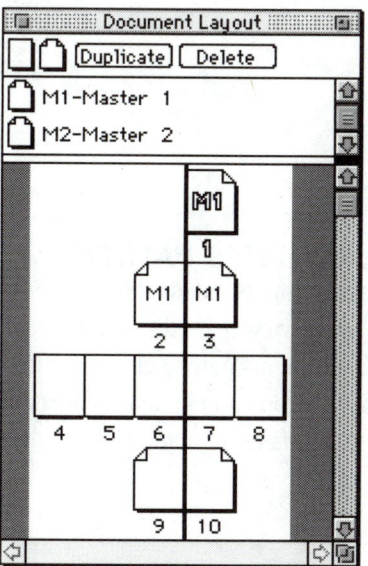

insert, delete, and move document pages; navigate through document pages and master pages; and create multi-page spreads.

THE LIBRARY PALETTE

A Library palette (Utilities ➤ Library), shown in Figure B.4, enables you to store and retrieve frequently used Items (text boxes, picture boxes, lines and groups).

THE MEASUREMENTS PALETTE

The Measurements palette (View ➤ Show Measurements), shown in Figure B.5, allows you to view and edit specific item contents. Information categories within the Measurements palette change as the item highlighted changes; e.g., text size element vs. drop cap element. A Measurements palette for each type of item is included in this graphic to illustrate the different information in each.

FIGURE B.5

The Measurements palette. (The palette will have a different appearance, depending upon what kind of item you are working with.)

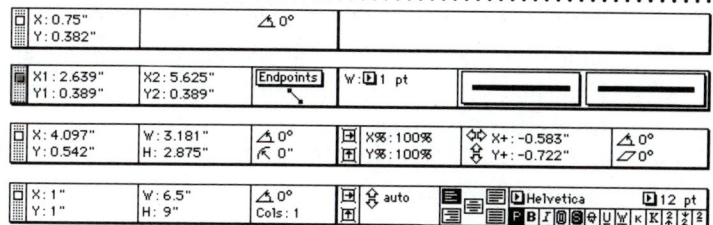

THE COLORS PALETTE

The Colors palette (View ➤ Show Colors), shown in Figure B.6, enables you to apply color and shade to box backgrounds, lines, frames, text, and pictures. You can also use the Colors palette to specify one- or two-color blends for box backgrounds. You can use this palette to open a Colors dialog box by holding down the ⌘ key and clicking on the color name.

FIGURE B.6

The Colors palette

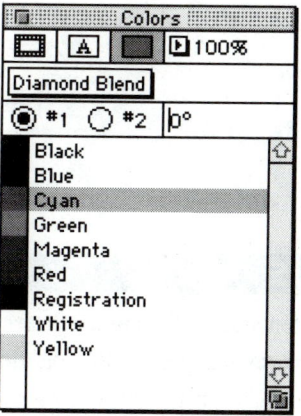

THE TRAP INFORMATION PALETTE

You can implement or override automatic and color-specific trapping settings on an item-by-item basis through the Trap Information palette (View ➤ Show Trap Information), as shown in Figure B.7. Specifications for custom trapping can vary from −36 to 36 points.

FIGURE B.7

The Trap Information palette

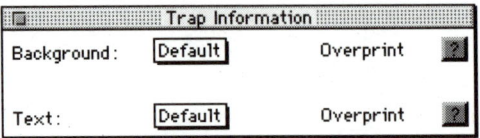

THE STYLE SHEETS PALETTE

The Style Sheets palette (View ➤ Show Style Sheets), shown in Figure B.8, may be used to view or select a style sheet name to apply to selected text. You can also open the Style Sheets dialog box by holding down the ⌘ key and clicking on a style sheet name.

FIGURE B.8

The Style Sheets palette

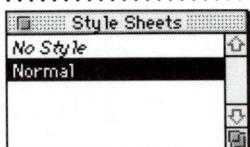

THE MENUS

This section shows the sundry QuarkXPress menus, listing the commands found on each. Remember the following principles:

▸ To display a menu, click on its title in the menu bar.

▸ If a command is dimmed, it is not available.

• A check mark to the left of a menu command indicates that an attribute is applied or a function is in effect.

Each menu includes one or more of the following elements:

Keyboard equivalents: These enable you to choose a menu command using the keyboard.

Submenu indicator: An arrowhead displayed to the right of a command indicates that choosing that command displays a submenu from which you can choose a command. You can use the right arrows to scroll through the list. To select a fill, click on its name or use the up or down arrow keys. Double-click on a file name to open the file.

Submenus: A submenu displays a list of commands related to the menu command that displays it. Choosing a submenu command either performs on actin or opens a dialog box.

Ellipsis (...): These indicate that choosing the command displays a dialog box.

THE FILE MENU

The File menu (shown in Figure B.9) includes commands that relate to entire documents (files). Groups of related commands are separated by lines in the menu.

The first group enables you to create and open documents. The second group enables you to close, save, and make a copy of a document, and to undo your last set of changes to a document. The third group enables you to import text and pictures into documents, save text in a variety of formats, and save document pages as EPS pictures. The fourth group enables you to change a document's page size while it is active and to control the way in which the document prints out. The last command enables you to exit the program.

File	
New	▶
Open...	⌘O
Close	⌘W
Save	⌘S
Save as...	⌘⌥S
Revert to Saved	
Get Text...	⌘E
Save Text...	
Save Page as EPS...	
Collect for Output...	
Document Setup...	⌘⌥⇧P
Page Setup...	⌘⌥P
Print...	⌘P
Quit	⌘Q

THE EDIT MENU

The Edit menu (shown in Figure B.10) includes commands for editing text, pictures, and items, for changing QuarkXPress default specifications, and for controlling text formatting features. Groups of related features are separated by lines.

The first command enables you to undo certain actions. The second group enables you to edit text and pictures or items, depending on whether the Content tool or the Item tool is selected in the Tool palette. The third group enables you to customize the way files imported into QuarkXPress are updated via OLE (Object Linking and Embedding). The fourth group enables you to display a window that shows the contents of the Clipboard. The fifth group includes commands that enable you to search for and replace text and character attributes; to define application, general, typographic, and tool default specifications; and to create and edit style sheets, colors, and hyphenation and justification specifications.

Edit	
Can't Undo	⌘Z
Cut	⌘X
Copy	⌘C
Paste	⌘U
Clear	
Select All	⌘A
Subscribe To...	
Subscriber Options...	
Show Clipboard	
Find/Change	⌘F
Preferences	▶
Style Sheets...	
Colors...	
H&Js...	⌘⌥H

THE VIEW MENU

The View menu (shown in Figure B.11) includes commands for controlling what you see on-screen and the way in which items and pages are displayed. Groups of related commands are separated by lines.

The first group enables you to specify the size of the document view. The second group enables you to control the way in which visual layout aids are displayed and operate. The third group enables you to display or hide palettes that provide tools, fields, and icons for working with items, text, pictures, document and master pages, style sheets, colors, and trapping.

View

Fit in Window	⌘0
50%	
75%	
Actual Size	⌘1
200%	
Thumbnails	
Windows	▶
Hide Guides	
Show Baseline Grid	
Snap to Guides	
Hide Rulers	⌘R
Show Invisibles	⌘I
Hide Tools	
Show Measurements	
Show Document Layout	
Show Style Sheets	
Show Colors	
Show Trap Information	

THE STYLE MENU

The commands in the Style menu vary according to the active item: a text box, a picture box, or a line. The Style menu for text (shown in Figure B.12) includes commands for specifying character attributes and paragraph formats. These commands are available when the Content tool is selected and a text box is active. Groups of related commands are separated by lines.

The first group enables you to apply and modify character attributes. You can specify font, size, type style, color, shade, and scale for characters, as well as intercharacter spacing and the position of characters relative to their baselines. The second group enables you to apply and modify paragraph formats. You can specify alignment, leading, indents, rules, and several other paragraph formats, and you can apply a style sheet to selected paragraphs.

The Style menu for text

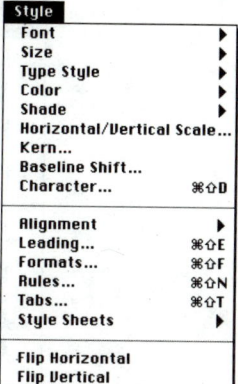

The Style menu for pictures (shown in Figure B.13) enables you to change the color and shade of a picture, to create a negative of a picture, to adjust the contrast of a picture, and to control the way in which QuarkXPress creates an electronic halftone of the picture. Groups of related commands are separated by lines.

Using the Style menu, you can modify pictures in TIFF (Tagged Image File Format), metafile color, grayscale, line art, color bitmaps, or black and white bitmaps. EPS (Encapsulated Postscript) pictures cannot be modified through the Style menu; use the original application for creating EPS documents to modify them.

The Style menu for lines (shown in Figure B.14) includes commands that enable you to specify line style, endcaps, width, color, and shade.

Style	
Color	▶
Shade	▶
Profile...	
Negative	⌘⇧-
Normal Contrast	⌘⇧N
High Contrast	⌘⇧H
Posterized	⌘⇧P
Other Contrast...	⌘⇧C
Normal Screen	
60-Line Line Screen/0°	
30-Line Line Screen/45°	
20-Line Dot Screen/45°	
Other Screen...	⌘⇧S
Flip Horizontal	
Flip Vertical	

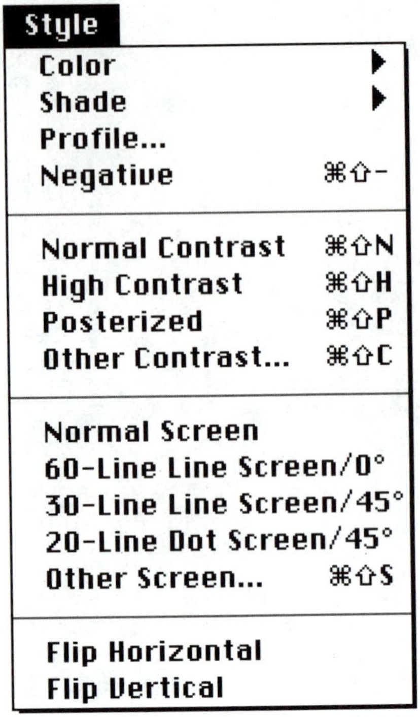

FIGURE B.14
The Style menu for lines

Style	
Line Style	▶
Endcaps	▶
Width	▶
Color	▶
Shade	▶

THE ITEM MENU

The Item menu (shown in Figure B.15) includes commands for working with all items; e.g., text boxes, picture, lines and groups. Groups of related commands are separated by lines.

The first group enables you to make specifications for boxes, lines, and groups, to place frames on boxes, and to control the way in which text flows in relation to items. The second group enables you to make one or more duplicates of an item and to remove items from a document. The third group enables you to create groups in which multiple items act as one and to prevent items from being moved or resized accidentally. The fourth group enables you to change the stacking order of items on a page and to control the spacing and alignment of items. The last group enables you to change the shape of a picture box at any time and to reshape polygon picture boxes.

FIGURE B.15

The Item menu

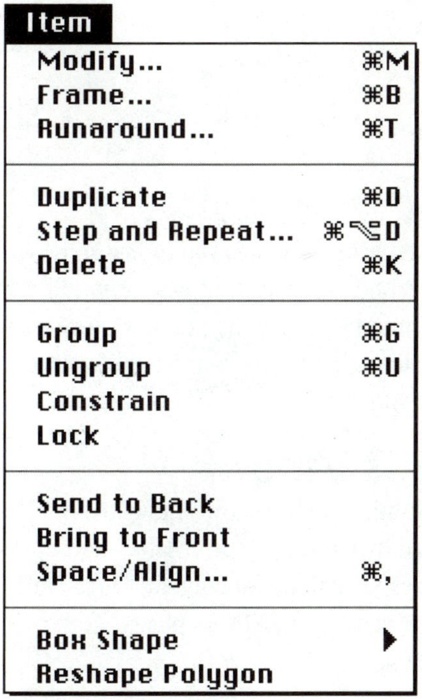

Item	
Modify...	⌘M
Frame...	⌘B
Runaround...	⌘T
Duplicate	⌘D
Step and Repeat...	⌘⬎D
Delete	⌘K
Group	⌘G
Ungroup	⌘U
Constrain	
Lock	
Send to Back	
Bring to Front	
Space/Align...	⌘,
Box Shape	▶
Reshape Polygon	

THE PAGE MENU

The Page menu (shown in Figure B.16) includes commands for arranging pages in a document and for navigating through a document. Groups of related commands are separated by lines.

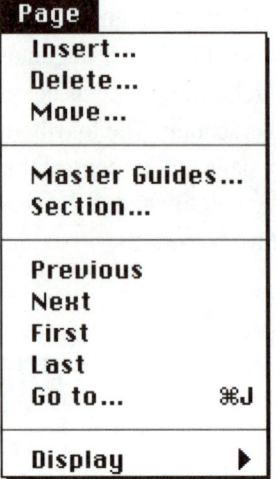

The first group enables you to insert, delete, and move pages within a document. The second group enables you to modify the placement of page builds on master pages and to change the numbering system of a document range of pages in a document. The third group enables you to navigate through a document. The last command enables you to display a master page or a document page.

THE UTILITIES MENU

The Utilities menu (shown in Figure B.17) includes commands for checking spelling and hyphenation, for creating and opening libraries, and for listing fonts and pictures used in the document. The Utilities menu also displays commands for XTensions to QuarkXPress placed in the program directory before launching the program.

The Utilities menu

```
┌─────────────────────────────────────┐
│ Utilities                            │
├─────────────────────────────────────┤
│ Check Spelling                    ▶  │
│ Auxiliary Dictionary...              │
│ Edit Auxiliary...                    │
├─────────────────────────────────────┤
│ Suggested Hyphenation...     ⌘H     │
│ Hyphenation Exceptions...            │
├─────────────────────────────────────┤
│ Font Usage...                        │
│ Picture Usage...                     │
│ Profile Usage...                     │
├─────────────────────────────────────┤
│ Tracking Edit...                     │
│ Kerning Table Edit...                │
└─────────────────────────────────────┘
```

DIALOG BOXES

A typical QuarkXPress dialog box is shown in Figure B.18. A dialog box is displayed on-screen when you choose a command that is followed by an ellipsis (for example, Modify, under the Item menu).

All dialog boxes contain one or more of the following elements:

Field: Enables you to enter specific values. You can add values to or subtract values from values in dialog box fields that control item specifications.

Dialog box name: Gives a good clue as to its function.

Area: QuarkXPress places a border around and assigns a name to an area that contains related fields, buttons, and/or drop-down lists. An area name can include a check box. The fields and controls in such an area become active when you check the box.

Drop-down list indicator: A drop-down list is a space-saving method of providing several options. Click and hold on the arrow to display the list.

Button: clicking a button does one of three things: it performs an operation, selects an option, or opens and closes a dialog box. To perform an operation or

*A dialog box (the Text
Box Specifications Box)*

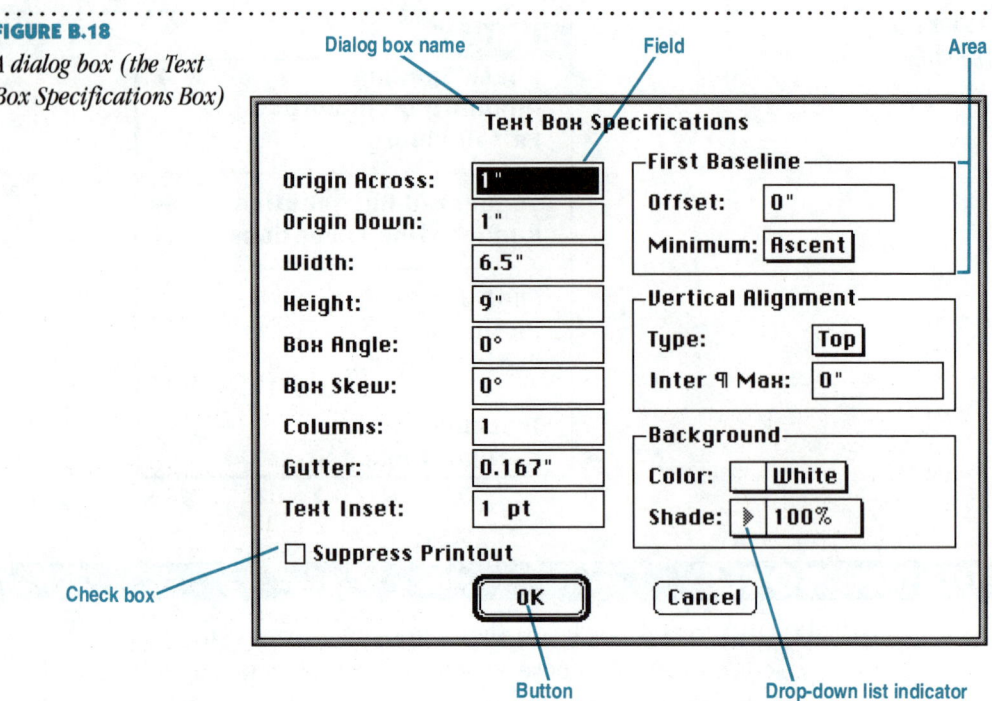

Dialog box name   Field   Area

Check box

Button   Drop-down list indicator

open a dialog box, move the arrow pointer over the button and click. If the button is surrounded by a thick border, pressing the Return key will perform the same operation as clicking the button. To select an option, click the button representing the option you want.

Check box: These represent options that you can turn on and off by clicking with the mouse. A checked box indicates that an option is turned on.

INDEX

Throughout this index, we have used certain typographical conventions to help you find information. Page numbers in **boldface** indicate primary explanations. Page numbers in *italic* indicate illustrations.

B

C

G

H

I

N

T

U

SYBEX

FREE BROCHURE!

Complete this form today, and we'll send you a full-color brochure of Sybex bestsellers.

Please supply the name of the Sybex book purchased.

_____

How would you rate it?

_____ Excellent   _____ Very Good   _____ Average   _____ Poor

Why did you select this particular book?

_____ Recommended to me by a friend

_____ Recommended to me by store personnel

_____ Saw an advertisement in _____

_____ Author's reputation

_____ Saw in Sybex catalog

_____ Required textbook

_____ Sybex reputation

_____ Read book review in _____

_____ In-store display

_____ Other _____

Where did you buy it?

_____ Bookstore

_____ Computer Store or Software Store

_____ Catalog (name: _____)

_____ Direct from Sybex

_____ Other: _____

Did you buy this book with your personal funds?

_____ Yes   _____ No

About how many computer books do you buy each year?

_____ 1-3   _____ 3-5   _____ 5-7   _____ 7-9   _____ 10+

About how many Sybex books do you own?

_____ 1-3   _____ 3-5   _____ 5-7   _____ 7-9   _____ 10+

Please indicate your level of experience with the software covered in this book:

_____ Beginner   _____ Intermediate   _____ Advanced

Which types of software packages do you use regularly?

_____ Accounting	_____ Databases	_____ Networks
_____ Amiga	_____ Desktop Publishing	_____ Operating Systems
_____ Apple/Mac	_____ File Utilities	_____ Spreadsheets
_____ CAD	_____ Money Management	_____ Word Processing
_____ Communications	_____ Languages	_____ Other _____
		(please specify)

Which of the following best describes your job title?

_____ Administrative/Secretarial   _____ President/CEO

_____ Director   _____ Manager/Supervisor

_____ Engineer/Technician   _____ Other _____
                                                                    (please specify)

Comments on the weaknesses/strengths of this book: _____

_____

_____

_____

_____

Name _____

Street _____

City/State/Zip _____

Phone _____

PLEASE FOLD, SEAL, AND MAIL TO SYBEX

SYBEX, INC.
Department M
2021 CHALLENGER DR.
ALAMEDA, CALIFORNIA USA
94501

SEAL

All caps format	⌘-Shift-K
Bold format	⌘-Shift-B
Bullet symbol (•)	Option-8
Center alignment	⌘-Shift-C
Center picture in box	⌘-Shift-M
Character Attributes dialog box	⌘-Shift-D
Close all document windows	Option-click on *close box*
Copyright symbol (©)	Option-G
Degree symbol (°)	Option-Shift-8
Delete all guide rulers	Option-click in ruler
Delete all tab stops on ruler	Option-click on tab ruler
Ellipsis symbol (…)	Option-;
En space	Option-spacebar
End of document	Control-D (or End)
Fit picture to box (maintain aspect ratio)	⌘-Option-Shift-F
Fit picture to box	⌘-Shift-F
Flex space (breaking)	Option-Shift-spacebar
Flex space (non-breaking)	⌘-Option-Shift-spacebar
Go to page	⌘-J
Import new picture/text	⌘-E
Italic format	⌘-Shift-I
Item ➤ Duplicate	⌘-D
Item ➤ Modify	⌘-M